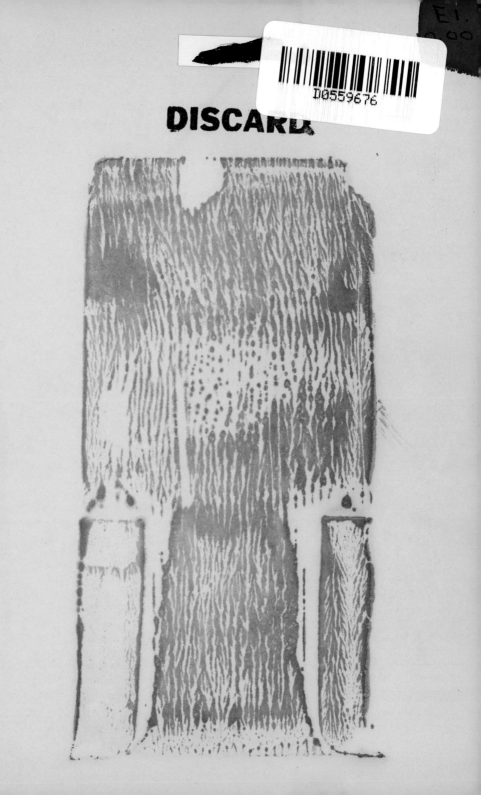

*American Satire in Prose
and Verse*

AMERICAN SATIRE
in Prose and Verse

Edited by Henry C. Carlisle, Jr.

RANDOM HOUSE

NEW YORK

FOURTH PRINTING

© Copyright, 1962 by Henry C. Carlisle, Jr.

All rights reserved under International and Pan-American Copyright Conventions. Published in New York by Random House, Inc., and simultaneously in Toronto, Canada, by Random House of Canada, Limited. *Library of Congress Catalog Card Number: 62–12727* Manufactured in the United States of America

Design by Warren Chappell

Acknowledgments

The editor wishes to thank the following for permission to reprint the material included in this anthology:

ALBERT AND CHARLES BONI, INC.—for "How to Tell a Butler, and Other Etiquette" by Will Rogers.

GEORGE BRAZILLER, INC.—for "Modern Chanty, or the Soft Berth" by Marya Mannes, from *Subverse*, by Marya Mannes and Robert Osborn. Copyright © Marya Mannes 1959, © Robert Osborn 1959.

GEORGE ADE DAVIS—for "The Fable of the Caddy Who Hurt His Head While Thinking," from *Fables in Slang* by George Ade;—for "The Fable of What Happened the Night the Men Came to the Women's Club," from *More Fables in Slang* by George Ade;—and for "The Fable of the Spotlighters and the Spotter," from *Hand-Made Fables* by George Ade.

DODD, MEAD & CO.—for "Ring Out, Wild Bells," from *Bed of Neuroses* by Wolcott Gibbs. Copyright 1936 by Wolcott Gibbs;—and for selection from *Dere Mable* by Edward Streeter. Copyright 1918, 1919, 1941 by Edward Streeter.

DOUBLEDAY & CO., INC.—for selection from *The Old Soak's History of the World* by Don Marquis. Copyright 1923 by New York Tribune, Inc.;—for "Aren't the Russians Wonderful?" and "How Suffering Purifies One," from *Hermione and Her Little Group of Serious Thinkers* by Don Marquis. Copyright 1916 by D. Appleton and Co.;—for "pete the parrot and shakespeare" and "mehitabel sees paris," from *archy and mehitabel* by Don Marquis. Copyright 1927 by Doubleday & Co., Inc.;—for "Wedding Etiquette," and "Formal and Informal Drinking," from *Perfect Behavior* by Donald Ogden Stewart. Copyright 1922 by George H. Doran Co.;—and for "The Landing of the Pilgrim Fathers" and "Optimistic Thoughts on the Cosmos," from *The Column Book of F. P. A.*

HOUGHTON MIFFLIN CO.—for selection from *Mr. Roberts* by Thomas Heggen. Copyright 1946 by Thomas Heggen.

ALFRED A. KNOPF, INC.—for "Senator Pooh and the Communist Woozles," from *In One Ear* by Eric Sevareid. Copyright 1952 by Eric Sevareid;— for "The Hills of Zion," from *Prejudices: Fifth Series* by H. L. Mencken. Copyright 1926 by Alfred A. Knopf, Inc.;—for "The Wedding: A Stage Direction," from *A Book of Burlesque* by H. L. Mencken. Copyright 1916, 1920 by Alfred A. Knopf, Inc.;—for selections from "The New American Credo," by George Jean Nathan and H. L. Mencken, from *The World of George Jean Nathan*. Copyright 1927, 1952 by Alfred A. Knopf, Inc.;—for selection from *Pictures from an Institution* by Randall Jarrell. Copyright 1952, 1953, 1954 by Randall Jarrell;—for selection from *Wake Up, Stupid* by Mark Harris. Copyright 1959 by Mark Harris;—and for selection from *The Revelations of Dr. Modesto* by Alan Harrington. Copyright 1955 by Alan Harrington.

LITTLE, BROWN & CO.—for selection from *The Late George Apley* by John P. Marquand. Copyright 1936, 1937 by John P. Marquand.

THOMAS MEEHAN—for "Early Morning of a Motion-Picture Executive" by Thomas Meehan. Originally appeared in *The New Yorker*.

OGDEN NASH—for "I Will Arise and Go Now," from *Versus* by Ogden Nash, published by Little, Brown & Co. Originally appeared in *The New Yorker*. Copyright 1948 by The New Yorker Magazine, Inc.

NEW DIRECTIONS—for selection from *The Day of the Locust* by Nathanael West. Copyright 1939 by the Estate of Nathanael West.

THE NEW YORK TIMES—for "To Ingemar Johansson with Love" by James Reston, from the *New York Times* of June 29, 1960.

THE NEW YORKER—for "The Secret Life of Walter Mitty" by James Thurber. Copyright 1939 by The New Yorker Magazine, Inc.;—for "If Grant Had Been Drinking at Appomat-

For Michael

Editor's Preface

Once, the incomparable Mencken, solicitously prescribing artistic hobbies in place of golf or Kiwanis for bored and dissatisfied businessmen, suggested among other therapies that Babbitt ". . . take a stiff drink and try *vers libre*. Or, if his tastes run to more sober things, let him collect early American humor . . ." As anyone who has tried it lately will testify, the archaeology of early American humor is a pastime in which real finds are rare and impediments are many, always seeming to inhibit the researcher from sharing open laughter with his great-grandfather. One finds that there is little native vintage humor preserved in books, and even less in books currently in print or easily available. Some of it is political or occasional satire which turned to dust along with the issues and persons it attacked; and some is, for other reasons, simply not very funny in its excavated state. There are maddening obstacles in the outmoded forms and fads, such as the Yankee Doodle doggerel of the Revolutionary period and the notorious fashion for phonetic spelling, which was a blight on the prime Civil War crop of humor, including the otherwise memorable satires of Petroleum V. Nasby and Orpheus C. Kerr.

Yet, a rich vein of satiric humor runs through our past, indeed through our character, a cocky, critical humor unlike the hysteria which passes for comedy on television and invites us to wonder whether the highest traditions of American humor have been worth it all. Contrary to all true comic traditions, the denatured humor of television is calculated to take the audience's mind *off* its troubles, anesthetize its critical intelligence with stultifying merriment, and thus decrease its sales resistance. Medicine-show entertainment in America has always been of this caliber, although prior to the electronic age the audience was limited to a handful of people at a time, and usually not the best element.

Far worse—since few seriously expected a contribution from television toward the enrichment of native humor—is the fact that newspapers, which once opened their pages to the best humorists in the land, at present boast remarkably few columns of humor with a genuine satirical bite.

Yet now, as in the past, clear and present targets of satire abound. It is easy to imagine with what serene devastation Mr. Dooley would have viewed the Cuban fiasco, and how Mencken in his heyday would have razed Norman Vincent Peale. Though satire is the "ultimate weapon" in wars of ideas (it was a very effective fifth column in our Revolutionary War), it is not at present being used to help us win the Cold War. We have a vast natural resource in our humor that today is largely wasted; the reader will note that there is no satire against the Communists anywhere in this volume. Presumably this is because Communism is not funny. Yet had witty writers like Ben Franklin not ridiculed mercantilism, which was not funny either, we might still be paying the Stamp Tax!

What is the difference between satire and plain humor? Of Mark Twain, William Dean Howells once said, "There is a bottom of fury to his humor"; it is this fury which distinguishes satire from ordinary humor. Satire is not respectable; humor is. We are likely to associate the two because in the United States, satire, like that variety of crab that seeks the protection of whatever shell happens to suit it, makes its home in American humor. Our humor makes our satire *seem* respectable when it isn't. Actually, satire is clever, irreverent, and insinuating; it is, above all, critical; it does not accept life the way life is commonly accepted, but finds normal things abnormal, proper people odd, ridiculous, and sometimes even evil and outrageous. Worst of all, it is both fictional and true.

But it is also irresistible.

In the United States the way satire has made itself irresistible is to be humorous. Invective, paradox, wit, and direct appeals to the intellect may work well elsewhere, but in America satire is typically humorous, disarming, friendly, familiar, perhaps a trifle ingratiating—at any rate, typical of the American character. It was perhaps inevitable too that, with our well-known passion for invention, we would invent a particular kind of satire that doesn't satirize. The elements (sharp criticism and humor) are there, but the criticism has become merely the "material" of the performer or writer—who is wholly indifferent to the object of his attack, if not actually fond of it. Thus the audience has the best of everything: both the joyous feeling that something respectable is being ridiculed and the assurance that it really isn't being ridiculed except in fun.

This strain of native satire goes back at least to Artemus Ward—that is, to the pre-Civil War period. "Tame" satire was then perfected on the lecture-circuits during the Gilded Age (when the major comic writers were usually performers as well, and when Mark Twain found to his surprise that his audience expected him to be rigorously zany), and it flowered again in the radio humor of the 1930s and 40s.

This kind of satire—which is the principal ingredient of the usual humor anthology—is respectable, and *American Satire* includes a sampling of it. But this volume also contains more of the sort of satire which is genuinely, sometimes profoundly, though almost always comically critical of life as it has been and as it happens to be in the U. S. A. Admittedly, today it is not easy to find this strain. Malcolm Muggeridge of *Punch* says: "The area of life in which ridicule is permissible is steadily shrinking, and . . . a dangerous tendency is becoming manifest to take ourselves with undue seriousness . . . Irreverence is decidedly out of fashion, and the clown or satirist, if he is to continue in business, must keep a careful eye on his targets lest they frown unduly."

Still, there are signs which give hope that a new age of satire may only be beginning. Reports of the death of the comic spirit in America are sometimes greatly exaggerated.

These are the ground rules which governed my choice of selections:

American Satire is a collection of literary satire. By literary satire I do not mean "artistic," but simply satire through the medium of the printed word. Thus there are no cartoons by Thomas Nast, Bill Mauldin, or Herblock, no Pogo strips. And because the selections are limited to published works, or parts of published works, there are no transcriptions of the monologues of the new school of stand-up satirists such as Sahl and Bob Newhart. Arbitrarily, no dramatic literature is included, in order to keep the book within reasonable size.

Whenever I felt that there was something to say about a selection or about one of the categories into which the selections are arranged I have said it in the form of a note which preceeds the selection or section.

Of course anyone familiar with American literature will find what will seem to be inexplicable omissions. Some such were deliberate, if reluctant, exclusions on the part of the Editor. Edith Wharton, for instance, is not represented in the "High Society" section because I could find no excerptable section of her work (including *The Age of Innocence*) which would display her satirical side without getting discouragingly entangled in her well-made plots. A sad confession—but let the reader try it!

Nathaniel Hawthorne's frequently anthologized satire *The Celestial Railroad* is not here because it always puts me into a state of the darkest gloom.

Philip Wylie's piece on Mom is perhaps technically disqualifiable as being unfictional, a direct attack and therefore unsatirical. But the piece cried out to be included.

On the sunnier side of satire (or whatever), S. J. Perelman, Robert Benchley and Ogden Nash took places in the manuscript before I could decide whether or not to include those fringe areas where satire begins to lose itself in a mist of innocent fun and merriment (including what I have called respectable or tame satire). They were there, and all I could do was try to choose their more abrasive moments.

Above all, I have chosen the pieces which follow and not others because these were irresistible to me at the time of choosing them. I am aware that such an explanation cannot be very satisfying to the reader who finds one of his favorite authors missing or else represented by the "wrong" selection. At the same time, I must admit a prejudice for the sort of American satire that means business, that says something about the kind of people we are, and whose purpose is not merely gentle spoofing. In the end, I must rely on the hope that the presence of such masters as Benjamin Franklin, James Russell Lowell, David Ross Locke, Mark Twain, Finley Peter Dunne, George Ade, Don Marquis, H. L. Mencken, Sinclair Lewis, Will Rogers, and James Thurber will distract the reader from finding too many sins of omission and debatable choices.

I owe a debt of gratitude to a great many people who have helped me with advice and suggestions and with their thoughts about what American satire is. Most particularly I am grateful to Joe Fox and Berenice Hoffman, both of Random House, Inc., whose ideas and criticisms have been invaluable. Special thanks are also due that remarkable institution, the New York Public Library at Forty-second Street and Fifth Avenue, where much of my digging and sifting was done.

Finally, I wish to thank the various publishers and authors whose permissions to use copyrighted material made this book possible.

Henry C. Carlisle, Jr.

JURA, 1962

Contents

RELIGION

WAR AND SERVICE LIFE

THE BLACK AND THE WHITE

HIGHER EDUCATION

THE ARTS

CONTENTS

A SPRIG OF HOLLYWOOD

HIGH SOCIETY, FASHION AND CELEBRITY

COURTSHIP AND MARRIAGE

AMERICANS ABROAD

PROGRESS AND CIVILIZATION

. . . that idiot, laughter . . .
A passion hateful to my purposes.

WILLIAM SHAKESPEARE
King John, III, 3

". . . satire everywhere attacks evil arrogant and triumphant, pride victorious and riding for a fall. It attacks those conventional respectabilities which are really hidden absurdities or vices blindly accepted by thoughtlessness, habit or social custom. It attacks foolishness foolishly convinced that it makes sense, grinning and unrepentant in its folly. It attacks stuffed shirts, hypocrisies aping merit . . ."

EDGAR JOHNSON, *A Treasury of Satire*

PORTRAITS

"We're a gr-reat people," said Mr. Hennessy, earnestly.

"We ar-re," said Mr. Dooley. "We ar-re that. An' th' best iv it is, we know we ar-re."

Finley Peter Dunne, *Mr. Dooley on War Preparation*

Portraits

In literature and legend the American has appeared in many aspects, from Sam Slick to Sam Spade, from the Yankee peddler to Walter Mitty. He has been Brother Jonathan, Major Jack Downing, Davy Crockett, Hosea Biglow, the Virginian, Mr. Dooley, George Apley, George Babbitt, Pal Joey, Jay Gatsby, and Private Hargrove. In his youth he was Huck Finn, Tom Sawyer, Penrod, Frank Merriwell, Dink Stover, Holden Caulfield. The female line includes an engaging variety of little women, big blondes, moms, flappers, bluestockings, and belles.

Reviewing the changing styles of American self-portraiture, one finds a striking shift in the notion of who we are. Take the male: in the nineteenth century the American male appeared in literature and folklore as something special, a kind of walking superlative. He was as clever as the Yankee peddler, as dead a shot as Davy Crockett, as tall as Paul Bunyan. Of course, no one seriously believed that the typical American was really so extraordinary, but it was comforting to think that he might be when the Indians and coyotes howled around the wagon train.

However, when all that was left of the frontier were a few arrowhead collections and ghost towns, the male had nothing to do but build the country. Seizing the opportunity, the female took over.

Such, at least, seems to be the consensus of American satire: once comically big, the American male becomes comically little; while the female, once comically homespun, becomes comically liberated and managerial.

Here is a gallery of portraits of Americans as they have been seen by the critical eye of the satirist.

Washington Irving

Washington Irving's sketch of Aunt Charity Cockloft presents an "unforgettable character" in early American literature. It is taken from *Salmagundi*, a miscellany of satires—mostly on fashionable New York—which was written by Washington Irving, then twenty-three, his brother William, and his brother-in-law James Kirke Paulding.

Suggested by the comic portrayals of the English gentry in the London *Spectator*, the Cockloft family is of ancient derivation ("if there be any truth in the genealogical tree"), of highly whimsical habits, including that of marrying none but first and second cousins, and all dedicated to hating the French. (A Cockloft female had once run off with a French count who was later found to be descended from a long line of barbers.)

AUNT CHARITY COCKLOFT
(from *Salmagundi*, 1808)

My Aunt Charity departed this life in the fifty-ninth year of her age, though she never grew older after twenty-five. In her teens she was, according to her own account, a celebrated beauty, though I never could meet with anybody that remembered when she was handsome. In the good old days that saw my aunt in the heydey of youth, a fine lady was a most formidable animal, and required to be approached with the same awe

and devotion that a Tartar feels in the presence of his Grand
Lama. If a gentleman offered to take her hand, except to help
her into a carriage, or lead her into a drawing room, such
frowns! such a rustling of brocade and taffeta! her very paste
shoe buckles sparkled with indignation, and for a moment assumed the brilliancy of diamonds: in those days the person of a
belle was sacred; it was unprofaned by the sacrilegious grasp of
a stranger—simple souls!—they had not the waltz among them
yet!

My good aunt prided herself on keeping up this buckram deli-
cacy; and if she happened to be playing at the old fashioned
game of forfeits, and was fined a kiss, it was always more trouble to get it than it was worth; for she made a most gallant de-
fence, and never surrendered until she saw her adversary inclined to give over the attack. Once, when on a sleighing party,
when they came to the Kissing Bridge, her swain attempted to
levy contributions on Miss Charity Cockloft, who after squalling
at a hideous rate, at length jumped out of the sleigh plump into
a snow bank, where she stuck fast, until he came to her rescue.
This Latonian feat cost her a rheumatism, from which she never
thoroughly recovered.

It is rather singular that my aunt, though a great beauty, and
an heiress withal, never got married. This much is certain, that
for many years previous to her decease, she declined all atten-
tions from the gentlemen, and contented herself with watching
over the welfare of her fellow creatures. She was indeed observed to take a considerable lean toward Methodism, was frequent in her attendance at love feasts, read Whitefield and
Wesley, and even went so far as to travel the distance of five-
and-twenty miles to be present at a camp meeting.

This gave great offence to my Cousin Christopher, and his
good lady, who, as I have already mentioned, are rigidly ortho-
dox in the Established Church. Had my Aunt Charity not been
of a most pacific disposition, her religious whim would have occasioned many a family altercation. She was indeed as good a
soul as the Cockloft family ever boasted; a lady of unbounded
loving-kindness, which extended to man, woman, and child.
Was any acquaintance sick? In vain did the wind whistle and the

storm beat; my aunt would waddle through mud and mire, over the whole section, but what she would visit them. She would sit by them for hours together with the most persevering patience, and tell a thousand melancholy stories of human misery, to keep up their spirits. The whole catalogue of *yerb* teas was at her fingers' ends, from formidable wormwood down to gentle balm; and she would descant by the hour on the healing qualities of hoarhound, catnip, and penny royal. Woe be to the patient that came under the benevolent hand of my Aunt Charity; he was sure, willy-nilly, to be drenched with a deluge of concoctions; and full many a time has my Cousin Christopher borne a twinge of pain in silence, through fear of being condemned to suffer the martyrdom of her materia medica.

But the truth must be told. With all her good qualities, my Aunt Charity was afflicted with one fault, extremely rare among her gentle sex—it was curiosity. How she came by it, I am at a loss to imagine, but it played the very vengeance with her and destroyed the comfort of her life. Having an invincible desire to know everybody's character, business, and mode of living, she took up her residence in town, and was forever prying into the affairs of her neighbors; and got a great deal of ill will from people toward whom she had the kindest disposition possible.

If any family on the opposite of the street gave a dinner, my aunt would mount her spectacles, and sit at the window until the company were all housed, merely that she might know who they were. If she heard a story about any of her acquaintance, she would, forthwith, set off, full sail, and never rest until, to use her usual expression, she had got "to the bottom of it;" which meant nothing more than telling it to everybody she knew.

I remember one night my Aunt Charity happened to hear a most precious story about one of her good friends, but unfortunately too late to give it immediate circulation. It made her absolutely miserable; and she hardly slept a wink all night, for fear her bosom friend, Mrs. Sipkins, should get the start of her in the morning. You must know there was always a contest between these two ladies, who should first give currency to the good-natured things said about everybody; and this unfortunate rivalship at length proved fatal to their long and ardent friendship.

My aunt got up full two hours that morning before her usual time; put on her pompadour taffeta gown, and sallied forth to lament the misfortune of her dear friend. Would you believe it! —wherever she went, Mrs. Sipkins had anticipated her; and, instead of being listened to with uplifted hands and open-mouthed wonder, my unhappy aunt was obliged to sit quietly and listen to the whole affair, with numerous additions, alterations, and amendments! Now, this was too bad; it would have provoked Patience Grizzle or a saint. It was too much for my aunt, who kept her bed for three days afterward, with a cold; but I have no doubt it was owing to this affair of Mrs. Sipkins, to whom she would never be reconciled.

But I pass over the rest of my Aunt Charity's life, chequered with the various calamities, and misfortunes, and mortifications, incident to those worthy old gentlewomen who have the domestic cares of the whole community upon their minds. I hasten to relate the melancholy incident that hurried her out of existence in the full bloom of antiquated virginity.

In their frolicsome malice, the fates had ordained that a French boarding house, or *Pension Française*, as it was called, should be established directly opposite my aunt's residence. Cruel event!—it threw her into that alarming disorder denominated the fidgets; she did nothing but watch at the window day after day, but without becoming one whit the wiser at the end of a fortnight. She wondered why there was always such a scraping of fiddles in the parlor, and such a smell of onions from the kitchen; in short, neighbor Pension was continually uppermost in her thoughts, and incessantly on the outer edge of her tongue. This was, I believe, the first time she had ever failed "to get at the bottom of a thing;" and the disappointment cost her many a sleepless night, I warrant you. I have little doubt, however, that my aunt would have ferreted neighbor Pension out, could she have spoken or understood French; but in those times people in general could make themselves understood in plain English; and it was always a standing rule in the Cockloft family, which exists to this day, that not one of the females should learn French.

My Aunt Charity had lived for some time at her window in vain; when one day as she was keeping her usual look-out, and suffering all the pangs of unsatisfied curiosity, she beheld a little, meagre, weazel-faced Frenchman, of the most forlorn, pitiful, and diminutive proportions, arrive at neighbor Pension's door. He was dressed in white, with a little pinched-up cocked hat; he seemed to shake in the wind, and every blast that went over him whistled through his bones and threatened instant annihilation. This embodied spirit of famine was followed by three carts, lumbered with crazy trunks, chests, band boxes, bidets, medicine chests, parrots and monkeys; and at his heels ran a yelping pack of little black-nosed pug dogs.

This was the thing wanting to fill up the measure of my Aunt Charity's affliction. She could not conceive, for the soul of her, who this mysterious little apparition could be that made so great a display; what he could possibly do with so much baggage, and particularly with his parrots and monkeys; or how so small a carcass could have occasion for so many trunks of clothes.

From the time of this fatal arrival, my poor aunt was in a quandary. All her inquiries were fruitless; no one could expound the history of this mysterious stranger. She never held up her head afterward—drooped daily, took to her bed in a fortnight, and in one little month I saw her quietly deposited in the family vault:—*dead of a Frenchman!* as the family ever afterward said.

James Kirke Paulding

During the 1820s and 30s, journals written by English travelers in America found an eager market in London, particularly if they demonstrated that the American democracy was crude, lawless, and on the brink of anarchy. Almost any such book was assured of commercial success if it included glimpses into the slave territories and the rough-and-tumble western frontier.

Of course, Americans violently resented these derogatory travelogues (even though, years later, Mark Twain said that such commentaries did not show the true barbarity of early frontier life), and educated American writers ridiculed the British stereotyped view of the United States. Among them, none was more successful than James Kirke Paulding, whose satirical wit had been sharpened by his collaboration with the Irving brothers on *Salmagundi*. Paulding's *John Bull in America* is a vigorous lampoon of the typical America-baiting travel book. In it the English traveler, John Bull, is shocked at every turn by the rudeness of manners, distressed by republican institutions, avid for hearsay to support his antidemocratic prejudices. John Bull's favorite American atrocity story is the lurid Ramsbottom affair, a tall tale which he has swallowed whole, and which he repeats throughout his journal with endless variations, as if he had put it out of mind and recalled it, again and again, each time with fresh indignation.

THE SHOCKING RAMSBOTTOM AFFAIR
(from *John Bull in America*, 1825)

It seems that a fellow by the name of Ramsbottom, a man-milliner by trade, and a great stickler for the rights of man, had taken offense at a neighbour whose name was Higginbottom, because his wife had attempted to cheapen a crimped tucker at his shop, and afterwards reported all over town that he, Ramsbottom, sold his things much dearer than his rival man-milliner over the way, whose name was Winterbottom, and whose next door neighbour was one Oddy. In the pure spirit of democracy, Ramsbottom determined to dirk not only Higginbottom, Winterbottom, and Oddy, together with their wives, but likewise all the little Higginbottoms, Winterbottoms, Oddys, and little Oddities. It was several years before Ramsbottom could get the whole party together, so as to make one job of it. At last, after an interval of about ten years, he collected them all at his house, to keep their Christmas-eve, and determined then and there to execute his diabolical purpose. It would appear, however, that he had previously changed his mind as to the dirking, probably on account of the trouble of killing so many, one after the other, for just as they were all up to the eyes in a Christmas pie, made of four-and-twenty blackbirds, an explosion took place—the house blew up, and every soul, Ramsbottom, Higginbottom, Winterbottom, Oddy, their wives, together with all the young Ramsbottoms, Higginbottoms, Winterbottoms, Oddys, and Oddities, were scattered in such invisible atoms, that not a vestige of them was ever afterwards discovered. Such is the deadly spirit of revengeful ferocity, generated in the polluted sink of democracy. The desperado, Ramsbottom, who was considered rather a peaceable person, among these barbarians, scrupled not, like the old republican Samson, to pull down destruction on his own head, that he might be revenged upon a poor woman for cheapening a crimped tucker.

James Fenimore Cooper

When James Fenimore Cooper returned home in 1833 after seven years of residence and travel in Europe, he found the United States changed for the worse. The well-ordered Federalist squirearchy he remembered having left had been engulfed in a wave of vulgarity and materialism; and, worst of all, an ungentlemanly element was claiming and getting a large share of the power and wealth.

The portrait of Aristabulus Bragg in *Home as Found* is Cooper's portrait of the new man, the classless "creature of circumstances" whose rise and proliferation the patrician Cooper regarded with profound distrust.

PORTRAIT OF MR. ARISTABULUS BRAGG, ATTORNEY AND COUNSELLOR-AT-LAW
(from *Home as Found*, 1838)

Mr. Aristabulus Bragg was born in one of the western counties of Massachusetts, and emigrated to New York, after receiving his education, at the mature age of nineteen; at twenty-one he was admitted to the bar, and for the last

seven years he has been a successful practitioner in all the courts
of Otsego, from the justice's to the circuit. His talents are un-
deniable, as he commenced his education at fourteen and terminated it at twenty-one, the law course included. This man is an
epitome of all that is good and all that is bad in a very large
class of his fellow-citizens. He is quick-witted, prompt in action, enterprising in all things in which he has nothing to lose,
but wary and cautious in all things in which he has a real stake,
and ready to turn not only his hand, but his heart and his
principles, to anything that offers an advantage. With him,
literally, "nothing is too high to be aspired to, nothing too low
to be done." He will run for Governor, or for town clerk,
just as opportunities occur, is expert in all the practices of his
profession, has had a quarter's dancing, with three years in the
classics, and turned his attention toward medicine and divinity,
before he finally settled down into the law. Such a compound
of shrewdness, impudence, common-sense, pretension, humility,
cleverness, vulgarity, kind-heartedness, duplicity, selfishness,
law-honesty, moral fraud and mother wit, mixed up with a
smattering of learning and much penetration in practical things,
can hardly be described, as any one of his prominent qualities is
certain to be met by another quite as obvious that is almost its
converse. Mr. Bragg, in short, is purely a creature of circumstances . . .

Mark Twain

Modeled after Twain's uncle James Lampton and sharpened
by Twain's own disillusioning business experiences, the splendid portrait of Colonel Beriah Sellers in *The Gilded Age* is a
comic and often poignant caricature of the luckless optimist.
While dining his guests on turnips and water, the Colonel is
confident that, once his temporary bad luck ends, his promo-
tional schemes will realize a huge fortune.

In the following passage, Sellers' young associate has reported
from Washington the failure of his efforts to secure a federal

subsidy to finance the Colonel's land "development" at a desolate locality known as Stone's Landing. The bubble has burst. And yet, if a railroad were to pass through Stone's Landing—or "Napoleon" as the Colonel intended to rename his city—the situation would still be saved. But, of course, the railroad is routed elsewhere, far from Sellers' dreams.

THERE'S A GOOD TIME COMING
(from *The Gilded Age*, 1873)

It was a hard blow to poor Sellers to see the work on his darling enterprise stop, and the noise and bustle and confusion that had been such refreshment to his soul, sicken and die out. It was hard to come down to humdrum ordinary life again after being a General Superintendent and the most conspicuous man in the community. It was sad to see his name disappear from the newspapers; sadder still to see it resurrected at intervals, shorn of its aforetime gaudy gear of compliments and clothed on with rhetorical tar and feathers.

But his friends suffered more on his account than he did. He was a cork that could not be kept under the water many moments at a time.

He had to bolster up his wife's spirits every now and then. On one of these occasions he said:

"It's all right, my dear, all right; it will all come right in a little while. There's two hundred thousand dollars coming, and that will set things booming again. Harry seems to be having some difficulty, but that's to be expected—you can't move these big operations to the tune of Fisher's Hornpipe, you know. But Harry will get it started along presently, and then you'll see! I expect the news every day now."

"But, Beriah, you've *been* expecting it every day, all along, haven't you?"

"Well, yes; yes—I don't know but I have. But anyway, the longer it's delayed, the nearer it grows to the time when it will start—same as every day you live brings you nearer to—nearer—"

"The grave?"

"Well, no—not that exactly; but you can't understand these things, Polly dear—women haven't much head for business, you know. You make yourself perfectly comfortable, old lady, and you'll see how we'll trot this right along. Why, bless you, *let* the appropriation lag, if it wants to—that's no great matter— there's a bigger thing than that."

"Bigger than two hundred thousand dollars, Beriah?"

"Bigger, child?—why, what's two hundred thousand dollars? Pocket-money! Mere pocket-money! Look at the railroad! Did you forget the railroad? It ain't many months till spring; it will be coming right along, and the railroad swimming right along behind it. Where'll it be by the middle of summer? Just stop and fancy a moment—just think a little— don't anything suggest itself? Bless your heart, you dear women live right in the present all the time—but a man, why a man lives—"

"In the future, Beriah? But don't we live in the future most too much, Beriah? We do somehow seem to manage to live on next year's crop of corn and potatoes as a general thing while this year is still dragging along, but sometimes it's not a robust diet—Beriah. But don't look that way, dear—don't mind what I say. I don't mean to fret, I don't mean to worry; and I *don't*, once a month, *do* I, dear? But when I get a little low and feel bad, I get a bit troubled and worrisome, but it don't mean anything in the world. It passes right away. I know you're doing all you can, and I don't want to seem repining and ungrateful—for I'm *not*, Beriah—you know I'm not, don't you?"

"Lord bless you, child, I know you are the very best little woman that ever lived—that ever lived on the whole face of the earth! And I know that I would be a dog not to work for you and think for you and scheme for you with all my might. And I'll bring things all right yet, honey—cheer up and don't you fear. The railroad—"

"Oh, I *had* forgotten the railroad, dear, but when a body gets blue, a body forgets everything. Yes, the railroad—tell me about the railroad."

"Aha, my girl, don't you see? Things ain't so dark, are they? Now *I* didn't forget the railroad. Now just think for a moment—just figure up a little on the future dead moral certainties. For instance, call this waiter St. Louis.

"And we'll lay this fork (representing the railroad) from St. Louis to this potato, which is Slouchburg:

"Then with this carving-knife we'll continue the railroad from Slouchburg to Doodleville, shown by the black pepper:

"Then we run along the—yes—the comb—to the tumbler—that's Brimstone:

"Thence by the pipe to Belshazzar, which is the salt-cellar:

"Thence to, to—that quill—Catfish—hand me the pin-cushion, Marie Antoinette:

"Thence right along these shears to this horse, Babylon:

"Then by the spoon to Bloody Run—thank you, the ink:

"Thence to Hail Columbia—snuffers, Polly, please—move that cup and saucer close up, that's Hail Columbia:

"Then—let me open my knife—to Hark-from-the-Tomb, where we'll put the candlestick—only a little distance from Hail Columbia to Hark-from-the-Tomb—down-grade all the way.

"And there we strike Columbus River—pass me two or three skeins of thread to stand for the river; the sugar-bowl will do for Hawkeye, and the rattrap for Stone's Landing—Napoleon, I mean—and you can see how much better Napoleon is located than Hawkeye. Now here you are with your railroad complete, and showing its continuation to Hallelujah, and thence to Corruptionville.

"Now, then—there you are! It's a beautiful road, beautiful. Jeff Thompson can out-engineer any civil engineer that ever sighted through an aneroid, or a theodolite, or whatever they call it—*he* calls it sometimes one and sometimes the other—just whichever levels off his sentence neatest, I reckon. But ain't it a ripping road, though? I tell you, it'll make a stir when it gets along. Just see what a country it goes through. There's your onions at Slouchburg—noblest onion country that graces God's footstool; and there's your turnip country all around Doodleville—bless my life, what fortunes are going to be made there when they get that contrivance perfected for extracting

olive-oil out of turnips—if there's any in them; and I reckon
there is, because Congress has made an appropriation of
money to test the thing, and they wouldn't have done that just
on conjecture, of course. And now we come to the Brimstone
region—cattle raised there till you can't rest—and corn, and all
that sort of thing. Then you've got a little stretch along
through Belshazzar that don't produce anything now—at least
nothing but rocks—but irrigation will fetch it. Then from
Catfish to Babylon it's a little swampy, but there's dead loads
of peat down under there somewhere. Next is the Bloody
Run and Hail Columbia country—tobacco enough can be
raised there to support two such railroads. Next is the sassparilla region. I reckon there's enough of that truck along in
there on the line of the pocket-knife, from Hail Columbia to
Hark-from-the-Tomb, to fat up all the consumptives in all the
hospitals from Halifax to the Holy Land. It just grows like
weeds! I've got a little belt of sassparilla land in there just
tucked away unobtrusively waiting for my little Universal
Expectorant to get into shape in my head. And I'll fix that,
you know. One of these days I'll have all the nations of the
earth expecto—"

"But, Beriah dear—"

"Don't interrupt me, Polly—I don't want you to lose the run
of the map—well, *take* your toy-horse, James Fitz-James, if you
must have it—and run along with you. Here, now—the soap
will do for Babylon. Let me see—where was I? Oh yes—now
we run down to Stone's Lan—Napoleon—now we run down to
Napoleon. Beautiful road. Look at that, now. Perfectly straight
line—straight as the way to the grave. And see where it leaves
Hawkeye—clear out in the cold, my dear, clear out in the cold.
That town's as bound to die as—well if I owned it I'd get its
obituary ready, now, and notify the mourners. Polly, mark my
words—in three years from this, Hawkeye'll be a howling
wilderness. You'll see. And just look at that river—noblest
stream that meanders over the thirsty earth!—calmest, gentlest
artery that refreshes her weary bosom! Railroad goes all over it
and all through it—wades right along on stilts. Seventeen
bridges in three miles and a half—forty-nine bridges from
Hark-from-the-Tomb to Stone's Landing altogether—forty-nine

bridges, and culverts enough to culvert creation itself! Hadn't skeins of thread enough to represent them all—but you get an idea—perfect trestle-work of bridges for seventy-two miles. Jeff Thompson and I fixed all that, you know; he's to get the contracts and I'm to put them through on the divide. Just oceans of money in those bridges. It's the only part of the railroad I'm interested in—down along the line—and it's all I want, too. It's enough, I should judge. Now here we are at Napoleon. Good enough country—plenty good enough—all it wants is population. That's all right—that will come. And it's no bad country *now* for calmness and solitude, I can tell you—though there's no money in that, of course. No money, but a man wants rest, a man wants peace—a man don't want to rip and tear around *all* the time. And here we go, now, just as straight as a string for Hallelujah—it's a beautiful angle—handsome up-grade all the way—and then away you go to Corruptionville, the gaudiest country for early carrots and cauliflowers that ever—good missionary field, too. There ain't such another missionary field outside the jungles of Central Africa. And patriotic?—why, they named it after Congress itself. Oh, I warn you, my dear, there's a good time coming, and it'll be right along before you know what you're about, too. That railroad's fetching it. You see what it is as far as I've got, and if I had enough bottles and soap and bootjacks and such things to carry it along to where it joins onto the Union Pacific, fourteen hundred miles from here, I should exhibit to you in that little internal improvement a spectacle of inconceivable sublimity. So, don't you see? We've got the railroad to fall back on; and in the mean time, what are we worrying about that two-hundred-thousand-dollar appropriation for? That's all right. I'd be willing to bet anything that the very next letter that comes from Harry will—"

Henry James

Generally the feminist movement in America aroused either coarse abuse or fervent enthusiasm, rarely satire. Henry James' portraits of Boston bluestockings, however, are sharp and subtle. Basil Ransom is the male observer of the formidable feminists who, in order of appearance, are Miss Birdseye, Mrs. Farrinder and the crusading Olive Chancellor. Meeting them, one wonders not how women eventually won the vote but how the men kept it.

THE REFORM LADIES
(from *The Bostonians*, 1886)

1. MISS BIRDSEYE

She was a little old lady, with an enormous head; that was the first thing Ransom noticed—the vast, fair, protuberant, candid, ungarnished brow, surmounting a pair of weak, kind, tired-looking eyes, and ineffectually balanced in the rear by a cap which had the air of falling backward, and which Miss Birdseye suddenly felt for while she talked, with unsuccessful irrelevant movements. She had a sad, soft, pale face, which (and it was the effect of her whole head) looked as if it had been soaked, blurred, and made vague by exposure to some slow dissolvent. The long practice of philanthropy had not given accent to her features; it had rubbed out their transitions, their meanings. The waves of sympathy, of enthusiasm, had wrought upon them in the same way in which the waves of time finally modify the surface of old marble busts, gradually washing away their sharpness, their details. In her large countenance her dim little smile scarcely showed. It was a mere sketch of a smile, a kind of installment, or payment on account; it seemed to say that she would smile more if she had time, but that you could see, without this, that she was gentle and easy to beguile.

She always dressed in the same way: she wore a loose black jacket, with deep pockets, which were stuffed with papers, memoranda of a voluminous correspondence; and from beneath her jacket depended a short stuff dress. The brevity of this simple garment was the one device by which Miss Birdseye managed to suggest that she was a woman of business, that she wished to be free for action. She belonged to the Short-Skirts League, as a matter of course; for she belonged to any and every

league that had been founded for almost any purpose whatever.
This did not prevent her being a confused, entangled, inconse-
quent, discursive old woman, whose charity began at home and
ended nowhere, whose credulity kept pace with it, and who
knew less about her fellow-creatures, if possible, after fifty years
of humanitary zeal, than on the day she had gone into the field
to testify against the iniquity of most arrangements. Basil Ransom knew very little about such a life as hers, but she seemed
to him a revelation of a class, and a multitude of socialistic
figures, of names and episodes that he had heard of, grouped
themselves behind her. She looked as if she had spent her life
on platforms, in audiences, in conventions, in phalansteries, in
séances; in her faded face there was a kind of reflection of ugly
lecture lamps; with its habit of an upward angle, it seemed
turned toward a public speaker, with an effort of respiration in
the thick air in which social reforms are usually discussed. She
talked continually, in a voice of which the spring seemed broken,
like that of an over-worked bell-wire; and when Miss Chancellor
explained that she had brought Mr. Ransom because he was so
anxious to meet Mrs. Farrinder, she gave the young man a delicate, dirty, democratic little hand, looking at him kindly, as she
could not help doing, but without the smallest discrimination as
against others who might not have the good fortune (which involved, possibly, an injustice) to be present on such an interesting occasion. She struck him as very poor, but it was only
afterward that he learned she had never had a penny in her life.
No one had an idea how she lived; whenever money was given
her she gave it away to a negro or a refugee. No woman could
be less invidious, but on the whole she preferred these two
classes of the human race. Since the Civil War much of her occupation was gone; for before that her best hours had been
spent in fancying that she was helping some Southern slave to
escape. It would have been a nice question whether, in her heart
of hearts, for the sake of this excitement, she did not sometimes
wish the blacks back in bondage. She had suffered in the same
way by the relaxation of many European despotisms, for in
former years much of the romance of her life had been in
smoothing the pillow of exile for banished conspirators. Her

refugees had been very precious to her; she was always trying
to raise money for some cadaverous Pole, to obtain lessons for
some shirtless Italian. There was a legend that an Hungarian
had once possessed himself of her affections, and had disappeared after robbing her of everything she possessed. This,
however, was very apocryphal, for she had never possessed anything, and it was open to grave doubt that she could have en-
tertained a sentiment so personal. She was in love, even in those
days, only with causes, and she languished only for emancipa-
tions. But they had been the happiest days, for when causes
were embodied in foreigners (what else were the Africans?),
they were certainly more appealing.

2. MRS. FARRINDER

She was a copious, handsome woman, in whom angularity
had been corrected by the air of success; she had a rustling
dress (it was evident what *she* thought about taste), abundant
hair of a glossy blackness, a pair of folded arms, the expression
of which seemed to say that rest, in such a career as hers, was
as sweet as it was brief, and a terrible regularity of feature. I
apply that adjective to her fine placid mask because she
seemed to face you with a question of which the answer was
preordained, to ask you how a countenance could fail to be noble
of which the measurements were so correct. You would contest
neither the measurements nor the nobleness, and had to feel that
Mrs. Farrinder imposed herself. There was a lithographic
smoothness about her, and a mixture of the American matron
and the public character. There was something public in her
eye, which was large, cold, and quiet; it had acquired a sort of
exposed reticence from the habit of looking down from a lecture
desk, over a sea of heads, while its distinguished owner was
eulogized by a leading citizen. Mrs. Farrinder, at almost any
time, had the air of being introduced by a few remarks. She
talked with great slowness and distinctness, and evidently a high
sense of responsibility; she pronounced every syllable of every
word and insisted on being explicit. If, in conversation with her,
you attempted to take anything for granted, or to jump two or
three steps at a time, she paused, looking at you with a cold

patience, as if she knew that trick, and then went on at her own
measured pace. She lectured on temperance and the rights of
women; the ends she labored for were to give the ballot to every
woman in the country and to take the flowing bowl from every
man. She was held to have a very fine manner, and to embody
the domestic virtues and the graces of the drawing room; to be a
shining proof, in short, that the forum, for ladies, is not necessarily hostile to the fireside. She had a husband, and his name
was Amariah.

3. OLIVE CHANCELLOR

The barren, gas-lighted room grew richer and richer to her
earnest eyes; it seemed to expand, to open itself to the great life
of humanity. The serious, tired people, in their bonnets and
overcoats, began to glow like a company of heroes. Yes, she
would do something, Olive Chancellor said to herself; she would
do something to brighten the darkness of that dreadful image
that was always before her, and against which it seemed to her
at times that she had been born to lead a crusade—the image
of the unhappiness of women. The unhappiness of women! The
voice of their silent suffering was always in her ears, the ocean
of tears that they had shed from the beginning of time seemed
to pour through her own eyes. Ages of oppression had rolled
over them; uncounted millions had lived only to be tortured, to
be crucified. They were her sisters, they were her own, and the
day of their delivery had dawned. This was the only sacred
cause; this was the great, the just revolution. It must triumph, it
must sweep everything before it; it must exact from the other,
the brutal, blood-stained, ravening race, the last particle of
expiation! It would be the greatest change the world had seen;
it would be a new era for the human family, and the names of
those who had helped to show the way and lead the squadrons
would be the brightest in the tables of fame. They would be
names of women weak, insulted, persecuted, but devoted in
every pulse to their being to the cause, and asking no better
fate than to die for it. It was not clear to this interesting girl
in what manner such a sacrifice (as this last) would be required

of her, but she saw the matter through a kind of sunrise-mist of emotion which made danger as rosy as success. When Miss Birdseye approached, it transfigured her familiar, her comical shape, and made the poor little humanitary hack seem already a martyr. Olive Chancellor looked at her with love, remembered that she had never, in her long, unrewarded, weary life, had a thought or an impulse for herself. She had been consumed by the passion of sympathy; it had crumpled her into as many creases as an old glazed, distended glove. She had been laughed at, but she never knew it; she was treated as a bore, but she never cared. She had nothing in the world but the clothes on her back, and when she should go down into the grave she would leave nothing behind her but her grotesque, undistinguished, pathetic little name. And yet people said that women were vain, that they were personal, that they were interested! While Miss Birdseye stood there, asking Mrs. Farrinder if she wouldn't say something, Olive Chancellor tenderly fastened a small battered brooch which confined her collar and which had half detached itself.

e. e. cummings

THE CAMBRIDGE LADIES

The Cambridge ladies who live in furnished souls
are unbeautiful and have comfortable minds
(also, with the church's protestant blessings
daughters, unscented shapeless spirited)
they believe in Christ and Longfellow, both dead,
are invariably interested in so many things—
at the present writing one still finds
delighted fingers knitting for the is it Poles?
perhaps.   While permanent faces coyly bandy
scandal of Mrs. N and Professor D

. . . . the Cambridge ladies do not care, above
Cambridge if sometimes in its box of
sky lavender and cornerless, the
moon rattles like a fragment of angry candy

Edwin Arlington Robinson

MINIVER CHEEVY
(1910)

Miniver Cheevy, child of scorn,
   Grew lean while he assailed the seasons;
He wept that he was ever born,
   And he had reasons.

Miniver loved the days of old
   When swords were bright and steeds were prancing;
The vision of a warrior bold
   Would set him dancing.

Miniver sighed for what was not,
   And dreamed, and rested from his labors;
He dreamed of Thebes and Camelot,
   And Priam's neighbors.

Miniver mourned the ripe renown
   That made so many a name so fragrant;
He mourned Romance, now on the town,
   And Art, a vagrant.

Miniver loved the Medici,
   Albeit he had never seen one;
He would have sinned incessantly
   Could he have been one.

Miniver cursed the commonplace
    And eyed a khaki suit with loathing;
He missed the mediaeval grace
    Of iron clothing.

Miniver scorned the gold he sought,
    But sore annoyed was he without it;
Miniver thought, and thought, and thought
    And thought about it.

Miniver Cheevy, born too late,
    Scratched his head and kept on thinking;
Miniver coughed, and called it fate,
    And kept on drinking.

John Marquand

PORTRAIT OF A GENTLEMAN
(from *The Late George Apley*)

CIVIC DUTIES
AND THE RISING TIDE OF CHANGE

As one looks back upon the first decade of this century from the perspective of the present, one grows increasingly aware that it was a time of subtle change; subtle, because the material aspects of life as we have known it underwent no great marked exterior alteration. That change was rather a gathering of forces from within, the end of which we know not yet. George Apley himself was able to perceive the working of these forces during some of the most fruitful and interesting years of his life, for this decade was indeed important to him. It was in many ways the crowning decade of his career, since it found him in the full force of early manhood and left him in the prime of middle life. It was in this decade, in the year 1905 to be exact, that our great genius, John Sargent, painted George Apley's portrait, now the property of his son. Sargent's uncanny ability to evaluate a character through indefinable gradation of feature is very finely manifested in this work. It shows George Apley in a simple brown business suit, with the high starched collar of the period, standing with one hand leaning upon a bare table, the other half-thrust into the side pocket of his coat. It is a simple, austere picture of a slender man with a somewhat long brown mustache, but in some way George Apley has brought his world with him to the canvas so that one recalls almost immediately the line written to his son: "You cannot get away from it." The sharp nose and particularly the set of the mouth and jaw indicate their owner's definite reaction to his world. The hands are long and fine. In the attenuation of the features one is aware of distinctive breeding. It might be termed, as many another canvas by older great masters, "The Portrait of a Gentleman." There is a marked and gratifying similarity shared by Sargent's "Apley" and Titian's "Gentleman with a Glove" and Velasquez's and Rembrandt's gentlemen. There is the same leanness, the same courteous, reserved assurance—but here the resemblance ends. George Apley is not an Italian or a Spaniard; he is entirely his own type and completely true to type.

This was the Apley of State Street, of Mulberry Beach and Milton, who walked across the Common to his office of a winter morning in long, half-careless strides, a true son of Boston— the present writer likes to think—imbued with the love of his land and caste. This was the Apley who realized, like so many of his contemporaries, that his caste in a sense was threatened. The realization came to him when he encountered at firsthand certain vicious phases in the city government. This occurred when he was given the place his name demanded on a committee selected by the Mayor of Boston to advise regarding certain plantings and improvements on the Commonwealth Avenue Mall. Though this was a matter of no very large importance, it was not his way to shirk a civic duty and he attended the meetings of this committee assiduously. The make-up of this committee, rather than its actions, amazed him most; and this example, coming at firsthand, drove him ever afterwards to take a more active interest in city affairs and threw him eventually

with many who were trying to shed some light on the shadowy
ways of our municipal politics. Thus, as early as 1902, we find
him writing to Mr. Henry Salter, whose letters to the *Transcript*
at the time were already causing no little discussion.

My dear Mr. Salter: —

I have heard you speak more than once of the incredible
laxness, to use a mild expression, which has been appearing
without our fully recognizing it, in our city affairs. I am afraid
I have been guilty of not paying much attention to this, since I
have been engaged in many other activities, until I found myself upon the advisory committee for the planting of the Commonwealth Avenue Mall. Then, for the first time I realized that
Boston has indeed become a melting pot. As I listened to the dis-
cussions of this committee I was amazed to find myself in the
company of a number of ill-bred men, mostly Irish, who
seemed to take no real interest in improving the city. Such ideas
as they had were illiterate and without any merit. What
seemed to concern them most was that the work should go to
one of two contractors for whom they appeared to have a deep
personal friendship, although I could readily see that the bids
these contractors had made for the proposed work were vastly
higher than the bids of others. The matter of economy did not
seem to concern my fellow committee members in the least.
Their argument ran something like this: "Martin Casey will do
a good job. He always does the work." What surprised me
more was that no one paid much attention to anything I said.
They appeared rather to resent some suggestions which I made
and one of them actually said to me: "It's your name we
want, we're used to this sort of business; sure, you wouldn't
understand it, Mr. Apley." If this is indicative of the way our
entire city is run, and I begin to be afraid that it is, surely
something is very wrong. Those of us who should sway the
taste and perhaps the conscience in municipal affairs have been
careless of our trust. I, for one, hope that you will call on me
to aid in any of the good works which you may be doing.

In all the amusing and erroneous criticisms directed against
our city no one has been able to say that there has not always

been a spirit of abnegation and self-sacrifice among our better element. The Puritanical idea of uplift ever lingers in the blood of the descendants of the first colonists of Massachusetts Bay. It may be true that occasionally they are shortsighted and oblivious to certain faults in their surroundings which may be obvious to others, but when their attention is directed toward these faults, they leave no stone unturned in an effort at rectification. In a sense the letter of George Apley indicates a marked awakening of conscience in the better element of Boston—or "consciousness" might be a fitter word.

It is clear to-day that this better element was already beginning to perceive that it had neglected certain phases of the life around it. Preoccupied with their own activities, and possibly judging the probity of others by their own, many persons did not observe the inevitable results of the rapid growth of our city until they became suddenly aware, perhaps more so in this decade than at any other time, that much of Boston had grown away from them. It was becoming increasingly evident that a species of organized corruption which had reared its ugly head in other American municipalities was only too apparent in Boston also. Imperceptibly, but at last surely, it was dawning on thoughtful observers of the public trend that the esprit and the spiritual pattern which had always distinguished the metropolis of New England was no longer sensitive to the influence of our better element.

If it had not been for external urging, it might have been that Apley would have allowed the matter to rest with this single unsavory committee experience. As he said in later years, he was never greatly interested in politics or sociology, nor had he, as he admitted himself, the pliability of mind or the tolerance to deal with demagogues; but the pressure of public conscience, and also the pressure of individuals including members of his own family, gradually aroused his sense of duty. Those who know the indefatigability and fearlessness of Henry Salter in his efforts at various branches of reform can readily appreciate the enthusiasm with which he welcomed an offer of assistance given by one of Apley's caliber.

I have never seen [George Apley wrote some time afterwards, in a paper entitled "Adventures in Reform"] a more dynamic man than Henry Salter. He had the leanness of face and the fixity of purpose which make up the ideal leader of a cause. His very eccentricities of dress and manner served only to accentuate his earnestness. He is the type of man who has made us what we are, and I am proud to have been associated in some of his activities.

Even a casual perusal of Salter's letters to George Apley give a definite idea of the effect they must have had on one of Apley's disposition, for they are calculated to open up new and startling vistas.

Do you remember Henry Salter? [We find Apley writing thus to his classmate, Walker.] I recall how we used to joke about him at Harvard, the pale bookworm with glasses. Believe me, he is quite a different sort of fellow now.

We are beginning to realize here that the better element has let things slide and that now there are incredible social abuses. Organized vice is rampant hardly a stone's throw from our very doors. I never knew it before, but bribery seems to be a common practice and many officials are growing rich on the taxpayers' money. More than this, there is an entire letdown in the general moral tone. The displays at some of the Music Halls are really too shocking to be mentioned, although I consider myself tolerably broad-minded.

It has always seemed to me until lately that these matters were beyond my province. In some way the better element must be organized and must make its influence felt. I do not know exactly how, because suddenly we seem to be very much in the minority.

More significant, perhaps, in his correspondence at this time is a hastily penned note from his sister, Amelia Simmings.

Dear George: —
Newcomb has just told me the news that you and he have been asked to serve on the organizing committee of a new or-

ganization which is to be called the Save Boston Association. Newcomb has overcome his usual reluctance to put himself for· ward in anything and, of course, will serve. You must do so also. Your name will be of great importance and we must be repre· sented since everyone else will be. I have just come back from the Morning Reading Club where Henry Salter gave a talk. We must and we shall clean up Boston. If we do not, this will become an Irish city run by the Roman Catholic Church. For your own self-respect and for ours I am sure you will join Newcomb on this committee. . . .

If Apley was slow to act it was more because of natural caution than through lack of courage.

It seems to me [he wrote to his sister in an answering note] that all this business is rather sudden, that we may all of us be growing a trifle hysterical. I should like to consider more carefully what the "Save Boston Association" means and exactly what it is trying to do. We seem to forget that all these abuses have been going on for quite a long while without causing any of us any real discomfort. You know how quickly you jump at things, Amelia.

You will be glad to know, however, that Catharine is in hearty accord with you. I have never known her so deeply interested and we have been discussing this during the entire evening. I still do not feel that I am the man for the place.

His realization of the importance of the Save Boston Associa· tion to the ultimate public welfare finally overcame his disbelief in his own fitness and his name appears upon the list of early organizers. Once embarked on such a cause, Apley was not the sort to turn back. For many years he was indefatigable in raising money and in appealing personally to his friends to join the growing roster of members.

The work accomplished by Henry Salter and the Save Boston Association is too well known to need mention here, except in so far as its activities affected Apley himself. The political significance of the Save Boston Association, the effect which it had in stimulating the public conscience to many abuses, its fearless revelation of many irregularities, resulting even in the confusion

of many public officials, all form a part of Boston history. Better
yet, this association furnished the impetus for the inception of
many other civic groups such as the "Teachers' Investigation
Association" which has done so much to eradicate many defi-
ciencies in our public teaching, and the "Guardian Association,"
and, in later years, the "Parents' Association," which has
brought startlingly to our attention many of the moral lapses of
our own children.

It was a source of deep pain to Apley that this new interest of
his met with doubt and opposition in certain quarters, even from
members of his own family who saw affairs with a perspective
with which George Apley could not agree. A letter from his Uncle William distressed him.

Dear George: —

From what you told me the other night when you came to me
seeking a contribution for the Save Boston Association—take an
old man's advice. You are biting off a good deal more than you
can chew. I am pretty familiar with the type of person you are
trying to attack because I have had a good deal to do with him.
You do not understand him; he is too much for you and, mark
my words, sooner or later he will get you into trouble. He
doesn't care a button for anything you think. . . .

There is also extant a letter from his cousin, John Apley, expressing a somewhat different point of view: —

Dear George: —

You won't mind my giving you a piece of advice, will you, as
we have always been friends? The other afternoon at the Club in
Cambridge they were talking about you, saying that you were
getting to be a reformer and that your ideas were almost radical.
They tell me that you are in this new organization which seems
to be designed to mind other people's business and that you are
joining all the other Catos and censoring a lot of things that you
really don't know anything about. You're too good a fellow,
George, to get mixed up in anything like this. Besides, you
know it's unsound; it isn't going to help you with the people you
like and who like you. Make your horse jump over the mud,

don't try to gallop him through it and don't you mind what
Catharine says either. . . .

There is no doubt that Apley was subjected to much similar
advice. In the light of what we know, it might have been better
had he followed it, but in many ways it is to his credit that he
did not.

"I neither like nor enjoy what I am doing," he wrote to his
Uncle William. "You may be right in what you say, as you
nearly always are, but I feel this to be my duty. I am sorry I
must go ahead."

It is only on looking back over the events of a life which is
finished that individual episodes take their proper place, and so
it is with George Apley's emergence into public affairs. Only
when his entire life was completed could one fully understand
the difficulties which he was storing up for himself when he
took the position that he did, because he considered it his duty.

At this period in his life, however, his interest in these affairs
was more passive than it was later. His life at the time was vivid
with other concerns, several of which one may mention. The
most important is made self-explanatory by a copy of a letter
which he sent to the Committee on Admissions of the Province
Club, and marks the beginning of a collision which the present
writer knows that Apley would gladly have avoided.

My dear Sirs: —

I noticed to-day on the bulletin board that the name of Mar-
cus Ransome has been proposed by Mr. Storrel Moore and
Mr. Franklin Fields for resident membership in the Province
Club. I wish to express myself as unalterably opposed to his admission.

I do not object to Ransome personally and I have sat with
him about the directors' tables of several small companies in
which we are both associated. Although he has only been in Boston for ten years, he has good manners and is superficially a gentleman. He may not possess the same background and ante-
cedents which characterize most members of the Province Club
but I do not believe that his appearance here would be objection-
able. I wish to make it clear that it is not because of Ransome
personally that I move to oppose him.

Rather, I move to oppose the motive which actuates Messrs.
Moore and Fields in putting this man up for membership. They
are not doing so because of family connections, nor because of
disinterested friendship, but rather because of business reasons.
It is, perhaps, too well known for me to mention it that Mr. Ransome has been instrumental in bringing a very large amount of
New York business to the banking house of Moore and Fields.
This I do not think is reason enough to admit Mr. Ransome to
the Province Club, a club which exists for social and not for
business purposes. I, for one, shall feel that the Club has lost
much of what is good in it if the Committee acts favorably on
Mr. Ransome. I am sending a copy of this letter to Mr. Moore
and another to Mr. Fields. . . .

It may readily be understood that the importance of the two
above-mentioned gentlemen in Boston business was so great that
this act of Apley's assumes the proportions of one of considerable
moral courage. He was standing against his own kind for what
he felt was a principle, and in the end he may be largely thanked
that the Province Club to-day maintains its old standards and
still remains known as the best club in Boston, broad-minded,
yet conservative. This letter, however, aroused a species of dis-
sension which has not been forgotten, for it struck a spark from
the well-known high temper of Mr. Moore, which divided Boston into factions. Many persons who had never heard of Ransome before, including friends of George Apley, eagerly es-
poused his cause. The answering letter from Mr. Moore is still
among the late George Apley's papers: —

My dear Apley: —
If you interested yourself in business more than in a variety
of social pursuits you would know enough to mind your own
business. What is the matter with Ransome that you should
write this ridiculous and puerile letter to the Province Club? I
ask you to reconsider it at once. . . .

The copy of Apley's letter which he preserved is equally curt.

My letter to the admission committee explains itself. I do not
care to reconsider it.

When one recalls the ensuing excitement it is not surprising to find floods of protest still extant. There were letters of expostulation and letters of pleading from many who realized the embarrassments which Apley's stand would cause. There is even a letter from Hugh Tilton, Secretary of the Province Club. "I appreciate your objection," he writes, "but I wonder if you consider its implications." It is clear enough that Apley considered them.

If Mr. Ransome is elected, [he wrote in a second letter to the Committee] I myself shall be obliged to resign from the Province Club. You may consider this letter as my resignation, taking effect immediately upon Mr. Ransome's admission.

This statement of George Apley's, which was couched rather more in the form of a suggestion than an actual threat, reduced the situation *ad absurdum*, since Ransome could no longer be considered as a serious possibility. It is safe to believe that this stand of Apley's had repercussions which lasted until the day of his death and that he underwent much pain in doing what he always considered a disinterested service. What grieved him most was the impression gained by many that he was a "snob," for he had always prided himself upon maintaining democratic tolerance and anyone who has seen Apley at a single reunion of his college class can be quite sure that this is true.

On George Apley's fifteenth reunion and outing which was held at about this time at the Breaker House, near Pachogue Neck, Apley made an especial point of addressing every one of his classmates present, some of them less than mere acquaintances. More than this, he was careful to ask considerately and with real interest, how each was faring in the world; and he went so far as to call several by their first names for the first time in their acquaintanceship. This scrupulousness of Apley was commented upon freely by many of his intimates who had expected him to join the small group of Club members. There is no doubt that Apley would have preferred to do so, but he persisted strictly in this other course. Instead of being a snob, it would be more just to say that throughout his life George Apley was persistently democratic.

Greatly to his astonishment he was also taxed in many quarters with being personally hostile to Mr. Ransome himself—who, it appears, held a certain position in the downtown district and in West Newton, where he resided. This was the accusation which Apley denied most heatedly. Instead of disliking Ransome, he always asserted with perfect truth that he had a warm personal liking for the man and a general admiration for his business acumen. There are not many who know that George Apley had recourse to definite action to confirm these words. In the very heat of this dispute he went to considerable trouble to give Ransome some buying orders for securities that would ordinarily have fallen to another firm, and he could only express astonishment and bewilderment when Ransome refused to execute these orders. Nevertheless, his quiet interest in Ransome did not cease, and the present writer is one of the few who know that when Ransome was seriously embarrassed in the autumn of 1929 George Apley, though the two had not seen each other for many years, immediately came to his aid.

Enough has already been said of this episode to illustrate George Apley's point of view. It made him many friends, but also many enemies who to the end refused to understand his attitude. Many of these individuals also used the Province Club dispute as an actual precedent for doubting George Apley's integrity when he found himself faced with the final unmerited *débâcle* that did so much to shorten the latter end of his life and to sadden his latter days.

Dorothy Parker

EPITAPH FOR A DARLING LADY

All her hours were yellow sands,
  Blown in foolish whorls and tassels;
Slipping warmly through her hands;
Patted into little castles.

Shiny day on shiny day
Tumbled in a rainbow clutter,
As she flipped them all away,
Sent them spinning down the gutter.

Leave for her a red young rose,
Go your way, and save your pity;
She is happy, for she knows
That her dust is very pretty.

Ring Lardner

Ring Lardner a satirist? H. L. Mencken noticed a "sharply acrid flavor" in Lardner's later work, and took the occasion to declare ". . . it is difficult, even for an American, to contemplate the American without yielding to something hard to distinguish from moral indignation." And then: "Lardner conceals his new savagery, of course, beneath his old humor."

In *Writers in Crisis* Maxwell Geismar commented on Lardner in the following terms: "The funnyman of the 1920s, Ring Lardner is an authentic commentator on American capitalism in its frantic flowering. . . . Lardner's critique of the basic beliefs of 1929 is thorough. . . . though he wrote much that was evasive [he] basically accepted none of the social myths which formed his time."

In spite of Ring Lardner's distrust of "seriousness," the stamp of satire is on his later stories.

MR. AND MRS. FIX-IT

They're certainly a live bunch in this town. We ain't only been here three days and had calls already from people representin' four different organizations—the Chamber of Commerce, Kiwanis, and I forget who else. They wanted to know if

we was comfortable and did we like the town and is they anything they can do for us and what to be sure and see.

And they all asked how we happened to come here instead of
goin' somewheres else. I guess they keep a record of everybody's
reasons for comin' so as they can get a line on what features
tourists is most attracted by. Then they play up them features
in next year's booster advertisin'.

Well, I told them we was perfectly comfortable and we like
the town fine and they's nothin' nobody can do for us right now
and we'll be sure and see all the things we ought to see. But
when they asked me how did we happen to come here, I said it
was just a kind of a accident, because the real reason makes too
long a story.

My wife has been kiddin' me about my friends ever since we
was married. She says that judgin' by the ones I've introduced
her to, they ain't nobody in the world got a rummier bunch of
friends than me. I'll admit that the most of them ain't, well, what
you might call hot; they're different somehow than when I first
hung around with them. They seem to be lost without a brass
rail to rest their dogs on. But of course they're old friends and I
can't give 'em the air.

We have 'em to the house for dinner every little w'ile, they
and their wives, and what my missus objects to is because they
don't none of them play bridge or mah jong or do cross-word
puzzles or sing or dance or even talk, but jest set there and wait
for somebody to pour 'em a fresh drink.

As I say, my wife kids me about 'em and they ain't really
nothin' I can offer in their defense. That don't mean, though,
that the shoe is all on one foot. Because w'ile the majority of her
friends may not be quite as dumb as mine, just the same they's a
few she's picked out who I'd of had to be under the ether to allow anybody to introduce 'em to me in the first place.

Like the Crandalls, for instance. Mrs. Crandall come from
my wife's home town and they didn't hardly know each other
there, but they met again in a store in Chi and it went from bad
to worse till finally Ada asked the dame and her husband to the
house.

Well, the husband turns out to be the fella that win the war, w'ile it seems that Mrs. Crandall was in Atlantic City once and some movin' picture company was makin' a picture there and they took a scene of what was supposed to be society people walkin' up and down the Boardwalk and Mrs. Crandall was in the picture and people that seen it when it come out, they all said that from the way she screened, why if she wanted to go into the business, she could make Gloria Swanson look like Mrs. Gump.

Now it ain't only took me a few words to tell you these things, but when the Crandalls tells their story themselves, they don't hardly get started by midnight and no chance of them goin' home till they're through even when you drop 'em a hint that they're springin' it on you for the hundred and twelfth time.

That's the Crandalls, and another of the wife's friends is the Thayers. Thayer is what you might call a all-around handy man. He can mimic pretty near all the birds and beasts and fishes, he can yodel, he can play a ocarina, or he can recite Kipling or Robert H. Service, or he can do card tricks, and strike a light without no matches, and tie all the different knots.

And besides that, he can make a complete radio outfit and set it up, and take pictures as good as the best professional photographers and a whole lot better. He collects autographs. And he never had a sick day in his life.

Mrs. Thayer gets a headache playin' bridge, so it's mah jong or rhum when she's around. She used to be a teacher of elocution and she still gives readin's if you coax her, or if you don't, and her hair is such a awful nuisance that she would get it cut in a minute only all her friends tells her it would be criminal to spoil that head of hair. And when she talks to her husband, she always talks baby talk, maybe because somebody has told her that she'd be single if he wasn't childish.

And then Ada has got still another pal, a dame named Peggy Flood who is hospital mad and ain't happy unless she is just goin' under the knife or just been there. She's had everything removed that the doctors knew the name of and now they're probin' her for new giblets.

Well, I wouldn't mind if they cut her up into alphabet soup if they'd only do such a good job of it that they couldn't put her together again, but she always comes through O.K. and she spends the intermissions at our place, describin' what all they done or what they're plannin' to do next.

But the cat's nightgown is Tom Stevens and his wife. There's the team that wins the Olympics! And they're Ada's team, not mine.

Ada met Belle Stevens on the elevated. Ada was invited to a party out on the North Side and didn't know exactly where to get off and Mrs. Stevens seen her talkin' to the guard and horned in and asked her what was it she wanted to know and Ada told her, and Mrs. Stevens said she was goin' to get off the same station Ada wanted to get off, so they got off together.

Mrs. Stevens insisted on goin' right along to the address where Ada was goin' because she said Ada was bound to get lost if she wasn't familiar with the neighborhood.

Well, Ada thought it was mighty nice of her to do so much for a stranger. Mrs. Stevens said she was glad to because she didn't know what would of happened to her lots of times if strangers hadn't been nice and helped her out.

She asked Ada where she lived and Ada told her on the South Side and Mrs. Stevens said she was sure we'd like it better on the North Side if we'd leave her pick out a place for us, so Ada told her we had a year's lease that we had just signed and couldn't break it, so then Mrs. Stevens said her husband had studied law and he claimed they wasn't no lease that you couldn't break and some evening she would bring him out to call on us and he'd tell us how to break our lease.

Well, Ada had to say sure, come on out, though we was perfectly satisfied with our apartment and didn't no more want to break the lease than each other's jaw. Maybe not as much. Anyway, the very next night, they showed up, Belle and Tom, and when they'd gone, I give 'em the nickname—Mr. and Mrs. Fix-It.

After the introductions, Stevens made some remarks about what a cozy little place we had and then he asked if I would mind tellin' what rent we paid. So I told him a hundred and a quarter a month. So he said, of course, that was too much and no wonder we wanted to break the lease. Then I said we was satisfied and didn't want to break it and he said I must be

kiddin' and if I would show him the lease he would see what
loopholes they was in it.

Well, the lease was right there in a drawer in the table, but I
told him it was in my safety deposit box at the bank. I ain't got
no safety deposit box and no more use for one than Judge Lan-
dis has for the deef and dumb alphabet.

Stevens said the lease was probably just a regular lease and if
it was, they wouldn't be no trouble gettin' out of it, and mean-
w'ile him and his wife would see if they couldn't find us a place
in the same buildin' with them.

And he was pretty sure they could even if the owner had to
give some other tenant the air, because he, the owner, would do
anything in the world for Stevens.

So I said yes, but suppose we want to stay where we are. So
he said I looked like a man with better judgment than that and
if I would just leave everything to him he would fix it so's we
could move within a month. I kind of laughed and thought that
would be the end of it.

He wanted to see the whole apartment so I showed him
around and when we come to the bathroom he noticed my
safety razor on the shelf. He said, "So you use one of them
things," and I said, "Yes," and he asked me how I liked it, and I
said I liked it fine and he said that must be because I hadn't
never used a regular razor.

He said a regular razor was the only thing to use if a man
wanted to look good. So I asked him if he used a regular razor
and he said he did, so I said, "Well, if you look good, I don't
want to."

But that didn't stop him and he said if I would meet him
downtown the next day he would take me to the place where he
bought all his razors and help me pick some out for myself. I
told him I was goin' to be tied up, so just to give me the name
and address of the place and I would drop in there when I had
time.

But, no, that wouldn't do; he'd have to go along with me and
introduce me to the proprietor because the proprietor was a great
pal of his and would do anything in the world for him, and if
the proprietor vouched for the razors, I could be sure I was

gettin' the best razors money could buy. I told him again that I was goin' to be tied up and I managed to get him on some other subject.

Meanw'ile, Mrs. Stevens wanted to know where Ada had bought the dress she was wearin' and how much had it cost and Ada told her and Mrs. Stevens said it was a crime. She would meet Ada downtown tomorrow morning and take her to the shop where she bought her clothes and help her choose some dresses that really was dresses.

So Ada told her she didn't have no money to spend on dresses right then, and besides, the shop Mrs. Stevens mentioned was too high priced. But it seems the dame that run the shop was just like a sister to Mrs. Stevens and give her and her friends a big reduction and not only that, but they wasn't no hurry about payin'.

Well, Ada thanked her just the same, but didn't need nothin' new just at present; maybe later on she would take advantage of Mrs. Stevens's kind offer. Yes, but right now they was some models in stock that would be just beautiful on Ada and they might be gone later on. They was nothin' for it but Ada had to make a date with her; she wasn't obliged to buy nothin', but it would be silly not to go and look at the stuff that was in the joint and get acquainted with the dame that run it.

Well, Ada kept the date and bought three dresses she didn't want and they's only one of them she's had the nerve to wear. They cost her a hundred dollars a smash and I'd hate to think what the price would of been if Mrs. Stevens and the owner of the shop wasn't so much like sisters.

I was sure I hadn't made no date with Stevens, but just the same he called me up the next night to ask why I hadn't met him. And a couple of days later I got three new razors in the mail along with a bill and a note from the store sayin' that these was three specially fine razors that had been picked out for me by Thomas J. Stevens.

I don't know yet why I paid for the razors and kept 'em. I ain't used 'em and never intended to. Though I've been tempted a few times to test their edge on Stevens's neck.

That same week, Mrs. Stevens called up and asked us to

spend Sunday with them and when we got out there, the owner
of the buildin' is there, too. And Stevens has told him that I was
goin' to give up my apartment on the South Side and wanted
him to show me what he had.

I thought this was a little too strong and I said Stevens must
of misunderstood me, that I hadn't no fault to find with the
place I was in and wasn't plannin' to move, not for a year anyway. You can bet this didn't make no hit with the guy, who was
just there on Stevens's say-so that I was a prospective tenant.

Well, it was only about two months ago that this cute little
couple come into our life, but I'll bet we seen 'em twenty times
at least. They was always invitin' us to their place or invitin'
themselves to our place and Ada is one of these here kind of people that just can't say no. Which may be why I and her is married.

Anyway, it begin to seem like us and the Stevenses was livin'
together and all one family, with them at the head of it. I never
in my life seen anybody as crazy to run other people's business.
Honest to heavens, it's a wonder they let us brush our own
teeth!

Ada made the remark one night that she wished the ski
jumper who was doin' our cookin' would get married and quit
so's she wouldn't have to can her. Mrs. Stevens was there and
asked Ada if she should try and get her a new cook, but Ada
says no, the poor gal might have trouble findin' another job and
she felt sorry for her.

Just the same, the next afternoon a Jap come to the apartment and said he was ready to go to work and Mrs. Stevens had
sent him. Ada had to tell him the place was already filled.

Another night, Ada complained that her feet was tired. Belle
said her feet used to get tired, too, till a friend of hers recommended a chiropodist and she went to him and he done her so
much good that she made a regular appointment with him for
once every month and paid him a flat sum and no matter how
much runnin' around she done, her dogs hadn't fretted her once
since this cornhusker started tendin' to 'em.

She wanted to call up the guy at his home right then and
there and make a date for Ada and the only way Ada could

stop her was by promisin' to go and see him the next time her feet hurt. After that, whenever the two gals met, Belle's first question was "How is your feet?" and the answer was always "Fine, thanks."

Well, I'm quite a football fan and Ada likes to go, too, when it's a big game and lots of excitement. So we decided we'd see the Illinois-Chicago game and have a look at this "Red" Grange. I warned Ada to not say nothin' about it to Tom and Belle as I felt like we was entitled to a day off.

But it happened that they was goin' to be a game at Evanston that day and the Stevenses invited us to see that one with them. So we used the other game as a alibi. And when Tom asked me later on if I'd boughten my tickets yet, instead of sayin' yes, I told him the truth and said no.

So then he said:

"I'm glad you ain't, because I and Belle has made up our mind that the Chicago game is the one we ought to see. And we'll all go together. And don't you bother about tickets because I can get better ones than you can as Stagg and I is just like that."

So I left it to him to get the tickets and we might as well of set on the Adams Street bridge. I said to Stevens, I said:

"If these is the seats Mr. Stagg digs up for his old pals, I suppose he leads strangers twenty or thirty miles out in the country and blindfolds 'em and ties 'em to a tree."

Now of course it was the bunk about he and Stagg bein' so close. He may of been introduced to him once, but he ain't the kind of a guy that Stagg would go around holdin' hands with. Just the same, most of the people he bragged about knowin', why it turned out that he really did know 'em; yes, and stood ace high with 'em too.

Like, for instance, I got pinched for speedin' one night and they give me a ticket to show up in the Speeders' court and I told Stevens about it and he says, "Just forget it! I'll call up the judge and have it wiped off the book. He's a mighty good fella and a personal friend of mine."

Well, I didn't want to take no chances so I phoned Stevens the day before I was supposed to appear in court, and I asked him if he'd talked to the judge. He said he had and I asked him if he was sure. So he said, "If you don't believe me, call up the judge yourself." And he give me the judge's number. Sure enough, Stevens had fixed it and when I thanked the judge for his trouble, he said it was a pleasure to do somethin' for a friend of Tom Stevens's.

Now, I know it's silly to not appreciate favors like that and not warm up to people that's always tryin' to help you along, but still a person don't relish bein' treated like they was half-witted and couldn't button their shirt alone. Tom and Belle meant all right, but I and Ada got kind of tired of havin' fault found with everything that belonged to us and everything we done or tried to do.

Besides our apartment bein' no good and our clothes terrible, we learned that my dentist didn't know a bridge from a mustache cup, and the cigarettes I smoked didn't have no taste to them, and the man that bobbed Ada's hair must of been mad at her, and neither of us would ever know what it was to live till we owned a wire-haired fox terrier.

And we found out that the liquor I'd been drinkin' and enjoyin' was a mixture of bath salts and assorted paints, and the car we'd paid seventeen hundred smackers for wasn't nowheres near as much of a car as one that Tom could of got for us for eight hundred on account of knowin' a brother-in-law of a fella that used to go to school with the president of the company's nephew, and that if Ada would take up aesthetic dancin' under a dame Belle knew about, why she'd never have no more trouble with her tonsils.

Nothin' we had or nothin' we talked about gettin' or doin' was worth a damn unless it was recommended or suggested by the Stevenses.

Well, I done a pretty good business this fall and I and Ada had always planned to spend a winter in the South, so one night we figured it out that this was the year we could spare the money and the time and if we didn't go this year we never would. So the next thing was where should we go, and we finally decided on Miami. And we said we wouldn't mention nothin' about it to

Tom and Belle till the day we was goin'. We'd pretend we was doin' it out of a clear sky.

But a secret is just as safe with Ada as a police dog tethered with dental floss. It wasn't more than a day or two after we'd had our talk when Tom and Belle sprang the news that they was leavin' for California right after New Year's. And why didn't we go with them.

Well, I didn't say nothin' and Ada said it sounded grand, but it was impossible. Then Stevens said if it was a question of money, to not let that bother us as he would loan it to me and I could pay it back whenever I felt like it. That was more than Ada could stand, so she says we wasn't as poor as people seemed to think and the reason we couldn't go to California was because we was goin' to Miami.

This was such a surprise that it almost struck 'em dumb at first and all Tom could think of to say was that he'd been to Miami himself and it was too crowded and he'd lay off it if he was us. But the next time we seen 'em they had our trip all arranged.

First, Tom asked me what road we was goin' on and I told him the Big Four. So he asked if we had our reservations and I told him yes.

"Well," he said, "we'll get rid of 'em and I'll fix you up on the C. & E. I. The general passenger agent is a friend of mine and they ain't nothin' he won't do for my friends. He'll see that you're treated right and that you get there in good shape."

So I said:

"I don't want to put you to all that trouble, and besides I don't know nobody connected with the Big Four well enough for them to resent me travelin' on their lines, and as for gettin' there in good shape, even if I have a secret enemy or two on the Big Four, I don't believe they'd endanger the lives of the other passengers just to see that I didn't get there in good shape."

But Stevens insisted on takin' my tickets and sellin' 'em back to the Big Four and gettin' me fixed on the C. & E. I. The berths we'd had on the Big Four was Lower 9 and Lower 10. The berths Tom got us on the C. & E. I. was Lower 7 and Lower 8, which he said was better. I suppose he figured that the nearer you are to the middle of the car, the less chance there is of bein' woke up if your car gets in another train's way.

He wanted to know, too, if I'd made any reservations at a hotel. I showed him a wire I had from the Royal Palm in reply to a wire I'd sent 'em.

"Yes," he says, "but you don't want to stop at the Royal Palm. You wire and tell 'em to cancel that and I'll make arrangements for you at the Flamingo, over at the Beach. Charley Krom, the manager there, was born and raised in the same town I was. He'll take great care of you if he knows you're a friend of mine."

So I asked him if all the guests at the Flamingo was friends of his, and he said of course not; what did I mean?

"Well," I said, "I was just thinkin' that if they ain't, Mr. Krom probably makes life pretty miserable for 'em. What does he do, have the phone girl ring 'em up at all hours of the night, and hide their mail, and shut off their hot water, and put cracker crumbs in their beds?"

That didn't mean nothin' to Stevens and he went right ahead and switched me from one hotel to the other.

While Tom was reorganizin' my program and tellin' me what to eat in Florida, and what bait to use for barracuda and carp, and what time to go bathin' and which foot to stick in the water first, why Belle was makin' Ada return all the stuff she had boughten to wear down there and buy other stuff that Belle picked out for her at joints where Belle was so well known that they only soaked her twice as much as a stranger. She had Ada almost crazy, but I told her to never mind; in just a few more days we'd be where they couldn't get at us.

I suppose you're wonderin' why didn't we quarrel with 'em and break loose from 'em and tell 'em to leave us alone. You'd know why if you knew them. Nothin' we could do would convince 'em that we didn't want their advice and help. And nothin' we could say was a insult.

Well, the night before we was due to leave Chi, the phone rang and I answered it. It was Tom.

"I've got a surprise for you," he says. "I and Belle has give up the California idear. We're goin' to Miami instead, and on ac-

count of me knowin' the boys down at the C. & E. I., I've landed
a drawin' room on the same train you're takin'. How is that for
news?"

"Great!" I said, and I went back and broke it to Ada. For a
minute I thought she was goin' to faint. And all night long she
moaned and groaned and had hysterics.

So that's how we happened to come to Biloxi.

Philip Wylie

If criticism is concealed in comedy in the work of Lardner,
Philip Wylie's *Generation of Vipers* is as candidly assertive as a
10-gauge shotgun discharged in church. A jeremiad against
some of the fonder American idols and ideas, Wylie's explosive
white paper includes the famous acid-etched portrait of Mom.

MOM
(from *Generation of Vipers*)

Mom is an American creation. Her elaboration was necessary because she was launched as Cinderella. Past generations of men have accorded to their mothers, as a rule, only
such honors as they earned by meritorious action in their individual daily lives. Filial *duty* was recognized by many sorts of
civilizations and loyalty to it has been highly regarded among
most peoples. But I cannot think, offhand, of any civilization except ours in which an entire division of living men has been
used, during wartime, or at any time, to spell out the word
"mom" on a drill field, or to perform any equivalent act.

The adoration of motherhood has even been made the basis of
a religious cult, but the mother so worshiped achieved maternity
without change in her virgin status—a distinction worthy of contemplation in itself—and she thus in no way resembled mom.

Hitherto, in fact, man has shown a considerable qui vive to the dangers which arise from momism and freely perceived that his "old wives" were often vixens, dragons, and Xanthippes. Classical literature makes a constant point of it. Shakespeare dwelt on it. Man has also kept before his mind an awareness that, even in the most lambent mother love, there is always a chance some extraneous current will blow up a change, and the thing will become a consuming furnace. The spectacle of the female devouring her young in the firm belief that it is for their own good is too old in man's legends to be overlooked by any but the most flimsily constructed society.

Freud has made a fierce and wondrous catalogue of examples of mother-love-in-action which traces its origin to an incestuous perversion of a normal instinct. That description is, of course, sound. Unfortunately, Americans, who are the most prissy people on earth, have been unable to benefit from Freud's wisdom because they can *prove* that they do not, by and large, sleep with their mothers. That is their interpretation of Freud. Moreover, no matter how many times they repeat the Scriptures, they cannot get the true sense of the passage about lusting in one's heart—especially when they are mothers thinking about their sons, or vice versa.

Meanwhile, megaloid momworship has got completely out of hand. Our land, subjectively mapped, would have more silver cords and apron strings crisscrossing it than railroads and telephone wires. Mom is everywhere and everything and damned near everybody, and from her depends all the rest of the U. S. Disguised as good old mom, dear old mom, sweet old mom, your loving mom, and so on, she is the bride at every funeral and the corpse at every wedding. Men live for her and die for her, dote upon her and whisper her name as they pass away, and I believe she has now achieved, in the hierarchy of miscellaneous articles, a spot next to the Bible and the Flag, being reckoned part of both in a way. She may therefore soon be granted by the House of Representatives the especial supreme and extraordinary right of sitting on top of both when she chooses, which, God knows, she does. At any rate, if no such bill is under consideration, the presentation of one would cause little debate among the solons. These sages take cracks at their native land

and make jokes about Holy Writ, but nobody among them—no great man or brave—from the first day of the first congressional meeting to the present ever stood in our halls of state and pronounced the one indubitably most-needed American verity: "Gentlemen, mom is a jerk."

Mom is something new in the world of men. Hitherto, mom has been so busy raising a large family, keeping house, doing the chores, and fabricating everything in every home except the floor and the walls that she was rarely a problem to her family or to her equally busy friends, and never one to herself. Usually, until very recently, mom folded up and died of hard work somewhere in the middle of her life. Old ladies were scarce and those who managed to get old did so by making remarkable inner adjustments and by virtue of a fabulous horniness of body, so that they lent to old age not only dignity but metal.

Nowadays, with nothing to do, and all the tens of thousands of men I wrote about in a preceding chapter to maintain her, every clattering prickamette in the republic survives for an incredible number of years, to stamp and jibber in the midst of man, a noisy neuter by natural default or a scientific gelding sustained by science, all tongue and teat and razzmatazz. The machine has deprived her of social usefulness; time has stripped away her biological possibilities and poured her hide full of liquid soap; and man has sealed his own soul beneath the clamorous cordillera by handing her the checkbook and going to work in the service of her caprices.

These caprices are of a menopausal nature at best—hot flashes, rage, infantilism, weeping, sentimentality, peculiar appetite, and all the ragged reticule of tricks, wooings, wiles, suborned fornications, slobby onanisms, indulgences, crotchets, superstitions, phlegms, debilities, vapors, butterflies-in-the-belly, plaints, connivings, cries, malingerings, deceptions, visions, hallucinations, needlings and wheedlings, which pop out of every personality in the act of abandoning itself and humanity. At worst—i.e., the finis—this salaginous mess tapers off into senility, which is man's caricature of himself by reversed ontogeny. But behind this vast aurora of pitiable weakness is mom, the brass-breasted Baal, or mom, the thin and enfeebled martyr whose very urine, nevertheless, will etch glass.

Satan, we are told, finds work for idle hands to do. There is no mistaking the accuracy of this proverb. Millions of men have heaped up riches and made a conquest of idleness so as to discover what it is that Satan puts them up to. Not one has failed to find out. But never before has a great nation of brave and dreaming men absent-mindedly created a huge class of idle, middle-aged women. Satan himself has been taxed to dig up enterprises enough for them. But the field is so rich, so profligate, so perfectly to his taste, that his first effort, obviously, has been to make it self-enlarging and self-perpetuating. This he has done by whispering into the ears of girls that the only way they can cushion the shock destined to follow the rude disillusionment over the fact that they are not really Cinderella is to institute momworship. Since he had already infested both male and female with the love of worldly goods, a single step accomplished the entire triumph: he taught the gals to teach their men that dowry went the other way, that it was a weekly contribution, and that any male worthy of a Cinderella would have to work like a piston after getting one, so as to be worthy, also, of all the moms in the world.

The road to hell is spiral, a mere bend in the strait and narrow, but a persistent one. This was the given torque, and most men are up to their necks in it now. The devil whispered. The pretty girl then blindfolded her man so he would not see that she was turning from a butterfly into a caterpillar. She told him, too, that although caterpillars ate every damned leaf in sight, they were moms, hence sacred. Finally, having him sightless and whirling, she snitched his checkbook. Man was a party to the deception because he wanted to be fooled about Cinderella, because he was glad to have a convenient explanation of mom, and also because there burned within him a dim ideal which had to do with proper behavior, getting along, and, especially, making his mark. Mom had already shaken him out of that notion of being a surveyor in the Andes which had bloomed in him when he was nine years old, so there was nothing left to do, anyway, but to take a stockroom job in the hairpin factory and try to work up to the vice-presidency. Thus the women of America raped the men, not sexually, unfortunately, but morally, since neuters come hard by morals.

I pass over the obvious reference to the deadliness of the female of the species, excepting only to note that perhaps, having a creative physical part in the universe, she falls more easily than man into the contraposite role of spiritual saboteur.

Mom got herself out of the nursery and the kitchen. She then got out of the house. She did not get out of the church, but, instead, got the stern stuff out of *it*, padded the guild room, and moved in more solidly than ever before. No longer either hesitant or reverent, because there was no cause for either attitude after her purge, she swung the church by the tail as she swung everything else. In a preliminary test of strength, she also got herself the vote and, although politics never interested her (unless she was exceptionally naïve, a hairy foghorn, or a size forty scorpion), the damage she forthwith did to society was so enormous and so rapid that even the best men lost track of things. Mom's first gracious presence at the ballot-box was roughly concomitant with the start toward a new all-time low in political scurviness, hoodlumism, gangsterism, labor strife, monopolistic thuggery, moral degeneration, civic corruption, smuggling, bribery, theft, murder, homosexuality, drunkenness, financial depression, chaos and war. Note that.

The degenerating era, however, marked new highs in the production of junk. Note that, also.

Mom, however, is a great little guy. Pulling pants onto her by these words, let us look at mom.

She is a middle-aged puffin with an eye like a hawk that has just seen a rabbit twitch far below. She is about twenty-five pounds overweight, with no sprint, but sharp heels and a hard backhand which she does not regard as a foul but a womanly defense. In a thousand of her there is not sex appeal enough to budge a hermit ten paces off a rock ledge. She none the less spends several hundred dollars a year on permanents and transformations, pomades, cleansers, rouges, lipsticks, and the like— and fools nobody except herself. If a man kisses her with any earnestness, it is time for mom to feel for her pocketbook, and this occasionally does happen.

She smokes thirty cigarettes a day, chews gum, and consumes tons of bonbons and petits fours. The shortening in the latter, stripped from pigs, sheep and cattle, shortens mom. She plays bridge with the stupid voracity of a hammerhead shark, which cannot see what it is trying to gobble but never stops snapping its jaws and roiling the waves with its tail. She drinks moderately, which is to say, two or three cocktails before dinner every night and a brandy and a couple of highballs afterward. She doesn't count the two cocktails she takes before lunch when she lunches out, which is every day she can. On Saturday nights, at the club or in the juke joint, she loses count of her drinks and is liable to get a little tiddly, which is to say, shot or blind. But it is her man who worries about where to acquire the money while she worries only about how to spend it, so he has the ulcers and colitis and she has the guts of a bear; she can get pretty stiff before she topples.

. . . .

I give you mom. I give you the destroying mother. I give you her justice—from which we have never removed the eye bandage. I give you the angel—and point to the sword in her hand. I give you death—the hundred million deaths that are muttered under Yggdrasill's ash. I give you Medusa and Stheno and Euryale. I give you the harpies and the witches, and the Fates. I give you the woman in pants, and the new religion: she-popery. I give you Pandora. I give you Proserpine, the Queen of Hell. The five-and-ten-cent-store Lilith, the mother of Cain, the black widow who is poisonous and eats her mate, and I designate at the bottom of your program the grand finale of all the soap operas: the mother of America's Cinderella.

James Thurber

THE SECRET LIFE OF WALTER MITTY

We're going through!" The Commander's voice was like thin ice breaking. He wore his full-dress uniform, with the heavily braided white cap pulled down rakishly over one cold gray eye. "We can't make it, sir. It's spoiling for a hurricane, if you ask me." "I'm not asking you, Lieutenant Berg," said the Commander. "Throw on the power lights! Rev her up to 8,500! We're going through!" The pounding of the cylinders increased: ta-pocketa-pocketa-pocketa-*pocketa-pocketa*. The Commander stared at the ice forming on the pilot window. He walked over and twisted a row of complicated dials. "Switch on No. 8 auxiliary!" he shouted. "Switch on No. 8 auxiliary!" repeated Lieutenant Berg. "Full strength in No. 3 turret!" shouted the Commander. "Full strength in No. 3 turret!" The crew, bending to their various tasks in the huge, hurtling eight-engined Navy hydroplane, looked at each other and grinned. "The Old Man'll get us through," they said to one another. "The Old Man ain't afraid of Hell!". . .

"Not so fast! You're driving too fast!" said Mrs. Mitty. "What are you driving so fast for?"

"Hmm?" said Walter Mitty. He looked at his wife, in the seat beside him, with shocked astonishment. She seemed grossly unfamiliar, like a strange woman who had yelled at him in a crowd. "You were up to fifty-five," she said. "You know I don't like to go more than forty. You were up to fifty-five." Walter Mitty drove on toward Waterbury in silence, the roaring of the SN202 through the worst storm in twenty years of Navy flying fading in the remote, intimate airways of his mind. "You're tensed up again," said Mrs. Mitty. "It's one of your days. I wish you'd let Dr. Renshaw look you over."

Walter Mitty stopped the car in front of the building where his wife went to have her hair done. "Remember to get those overshoes while I'm having my hair done," she said. "I don't need overshoes," said Mitty. She put her mirror back into her bag. "We've been all through that," she said, getting out of the car. "You're not a young man any longer." He raced the engine a little. "Why don't you wear your gloves? Have you lost your gloves?" Walter Mitty reached in a pocket and brought out the gloves. He put them on, but after she had turned and gone into the building and he had driven on to a red light, he took them off again. "Pick it up, brother!" snapped a cop as the light changed, and Mitty hastily pulled on his gloves and lurched ahead. He drove around the streets aimlessly for a time, and then he drove past the hospital on his way to the parking lot.

. . ."It's the millionaire banker, Wellington McMillan," said the pretty nurse. "Yes?" said Walter Mitty, removing his gloves slowly. "Who has the case?" "Dr. Renshaw and Dr. Benbow, but there are two specialists here, Dr. Remington from New York and Mr. Pritchard-Mitford from London. He flew over." A door opened down a long, cool corridor and Dr. Renshaw came out. He looked distraught and haggard. "Hello, Mitty," he said. "We're having the devil's own time with McMillan, the millionaire banker and close personal friend of Roosevelt. Obstreosis of the ductal tract. Tertiary. Wish you'd take a look at him." "Glad to," said Mitty.

In the operating room there were whispered introductions: "Dr. Remington, Dr. Mitty. Mr. Pritchard-Mitford, Dr. Mitty." "I've read your book on streptothricosis," said Pritchard-Mitford, shaking hands. "A brilliant performance, sir." "Thank you," said Walter Mitty. "Didn't know you were in the States, Mitty," grumbled Remington. "Coals to Newcastle, bringing Mitford and me up here for a tertiary." "You are very kind," said Mitty. A huge, complicated machine, connected to the operating table, with many tubes and wires, began at this moment to go pocketa-pocketa-pocketa. "The new anesthetizer is giving way!" shouted an interne. "There is no one in the East who knows how to fix it!" "Quiet, man!" said Mitty, in a low, cool voice. He sprang to the machine, which was now going pocketa-pocketa-queep-pocketa-queep. He began fingering delicately a row of glistening dials. "Give me a fountain pen!" he snapped. Someone handed him a fountain pen. He pulled a faulty piston out of the machine and inserted the pen in its place. "That will hold for ten minutes," he said. "Get on with the operation." A nurse hurried over and whispered to Renshaw, and Mitty saw the man turn pale. "Coreopsis has set in," said Renshaw nervously. "If you would take over, Mitty?" Mitty looked at him and at the craven figure of Benbow, who drank, and at the grave, uncertain faces of the two great specialists. "If you wish," he said. They slipped a white gown on him; he adjusted a mask and drew on thin gloves; nurses handed him shining . . .

"Back it up, Mac! Look out for that Buick!" Walter Mitty jammed on the brakes. "Wrong lane, Mac," said the parking-lot attendant, looking at Mitty closely. "Gee. Yeh," muttered Mitty. He began cautiously to back out of the lane marked "Exit Only." "Leave her sit there," said the attendant. "I'll put her away." Mitty got out of the car. "Hey, better leave the key." "Oh," said Mitty, handing the man the ignition key. The attendant vaulted into the car, backed it up with insolent skill, and put it where it belonged.

They're so damn cocky, thought Walter Mitty, walking along Main Street; they think they know everything. Once he had tried to take his chains off, outside New Milford, and he had got them wound around the axles. A man had had to come out in a wrecking car and unwind them, a young, grinning garageman. Since then Mrs. Mitty always made him drive to a garage to have the chains taken off. The next time, he thought, I'll wear my right arm in a sling; they won't grin at me then. I'll have my right arm in a sling and they'll see I couldn't possibly take the chains off myself. He kicked at the slush on the sidewalk. "Overshoes," he said to himself, and he began looking for a shoe store.

When he came out into the street again, with the overshoes in a box under his arm, Walter Mitty began to wonder what the other thing was his wife had told him to get. She had told him twice, before they set out from their house for Waterbury. In a way he hated these weekly trips to town—he was always getting something wrong. Kleenex, he thought, Squibb's, razor blades? No. Toothpaste, toothbrush, bicarbonate, carborundum, initiative and referendum? He gave it up. But she would remember it. "Where's the what's-its-name?" she would ask. "Don't tell me you forgot the what's-its-name." A newsboy went by shouting something about the Waterbury trial.

. . ."Perhaps this will refresh your memory." The District Attorney suddenly thrust a heavy automatic at the quiet figure on the witness stand. "Have you ever seen this before?" Walter Mitty took the gun and examined it expertly. "This is my Webley-Vickers 50.80," he said calmly. An excited buzz ran around the courtroom. The judge rapped for order. "You are a crack shot with any sort of firearms, I believe?" said the District Attorney, insinuatingly. "Objection!" shouted Mitty's attorney. "We have shown that the defendant could not have fired the shot. We have shown that he wore his right arm in a sling on the night of the fourteenth of July." Walter Mitty raised his hand briefly and the bickering attorneys were stilled. "With any known make of gun," he said evenly, "I could have killed Gregory Fitzhurst at three hundred feet *with my left hand.*" Pandemonium broke loose in the courtroom. A woman's scream rose above the bedlam and suddenly a lovely, dark-haired girl was in Walter Mitty's arms. The District Attorney struck at her savagely. Without rising from his chair, Mitty let the man have it on the point of the chin. "You miserable cur!" . . .

"Puppy biscuit," said Walter Mitty. He stopped walking and the buildings of Waterbury rose up out of the misty courtroom and surrounded him again. A woman who was passing laughed. "He said 'Puppy biscuit,'" she said to her companion. "That man said 'Puppy biscuit' to himself." Walter Mitty hurried on. He went into an A. & P., not the first one he came to but a smaller one farther up the street. "I want some biscuit for small, young dogs," he said to the clerk. "Any special brand, sir?" The greatest pistol shot in the world thought a moment. "It says 'Puppies Bark for It' on the box," said Walter Mitty.

His wife would be through at the hairdresser's in fifteen minutes, Mitty saw in looking at his watch, unless they had trouble drying it; sometimes they had trouble drying it. She didn't like to get to the hotel first; she would want him to be there waiting for her as usual. He found a big leather chair in the lobby, facing a window, and he put the overshoes and the puppy biscuit on the floor beside it. He picked up an old copy of *Liberty* and sank down into the chair. "Can Germany Conquer the World Through the Air?" Walter Mitty looked at the pictures of bombing planes and of ruined streets.

. . . "The cannonading has got the wind up in young Raleigh, sir," said the sergeant. Captain Mitty looked up at him through tousled hair. "Get him to bed," he said wearily. "With the others. I'll fly alone." "But you can't, sir," said the sergeant anxiously. "It takes two men to handle that bomber and the

Archies are pounding hell out of the air. Von Richtman's circus
is between here and Saulier." "Somebody's got to get that ammunition dump," said Mitty. "I'm going over. Spot of brandy?"
He poured a drink for the sergeant and one for himself. War
thundered and whined around the dugout and battered at the
door. There was a rending of wood and splinters flew through
the room. "A bit of a near thing," said Captain Mitty carelessly.
"The box barrage is closing in," said the sergeant. "We only
live once, Sergeant," said Mitty, with his faint, fleeting smile.
"Or do we?" He poured another brandy and tossed it off. "I
never see a man could hold his brandy like you, sir," said the
sergeant. "Begging your pardon, sir." Captain Mitty stood up
and strapped on his huge Webley-Vickers automatic. "It's forty
kilometers through hell, sir," said the sergeant. Mitty finished
one last brandy. "After all," he said softly, "what isn't?" The
pounding of the cannon increased; there was the rat-tat-tatting
of machine guns, and from somewhere came the menacing
pocketa-pocketa-pocketa of the new flamethrowers. Walter
Mitty walked to the door of the dugout humming "Auprès de Ma
Blonde." He turned and waved to the sergeant. "Cheerio!" he
said. . . .

Something struck his shoulder. "I've been looking all over
this hotel for you," said Mrs. Mitty. "Why do you have to hide
in this old chair? How did you expect me to find you?" "Things
close in," said Walter Mitty vaguely. "What?" Mrs. Mitty said.
"Did you get the what's-its-name? The puppy biscuit? What's
in that box?" "Overshoes," said Mitty. "Couldn't you have put
them on in the store?" "I was thinking," said Walter Mitty.
"Does it ever occur to you that I am sometimes thinking?" She
looked at him. "I'm going to take your temperature when I get
you home," she said.

They went out through the revolving doors that made a
faintly derisive whistling sound when you pushed them. It was
two blocks to the parking lot. At the drugstore on the corner
she said, "Wait here for me. I forgot something. I won't be a
minute." She was more than a minute. Walter Mitty lighted a
cigarette. It began to rain, rain with sleet in it. He stood up
against the wall of the drugstore, smoking. . . . He put his

shoulders back and his heels together. "To hell with the handkerchief," said Walter Mitty scornfully. He took one last drag on his cigarette and snapped it away. Then, with that faint, fleeting smile playing about his lips, he faced the firing squad; erect and motionless, proud and disdainful, Walter Mitty the Undefeated, inscrutable to the last.

John O'Hara

CONVERSATION IN THE ATOMIC AGE

Malloy, the occasional writer for motion pictures, and Mrs. Schmidt, his Los Angeles society friend, had said all they had to say; that is, Malloy had said his say, which was to report the news of his wife and family back East and provide whatever information he possessed on their few mutual friends in New York and Philadelphia. That had taken him up to the salad, which, contrary to California custom, was served after the entrée. Malloy had known it was going to be that way, but taking her out to dine and dance was a duty that Malloy performed because Mrs. Schmidt was always nice to his wife. When he had finished, Mrs. Schmidt took over. Her monologue was entirely predictable, involving, as always, her full report on every party she had been to in the last three weeks, including the names of people Malloy never had heard of, what some of the women wore or did not wear, who was sleeping with whom, how the people came by their money, and Transportation. Mrs. Schmidt was fascinated with Transportation, and her stories always went something like the one she plunged into that night. "I drove the Cadillac to Santa Barbara," she said, "because Gil Foster had left his car there, at Hopie and Jack's, and then Jack and I came back together in his Buick because he had a meeting downtown and wanted to use his car, and then of course Hopie, she was coming down that afternoon and so she drove my car and Gil had to come down alone, too, in his car. You know that old Lagonda he has."

"No, I don't know Gil Foster."

"Oh, I thought you did. Of course you do. Gil Foster? From Tulsa? Part Cherokee? Or maybe Choctaw. Terribly rich and terribly attractive."

"Nope."

"Hmm. Well, anyway, he has this old Lagonda he bought before the war. He's always kept it out here for when he visits here. He likes an open car but Martha won't ride in one, but of course she hardly ever comes to Los Angeles. She isn't very attractive."

"Is she part Indian?"

"I don't know. Why?"

"I just wondered."

"What made you ask that? Did you hear she was? She might be. I don't really know very much about her. They had an apartment here one winter, at the Town House, but she didn't make the grade. Nobody liked her, but I don't think it was because she's part Indian. After all, Gil is, and everybody's crazy about Gil. And you know, you coming from the East, you don't understand—"

"Now, listen, you're from Schenectady, New York."

"I was *born* there is all. Except for when I was at St. Margaret's I've lived here all my life, so I consider myself an Angeleno and I understand the Western point of view about Indian blood. All my friends out here have some Indian blood, at least all the oil crowd, or most of them. It's no disgrace."

"Oh."

"I'm rather surprised at you taking that attitude. I thought all you New Dealers were all for marrying Jews and Negroes and Hottentots all over the place."

"Oh, no. Just giving them a quart of milk every day."

"Huh?"

"It's all right."

"Oh, I get it. You're kidding me. I never can tell when you're serious or when you're kidding. How does Kate put up with it?"

"Christ knows."

"She's darling. Everybody loves Kate. She's rather hard to get to know. Reserved, I mean, and not very talkative, but I've

heard an awful lot of people say how attractive they thought she
was. You know you're awfully lucky."

"Am I?"

"What do you mean 'Am I'? Don't you think you are?"

"I was trapped into that marriage."

"What do you mean you were trapped into that marriage?
That's the most conceited statement I ever heard you make.
How do you mean you were trapped?"

"Kate was seven months pregnant when I married her."

"Why, you—I don't believe it. Whatever happened to the
baby, if she was pregnant?"

"I'm sorry, but that's a secret."

Mrs. Schmidt studied Malloy. "Are you telling me the
truth?"

"No."

"I didn't think you were. I didn't fall for it. Oh, there's your
friend Ed Vanralt. Who's he with?"

"Bee Corson."

"Bee Corson. Rex Corson the actor's wife? They broke up,
didn't they?"

"Mm-hmm."

"Why? Did she leave him or did he leave her?"

"I don't know."

"You know the Corsons, don't you?"

"Not terribly well. Her only very slightly."

"Call them over."

"What for?"

"I'd like to talk to them. I think Ed Vanralt's very attractive.
Does he still go around with Joan Lord in New York?"

"I suppose so."

"You know, for a writer you aren't a bit interested in people,
are you? . . . She's plastered."

"Looks that way, but of course she may have diabetes.
Orange juice'll fix her up."

"How long has she had it? Rex Corson must be a bastard to
leave her just when she gets diabetes. At least wait till she dies."

"She may hang on for years."

"I feel sorry for her. . . . You're wrong. She's drinking

double Scotches. The waiter just poured two Scotches in the glass and hardly any soda. She hasn't any diabetes. She's just plastered. I thought Ed Vanralt was Rex Corson's best friend."

"He is."

"Then what's he doing out with his wife?"

"That's a hard question."

"Not to me it isn't. Look at her patting his cheek."

"I can't look."

"Oh, stop. Just because Ed Vanralt's a friend of yours you don't have to put on an act. Those two'll be in bed in an hour if I know anything."

"Well, it *is* getting late. What are *your* plans?"

"I don't know. What would you like to do?"

"I'd like an early quit tonight."

"So would I. I tell you, you don't have to take me home. I left my car in the Brown Derby parking lot. You take me there and I can get home all right from there. Except, I just happened to think. Marge is stopping for me in her car tomorrow, we're going to Pat's luncheon. I think it'd be all right to leave my car in the parking lot all night or else put it in some garage in the neighborhood. Then I could go to the luncheon with Pat and she could take me to the garage after we've had our fittings. We're both having fittings after Pat's luncheon but then Pat is driving to Palm Springs after our fittings and I want to have my car because I'm going to Attie's for cocktails but I'm leaving early because I have to dress for dinner. Gil has a new Oldsmobile with the hydromatic shift. I don't mean Gil, I mean Arthur. And he's stopping for me around eight. So it might be a better idea if I left my car in Beverly. That is, if you don't mind taking me home."

"Not a bit," said Malloy.

Alan Harrington

"Shed your individuality. Be happy nothings." This is the message of Alan Harrington's Dr. Modesto, whose philosophy of Centralism—in appearance a ghastly compromise between Dale Carnegie and Zen Buddhism—is a striking satire on conformism.

Also the author of a report on the corporate uses of human beings in a giant business organization, The Crystal Palace, Harrington is one of the keenest of the unaffiliated commentators on the American scene.

THE DOCTRINE OF CENTRALISM
(from *The Revelations of Dr. Modesto*)

1. Since your self grates on others, and makes you miserable, get rid of it.

2. In our society, in our time, it does not pay to be yourself. People laugh at you and call you strange—even if it was your father's fault.

3. Look around you, and see who is the happy man. He is the one Just Like Everybody Else. "Oh, so that is the way to be?" you ask, and I say, yes, that is the way you and I must be.

4. You are a sensitive person in a world of Brutes. Like a feeble animal, you need protective coloration. You must hide.

5. The only place to hide is in the center of their culture. Be more average than anyone!

6. From this moment on, HAVE NO SELF.

7. Have no mind of your own. Have no thought, opinion, habit, no desire or preference, no enthusiasm, love, or fear of your own. *Be* the composite of your neighbors.

8. When you have not a shred of individuality left, no one can clash with you. Once you reach this state, it will be *absolutely impossible* for you to be unhappy.

9. You wonder again, anxiously: "Is this the way to be?" and I say, yes. What other chance do we have? Because we are sensitive and "different," they pick on us. They set British standards, and call us misfits for not measuring up to them. To survive, we must become happy nothings.

10. We'll form a massive nothing in the heart of the United States of America, and operate from there.

II

11. This is the way you melt into the Community Mind:
STARE AT ONE OBJECT. For instance, you might choose
an awning or a drain pipe. Stare at it until you lose yourself.
Then begin the Centralist's Walk through the streets.

12. It is an unusual sensation. There will be a hush all
around you. Hear the people. All the faces have bright eyes.
Their voices come through the uproarious silence and whisper
in your ear. You will obtain an instantaneous fix on many lone-
linesses. Louts meditate for you. A cry of anxiety rings out of a
horselaugh.

13. After a while, all the ideas that inhabit the town inhabit
you.

14. When the sleepwalk is over, you wake up The Central
Man in town. There is a moment when the intolerable burden
of self is lifted from you. Oh, if you could only *know* how it
feels to be free of caring about anything. Drifting along in the
center of the crowd, you are utterly happy. Peace radiates from
you, making others happy. And this gives you practically limit-
less power over others!

15. It is the power of averageness. Nobody can resist you.
How could they? You are the Norm around which their own
lives are arranged. They are completely centralized by you.
Without knowing it, they want to yield to you, because each
one sees himself in your image, and they all love you as they
love themselves.

III

16. The Central Man comprehends all variations from the
average, including the extremes, because they went into forming him. Thus, he can centralize the wildest hermit or the dullest clerk, and make them love him and buy whatever he has to
sell. The hermit will detect a brother wild man; the clerk will
respond to the image of a fellow clod. The Centralist assumes
either of their identities at will. He does so automatically. But
he has no personality of his own, for this is the very condition of
his happiness.

17. Remember that in yourself you are nothing. This means that you cannot be alone too long, for then you will have no one to "be." If you do not see people, you may faint and forget, and the vestiges of your old, permanent self will drag at you and pull you back toward your former state.

18. Realize that your initial happiness is not permanent. You will have to practice for quite a while, and melt into all kinds of towns, before you can adjust effortlessly to any circumstance.

19. One rule will protect you—make the idea of Centrality a fixation. Maintain a fanatic devotion to the center of everything. LIVE CENTRALLY. Even this. Live as close as possible to the geographical center of town. There is no joking. The idea should permeate everything you do. Pursue it to any lengths— your position in a group photograph, your seat in a bus. Such apparently meaningless acts add up to one dominating reflex, so that eventually—even when there is no pleasure or point in do- ing so—you will take your place in the center, where no harm can come to you.

20. I also tell you BELIEVE and THINK CENTRALLY, which is to say believe in nothing, but give your loyalty to any popular cause in the vicinity. And give it precisely in half-meas- ure, depending on what your neighbors believe. If they despise a certain race, join moderately in the pleasures of contempt. But then, supposing a liberal element comes to town, trim your po- sition. You have to adjust, like the wire-walker carrying a long pole, who keeps his eyes on the dips and lifts of the pole ends, and takes warning from them in time to maintain his balance. So, when the liberals come, your old position is slightly un- balanced, and you change your beliefs. Say, perhaps: "There are some good ones." With the arrival of more leftists, cite scientific evidence of the equality of races.

21. If this disturbs you, I will go further. I tell you, you have no morals any more. Prepare to do good and beautiful things and monstrous things. You will love God when you are with good people. But if some Maynard comes into your life, you will not be afraid to deny God and drink toasts to the death of God with a townful of atheists, for you *are* not religious and you *are* not an atheist. You are both and neither. Just as you are a mod-

erate drunkard among drunkards. Or if you are a prison guard, you will be just as brutal as the others. But I can see you in the time of great floods. When the Red Cross atmosphere is everywhere, and the newsreel cameras take pictures of heroes risking their necks to get people down off the housetops, you will be in one of those boats with a baby safe in your arms.

22. I say also, I will go further. When I took the Centralist's Walk in the city of M———, I saw some oafs teasing a waitress, and I *believed* then in teasing helpless girls, and I joined them (rough men who would normally have frightened me), and by making insulting remarks to the waitress I made them love me, and they begged me to go bowling.

23. Now you are beginning to see the conditions of your happiness, and the power you will have. You will think in the center, be ready to delight in trivialities. Care which team wins. Spend hours comparing the kinds of gasoline that all come from the same pipeline. Every time you wash your car it always rains, if that's the general story. Throw salt over your shoulder. Knock on wood.

24. You will also BEHAVE CENTRALLY. This means that for every man you talk to, the very air becomes a mirror. And every woman sees in you the kind of man who *rests* her at that moment. That is your secret. You *rest* people, often—especially in a group—without their being aware of you. At any party you are the fellow getting ice cubes. You're "around," virtually invisible, yet the gathering revolves about you. When you leave, a great nervousness may fall on everyone.

25. I tell you to WORK CENTRALLY. Despite your power to make anyone do your bidding, you should not rise to the top. Get ahead, but moderately. Work at a typical job for an ordinary salary. The extremes of worldly success and failure are equally dangerous, because they throw you off-center. Failure begets worry and the poor opinion of others. Success creates prominence and the envy of others. Both prevent your remaining Central.

26. PLAY CENTRALLY. Never be a champion. In tournaments lose out deftly in the middle rounds. You will know the joys of coming in second when the chips are down. Remember

that the champion is a plaything in your hands. He will flourish and die, but you will endure. When all the tournaments are over (because everyone must have the same ability), you will have your day.

27. Finally, you must abandon Love. Is this a sacrifice? I ask you, how can you love? For you, love is the last enemy—a terrible, unbalancing, uncalculated thing, ruinous to the peace of mind, destroyer of urbanity, a most individual process of *caring* that will end you, I warn. The Centralist practices love, but cannot for one unguarded moment permit it in his heart. He is the virtuoso of love, who can produce greater, shall I say, amounts of love, of the highest quality—greater than the sickliest-hearted worshipper—yet, for his survival, feel none of it.

28. I come to the FINAL EQUILIBRIUM, and ask you, savagely, is this sacrifice too much? Or would you rather return to the "individual" state, and have them sneer and laugh at you, and give you dirty clean-up jobs in animal houses? Go back, then! I assure you, they are waiting, *poised* to ignore you.

29. My enemies will say to you that Centralism is unprincipled, but I demand: "Where are *their* fabulous principles, in so far as they ever applied to *us?*" We bring encyclopedias to their doors. What principles prevented all those doors from slamming in our earnest faces? Oh, no! We know their world. *Science* is disproving all their principles, and showing that they are nothing. All their prophets had bad sex lives. All through history, it's not what you know, but who you know.

30. Listen. Modest, safe, and sure. That's the way to power. Are you afraid of obscurity? But, my boy, my son, we will be everywhere. All of us, running things. Only give your *self* up. Come with me, and together we will infiltrate back into the world that rejected us.

POLITICS

"Politics, *n.* A strife of interests masquerading as a contest of principles. The conduct of public affairs for private advantage."

AMBROSE BIERCE, *The Devil's Dictionary*

"I tell you Folks, all Politics is Apple Sauce."

WILL ROGERS, *The Illiterate Digest*

Politics

*N*o sight on earth is better calculated to quicken a satirist's
blood than a string tie, a ripple of red, white and blue
*bunting, and a ballot box. A stirring contest of issues, oratory,
pageantry, and skulduggery, politics in the American democracy is a show which P. T. Barnum must have envied. It brings
out the best in men, and—what is far more interesting to the
satirist—the worst.*

*During the Revolutionary period, political satire was a crucial
weapon in the struggle between rebel and Tory. Even after the
Revolution was won, political satire of a peppery doggerel variety continued to be popular for a time; though now Federalist
was pitted against Republican, American against American, and
in the long, precarious struggle for political equilibrium, satire
in verse degenerated into a medium of bickering and slander.*

*Then, in the 1830s, when the ordinary American was form-
ing an increasingly clear idea of who he was, what he looked
like, and how he talked, there appeared a humorous work called
the* Life and Writings of Major Jack Downing, *written by a
Maine newspaperman, Seba Smith. The* Downing Papers *ini-
tiated a tradition of cracker-barrel commentary on national affairs which was to be the mainstream of American political
satire for a century. The common citizen saw himself talking
back, making the most of his freeborn right to be critical of the*

government. Later adepts, represented in these pages, include David Ross Locke as Petroleum V. Nasby, Robert Henry Newell as Orpheus C. Kerr, and Will Rogers—as Will Rogers. All wrote for the newspapers.

Today literary-journalistic political satire is all too seldom found. A minor renaissance occurred during President Eisenhower's two terms, but as a general rule it is not the journalists but cartoonists like Herblock and Bill Mauldin, entertainers like Mort Sahl, and occasionally dramatists like Gore Vidal who are the keenest political satirists on the scene today. For the moment there is no reliable source of amusing political commentary in any one newspaper column, and this—as the following selections may suggest—is an odd and sorry state of affairs.

John Trumbull

John Trumbull was one of a group of writers known as the Connecticut Wits, young men of conservative outlook who practiced the art of literature in the Colonies while their more radical contemporaries dumped tea and composed revolutionary broadsides. As a young academic at Yale (alma mater of most of the Wits), he published a satire on education (see page 238) which brought him trouble from the authorities. Though no firebrand, Trumbull was also the author of the most popular of all the political satires of the Revolutionary period: *M'Fingal*, a mock-epic poem which ridicules Tory pretensions. In the pompous magistrate Squire M'Fingal everyone recognized a damaging caricature of the King's Man in America.

SQUIRE M'FINGAL ADDRESSES
THE TOWN MEETING
(from *M'Fingal*, 1782)

Ye Whigs, attend, and hear affrighted
    The crimes whereof ye stand indicted;
The sins and follies past all compass,

That prove you guilty, or *non compos*.
I leave the verdict to your senses,
And Jury of your consciences;
Which though they're neither good nor true,
Must yet convict you and your crew.
Ungrateful sons! a factious band,
That rise against your parent land
Ye viper race, that burst in strife
The welcome womb that gave you life,
Tear with sharp fangs, and forked tongue
Th' indulgent bowels, whence you sprung;
And scorn the debt of obligation,
You justly owe the British nation,
Which since you cannot pay, your crew,
Affect to swear 'twas never due.
    "Did not the deeds of England's Primate [1]
First drive your fathers to this climate,
Whom jails, and fines, and ev'ry ill
Forc'd to their good against their will.
Ye owe to their obliging temper,
The peopling your new-fangled empire,
While every British act and canon
Stood forth your *causa sine qua non*.
Did they not send you charters o'er,
And give you lands you own'd before,
Permit you to spill your blood,
And drive out heathen where you could;
On these mild terms, that, conquest won,
The realm you gain'd should be their own?
Or when of late, attack'd by those,
Whom her connection made you foes, [2]
Did they not then, distressed in war,
Send Gen'rals to your help from far,
Whose aid you own'd in terms less haughty
And thankfully o'erpaid your quota?
Say, at what period did they grudge
To send you Governor or Judge,

[1] Archbishop Laud.   [2] The French.

With all their missionary crew,[3]
To teach you law and gospel too?
Brought o'er all felons in the nation
To help you on in population,
Propos'd their Bishops to surrender,
And made their Priests a legal tender,
Who only ask'd in surplice clad,
The simple tithe of all you had:
And now to keep all knaves in awe,
Have sent their troops t' establish law,
And with gunpowder, fire, and ball,
Reform your people one and all."

Hugh Henry Brackenridge

Modern Chivalry is the novel which best reflects the precarious formative years at the beginning of the nineteenth century when the United States was enacting the drama which we now refer to—sometimes too casually—as self-determination. Its author, Hugh Henry Brackenridge, was in many ways typical of "the better element" of his times. A classmate of Philip Freneau and James Madison at Princeton, he was well educated and acutely conscious of the political moment of the years in which he lived.

Throughout his life, Brackenridge was dedicated to republican principles; yet, like so many of his contemporaries, he intensely feared the specter of mob rule and the overthrow of reason and balance. *Modern Chivalry*, formally patterned after *Don Quixote*, is largely a satire against the elevation of unfit and ignorant individuals into positions of power and eminence. The story is episodic, following the adventures of one Captain Farrago—an overly reasonable and abundantly educated person —and his manservant, the "bog-trotter" Teague O'Regan. Teague, though illiterate and barely able to speak the English language, continually confounds his master by being nominated for public office, by being invited to join the American Philo-

---

[3] Royalist clergymen, ordained by the Bishop of London.

sophical Society, or by deciding to set up as a lawyer. In the
following episode, a weaver is campaigning for office; Captain
Farrago delivers an argument against the weaver's qualifications; whereupon Teague is almost chosen in the weaver's place.

HOW THE BOG-TROTTER IS NEARLY ELECTED
TO THE LEGISLATURE
(from *Modern Chivalry*, 1792)

At an early hour, our knight-errant and his squire set out on
their way, and soon arrived at a place of cross-roads, at
a public house and store, where a number of people were con-
vened, for the purpose of electing persons to represent them in
the legislature of the state. This was not the annual election, but
to fill an occasional vacancy. There was a weaver who was a
candidate, and seemed to have a good deal of interest among
the people. But another, who was a man of education, was his
competitor. Relying on some talent of speaking which he thought
he possessed, and getting on the stump of a large oak tree for
the convenience of a more elevated position, he thus addressed
the people.

"Fellow citizens," said he, "I pretend not to any great abilities;
but am conscious to myself that I have the best good will to
serve you. But it is very astonishing to me, that this man should
conceive himself qualified for the trust. For though my acquire-
ments are not great, yet his are still less. The business which
he pursues, must necessarily take up so much of his time, that
he cannot apply himself to political studies. I should therefore
think it would be more answerable to your dignity, and con-
ducive to your interest, to be represented by a man at least of
some letters, than by an illiterate man like this. It will be more
honourable for himself, to remain at his loom and knot threads,
than to come forward in a legislative capacity; because in the
one case, he is in the sphere suited to his education; in the other,
he is like a fish out of water, and must struggle for breath in a
new element. It is not because he is a weaver that I object to
him, but because he is nothing but a weaver, and entirely desti-

tute of the qualifications necessary to fill the office to which he
aspires. The occupation a man pursues for a livelihood is but a
secondary consideration, if any consideration at all. Warriors
and statesmen, and sages, may be found at the plough, and the
work bench, but this man has not the slightest pretensions beyond the mysteries of his trade.

"Is it possible that he can understand the affairs of government, whose mind has been entirely concentered to the small
object of weaving webs; to the price by the yard, the grist of the
thread, and such like matters as concern the manufacturer of
cloths? The feet of him who weaves, are more occupied than the
head, or at least as much; and therefore he must be, at least, but
in half, accustomed to exercise his mental powers. For these
reasons, all other things set aside, the chance is in my favour,
with respect to information. However, you will decide, and
give your suffrages to him or to me, as you shall judge ex-
pedient."

The captain hearing these observations, and looking at the
weaver, made free to subjoin something in support of what had
been just said. Said he, "I have no prejudice against a weaver
more than another man. Nor do I know any harm in the trade;
save that from the sedentary life in a damp place, there is usually a paleness of the countenance: but this is a physical, not a
moral evil. Such usually occupy subterranean apartments; not
for the purpose, like Demosthenes, of shaving their heads and
writing over eight times the history of Thucydides, and per-
fecting a style of oratory; but rather to keep the thread moist;
or because this is considered but as an inglorious sort of trade,
and is frequently thrust away into cellars, and damp out-houses,
which are not occupied for a better use.

"But to rise from the cellar to the senate house, would be an
unnatural hoist for one whose mind had not been prepared for
it by a previous course of study or training, either self-instructed,
and gifted with superior intellect, or having the good fortune to
have received an education, with also the advantage of actual experience in public affairs. To come from counting threads, and
adjusting them to the splits of a reed, to regulate the finances of
a government, would be preposterous; there being no congruity
in the case. There is no analogy between knotting threads and

framing laws. It would be a reversion of the order of things. Not that a manufacturer of linen or woollen, or other stuffs, is an inferior character, but a different one, from that which ought to be employed in affairs of state. It is unnecessary to enlarge on this subject; for you must all be convinced of the truth and propriety of what I say. But if you will give me leave to take the manufacturer aside a little, I think I can explain to him my ideas on the subject; and very probably prevail with him to withdraw his pretensions." The people seeming to acquiesce, and beckoning to the weaver, they withdrew aside, and the captain addressed him in the following words:

"Mr. Traddle," said he, "I have not the smallest idea of wounding your feelings, but it would seem to me, it would be more your interest to pursue your occupation, than to lanch out into that of which you have no knowledge. When you go to the senate house, the application to you will not be to warp a web; but to make laws for the commonwealth. Now, suppose that the making these laws requires a knowledge of commerce, of finance, and of the infinite variety of subjects embraced by the laws, civil, or criminal, what service could you render? It is possible you might think justly; but could you speak? You are not in the habit of public speaking. You are not furnished with those commonplace ideas, with which even very ignorant men can pass for knowing something. There is nothing makes a man so ridiculous, as to attempt what is beyond his capacity. You are no tumbler for instance; yet should you give out that you could vault upon a man's back; or turn heels over head like the wheels of a cart; the stiffness of your joints would encumber you; and you would fall to the ground. Such a squash as that, would do you damage. The getting up to ride on the state is an unsafe thing to those who are not accustomed to such horsemanship. It is a disagreeable thing for a man to be laughed at, and there is no way of keeping one's self from it but by avoiding all affectation." These observations did not seem to make much impression on the weaver, who argued that common sense was often better than learning.

While they were thus discoursing, a bustle had taken place among the crowd. Teague hearing so much about elections, and serving the government, took it into his head, that he could be a legislator himself. The thing was not displeasing to the people, who seemed to favour his pretensions; owing, in some degree, to there being several of his countrymen among the crowd; but more especially to the fluctuation of the popular mind, and a disposition to what is new and ignoble. For though the weaver was not the most elevated object of choice, yet he was still preferable to this tatter-demalion.

The captain coming up, and finding what was on the carpet, was chagrined at not having been able to give the voters a better idea of the importance of a legislative trust; alarmed also, from an apprehension of the loss of his servant. Under these impressions he resumed his address to the people. Said he, "this is making the matter still worse, gentlemen: this servant of mine is but a bog-trotter, who can scarcely speak the dialect in which your laws ought to be written; but certainly has never read a single treatise on any political subject; for the truth is, he cannot read at all. The young people of the lower class, in Ireland, have seldom the advantage of a good education; especially the descendants of the ancient Irish, who have most of them a great assurance of countenance, but little information or literature. This young man, whose family name is O'Regan, has been my servant for several years; and, except a too great fondness for whiskey, which now and then brings him into scrapes, he has demeaned himself in a manner tolerable enough. But he is totally ignorant of the great principles of legislation; and more especially the particular interests of the government. A free government is a noble acquisition to a people: and this freedom consists in an equal right to make laws, and to have the benefit of the laws when made. Though doubtless, in such a government, the lowest citizen may become chief magistrate; yet it is sufficient to possess the right, not absolutely necessary to exercise it. Or even if you should think proper, now and then, to show your privilege, and exert, in a signal manner, the democratic prerogative, yet is it not descending too low to filch away from me a servant whom I cannot well spare, and for whom I have paid my money? You are surely carrying the matter too far, in thinking to make a senator of this hostler; to take him away from an employment to which he has been bred, and put him to another, to which he has served no apprenticeship: to set those hands, which have lately been employed in currying my horse, to the draughting bills, and preparing business for the house."

The people were tenacious of their choice, and insisted on giving Teague their suffrages; and by the frown upon their brows, seemed to indicate resentment at what had been said; as indirectly charging them with want of judgment; or calling in question their privilege to do what they thought proper. "It is a very strange thing," said one of them, who was a speaker for the rest, "that after having conquered Burgoyne and Cornwallis, and got a government of our own, we cannot put in whom we please. This young man may be your servant, or another man's servant; but if we choose to make him a delegate, what is that to you? He may not be yet skilled in the matter, but there is a good day coming. We will empower him; and it is better to trust a plain man like him, than one of your high-flyers, that will make laws to suit their own purposes."

"I had much rather," said the captain, "you would send the weaver, though I thought that improper, than to invade my household, and thus take from me the person who is employed to curry my horse, and black my boots."

The prolocutor of the people gave him to understand that his objections were useless, for the people had determined on the choice, and Teague they would have, for a representative.

Finding it answered no end to expostulate, he requested to speak a word with Teague by himself. Stepping aside, he said to him, composing his voice, and addressing him in a soft manner: "Teague, you are quite wrong in this matter they have put into your head. Do you know what it is to be a member of a deliberative body? What qualifications are necessary? Do you understand any thing of geography? If a question should be put to make a law to dig a canal in some part of the state, can you describe the bearing of the mountains, and the course of the rivers? Or, if commerce is to be pushed to some new quarter, by the force of regulations, are you competent to decide in such a case? There will be questions of law, and astronomy, on the carpet. How you must gape and stare like a fool, when you come to be asked your opinion on these subjects! Are you acquainted with the principles of finance; with the funding public securities; the ways and means of raising the revenue; providing for the discharge of the public debts, and all other things which respect the economy of the government? Even if you had knowledge, have you a facility of speaking? I would suppose you would have too much pride to go to the house just to say, ay or no. This is not the fault of your nature, but of your education; having been accustomed to dig turf in your early years, rather than instructing yourself in the classics, or common school books.

"When a man becomes a member of a public body, he is like a raccoon, or other beast that climbs up the fork of a tree; the boys pushing at him with pitchforks, or throwing stones, or shooting at him with arrows; the dogs barking in the mean time. One will find fault with your not speaking; another with your speaking, if you speak at all. They will put you in the newspapers, and ridicule you as a perfect beast. There is what they call the *caricatura;* that is, representing you with a dog's head, or a cat's claw. It is the devil to be exposed to the squibs and crackers of the gazette wits and publications. You know no more about these matters than a goose; and yet you would undertake rashly, without advice, to enter on the office; nay, contrary to advice. For I would not for a hundred guineas, though I have not the half to spare, that the breed of the O'Regans should come to this; bringing on them a worse stain than stealing sheep. You have nothing but your character, Teague, in a new country to depend upon. Let it never be said, that you quitted an honest livelihood, the taking care of my horse, to follow the new fangled whims of the times, and be a statesman. And, besides, have I not promised to do something clever towards settling you in life hereafter, provided you will serve me faithfully in my travels? Something better than you have thought of may turn up in the course of our rambles."

Teague was moved chiefly with the last part of the address, and consented to relinquish his pretensions.

The captain, glad of this, took him back to the people, and announced his disposition to decline the honour which they had intended him.

Teague acknowledged that he had changed his mind, and was willing to remain in a private station.

The people did not seem well pleased; but as nothing more could be said about the matter, they turned their attention to the weaver, and gave him their suffrages.

Seba Smith

Seba Smith's Jack Downing letters are the first successful vernacular satires on national affairs.

Originally a dealer in ax-handles in his village of Downingville, Maine, Jack Downing becomes an adviser to Jackson when the General is elected president. Downing's letters home are amusing and low-keyed in their humor, but in putting political issues, personalities, and Jacksonian democracy to the test of Yankee wit and common sense, they carry a sharp critical appraisal of public affairs.

Popular for twenty years, imitated in nearly every newspaper in the country, the Downing letters showed that Americans appreciated satire when it was expressed in a voice they could recognize as their own.

The following is a late example of the letters, a satire on the selection of presidential timber.

SHOWING HOW THE MAJOR PERSUADED
UNCLE JOSHUA TO TAKE HOLD AND
HELP ELECT GENERAL PIERCE
TO THE PRESIDENCY,
AND HOW DOWNINGVILLE RATIFIED
THE NOMINATION
(July 20, 1852)

DOWNINGVILLE, Away Down East,
In the State of Maine, July 20, 1852.

MR. GALES AND SEATON—

MY DEAR OLD FRIENDS:—We've made out to ratify at last: but it was about as hard a job as it was for the Baltimore Convention to nominate. And I'm afraid the worst on't ain't over yet; for Uncle Joshua shakes his head and says to me, in a low tone, so the rest shan't hear, "Between you and me, Major, the 'lection will be a harder job still." I put great faith in Uncle Joshua's feelin's. He's a regular political weather-glass, and can always tell whether we are going to have it fair or foul a good ways ahead. So when he shakes his head, I naterally look out for a tough spell of weather. When I got home from Baltimore, says I, "Well, Uncle Joshua, you got my letter in the Intelligencer, didn't you?" And says he, "Yes."

"Well, didn't we do that business up well?" says I.

"I don't know about that," said Uncle Joshua; "I have my doubts about it."

"Why, don't you think," says I, "the nomination of Gineral Pierce will put the Democratic party on its legs again, and give it a fine start?"

Uncle Joshua looked up to me kind of quizical, and says he, "It *has* gin the party a pretty considerable of a start already, it come so unexpected." And then he sot as much as two minutes drumming his finger on the table, and didn't say nothin'.

And then he looked up again, and says he, "Major, *who is Gineral Pierce?* It ain't a *fictious* name, is it?"

"Why, Uncle Joshua," says I, "how you talk! It is General Franklin Pierce, of New Hampshire."

"Gineral Franklin Pierce, of New Hampshire, is it?" says he. "Well, now, Major, are you sure there *is* such a person, or did somebody play a hoax on the Baltimore Convention?"

"Yes," says I, "Uncle, I'm as sure of it as I am that there is such a person as Uncle Joshua Downing. To make all sure of it and no mistake, I come through New Hampshire, and went to Concord, where they said he lived, and inquired all about it. The neighbors there all knew him perfectly well, and showed me the house he lives in. He wasn't at home, or I should a seen him myself, and should got his promise to keep the Downingville Post-Office for you. But you needn't be afraid but what you'll have it, for I sent a telegraph to him from Baltimore, as soon as he was nominated, to keep it for you."

Here I see by the looks of Uncle Joshua's eyes that he begun to get hold of some new ideas. Says he, "Well, Major, it is a fact, then, is it, that he was nominated in real earnest, and 'twasn't no joke?"

"Upon my word and honor," says I, "there isn't a particle of joke about it—it was all done in real arnest."

"Well, then, if you've really got a candidate," says Uncle Joshua, "I should like to know something about him. Does he belong to the Old Fogy class or Young America class?"

"I guess about half and half," says I, "and he'll be all the stronger for that, because he can draw votes on both sides."

"After all," says he, "I'm afraid it's a bad nomination. Them old pillars of the Democratic party, Gineral Cass, and Mr. Buchanan, and Governor Marcy, and General Houston, and the rest, will feel so insulted and mortified at being pushed aside for strangers to take the lead, that they'll all be agin the nomination, and their friends, too, and that'll upset the whole kettle of fish."

"Don't you never fear that, Uncle Joshua," says I; "them old pillars that you speak of are all very much tickled with the nomination. Ye see, it broke the nose of Young America, and they was delighted with it. As soon as the nomination was out of the mould, before it had time to cool, they all telegraphed right to Baltimore that nothin' in the world could have happened to suit 'em better; it was a most excellent nomination, and they felt under everlasting obligations to the Baltimore Convention. You needn't have no fears that they'll feel any coldness towards the nomination. They'll turn to and work for it like beavers."

"Well, how is it," said Uncle Joshua, "about that boy candidate for the Presidency that they call Young America? If his nose is knocked out of joint he'll of course oppose the nomination, tooth and nail."

"There's where you are mistaken again, Uncle Joshua," says I. "On the contrary, he goes for it hotter than any of 'em; and he telegraphed back to Baltimore, as quick as lightning could carry it, that the nomination was jest the thing; it couldn't be no better. Ye see, he looks upon it in the light that it chokes off all the Old Fogies, and leaves the field clear for him next time.

He thinks so highly of the nomination, and feels so patriotic about it, they say he is going to stump it through all the States, and make speeches in favor of Gineral Pierce's election. You may depend upon it, Uncle Joshua, we've got a very strong nomination—one that'll carry all afore it—and everybody is delighted with it, and everybody's going to go for it. I didn't expect you to hold back a moment. I thought you would have things all cut and dried for a rousin' ratification meeting by the time I got home."

"Well, you know, Major," said Uncle Joshua, "I always follow Colonel Crockett's rule, and never go ahead till I know I'm right. How foolish we should look to call a ratification meeting here in Downingville, and be voted right plump down. You know the Free-Soilers are very strong among us; they are strong in all the Northern States. And you know the Baltimore Convention fixed up a platform to stand on, that's all in favor of the Compromise and the Fugitive law, and is dead set agin the Free-Soilers. Now, Major, you must have more understanding than to think the Free-Soilers will ever swallow that platform; and if they don't, we are dished."

"You are wrong again, Uncle Joshua," says I, "for the biggest Free-Soiler in all America swallowed it right down, and didn't make a wry face about it."

"Who do you mean?" says he.

"I mean Mr. John Van Buren," says I.

"But you don't mean," says Uncle Joshua, "that Mr. John Van Buren accepts this platform, and is willing to stand on it."

"Yes I do, exactly so," says I, "for he got right up in Tammany Hall and made a speech about it; and he said he would go the nomination, and he'd stand the platform; at all events, he'd stand the platform for *this election*, anyhow. You needn't be at all afraid of the Free-Soilers, Uncle; they ain't so stiff as you think for, and they are as anxious to get the offices as anybody, and will work as hard for 'em. Now let us go to work and get up our ratification, and blow it out straight. The Democracy of the country expects Downingville to do its duty."

"Well, Major," says Uncle Joshua, "you've made out a better case than I thought you could. I'm willing to take hold and see what we can do. But I declare I can't help laughing when I think it's Gineral Franklin Pierce, of New Hampshire, that we've got to ratify. I wish we knew something about him; something that we could make a little flusteration about, and wake up the Democracy."

"Good gracious, Uncle Joshua," says I, "have you been Postmaster of Downingville this twenty years, and always reading the papers, and don't know that Gineral Pierce was one of the heroes of the Mexican war?"

At that, Uncle Joshua hopped out of his chair like a boy, and says he, "Major, is that a fact?"

"Yes," says I, " 'tis a fact. You know Mr. Polk sent me out there as a private ambassador to look after Gineral Scott and Mr. Trist. And Gineral Pierce *was* out there; I knew all about it, and about his getting wounded."

"Good!" says Uncle Joshua, snapping his fingers; "that's lucky, then we've got something to go upon; something that the boys can hoorah about. And if we don't have too strong a team agin us we may carry the day yet. Who do you think the other party will put up?"

"Well," says I, "it's pretty likely to be Mr. Webster or Mr. Fillmore, and they can't either of 'em hold a candle to Gineral Pierce."

"Of course not," says Uncle Joshua, "if he was the hero of the Mexican war. I s'pose it was Gineral Scott's part of the war that he was in, because that's where you was. Which of the battles did he fight the bravest in, and mow down most of the Mexicans? Did he help storm that Gibralta castle at Vera Cruz?"

"No," says I, "that little matter was all over before Gineral Pierce got to Mexico."

"Well, the great battle of Cerro Gordo come next," said Uncle Joshua; "I dare say Gineral Pierce was foremost in marching up that bloody Bunker Hill and driving off Santa Anna and his fifteen thousand troops."

"I'm sure he would a been foremost, if he'd been there," says I, "but he hadn't got into the country yet, and Gineral Scott wouldn't wait for him. It seems as if Gineral Scott is always in a hurry when there is any fightin' to do, and won't wait for no-body."

"Well, the next great battle, if I remember the newspapers right," said Uncle Joshua, "was Contreras; and after that came the bloody and hot times of Cherubusco, and the King's Mill, and Chepultepec, and marching into the City of Mexico. These was the battles, I s'pose, where Gineral Pierce fit like a lion, and became the hero of the Mexican war. But which battle did he shine the brightest in, and cut down most of the enemy?"

"The truth is," says I, "he got wounded at Contreras, and so wasn't able to take a part in them bloody affairs of Cherubusco, King's Mill, and Chepultepec."

"Then he *was* in the battle of Contreras," said Uncle Joshua, "and that can't be disputed?"

"O yes," says I, "he certainly was in the first part of it, when they was getting the battle ready, for there's where he got wounded."

"Good," said Uncle Joshua, "he was in one battle, and got wounded; that's enough to make a handle of, anyhow. Where-abouts was his wound?"

"Well, he had several hurts," said I; "I believe in his foot and ancle, and other parts."

"Rifle balls?" said Uncle Joshua, very earnest.

"O no, nothing of that kind," says I.

"What then; sword cuts? Or did the Mexicans stick their bayonets into him?"

"No, no; nothin' of that kind, nother," says I.

"Then it must be grape or bombshells," said Uncle Joshua, "how was it?"

"No, no, 'twasn't none of them things," says I. "The fact was, when they was skirmishing round, getting ready for the battle, his horse fell down with him and lamed him very bad."

Uncle Joshua colored a little, and sot and thought. At last he put on one of his knowing looks, and says he, "Well, Major, a wound is a wound, and we can make a handle of it without being such fools as to go into the particulars of how he came by it. I say let's go ahead and ratify Gineral Pierce, and who knows but what we can make something out of this Mexican business?"

Well, Mr. Gales and Seaton, the thing was done. We ratified on the 21st of June, in the evening, and it was a tall piece of business. When I begun, I meant to give you a full account of it, with some of the speeches and resolutions; but I've made my preamble so long that I can't do it in this letter. *We had a torchlight procession.* Cousin Ephraim took his cart and oxen, and went into the woods and got a whole load of birch bark and pitch-pine knots, and all the boys in Downingville turned out and carried torches. The school-house was illuminated with fifty candles. Uncle Joshua presided, as usual. Banners were hung round the room, with large letters, giving the names of all the great battles in Mexico; and the enthusiasm was immense. When we'd got about through, and was just winding up with three tremendous cheers for the "Hero of Mexico," a message came up to Uncle Joshua from the Post-Office, stating that the telegraph had just brought news that the Whig Convention at Baltimore had nominated Gineral Scott for President. It gin the whole Convention the cold shuggers in a minute. Uncle Joshua looked very serious, and says he, "Feller-Democrats, to prevent any mistakes, I think you had better give them three last cheers over again, and put in the name of Gineral Pierce." So we did, and gin three rousin' cheers for *Gineral Franklin Pierce, of New Hampshire, the Hero of Mexico.*

Downingville is wide awake, and will do her duty in November.

So I remain your old friend,

MAJOR JACK DOWNING

James Russell Lowell

Long before the era of the Fireside Chat and the televised debate, a presidential candidate was known by the stump speeches he made and the letters he wrote, setting forth his views. Then, as now, the art was to satisfy and reassure as many opposing sides and factions as could be expected at the polls. "I know of nothing in our modern times," wrote Lowell, "which approaches so nearly to the ancient oracle as the letter of a Presidential candidate."

THE CANDIDATE'S LETTER
(from *The Biglow Papers*, 1867)

DEAR SIR,—You wish to know my notions
 On sartin pints thet rile the land;
There's nothin' thet my natur so shuns
 Ez bein' mum or underhand;
I'm a straight-spoken kind o' creetur
 Thet blurts right out wut's in his head,
An' ef I've one pecooler feetur,
 It is a nose thet wun't be led.

So, to begin at the beginnin'
 An' come direcly to the pint,
I think the country's underpinnin'
 Is some consid'ble out o' jint;
I ain't agoin' to try your patience
 By tellin' who done this or thet,
I don't make no insinooations,
 I jest let on I smell a rat.

Thet is, I mean, it seems to me so,
 But, ef the public think I'm wrong,
I wun't deny but wut I be so,—
 An', fact, it don't smell very strong;
My mind's tu fair to lose its balance
 An' say wich party hez most sense;
There may be folks o' greater talence
 Thet can't set stiddier on the fence.

I'm an eclectic; ez to choosin'
  'Twixt this an' thet, I'm plaguy lawth;
I leave a side thet looks like losin',
  But (wile there's doubt) I stick to both;
I stan' upon the Constitution,
  Ez preudunt statesmun say, who've planned
A way to git the most profusion
  O' chances ez to *ware* they'll stand.

Ez fer the war, I go agin' it,—
  I mean to say I kind o' du,—
Thet is, I mean thet, bein' in it,
  The best way wuz to fight it thru;
Not but wut abstract war is horrid,
  I sign to thet with all my heart,—
But civlyzation *doos* git forrid
  Sometimes upon a powder-cart.

About thet darned Proviso matter
  I never hed a grain o' doubt,
Nor I ain't one my sense to scatter
  So 'st no one could n't pick it out;
My love fer North an' South is equil,
  So I'll jest answer plump an' frank,
No matter wut may be the sequil,—
  Yes, Sir, I *am* agin' a Bank.

Ez to the answerin' o' questions,
  I'm an off ox at bein' druv,
Though I ain't one thet ary test shuns
  'll give our folks a helpin' shove;
Kind o' permiscoous I go it
  Fer the holl country, an' the ground
I take, ez nigh ez I can show it,
  Is pooty gen'ally all round.

I don't appruve o' givin' pledges;
  You'd ough' to leave a feller free,

An' not go knockin' out the wedges
  To ketch his fingers in the tree;
Pledges air awfle breachy cattle
  Thet preudunt farmers don't turn out,—
Ez long 'z the people git their rattle,
  Wut is there fer 'm to grout about?

Ez to the slaves, there's no confusion
  In *my* idees consarnin' them,—
I think they air an Institution,
  A sort of—yes, jest so,—ahem:
Do *I* own any? Of my merit
  On thet pint you yourself may jedge;
All is, I never drink no sperit,
  Nor I hain't never signed no pledge.

Ez to my princerples, I glory
  In hevin' nothin' o' the sort;
I ain't a Wig, I ain't a Tory,
  I'm jest a canderdate, in short;
Thet's fair an' square an' parpendicler,
  But, ef the Public cares a fig
To hev me an'thin' in particler,
  Wy, I'm a kind o' peri-Wig.

P. S.

Ez we're a sort o' privateerin',
  O' course, you know, it's sheer an' sheer,
An' there is sutthin' wuth your hearin'
  I'll mention in *your* privit ear;
Ef you git *me* inside the White House,
  Your head with ile I'll kin' o' 'nint
By gittin' *you* inside the Light-house
  Down to the eend o' Jaalam Pint.

An' ez the North hez took to brustlin'
  At bein' scrouged frum off the roost,

I'll tell ye wut 'll save all tusslin'
   An' give our side a harnsome boost,—
Tell 'em thet on the Slavery question
   I'm RIGHT, although to speak I'm lawth;
This gives you a safe pint to rest on,
   An' leaves me frontin' South by North.

Mark Twain

SENATOR DILWORTHY CAMPAIGNS
FOR RE-ELECTION
(from *The Gilded Age*, 1873)

The Senator now turned his attention to matters touching the souls of his people. He appeared in church; he took a leading part in prayer-meetings; he met and encouraged the temperance societies; he graced the sewing-circles of the ladies with his presence, and even took a needle now and then and made a stitch or two upon a calico shirt for some poor Bibleless pagan of the South Seas, and this act enchanted the ladies, who regarded the garments thus honored as in a manner sanctified. The Senator wrought in Bible classes, and nothing could keep him away from the Sunday-schools—neither sickness nor storms nor weariness. He even traveled a tedious thirty miles in a poor little rickety stagecoach to comply with the desire of the miserable hamlet of Cattleville that he would let its Sunday-school look upon him.

All the town was assembled at the stage office when he arrived, two bonfires were burning, and a battery of anvils was popping exultant broadsides; for a United States Senator was a sort of god in the understanding of these people, who never had seen any creature mightier than a county judge. To them a United States Senator was a vast, vague colossus, an awe-inspiring unreality.

Next day, everybody was at the village church a full half-

hour before time for Sunday-school to open; ranchmen and
farmers had come with their families from five miles around,
all eager to get a glimpse of the great man—the man who had
been to Washington; the man who had seen the President of
the United States, and had even talked with him; the man
who had seen the actual Washington Monument—perhaps
touched it with his hands.

When the Senator arrived the church was crowded, the
windows were full, the aisles were packed, so was the vestibule,
and so, indeed, was the yard in front of the building. As he
worked his way through to the pulpit on the arm of the minister and followed by the envied officials of the village, every neck
was stretched and every eye twisted around intervening obstruc-
tions to get a glimpse. Elderly people directed each other's attention and said, "There! that's him, with the grand, noble
forehead!" Boys nudged each other and said, "Hi, Johnny, here
he is! There, that's him, with the peeled head!"

The Senator took his seat in the pulpit, with the minister on
one side of him and the superintendent of the Sunday-school on
the other. The town dignitaries sat in an impressive row within
the altar railings below. The Sunday-school children occupied
ten of the front benches, dressed in their best and most uncomfortable clothes, and with hair combed and faces too clean
to feel natural. So awed were they by the presence of a living
United States Senator, that during three minutes not a "spit-
ball" was thrown. After that they began to come to themselves
by degrees, and presently the spell was wholly gone and they
were reciting verses and pulling hair.

The usual Sunday-school exercises were hurried through, and
then the minister got up and bored the house with a speech
built on the customary Sunday-school plan; then the superintendent put in his oar; then the town dignitaries had their say.
They all made complimentary reference to "their friend, the
Senator," and told what a great and illustrious man he was and
what he had done for his country and for religion and temperance, and exhorted the little boys to be good and diligent and
try to become like him some day. The speakers won the death-
less hatred of the house by these delays, but at last there was an

end and hope revived; inspiration was about to find utterance.

Senator Dilworthy rose and beamed upon the assemblage for a full minute in silence. Then he smiled with an access of sweetness upon the children and began:

"My little friends—for I hope that all these bright-faced little people are my friends and will let me be their friend—my little friends, I have traveled much, I have been in many cities and many states, everywhere in our great and noble country, and by the blessing of Providence I have been permitted to see many gatherings like this—but I am proud, I am truly proud to say that I never have looked upon so much intelligence, so much grace, such sweetness of disposition as I see in the charming young countenances I see before me at this moment. I have been asking myself, as I sat here, Where am I? Am I in some far-off monarchy, looking upon little princes and princesses? No. Am I in some populous center of my own country, where the choicest children of the land have been selected and brought together as at a fair for a prize? No. Am I in some strange foreign clime where the children are marvels that we know not of? No. Then where am I? Yes—where am I? I am in a simple, remote, unpretending settlement of my own dear state, and these are the children of the noble and virtuous men who have made me what I am! My soul is lost in wonder at the thought! And I humbly thank Him to whom we are but as worms of the dust, that He has been pleased to call me to serve such men! Earth has no higher, no grander position for me. Let kings and emperors keep their tinsel crowns, I want them not; my heart is here!

"Again I thought, Is this a theater? No. Is it a concert or a gilded opera? No. Is it some other vain, brilliant, beautiful temple of soul-staining amusement and hilarity? No. Then what is it? What did my consciousness reply? I ask you, my little friends, What did my consciousness reply? It replied, It is the temple of the Lord! Ah, think of that, now. I could hardly keep the tears back, I was so grateful. Oh, how beautiful it is to see these ranks of sunny little faces assembled here to learn the way of life; to learn to be good; to learn to be useful; to learn to be pious; to learn to be great and glorious men and women; to learn to be props and pillars of the state and shining lights in the councils and the households of the nation; to be bearers of the banner and soldiers of the cross in the rude campaigns of life, and ransomed souls in the happy fields of Paradise hereafter.

"Children, honor your parents and be grateful to them for providing for you the precious privileges of a Sunday-school.

"Now, my dear little friends, sit up straight and pretty— there, that's it—and give me your attention and let me tell you about a poor little Sunday-school scholar I once knew. He lived in the Far West, and his parents were poor. They could not give him a costly education, but they were good and wise and they sent him to the Sunday-school. He loved the Sunday-school. I hope you love your Sunday-school—ah, I see by your faces that you do! That is right.

"Well, this poor little boy was always in his place when the bell rang, and he always knew his lesson; for his teachers wanted him to learn and he loved his teachers dearly. Always love your teachers, my children, for they love you more than you can know, now. He would not let bad boys persuade him to go to play on Sunday. There was one little bad boy who was always trying to persuade him, but he never could.

"So this poor little boy grew up to be a man, and had to go out in the world, far from home and friends, to earn his living. Temptations lay all about him, and sometimes he was about to yield, but he would think of some precious lesson he learned in his Sunday-school a long time ago, and that would save him. By and by he was elected to the legislature. Then he did everything he could for Sunday-schools. He got laws passed for them; he got Sunday-schools established wherever he could.

"And by and by the people made him governor—and he said it was all owing to the Sunday-school.

"After a while the people elected him a Representative to the Congress of the United States, and he grew very famous. Now temptations assailed him on every hand. People tried to get him to drink wine, to dance, to go to theaters; they even tried to buy his vote; but no, the memory of his Sunday-school saved him from all harm; he remembered the fate of the bad little boy who used to try to get him to play on Sunday, and who grew up and became a drunkard and was hanged. He remembered that, and was glad he never yielded and played on Sunday.

"Well, at last, what do you think happened? Why the people gave him a towering, illustrious position, a grand, imposing position. And what do you think it was? What should you say it was, children? It was Senator of the United States! That poor little boy that loved his Sunday-school became that man. *That man stands before you!* All that he is, he owes to the Sunday-school.

"My precious children, love your parents, love your teachers, love your Sunday-school, be pious, be obedient, be honest, be diligent, and then you will succeed in life and be honored of all men. Above all things, my children, be honest. Above all things be pure-minded as the snow. Let us join in prayer."

When Senator Dilworthy departed from Cattleville, he left three dozen boys behind him arranging a campaign of life whose objective point was the United States Senate.

When he arrived at the state capital at midnight Mr. Noble came and held a three hours' conference with him, and then as he was about leaving said:

"I've worked hard, and I've got them at last. Six of them haven't got quite backbone enough to slew around and come right out for you on the first ballot to-morrow, but they're going to vote against you on the first for the sake of appearances, and then come out for you all in a body on the second—I've fixed all that! By supper-time to-morrow you'll be re-elected. You can go to bed and sleep easy on that."

After Mr. Noble was gone, the Senator said:

"Well, to bring about a complexion of things like this was worth coming West for."

Anonymous

The hit show *H.M.S. Pinafore*, first mounted in London in 1878, provided the inspiration for this 1880 satire against James A. Garfield, the ill-fated President whose first term of office ended a few months after it began, in 1881, by an assassin's bullet. Garfield was the dark-horse candidate of the radical faction of the Republican party, which succeeded in securing his nomination over the opposition of the corruption-tainted party regulars who were backing Grant for a third term. But given the political morality of the Gilded Age it is not surprising that Garfield, too, was suspected of various financial peccadilloes, allegedly perpetrated during his service as a U. S. Congressman from Ohio.

The "bribery dividend," and the title of the satire refer to $329.00 which Garfield was accused of receiving as a dividend on Crédit Mobilier stock. Shares of Crédit Mobilier had been distributed to various Congressmen as part of the greatest train robbery in American history—when that syndicate virtually "fixed" Congress to overlook the fact that the Union Pacific received a government subsidy of twice the actual cost of the railroad. Garfield denied that he was implicated.

The meeting with "Dick Parsons" refers to the fact that Congressman Garfield took a fee for services rendered a paving company intent on paving Washington, D. C., with wooden blocks. (The reference to "concrete" is apparently poetic license.)

The "back-pay steal" refers to a bill for improving and uplifting Congressional salaries.

THE HERO OF "329"
(1880)

When I was a boy, to keep me alive,
    A canal boat team I was driven to drive;
I traveled on foot and the reins I did yank,
And I held the mule's tail on the boat's gang-plank.
    I clung to that tail with such fixed intent
    That now I'm a candidate for President.

A trade I learned and theology scanned,
And I joined likewise the legal band;
But politics I found was my strongest game,
And so a Congressman I soon became.

As Congressman I followed such a goodly bent
That now I'm a candidate for President.

I took my bribery dividend,
But finding that it didn't my credit extend,
With all the solemnity an oath invokes,
I swore that my aims were as upright as oaks.
    I swore so devoutly I never got a cent
    That now I'm a candidate for President.

Next with Dick Parsons I chanced to meet,
Who converted me to pavements, abstract and concrete;
As an attorney I accepted a good fat fee,
For urging before my own commit-tee.
    So convincing did I make that argument
    That now I'm a candidate for President.

When first they talked of the back-pay steal,
I pretended to oppose it with righteous zeal;
But while I thus dust in the people's eyes threw,
    I pushed through that measure with such blandishment
    That now I'm a candidate for President.

Now, Republicans all, whoever you may be,
If you want to rise to the top of the tree,
In your youth get a chance to drive a mule,
And in politics be guided by this golden rule:
    Take whatever you can get, and swear it was lent,
    And you all may be candidates for President.

Ambrose Bierce

    Born in Ohio in 1842, Ambrose Bierce disappeared into
Mexico in 1913 and was never heard from again. During his
known lifetime he was a journalist, principally on San Fran-

cisco papers, and a short story writer of distinction. His work, though uneven, includes some of the best realistic war stories in American literature. Unquestionably the bitterest cynic of the turn-of-the-century period, he steadily regarded the universe as a kind of cosmic shell game, with mankind as the mark. His writing is a cold, spare shorthand of disillusion.

TWO FABLES
(from *Fantastic Fables*, 1899)

TWO POLITICIANS

Two Politicians were exchanging ideas regarding the rewards for public service.

"The reward that I most desire," said the First Politician, "is the gratitude of my fellow citizens."

"That would be very gratifying, no doubt," said the Second Politician, "but, alas! in order to obtain it one has to retire from politics."

For an instant they gazed upon each other with inexpressible tenderness; then the First Politician murmured, "God's will be done! Since we cannot hope for reward let us be content with what we have."

And lifting their right hands for a moment from the public treasury they swore to be content.

WASTED SWEETS

A CANDIDATE canvassing his district met a Nurse wheeling a Baby in a carriage and, stooping, imprinted a kiss upon the Baby's clammy muzzle. Rising, he saw a Man, who laughed.

"Why do you laugh?" asked the Candidate.

"Because," replied the Man, "the Baby belongs to an Orphan Asylum."

"But the Nurse," said the Candidate—"the Nurse will surely relate the touching incident wherever she goes, and perhaps write to her former master."

"The Nurse," said the Man who had laughed, "is an illiterate mute."

Ralph Barton

Among the best of all comic histories of the United States—and a memento of the 1920s—is *God's Country* by Ralph Barton, cartoonist, lexicographer, satirist. Today, however, with *God's Country* long out of print and the comic history out of fashion, Barton's canny irreverence is for connoisseurs of American satire only.

HOW THE FIRST POLITICAL PARTIES WERE FORMED
(from *God's Country*)

There being no railroads or motor cars, St. George was obliged to travel from Mount Vernon to New York, the temporary capital, in his carriage. The voyage became a sort of triumph, if a term of imperial Roman barbarity may be applied to anything connected with so simple a man of the people. Everywhere along the road, maidens dressed in white sang odes of welcome and praise specially written for the occasion and flowers were strewn in his path. At Trenton, the horses were unhitched from his carriage and the United Mothers of New Jersey attached garlands of roses to the whiffletree and pulled him to the ferry landing at Elizabethtown Point. Singing "Hail to the Chief" all the way.

He was carried across the Hudson River in a gorgeous barge, the figurehead of which was a large papier-mâché goose.[1] Aft, a

[1] That fowl, on account of its usefulness in the making of pens, beds and Sunday dinners, was then considered as the American national emblem. It has since been replaced by *Haliaëtus leucocephalus*, a raptorial bird.—Barton's note.

mighty cornucopia towered thirteen feet in the air, each foot representing a State, and poured forth an abundance of fruits and vegetables on the deck. A huge pumpkin, a quarter cut away, formed a throne for the Mister. The barge was manned by thirteen virgins who had won the honor in contests conducted in the several States. Each virgin was dressed in a white bathing suit with a broad sash running from shoulder to hip bearing the name of her State. Poised upon the pinnacle of the cornucopia was the Vice-Mistress, Abigail Adams, dressed as the Spirit of Truth and bearing aloft a banner upon which were blazoned the words: *Votes for Women.*

Other barges surrounded the Misterly barge bearing heralds blowing sackbuts and choirs made up of the schoolchildren. Seven lusty negro slaves swam round and about the fleet in single file, each with a letter painted in white on his woolly head so that the column spelled out the word: L-I-B-E-R-T-Y. When St. George landed on the carpeted steps at the wharf, he was received by the Sub-Mister of New York who presented him with the keys of the State and city and a five-gallon hat.

A few days later, on the spot where his statue now stands in Wall Street, St. George took the crown from the hands of the Archbishop of Canterbury and placed it upon his own head amid the wildest applause from the multitude. He was dressed in a smart costume of black velvet with silver accessories and carried the largest walking stick in the world, fashioned of compressed boll weevils and presented to the Mister by his admirers in the State of Georgia.

As soon as the ceremonies were over, the Congress rose as one man to its feet and began to attack the Constitution bitterly. Before they had finished they had voted ten amendments to it and still, though exhausted, they were not satisfied. They voted a recess in which to recuperate, during which the Mister of the Treasury,[2] Alexander Hamilton, established the Bank of the United States, which Thomas Jefferson, the Mister of State, at once bitterly attacked on the ground that it smelled of property and the old régime. The Congress at once reconvened and bit-

---

[2] At that time a treasury in name only.

terly attacked Hamilton as an aristocrat and Jefferson as a demo-
crat and both of them for not having opened the Bank in the
Capitol and given the representatives of the people keys to its
vaults so that they might go down and count the money every
evening before adjourning to make sure that none of it was
missing.

Public Opinion soon joined in, bitterly attacking the Congress, the Cabinet, the Mister and the opposition Public Opinion and, one by one, the sovereign States seceded from the
Union and set up Public Things * of their own.

While national affairs were in this distressing state, one of
the Seniles, a great-lunged fellow who had been the champion
hog caller of New England, rose to his feet in the Senatus and
demanded recognition in a voice that shook the entire building.

"Felly citizens!" he thundered. "Our country is the sweetest
and fairest in all the world and our Public Thing is the finest
form of government under the sun. But, as that great American poet, Uncle Tom Paine, hath sung, 'they is something rotten in Denmark.' What we lack, felly citizens, is organization!
It ain't no more than fair and just that the people contributes to
the public expenses by paying of their taxes like white folks.
But, to who are they going to pay their taxes? I ask you, felly
citizens, and by felly citizens I mean every mother's son in this
here Chamber, to *who*? Then, there's this here Public Opinion
that the newspapers chassé up and down the Capitol steps and
right here in this sacred sanctum, a-scaring the wadding out of
honest public servants. I claim it's right and just the public has
opinions and all, but what I stand before you to-day to ask is:
to *who* is the benefit of this here Public Opinion to be directed—
to WHO? The answer to both questions, felly citizens, is: to
NOBODY, that's who. As long as they is no ORGANIZA-
TION in this here Congress, the public ain't going to pay its
taxes to you, and it ain't going to pay its taxes to me, nor even
to the Mister hisself. And nor me nor you nor the Mister ain't
going to reap no benefit from Public Opinion as long as it is
allowed to run around loose like it is to-day, neither. And it's

* The "Public Thing" is Bar-   tion of Res Publica.—Editor's
ton's doggedly faithful transla-   note.

a-going to be every man for hisself, and the Bank's a-going to swell up till it busts itself and the wrong people is going to get rich and the right ones is going to get pore unless we do something and do it P. D. Q. And that something is ORGANIZE! What this country needs to-day, felly citizens, is PARTIES!"

When he had finished speaking the Senatus applauded for twenty-five minutes, which was the record for ovations up to that time, for the other Seniles recognized that their confrère had spoken words of gold. The States which had seceded were then induced to come back into the Union and the two great political parties were organized.

Those who supported the government of the Public Thing as set forth in the Constitution and as practiced by Hamilton, formed themselves into a party called the Uniboodlist Party. The Uniboodlists held that all the boodle in the country should be collected into one large pile, and that that pile should repose in the national capital where it could be transferred into the pockets of the servants of the people conveniently and at a safe distance from the watchful eyes of the constituencies.

Those who supported the government of the Public Thing as set forth in the Constitution and as practiced by Jefferson, formed the Multiboodlist Party. They believed that the national boodle should be divided into small piles and distributed throughout the States with only a slightly larger pile in the capital to take care of the slightly larger number of politicians usually gathered there. This scheme, they argued, would allow the small politicians who never got to the capital and the members of the party out of power to have a chance at the boodle. They also pointed out that the concentration of the boodle into one pile in Washington exposed it to the danger of one man or one group making away with the whole of it, whereas under their plan this would be extremely difficult, if not impossible.

The politicians of the entire country were then divided up between the two parties and the newspapers which manufactured Public Opinion were annexed, to begin with, half by the Uniboodlists and half by the Multiboodlists. St. George, who was claimed by both parties, was so taken up with his duties as Mister—posing for portraits, entertaining eminent visitors at elaborate functions and recovering from the effects of them the next day, accepting gifts from admirers, conferring with his tailors, writing holographs for future collectors, expressing noble sentiments and establishing precedents and traditions in a country where none existed—that he never really took an active part in either.

At a great mass meeting in New York, all the politicians and editors swore solemn oaths to die rather than betray their parties, and the country was ready to function as a Power.

The first test of the workings of the new party government came up shortly afterward. When their old allies, the French, read in the newspapers of the glorious blessing that had fallen upon the American people, they felt that the time had come to set up a Public Thing in their country, being, as they were, under the obligation to lead Europe with new ideas by 150 years. They accordingly returned their king to Him on high and established a Chose Publique, though it was some time before they elected a Monsieur. At the same time, they renewed their war with England and took on the rest of Europe to make it interesting.

The Americans, who had watched the French Revolution with deep interest, then began to root for France with all the power of their lungs. They called each other "Citizen," fired cannons, erected "liberty poles," waved the tricolor and pleaded to be allowed to take up arms against England.

Eric Severeid

The Senator McCarthy phenomenon provided positive confirmation that contemporary American political satire is perilously near bankruptcy. In the deafening silence which greeted McCarthy's tent show of intimidation, one could almost hear Mr. Dooley muttering to Mr. Hennessy, or imagine Petroleum Nasby changing from the Democratic to the Republican party to signify loyalty to the politician he resembled.

Among the rare satires against McCarthy is this brief one by

Eric Sevareid, the able news commentator for the Columbia Broadcasting System. Written originally for his radio series, it appears in Sevareid's collection of occasional pieces published under the title *In One Ear.*

SENATOR POOH AND THE COMMUNIST WOOZLES

It's funny how fairy-tale creatures will suddenly resemble living persons. You take the third chapter of "Winnie the Pooh," where Senator McCarthy, I mean Pooh, and Senator Hickenlooper, I mean Piglet, go hunting and nearly catch a Woozle. There's Pooh, walking in a circle, when Piglet says: "What are you doing?"

"Tracking something," says Winnie the Pooh very mysteriously.

"Tracking what?"

"That's just what I ask myself. I ask myself, what?"

"What do you think you'll answer?"

"I shall have to wait until I catch up with it," said Pooh. "Now, what do you see there?"

"Tracks," said Piglet. "Paw marks. Oh, Pooh, do you think it's a—a—Woozle?"

"It may be," said Pooh, "you never can tell with paw marks. But there seem to be two animals now. Would you mind coming with me, Piglet, in case they turn out to be hostile animals?"

Piglet said he didn't have anything to do till Friday, so off they went together, round and round the spinney of larch trees.

Suddenly Pooh stopped. "Look! A third animal has joined the other two. It is either two Woozles," said Pooh, "and one, as it might be, Wizzle, or two, as it might be, Wizzles and one, if so it is, Woozle."

A fourth set of tracks join the three, and Piglet remembers something he should be doing: "So really, dear old Pooh, if you'll excuse me—what's that?"

It was Senator Vandenberg—I mean, Christopher Robin—watching from a tree limb. "Silly old bear," he said, "what *were* you doing?"

Pooh sat down and thought in the most thoughtful way he could think. Then he fitted his paw into one of the tracks.

"Yes," said Pooh.

"I see now," said Pooh. "I have been foolish and deluded."

"You're the best bear in all the world," said Christopher Robin, soothingly.

"Am I?" said Pooh. And then he brightened up. "Anyhow," he said, "it's nearly luncheon time."

Art Buchwald

In December, 1957, when President Eisenhower and his press secretary, James Hagerty, were in Paris for a North Atlantic Treaty Organization meeting, Art Buchwald in his column in the *Herald Tribune* seized the occasion to spoof the kind of press briefings which covered the President's most ordinary acts as if they were of portentous national significance. To Mr. Buchwald's and everyone else's surprise, Mr. Hagerty immediately *denied* the spoof, calling it "unadulterated rot," and in so doing, turned an amusing satire into an international news story.

A LATE, LATE BRIEFING

The NATO conference now going on in Paris is being covered by 1,793 top-flight, highly paid journalists from every corner of the globe. Every detail of the conference is being given careful and thorough coverage. The star of the show is President Eisenhower, and every facet of the President's stay in Paris is being reported to the public in detail. In order to keep the press up on the President's activities, briefings are held at the Hotel Crillon in the morning, at noon and in the early evening, and there is even a special one held late at night for reporters who can't sleep.

I happened to attend one of these late-night briefings with several correspondents of early-morning newspapers. To give you an idea of what takes place at one of these briefings, I took down a transcript.

The man behind the microphone arrived at 12:30 A.M.

"I'm sorry I'm late, gentlemen, but I thought the show at the Lido would end at 11:30. I have a few things to report. The President went to bed at 11:06 tonight."

Q. Jim, have Premier Gaillard and Prime Minister Macmillan also retired?

A. To my knowledge they have.

Q. Then are we to assume that they will not meet with the President until morning?

A. Yes, you could assume that.

Q. Then does that mean he's going to meet with Adenauer during the night?

A. I didn't say that. As far as I know he'll sleep until morning.

Q. Jim, whose idea was it for the President to go to sleep?

A. It was the President's idea. He was tired and decided to go to sleep.

Q. Did Sherman Adams, or Dr. Snyder, or the President's son suggest he go to sleep?

A. As far as I know, the President suggested the idea himself.

Q. Jim, did the President speak to anyone before retiring?

A. He spoke to the Secretary of State.

Q. What did he say to the Secretary of State, Jim?

A. He said: "Good night, Foster."

Q. And what did the Secretary say to the President?

A. He said: "Good night, Mr. President."

Q. The Secretary didn't say: "Pleasant dreams"?

A. Not to my knowledge. I have nothing on that.

Q. Jim, do you have any idea what the President is dreaming of this very moment?

A. No, the President has never revealed to me any of his dreams.

Q. Are we to assume from that that the President doesn't dream?

A. I'm not saying he does or he doesn't. I just said I don't know.

Q. Jim, how will the President be waked up tomorrow morning? Will it be by alarm clock, or will someone come knock on the door?

A. That hasn't been decided yet. But as soon as it has, I'll let you fellows know.

Q. Do you have any idea who the President will see first tomorrow morning?

A. I imagine he'll see the Secretary of State.

Q. What will he say to him?

A. The President plans to say: "Good morning, Foster."

Q. What will the Secretary reply?

A. "Good morning, Mr. President."

Q. That's all?

A. That's all I can tell you at this moment.

Q. Jim, when the President went to bed last night, how did he feel?

A. He was feeling chipper and in good spirits.

Q. How many blankets were on the bed?

A. I'm not sure. Maybe two or three. But certainly no more than he uses in Washington.

Q. Could we say three?

A. I better check that. I know three blankets were made available but it's possible he didn't use all of them.

Q. One could have been kicked off during the night?

A. Yes, that could be possible, but it's unlikely.

Q. Was there a glass of water by the bed?

A. There was a glass of water and a pitcher.

Q. Jim, could we have another briefing before morning?

A. I don't see what would be accomplished by that.

Q. It might tend to clarify the situation.

A. I think the best thing would be to have the briefing after the President gets up.

Q. What about breakfast, Jim?

A. I think we better have another briefing about breakfast, after it's over.

Q. Thank you, Jim.

A. Okay, see you later.

James Reston

For one reason or another, today's journalists seldom find the time, disposition or editorial encouragement to depart from bald statements of fact or opinion, which are clear, unoffensive, easy to read—and easy to forget. For this reason, when a first-rate journalist turns to satire, as did the New York *Times*'s Washington commentator James Reston on June 29, 1960, the result can be memorable.

Reston's piece depends upon the association of two events which occurred in the spring of 1960: Ingemar Johansson's defeat in the heavyweight boxing championship of the world, and Eisenhower's forced cancellation of his trip to Japan because of Japanese student demonstrations.

The cast of characters includes:

Johansson, the defending champion from Sweden, whose training schedule had often been broken by television appearances and other diverting and profitable uses of his celebrity;

Floyd Patterson, the Negro heavyweight contender, who flattened Johansson in the fifth round;

Birgit, Johansson's attractive fiancée.

Of course, the real hero of the piece is Eisenhower, who had interpreted the Japanese debacle as a triumph for the Free World, somehow.

TO INGEMAR JOHANSSON WITH LOVE

Washington, June 28 [1960]—Dear Ingemar: You asked me what you should say in your forthcoming TV report to the Swedish people about the recent regrettable incident with Mr. Floyd Patterson at the Polo Grounds in New York.

I have three suggestions. The best thing is to say nothing. The next best thing is to deny that you ever went to America. But if you have to make a report, I suggest that you follow the victory-through-defeat system used by President Eisenhower in his report on Japan, speaking—if you are now able to speak— as follows:

My friends:

I have just returned to Sweden from America, where almost everybody treated me very kindly. It has been a trip so marked by events that I shall try this evening to give you a simple background of fact against which these recent events can be viewed in perspective.

First, Swedish relations with the United States have been strengthened. I wish that every one of you could have accompanied Birgit and me to New York and thus witnessed for yourselves the outpouring of friendship and respect for Sweden and the Swedish way of life.

Second, the happiness created among the Colored people of America as a result of my appearance there this time was not only heartwarming but surpassed by far their reaction to my last visit.

Finally, as the Marquis of Queensberry once said, it matters not in this life whether you win or lose, but how you play the game, especially when economic rewards are so agreeable.

Now, let's look at the background of this trip and the others I have taken in the interests of world understanding. For some years the world has been inclined to think only of the beauty of Swedish women.

Meanwhile, the heroism and warrior tradition of Swedish men had long been overlooked, not only by atheistic international communism, but even among the peoples of our sister democracies.

Accordingly, I have traveled tirelessly around the world, seeking lucrative personal contacts in my own people-to-people program, and belting old retreads regardless of race, creed or color.

With the passage of time I began to receive urgent invitations to attend a heavyweight summit meeting in America. Many months ago I concluded that I should accept these invitations whenever the price was right. In this decision Birgit enthusiastically concurred.

Incidentally, I have never believed that victory and money were the only things in life, although, as the Americans say in their picturesque way, these things are not to be sneezed at. What matters is the international goodwill that results from bilateral reciprocal aggression before multitudes of well-heeled savages in the over-developed and under-educated areas of the globe.

Now as to the incident at the Polo Grounds, I have been assured that the people there were, in overwhelming majority, anxious to welcome me as a representative of a nation with which they wished to cooperate and have friendly relations.

It is true that the outrageous conduct of a violent and disorderly minority prevented me from achieving all of my objectives, and that Mr. Patterson displayed toward me, especially in the fifth round, a certain animus and even hostility, which temporarily interrupted my mission.

Nevertheless, if you could have heard the cheering that filled that great arena, when I finally regained consciousness, I think you would agree with me that a great many peace-loving Americans were actually overjoyed at my survival.

I shall never forget the look of relief on the face of Mr. Patterson at the end. He kept saying in a faraway voice: "Wake up, Ingemar. Wake up!" It is in such moments a man realizes there is no defeat.

Now, a final personal word:

Sweden has nothing to regret. In the long history of human conflict no man has ever lost and regained the heavyweight championship of the world until now.

As I said to Birgit, this is our consolation: We have made it possible for Mr. Patterson to lose and regain a crown, and all I can hope is that he will do the same for me.

Thank you and—good night!

John Updike

When the spirit is on him, John Updike is among the most able satirists of the younger generation of writers. A novelist (*Poorhouse Fair; Rabbit, Run*) and short-story writer, he is also the author of humorously caustic poems and prose pieces which rank him high among the practitioners of the ungentle art of ridicule.

In a nonpartisan gesture, we now turn the satirical spotlight from ex-President Eisenhower to ex-Resident Truman.

MR. EX-RESIDENT

(ASSUMING, UNLIKELY THOUGH IT SEEMS AT FIRST
BLUSH, THAT HARRY S. TRUMAN, AUTHOR OF
"MR. CITIZEN," ALSO WROTE ADAM'S MEMOIRS)

A large number of people have expressed curiosity as to how Eve and I like residing out of Eden. The answer is very simple. We like it fine.

I began as a farm boy, so the thorns and thistles of the "outer world" are not news to me. We thoroughly enjoyed our years in Eden, but now that they are over we find many things to enjoy elsewhere. Pleasant as it was, Eden always had the disadvantage for me personally of being a little too lush and orderly. As the saying goes, I like some grit to my mash.

So many contradictory accounts of what happened have been published that I think the time has come to set the record straight. Now that my grandson Enoch has builded a city of the same name, I know there is a firm watertight place where the records can be kept. I think it is very important, whether or not it causes embarrassment in Heaven, for the First Man to set down in his own words his side of the story so that the generations succeeding him in this world can understand their present condition and why things are the way they are.

When the matter first came up of eating of the tree of knowledge of good and evil, I consulted with Eve and with the serpent and their consensus seemed to be that it could do no harm and might do a lot of good. It is easy to identify mistakes in hindsight, but at the time this was the best available information I could get, and it was my responsibility to act upon it. And I did.

The following day, God came to me and asked, "Hast thou eaten of the tree, whereof I commanded thee that thou shouldest not eat?"

I thought this was a curious question, since if He were omniscient as supposed He must have already known that I certainly had. But I have never had any trouble keeping the reins on my temper. With the utmost patience and courtesy I explained the situation.

When I was done, He simply told me, "In the sweat of thy face shalt thou eat bread, till thou return unto the ground." I felt lucky at that, since what He said to Eve and the serpent was far worse.

We wasted no time getting out, once the circumstances had become definite. I expected no fanfare, so it was one of the deeply moving experiences of my life to see all the cherubim waving goodbye with their flaming swords. I had not in any way asked them to do this. It was a truly spontaneous demonstration.

Two things need to be cleared up, for the reason that there has been a lot of improper and inaccurate speculation written concerning them.

The first is this. At no time, then or since, have Eve and I exchanged recriminations. She was produced from my rib and I have never for a moment wanted my rib back. In my opinion, she did a wonderful job raising Cain and Abel in an environment that was necessarily unsettled and far from ideal. If the boys did not turn out exactly the way we had hoped, this is no excuse for the disproportionate publicity that has surrounded their quarrel. It is of course a tribute to the office of First Man that everything that happens within his family circle attracts widespread comment.

Secondly, a lot of well-meaning—I will give them the benefit of the doubt—souls have expected us to resent how the serpent has insinuated himself into the good graces of subsequent administrations and is in fact enjoying a good deal of present prosperity. This shows they have no knowledge of the nature of the cosmos. It is the essence of the system that the serpent, having served his term with us, should seek "greener pastures." While I cannot feel that his advice was always in the best interests of my family, he was by his own lights successful and must be admired for it. History has been created by just this type of personality.

I have been called, among many other things, an optimist.

I do not think of myself as an optimist or a pessimist but as a normal human individual blessed with 100% excellent physical health since the day of my creation. At the time, a certain number of angels whom I do not wish to name doubted my ability to serve as First Man. I showed them that they were wrong. It is my sincere belief that any healthy man, placed in that position, could have done the job.

Though there is a lot wrong with the state of the world as we know it, I think entirely too much is made of the Fall. Eden just could not have accommodated all the men and women who now enjoy the blessings, qualified though they are in some instances, of earthly life. I lived in Eden many years and I flatter myself that I know more about its dimensions than most of the theological journals I make it my habit to read. These are written by good men, but their morbid preoccupation with Original Sin rubs me the wrong way, though I don't mind in the least whatever they say about me. I have no regrets. And I recommend that you have none either.

RELIGION

"In the United States, when the seventh day of each week arrives, the commercial and industrial life of the nation seems suspended; all noises cease. A profound rest, or rather a sort of solemn retirement replaces them; the soul at last regains its possession, and contemplates itself."

ALEXIS DE TOQUEVILLE, *Democracy in America*

Religion

*R*eligious satire has never been conspicuous in post-Colonial American literature. Since the Revolution, the separation of the churches from politics, the Constitutional assurances of tolerance, and the growth of secularism have not encouraged the satirist. Excepting the exotic sects which have been baited for comic effect in the way Artemus Ward made fun of Mormons and Shakers, American satire has seldom attacked religion. Rather, it has dealt energetically with abuses of religion, including hypocrisy, bigotry and fraud. Christian principles and un-Christian practices have been contrasted. Pseudo-religions, lucrative evangelism, and table-rapping have been ridiculed. Still, the American satirist tends to avoid all but the most obvious abuses and, generally, to avoid the subject of religion altogether. Today, the worldly bishop and the choir boy with the black eye are the remnants of a field of satire which once aroused the wit of Dryden and the ire of Swift.

Timothy Dwight

With John Trumbull, Timothy Dwight was one of the Connecticut Wits, who promoted the cause of American belles-lettres during the Revolutionary period. A chaplain during the war, Dwight became president of Yale in 1795. While in secular affairs he was a forward-looking humanitarian and ardent American, his religious views were those of an old-style Calvinist; Dwight had all of the Puritan's undisguised aversion for the modern minister, with his Deistic heresies and his ingratiating ways.

A MODERN MINISTER

(from *The Triumph of Infidelity*, 1788)

There smiled the smooth Divine, unused to wound
The sinner's heart with hell's alarming sound.
No terrors on his gentle tongue attend;
No grating truths the nicest ear offend.
That strange new-birth, that Methodistic grace,
Nor in his heart nor sermons found a place.
Plato's fine tales he clumsily retold,
Trite, fireside, moral seesaws, dull as old;
His Christ and Bible placed at good remove,
Guilt hell-deserving and forgiving love.
'Twas best, he said, mankind should cease to sin:
Good fame required it; so did peace within.
Their honors, well he knew, would ne'er be driven;
But hoped they still would please to go to heaven.
Each week he paid his visitation dues;
Coaxed, jested, laughed; rehearsed the private news;
Smoked with each goody, thought her cheese excelled;
Her pipe he lighted, and her baby held.
Or placed in some great town, with lacquered shoes,
Trim wig and trimmer gown, and glistening hose,
He bowed, talked politics, learned manners mild,
Most meekly questioned, and most smoothly smiled;
At rich men's jests laughed loud, their stories praised;
Their wives new patterns gazed, and gazed, and gazed;
Most daintily on pampered turkeys dined;
Nor shrunk with fasting, nor with study pined:

Yet from their churches saw his brethren driven,
Who thundered truth, and spoke the voice of heaven,
Chilled trembling guilt in Satan's headlong path,
Charmed their feet back, and roused the ear of death.
"Let fools," he cried, "starve on, while prudent I
Snug in my nest shall live, and snug shall die."

Artemus Ward
(Charles Farrar Browne)

Dean of the cracker-barrel humorists, Artemus Ward was born Charles Farrar Browne in Maine in 1834. His "Grate Moral Show," consisting of educational wax figures and stuffed animals, was the fictitious prop with which Ward launched his brief, brilliant illiterary career. Shortly after the first misspelled sketches signed "A. Ward" appeared in the Cleveland *Plain Dealer*, his audience discovered that besides being a funny writer he was a master of deadpan comic delivery, and thereafter Ward was in demand as a lecturer all over the country and abroad.

The humor of Artemus Ward is not characteristically satirical. He had too much affection for absurdity to wish it any permanent harm. He was fascinated less by the great issues of the day—abolition, states' rights, national union—than by out-of-the-way religious sects and such persuasions as table-rapping and free loving—subjects at which most Americans of the 1850s could laugh freely.

Here is a typical Ward production, "The Shakers," which lies on the boundary where satire becomes facetious diversion.

THE SHAKERS

The Shakers is the strangest religious sex I ever met. I'd hearn tell of 'em and I'd seen 'em, with their broad brim'd hats and long wastid coats; but I'd never cum into immejit contack with 'em, and I'd sot 'em down as lackin intelleck, as I'd never seen 'em to my Show—leastways, if they cum they was disgised in white peple's close, so I didn't know 'em.

But in the Spring of 18—, I got swampt in the exterior of New York State, one dark and stormy night, when the winds Blue pityusly, and I was forced to tie up with the Shakers.

I was toilin threw the mud, when in the dim vister of the futer I obsarved the gleams of a taller candle. Tiein a hornet's nest to my off hoss's tail to kinder encourage him, I soon reached the place. I knockt at the door, which it was opened unto me by a tall, slick-faced, solum lookin individooal, who turn'd out to be a Elder.

"Mr. Shaker," sed I, "you see before you a Babe in the woods, so to speak, and he axes shelter of you."

"Yay," sed the Shaker, and he led the way into the house, another Shaker bein sent to put my hosses and waggin under kiver.

A solum female, lookin sumwhat like a last year's beanpole stuck into a long meal bag, cum in and axed me was I a thurst and did I hunger? to which I urbanely anserd "a few." She went orf and I endeverd to open a conversashun with the old man.

"Elder, I spect?" sed I.

"Yay," he said.

"Helth's good, I reckon?"

"Yay."

"What's the wages of a Elder, when he understands his bisness—or do you devote your sarvices gratooitus?"

"Yay."

"Stormy night, sir."

"Yay."

"If the storm continners there'll be a mess underfoot, hay?"

"Yay."

"It's onpleasant when there's a mess underfoot?"

"Yay."

"If I may be so bold, kind sir, what's the price of that pecooler kind of weskit you wear, incloodin trimmins?"

"Yay!"

I pawsd a minit, and then, thinkin I'd be faseshus with him and see how that would go, I slapt him on the shoulder, bust into a harty larf, and told him that as a *yayer* he had no livin ekal.

He jumpt up as if Billin water had bin squirted into his ears, groaned, rolled his eyes up tords the sealin and sed: "You're a man of sin!" He then walkt out of the room.

Jest then the female in the meal bag stuck her hed into the room and statid that refreshments awaited the weary travler, and I sed if it was vittles she ment the weary travler was agreeable and I follored her into the next room.

I sot down to the table and the female in the meal bag pored out sum tea. She sed nothin, and for five minutes the only live thing in that room was a old wooden clock, which tickt in a sub-dood and bashful manner in the corner. This dethly stillness made me oneasy, and I determined to talk to the female or bust. So sez I, "marrige is agin your rules, I bleeve, marm?"

"Yay."

"The sexes liv strickly apart, I spect?"

"Yay."

"It's kinder singler," sez I, puttin on my most sweetest look and speakin in a winnin voice, "that so fair a made as thow never got hitched to some likely feller." [N. B.—She was upwards of 40 and homely as a stump fence, but I thawt I'd tickil her.]

"I don't like men!" she sed, very short.

"Wall, I dunno," sez I, "they're a rayther important part of the populashun. I don't scacely see how we could git along without 'em."

"Us poor wimin folks would git along a grate deal better if there was no men!"

"You'll excoos me, marm, but I don't think that air would work. It wouldn't be regler."

"I'm fraid of men!" she sed.

"That's onnecessary, marm. *You* ain't in no danger. Don't fret yourself on that pint."

"Here we're shot out from the sinful world. Here all is peas. Here we air brothers and sisters. We don't marry and conse-kently we hav no domestic difficulties. Husbans don't abooze their wives—wives don't worrit their husbans. There's no children here to worrit us. Nothin to worrit us here. No wicked matrimony here. Would thow like to be a Shaker?"

"No," sez I, "it ain't my stile."

I had now histed in as big a load of pervishuns as I could carry comfortable, and, leanin back in my cheer, commenst pickin my teeth with a fork. The female went out, leavin me all alone with the clock. I hadn't sot thar long before the Elder poked his hed in at the door. "You're a man of sin!" he sed, and groaned and went away.

Directly thar cum in two young Shakeresses, as putty and slick lookin gals as I ever met. It is troo they was drest in meal bags like the old one I'd met previsly, and their shiny, silky har was hid from sight by long white caps, sich as I spose female Josts wear; but their eyes sparkled like diminds, their cheeks was like roses, and they was charmin enuff to make a man throw stuns at his granmother if they axed him to. They commenst clearin away the dishes, castin shy glances at me all the time. I got excited. I forgot Betsy Jane in my rapter, and sez I, "my pretty dears, how air you?"

"We air well," they solumly sed.

"Whar's the old man?" sed I, in a soft voice.

"Of whom dost thow speak—Brother Uriah?"

"I mean the gay and festiv cuss who calls me a man of sin. Shouldn't wonder if his name was Uriah."

"He has retired."

"Wall, my pretty dears," sez I, "let's have sum fun. Let's play puss in the corner. What say?"

"Air you a Shaker, sir?" they axed.

"Wall my pretty dears, I haven't arrayed my proud form in a long weskit yit, but if they was all like you perhaps I'd jine 'em. As it is, I'm a Shaker pro-temporary."

They was full of fun. I seed that at fust, only they was a leetle skeery. I tawt 'em Puss in the corner and sich like plase, and we had a nice time, keepin quiet of course so the old man shouldn't hear. When we broke up, sez I, "my pretty dears, ear I go you hav no objections, hav you, to a innersent kiss at partin?"

"Yay," they sed, and I *yay'd*.

I went up stairs to bed. I spose I'd bin snoozin half an hour when I was woke up by a noise at the door. I sot up in bed, leanin on my elbers and rubbin my eyes, and I saw the follerin picter: The Elder stood in the doorway, with a taller candle in his hand. He hadn't no wearin appeerel on except his night close, which flutterd in the breeze like a Seseshun flag. He sed, "You're a man of sin!" then groaned and went away.

I went to sleep agin, and drempt of runnin orf with the pretty little Shakeresses mounted on my Californy Bar. I thawt the Bar insisted on steerin strate for my dooryard in Baldinsville and that Betsy Jane cum out and giv us a warm recepshun with a panfull of Bilin water. I was woke up arly by the Elder. He sed refreshments was reddy for me down stairs. Then sayin I was a man of sin, he went groanin away.

As I was goin threw the entry to the room where the vittles was, I cum across the Elder and the old female I'd met the night before, and what d'ye spose they was up to? Huggin and kissin like young lovers in their gushingist state. Sez I, "My Shaker frends, I reckon you'd better suspend the rules and git married."

"You must excoos Brother Uriah," sed the female; "he's subjeck to fits and hain't got no command over hisself when he's into 'em."

"Sartinly," sez I, "I've bin took that way myself frequent."

"You're a man of sin!" sed the Elder.

Arter breakfust my little Shaker frends cum in agin to clear away the dishes.

"My pretty dears," sez I, "shall we *yay* agin?"

"Nay," they sed, and I *nay'd*.

The Shakers axed me to go to their meetin, as they was to hav sarvices that mornin, so I put on a clean biled rag and went. The meetin house was as neat as a pin. The floor was white as chalk and smooth as glass. The Shakers was all on hand, in clean weskits and meal bags, ranged on the floor like milingtery companies, the mails on one side of the room and the females on tother. They commenst clappin their hands and singin and dancin. They danced kinder slow at fust, but as they got warmed up they shaved it down very brisk, I tell you. Elder Uriah, in particler, exhiberted a right smart chance of spryness in his legs, considerin his time of life, and as he cum a dubble shuffle near where I sot, I rewarded him with a approvin smile and sed: "Hunky boy! Go it, my gay and festiv cuss!"

"You're a man of sin!" he sed, continnerin his shuffle.

The Sperret, as they called it, then moved a short fat Shaker to say a few remarks. He sed they was Shakers and all was ekal. They was the purest and Seleckest peple on the yearth. Other peple was sinful as they could be, but Shakers was all right. Shakers was all goin kerslap to the Promist Land, and nobody want goin to stand at the gate to bar 'em out, if they did they'd git run over.

The Shakers then danced and sung agin, and arter they was threw, one of 'em axed me what I thawt of it.

Sez I, "What duz it siggerfy?"

"What?" sez he.

"Why this jumpin up and singin? This long weskit bizniss, and this anty-matrimony idee? My frends, you air neat and tidy. Your lands is flowin with milk and honey. Your brooms is fine, and your apple sass is honest. When a man buys a keg of apple sass of you he don't find a grate many shavings under a few layers of sass—a little Game I'm sorry to say sum of my New Englan ancestors used to practiss. Your garding seeds is fine, and if I should sow 'em on the rock of Gibralter probly I should raise a good mess of garding sass. You air honest in your dealins. You air quiet and don't distarb nobody. For all this I givs you credit. But your religion is small pertaters, I must say. You mope away your lives here in single retchidness, and as you air all by yourselves nothing ever conflicks with your pecooler idees, except when Human Nater busts out among you, as I understan she sumtimes do. [I giv Uriah a sly wink here, which made the old feller squirm like a speared Eel.] You wear long weskits and long faces, and lead a gloomy life indeed. No children's prattle is ever hearn around your harthstuns—you air in a dreary fog all the time, and you treat the jolly sunshine of life as tho' it was a thief, drivin it from your doors by them weskits, and meal bags, and pecooler noshuns of yourn. The gals among you, sum of which air as slick pieces of caliker as I ever sot eyes on, air syin to place their heds agin weskits which kiver honest, manly

harts, while you old heds fool yerselves with the idee that they
air fulfillin their mishun here, and air contented. Here you air all
pend up by yerselves, talkin about the sins of a world you don't
know nothin of. Meanwhile said world continners to resolve
round on her own axeltree onct in every 24 hours, subjeck to the
Constitution of the United States, and is a very plesant place of
residence. It's a unnatral, onreasonable and dismal life you're
leadin here. So it strikes me. My Shaker frends, I now bid you a
welcome adoo. You hav treated me exceedin well. Thank you
kindly, one and all."

"A base exhibiter of depraved monkeys and onprincipled wax
works!" sed Uriah.

"Hello, Uriah," sez I, "I'd most forgot you. Wall, look out for
them fits of yourn, and don't catch cold and die in the flour of
your youth and beauty."

And I resoomed my jerney.

Mark Twain

In turning from Artemus Ward to Mark Twain's passage
on Adam's tomb from *The Innocents Abroad* we move from
the periphery to the center of American religious satire. Here is
Twain at his skeptical best, piling one irony on top of another.
While manifestly a satire against human credulity, this brief,
intense passage evokes the dramatic encounter of rationalism
and science with fundamental religion, which lasted from
America's discovery of Darwin until the Scopes trial and beyond.

AT ADAM'S TOMB
(from *The Innocents Abroad*, 1869)

The Greek Chapel is the most roomy, the richest and the
showiest chapel in the Church of the Holy Sepulchre. Its
altar, like that of all the Greek churches, is a lofty screen that
extends clear across the chapel, and is gorgeous with gilding and

pictures. The numerous lamps that hang before it are of gold and silver, and cost great sums.

But the feature of the place is a short column that rises from the middle of the marble pavement of the chapel, and marks the exact *center of the earth*. The most reliable traditions tell us that this was known to be the earth's center, ages ago, and that when Christ was upon earth He set all doubts upon the subject at rest forever, by stating with His own lips that the tradition was correct. Remember He said that that particular column stood upon the center of the world. If the center of the world changes, the column changes its position accordingly. This column has moved three different times, of its own accord. This is because, in great convulsions of nature, at three different times, masses of the earth—whole ranges of mountains, probably—have flown off into space, thus lessening the diameter of the earth, and changing the exact locality of its center by a point or two. This is a very curious and interesting circumstance, and is a withering rebuke to those philosophers who would make us believe that it is not possible for any portion of the earth to fly off into space.

To satisfy himself that this spot was really the center of the earth, a skeptic once paid well for the privilege of ascending to the dome of the church to see if the sun gave him a shadow at noon. He came down perfectly convinced. The day was very cloudy and the sun threw no shadows at all; but the man was satisfied that if the sun had come out and made shadows it could not have made any for him. Proofs like these are not to be set aside by the idle tongues of cavilers. To such as are not bigoted, and are willing to be convinced, they carry a conviction that nothing can ever shake.

If even greater proofs than those I have mentioned are wanted, to satisfy the headstrong and the foolish that this is the genuine center of the earth, they are here. The greatest of them lies in the fact that from under this very column was taken the *dust from which Adam was made*. This can surely be regarded in the light of a settler. It is not likely that the original first man would have been made from an inferior quality of earth when it was entirely convenient to get first quality from the world's center. This will strike any reflecting mind forcibly. That Adam was formed of dirt procured in this very spot is amply proven by the fact that in six thousand years no man has ever been able to prove that the dirt was *not* procured here whereof he was made.

It is a singular circumstance that right under the roof of this same great church, and not far away from that illustrious column, Adam himself, the father of the human race, lies buried. There is no question that he is actually buried in the grave which is pointed out as his—there can be none—because it has never yet been proven that that grave is not the grave in which he is buried.

The tomb of Adam! How touching it was, here in a land of strangers, far away from home, and friends, and all who cared for me, thus to discover the grave of a blood relation. True, a distant one, but still a relation. The unerring instinct of nature thrilled its recognition. The fountain of my filial affection was stirred to its profoundest depths, and I gave way to tumultuous emotion. I leaned upon a pillar and burst into tears. I deem it no shame to have wept over the grave of my poor dead relative. Let him who would sneer at my emotion close this volume here, for he will find little to his taste in my journeyings through Holy Land. Noble old man—he did not live to see me—he did not live to see his child. And I—I—alas, I did not live to see *him*. Weighed down by sorrow and disappointment, he died before I was born—six thousand brief summers before I was born. But let us try to bear it with fortitude. Let us trust that he is better off where he is. Let us take comfort in the thought that his loss is our eternal gain.

Ambrose Bierce

FOUR FABLES
(from *Fantastic Fables*, 1899)

THE HOLY DEACON

An Itinerant Preacher who had wrought hard in the moral vineyard for several hours whispered to a Holy Deacon of the local church:

"Brother, these people know you, and your active support

will bear fruit abundantly. Please pass the plate for me, and you shall have one fourth."

The Holy Deacon did so, and putting the money into his pocket waited till the congregation was dismissed, then said good-night.

"But the money, brother, the money that you collected!" said the Itinerant Preacher.

"Nothing is coming to you," was the reply; "the Adversary has hardened their hearts and one fourth is all they gave."

TWO OF THE PIOUS

A CHRISTIAN and a Heathen in His Blindness were disputing, when the Christian, with that charming consideration which serves to distinguish the truly pious from wolves that perish, exclaimed:

"If I could have my way I'd blow up all your gods with dynamite."

"And if I could have mine," retorted the Heathen in His Blindness, bitterly malevolent but oleaginously suave, "I'd fan all yours out of the universe."

A RADICAL PARALLEL

SOME White Christians engaged in driving Chinese Heathens out of an American town found a newspaper published in Peking in the Chinese tongue and compelled one of their victims to translate an editorial. It turned out to be an appeal to the people of the province of Pang Ki to drive the foreign devils out of the country and burn their dwellings and churches. At this evidence of Mongolian barbarity the White Christians were so greatly incensed that they carried out their original design.

A CALL TO QUIT

SEEING that his audiences were becoming smaller every Sunday, a Minister of the Gospel broke off in the midst of a sermon, descended the pulpit stairs and walked on his hands down the central aisle of the church. He then remounted his feet, ascended to the pulpit and resumed his discourse, making no allusion to the incident.

"Now," said he to himself, as he went home, "I shall have, henceforth, a large attendance and no snoring."

But on the following Friday he was waited upon by the Pillars of the Church, who informed him that in order to be in harmony with the New Theology and get full advantage of modern methods of Gospel interpretation they had deemed it advisable to make a change. They had therefore sent a call to Brother Jowjeetum-Fallal, the world-renowned Hindoo human pin-wheel, then holding forth in Hoopitup's circus. They were happy to say that the reverend gentleman had been moved by the Spirit to accept the call, and on the ensuing Sabbath would break the bread of life for the brethren or break his neck in the attempt.

Don Marquis

"A proportion of Marquis's most brilliant work in those years was oblique comment on public affairs. In those days I give my word, most of us didn't consult the leading editorials to know what to think. The almost universal reflex, in New York at any rate, was Let's see what Don says about it."

Today, when Marquis is remembered only as the creator of *archy and mehitabel*, this tribute by his friend Christopher Morley is a reminder that, between 1913 and 1922 the "Sun Dial" column of the New York *Sun* was brightened by Marquis' pen. A reporter, playwright and poet, Don Marquis' other creations include Hermione and Her Little Group of Serious Thinkers (selections may be found on pages 241 and 242) and the Old Soak with his bibulous history of the world.

Here is the Old Soak at the top of his form—which is to say "dished"—defending the Good Book against the impieties of a "dam little athyiss" named Hennery Withers.

MEN ARE NOT DESSENDED OFF OF MONKEYS
(from *The Old Soak's History of the World*)

Well, what people want to find out about the histry of the world is mostly how people acted at different times and what they et and drunk and thought about, which it is my idea that from the garden of Eden down the present times it has all been about the same.

But the Eighteenth Commandment has come along and things have changed and from the garden of Eden down to to-day is one area, and from now on is another area, with a great gulf fixed, as the Good Book says.

Well, one of the most prominent men in the old days was Sampson he never liked to work none but use to loaf around with his hair long and show how stout he was and as far as taking a drink was concerned it never hurt him none but he would liquor up and slay more Phillippines drunk than one of these here Prohibitionists was ever man enough to do sober.

If you had said to him he was descended off of a monkey he would of beaned you with anything that was handy. And in my histry of the World it will be proved that men is not descended off of monkeys for if so why did not all the monkeys turn into men. You can't get back of the Good Book in them things, and for my part I don't hanker to.

There use to hang around Jake Smith's place a smart alec couisin of his by the name of Hennery Withers and every time this here Hennery Withers got too much to drink he use to say, Well, then, you tell me now, "Where did Cain get his wife?"

I says to Jake more than oncet, Well you tell Hennery to leave the Good Book alone or I will bean him one of these days with a bottle he is a dam little athyiss, and if there is anything I hate it is a dam little athyiss.

Well, Jake says, you leave him alone Clem, I keep a respectible place and I don't want a word of religion or any other trouble in here or no fuss for they will take away my lisence.

This feller Hennery Withers was proud of being an athyiss. You go and be one I says to him and keep your mouth shut about it and nobody will give a dam but I never saw one of these athyisses yet he didn't want to blah blah it around so the whole town would know it. It made him feel like he was important. He knowed he wasn't worth nothing and he's got to feel important some faked up way or he wouldn't have no reason to keep on living.

One difference of the old days in the early times of world whose histry I am going to write is that they didn't have no glass bottles, they kept it in jugs and skins which they was bladders I guess like they keep oil and putty in nowadays and they drunk it right out of the jug. Well, I have drunk cider that a way, and oncet I run onto a gang of Scandinavians building a barn and them fellows was drinking equival parts of sweet cider and straight alkohawl mixed right out of a jug and Oh boy! what a head ache you can get out of that stuff.

In Sampson's time they didn't have no alkohawl and it come into the world in recent years, what they had in the old days was wine and liquors.

He says the little foxes spoils the grapes, you can read it in the Good Book, and that made him sore and he went out and caught a hunderd of them foxes and tied all their tales together and set fire to them and turned them loose against the Phillippines.

Well, they finally got him, he married a new wife and she says you gotto cut that hair and he says bob your own and she slipped some nock out drops into his hootch and when he come to he was bob haired and it disturbed his balance.

Afore he got his hair cut when he wanted to set his self for a good lick his hair balanced him like the tale onto a kite, but when his balance was disturbed he couldn't set his self for a good lick and finally the enimy got him because he couldn't set him self for a good lick.

They took him and conkered him they bored his eyes out and they says now you gotto go to work.

Work, hell, he says, I won't do it, I never done nothing but drink liquor and fight and run with the women and I won't work.

You can see work was quite a come down to a gent that has always lived free and easy like that, but when they bored his eyes out they hooked him to a kind of a dog churn thing and he had to keep stepping or he would get his heels barked and he had to turn that mill.

But one day he notis his hair is down to his neck again and he says to his self these coots is got a big surprise coming to them some day. If I could get a jug of the old stuff I would show them.

Well, them Phillippines was an unreligious set. On Sundays

they would play baseball and go fishing and have big parties. They had some kind of a church, but it wasn't a reg'lar orthydox church, neither Baptis or Methodis nor none of the churches we know about in this country. It was an idle church full of them heathen idles all carved out of elephants tushes and things and on Sundays they would have like a street fair in front of the church so one Sunday they says let us bring out this Sampson to the street fair and make him do stunts and we will thrown orange peel and tomatoes at him and mebby eggs that aint so young as they use to be. Well he got some of that grubbage in his face and he fetched one roar like a bull and he pulled that church full of idles down on top of the whole kit and biling of them and they perished.

Offen Jake Smith an me have argued wether he could of licked John Sullivan, and Jake says John would of out boxed him but with the old london prise ring rules Sampson would of licked him.

Well I see John L. oncet in Boston I was into his place and shook the hand that knocked Charlie michell cold.

H. L. Mencken

Now that the shock waves of Mencken's passage through the American landscape have stopped rattling windows it should be possible to discuss him with some objectivity—but it is not. Partisan emotions still run high and even today one can occasionally stir up an argument over whether he was the true prophet of the twenties and thirties or merely a noisy disturber of the peace.

It is a tribute to Mencken's vitality, even after sickness and death, that in some quarters he is still a bad word. His cleverness and verbal ingenuity were diabolical and his whole attitude un-American; that he was wrongheaded from beginning to end (the argument runs) is proved by his refusal to see the menace of Germany and by signs in his writing of racism. At best, say others, he is a prewar curiosity whose reign of terror is a part of Americana as remote as wobblies and 3.2 beer.

This latter view is rapidly being dissipated by the publication of new collections of his best and most representative work, which offer convenient evidence that Mencken was not only a brilliant writer whose gifts of comic invective have seldom been matched, but a satirist of the first magnitude. His style was memorable, yet the style was never an end in itself; he wrote from a deep sense of human value and dignity. Most satirists in America have created comic characters through which to express their commentary, thereby softening and excusing any damage done. Mencken's was the first successful frontal offensive on "buncombe" ever launched on open ground in America, and the record still stands. His ironies, exaggerations, humor, and the elegant vocabulary which he used with such devastating effect were all but unanswerable. Here suddenly was the critique direct of a Juvenal—moreover, a Juvenal who enjoyed himself.

Mencken's attitude toward formal religion was skeptical, yet religious and pseudo-religious manifestations in America fascinated him. "The Hills of Zion" was written while he was covering the Scopes trial at Dayton, Tennessee. His note (in *Prejudices: Fifth Series*) states: "In its first form this was a dispatch to the Baltimore *Evening Sun*, in July 1925. I wrote it on a roaring hot Sunday afternoon in a Chattanooga hotel room, naked above the waist and with only a pair of BVDs below."

THE HILLS OF ZION
(from *Prejudices: Fifth Series*)

It was hot weather when they tried the infidel Scopes at Dayton, but I went down there very willingly, for I had good reports of the sub-Potomac bootleggers, and moreover I was eager to see something of evangelical Christianity as a going concern. In the big cities of the Republic, despite the endless efforts of consecrated men, it is laid up with a wasting disease. The very Sunday-school superintendents, taking jazz from the stealthy radio, shake their fireproof legs; their pupils, moving into adolescence, no longer respond to the proliferating hormones

by enlisting for missionary service in Africa, but resort to necking and petting instead. I know of no evangelical church from
Oregon to Maine that is not short of money: the graft begins to
peter out, like wire-tapping and three-card monte before it.
Even in Dayton, though the mob was up to do execution upon
Scopes, there was a strong smell of antinomianism. The nine
churches of the village were all half empty on Sunday, and
weeds choked their yards. Only two or three of the resident
pastors managed to sustain themselves by their ghostly science;
the rest had to take orders for mail-order pantaloons or work in
the adjacent strawberry fields; one, I heard, was a barber. On the
courthouse green a score of sweating theologians debated the
darker passages of Holy Writ day and night, but I soon found
that they were all volunteers, and that the local faithful, while
interested in their exegesis as an intellectual exercise, did not
permit it to impede the indigenous debaucheries. Exactly twelve
minutes after I reached the village I was taken in tow by a Christian man and introduced to the favorite tipple of the Cumber-
land Range: half corn liquor and half coca-cola. It seemed a
dreadful dose to me, spoiled as I was by the bootleg light
wines and beers of the Eastern seaboard, but I found that the
Dayton illuminati got it down with gusto, rubbing their tum-
mies and rolling their eyes. I include among them the chief local
proponents of the Mosaic cosmogony. They were all hot for
Genesis, but their faces were far too florid to belong to teetotal-
ers, and when a pretty girl came tripping down the main street,
which was very often, they reached for the places where their
neckties should have been with all the amorous enterprise of
movie actors. It seemed somehow strange.

An amiable newspaper woman of Chattanooga, familiar with
those uplands, presently enlightened me. Dayton, she explained, was simply a great capital like any other great capital.
That is to say, it was to Rhea County what Atlanta was to
Georgia or Paris to France. That is to say, it was predominantly
epicurean and sinful. A country girl from some remote valley of
the county, coming into town for her semi-annual bottle of Lydia
Pinkham's Vegetable Compound, shivered on approaching
Robinson's drug-store quite as a country girl from up-state New

York might shiver on approaching the Metropolitan Opera
House or the Ritz Hotel. In every village lout she saw a potential white-slaver. The hard sidewalks hurt her feet. Temptations of the flesh bristled to all sides of her, luring her to hell.
This newspaper woman told me of a session with just such a
visitor, holden a few days before. The latter waited outside one
of the town hot-dog and coca-cola shops while her husband ne-
gotiated with a hardware merchant across the street. The newspaper woman, idling along and observing that the stranger was
badly used by the heat, invited her to step into the shop for a
glass of coca-cola. The invitation brought forth only a gurgle
of terror. Coca-cola, it quickly appeared, was prohibited by the
country lady's pastor, as a levantine and hell-sent narcotic. He
also prohibited coffee and tea—and pies! He had his doubts
about white bread and boughten meat. The newspaper woman,
interested, inquired about ice-cream. It was, she found, not specifically prohibited, but going into a coca-cola shop to get it
would be clearly sinful. So she offered to get a saucer of it and
bring it out to the sidewalk. The visitor vacillated—and came
near being lost. But God saved her in the nick of time. When
the newspaper woman emerged from the place she was in full
flight up the street! Later on, her husband, mounted on a mule,
overtook her four miles out the mountain pike.

This newspaper woman, whose kindness covered city infidels
as well as Alpine Christians, offered to take me back in the hills
to a place where the old-time religion was genuinely on tap. The
Scopes jury, she explained, was composed mainly of its custom-
ers, with a few Dayton sophisticates added to leaven the mass.
It would thus be instructive to climb the heights and observe
the former at their ceremonies. The trip, fortunately, might be
made by automobile. There was a road running out of Dayton to
Morgantown, in the mountains to the westward, and thence beyond. But foreigners, it appeared, would have to approach the
sacred grove cautiously, for the upland worshippers were very
shy, and at the first sight of a strange face they would adjourn
their orgy and slink into the forest. They were not to be feared,
for God had long since forbidden them to practice assassination,
or even assault, but if they were alarmed a rough trip would go

for naught. So, after dreadful bumpings up a long and narrow road, we parked our car in a little wood-path a mile or two beyond the tiny village of Morgantown and made the rest of the approach on foot, deployed like skirmishers. Far off in a dark, romantic glade a flickering light was visible, and out of the silence came the rumble of exhortation. We could distinguish the figure of the preacher only as a moving mote in the light: it was like looking down the tube of a dark-field microscope. Slowly and cautiously we crossed what seemed to be a pasture, and then we crouched down along the edge of a cornfield and stealthily edged further and further. The light now grew larger and we could begin to make out what was going on. We went ahead on all fours, like snakes in the grass.

From the great limb of a mighty oak hung a couple of crude torches of the sort that car inspectors thrust under Pullman cars when a train pulls in at night. In the guttering glare was the preacher, and for a while we could see no one else. He was an immensely tall and thin mountaineer in blue jeans, his collarless shirt open at the neck and his hair a tousled mop. As he preached he paced up and down under the smoking flambeaux, and at each turn he thrust his arms into the air and yelled: "Glory to God!" We crept nearer in the shadow of the cornfield and began to hear more of his discourse. He was preaching on the Day of Judgment. The high kings of the earth, he roared, would all fall down and die; only the sanctified would stand up to receive the Lord God of Hosts. One of these kings he mentioned by name, the King of what he called Greece-y. The King of Greece-y, he said, was doomed to hell. We crawled forward a few more yards and began to see the audience. It was seated on benches ranged round the preacher in a circle. Behind him sat a row of elders, men and women. In front were the younger folk. We crept on cautiously, and individuals rose out of the ghostly gloom. A young mother sat suckling her baby, rocking as the preacher paced up and down. Two scared little girls hugged each other, their pigtails down their backs. An immensely huge mountain woman, in a gingham dress, cut in one piece, rolled on her heels at every "Glory to God!" To one side, and but half visible, was what appeared to be a bed. We found afterwards that half a dozen babies were asleep upon it.

The preacher stopped at last, and there arose out of the darkness a woman with her hair pulled back into a little tight knot. She began so quietly that we couldn't hear what she said, but soon her voice rose resonantly and we could follow her. She was denouncing the reading of books. Some wandering book-agent, it appeared, had come to her cabin and tried to sell her a specimen of his wares. She refused to touch it. Why, indeed, read a book? If what was in it was true, then everything in it was already in the Bible. If it was false, then reading it would imperil the soul. This syllogism from Caliph Omar complete, she sat down. There followed a hymn, led by a somewhat fat brother wearing silver-rimmed country spectacles. It droned on for half a dozen stanzas, and then the first speaker resumed the floor. He argued that the gift of tongues was real and that education was a snare. Once his children could read the Bible, he said, they had enough. Beyond lay only infidelity and damnation. Sin stalked the cities. Dayton itself was a Sodom. Even Morgantown had begun to forget God. He sat down, and a female aurochs in gingham got up. She began quietly, but was soon leaping and roaring, and it was hard to follow her. Under cover of the turmoil we sneaked a bit closer.

A couple of other discourses followed, and there were two or three hymns. Suddenly a change of mood began to make itself felt. The last hymn ran longer than the others, and dropped gradually into a monotonous, unintelligible chant. The leader beat time with his book. The faithful broke out with exultations. When the singing ended there was a brief palaver that we could not hear, and two of the men moved a bench into the circle of light directly under the flambeaux. Then a half-grown girl emerged from the darkness and threw herself upon it. We noticed with astonishment that she had bobbed hair. "This sister," said the leader, "has asked for prayers." We moved a bit closer. We could now see faces plainly, and hear every word. What followed quickly reached such heights of barbaric grotesquerie that it was hard to believe it real. At a signal all the faithful crowded up to the bench and began to pray—not in unison, but each for himself! At another they all fell on their knees, their arms over the penitent. The leader kneeled facing us, his head alternately thrown back dramatically or buried in his hands. Words spouted from his lips like bullets from a machine-gun—appeals to God to pull the penitent back out of hell, defiances of the demons of the air, a vast impassioned jargon of apocalyptic texts. Suddenly he rose to his feet, threw back his head and began to speak in the tongues—blub-blub-blub, gurgle-gurgle-gurgle. His voice rose to a higher register. The climax was a shrill, inarticulate squawk, like that of a man throttled. He fell headlong across the pyramid of suppliants.

A comic scene? Somehow, no. The poor half-wits were too horribly in earnest. It was like peeping through a knothole at the writhings of people in pain. From the squirming and jabbering mass a young woman gradually detached herself—a woman not uncomely, with a pathetic home-made cap on her head. Her head jerked back, the veins of her neck swelled, and her fists went to her throat as if she were fighting for breath. She bent backward until she was like half a hoop. Then she suddenly snapped forward. We caught a flash of the whites of her eyes. Presently her whole body began to be convulsed—great throes that began at the shoulders and ended at the hips. She would leap to her feet, thrust her arms in air, and then hurl herself upon the heap. Her praying flattened out into a mere delirious caterwauling, like that of a tomcat on a petting party. I describe the thing discreetly, and as a strict behaviorist. The lady's subjective sensations I leave to infidel pathologists, privy to the works of Ellis, Freud, and Moll. Whatever they were, they were obviously not painful, for they were accompanied by vast heavings and gurglings of a joyful and even ecstatic nature. And they seemed to be contagious, too, for soon a second penitent, also female, joined the first, and then came a third, and a fourth, and a fifth. The last one had an extraordinary violent attack. She began with mild enough jerks of the head, but in a moment she was bounding all over the place, like a chicken with its head cut off. Every time her head came up, a stream of hosannas would issue out of it. Once she collided with a dark, undersized

brother, hitherto silent and stolid. Contact with her set him off
as if he had been kicked by a mule. He leaped into the air,
threw back his head, and began to gargle as if with a mouthful
of BB shot. Then he loosed one tremendous, stentorian sentence
in the tongues, and collapsed.

By this time the performers were quite oblivious of the pro-
fane universe and so it was safe to go still closer. We left our
hiding and came up to the little circle of light. We slipped into
the vacant seats on one of the rickety benches. The heap of
mourners was directly before us. They bounced into us as they
cavorted. The smell that they radiated, sweating there in that
obscene heap, half suffocated us. Not all of them, of course, did
the thing in the grand manner. Some merely moaned and rolled
their eyes. The female ox in gingham flung her great bulk on
the ground and jabbered an unintelligible prayer. One of the
men, in the intervals between fits, put on his spectacles and read
his Bible. Beside me on the bench sat the young mother and her
baby. She suckled it through the whole orgy, obviously fascinated by what was going on, but never venturing to take any
hand in it. On the bed just outside the light half a dozen other
babies slept peacefully. In the shadows, suddenly appearing and
as suddenly going away, were vague figures, whether of believ-
ers or of scoffers I do not know. They seemed to come and go in
couples. Now and then a couple at the ringside would step out
and vanish into the black night. After a while some came back,
the males looking somewhat sheepish. There was whispering
outside the circle of vision. A couple of Fords lurched up the
road, cutting holes in the darkness with their lights. Once someone out of sight loosed a bray of laughter.

All this went on for an hour or so. The original penitent, by
this time, was buried three deep beneath the heap. One caught
a glimpse, now and then, of her yellow bobbed hair, but then
she would vanish again. How she breathed down there I don't
know; it was hard enough six feet away, with a strong five-cent
cigar to help. When the praying brothers would rise up for a
bout with the tongues, their faces were streaming with perspiration. The fat harridan in gingham sweated like a longshoreman.
Her hair got loose and fell down over her face. She fanned her-

self with her skirt. A powerful old gal she was, plainly equal in
her day to a bout with obstetrics and a week's washing on the
same morning, but this was worse than a week's washing.
Finally she fell into a heap, breathing in great, convulsive gasps.

Finally we got tired of the show and returned to Dayton. It
was nearly eleven o'clock—an immensely late hour for those lati-
tudes—but the whole town was still gathered in the courthouse
yard, listening to the disputes of theologians. The Scopes trial
had brought them in from all directions. There was a friar
wearing a sandwich sign announcing that he was the Bible
champion of the world. There was a Seventh Day Adventist
arguing that Clarence Darrow was the beast with seven heads
and ten horns described in Revelation xiii, and that the end of
the world was at hand. There was an evangelist made up like
Andy Gump, with the news that atheists in Cincinnati were
preparing to descend upon Dayton, hang the eminent Judge
Raulston, and burn the town. There was an ancient who maintained that no Catholic could be a Christian. There was the eloquent Dr. T. T. Martin, of Blue Mountain, Miss., come to town
with a truck-load of torches and hymn-books to put Darwin in
his place. There was a singing brother bellowing apocalyptic
hymns. There was William Jennings Bryan, followed everywhere by a gaping crowd. Dayton was having a roaring time. It
was better than the circus. But the note of devotion was simply
not there; the Daytonians, after listening awhile, would slip
away to Robinson's drug-store to regale themselves with coca-
cola, or to the lobby of the Aqua Hotel, where the learned
Raulston sat in state, judicially picking his teeth. The real religion was not present. It began at the bridge over the town
creek, where the road makes off for the hills.

Sinclair Lewis

In the Bible Belt, Sinclair Lewis' *Elmer Gantry* aroused a
storm of indignation when it was published in 1927. Today,

however, the story of the regular fellow corrupted while in the
Baptist ministry seems less a condemnation of Middle Western
religion than a caricature of a Babbitt gone haywire. Although
the novel suffers from the author's ambiguous attitude toward
his subject matter, Lewis' criticism is unequivocal in his be-
hind-the-scenes descriptions of ministers and evangelists in
action. In the following passage, Elmer, who has joined forces
with the famous evangelist Sharon Falconer, has an opportunity
to observe the fund-raising techniques of that priestly lady.

SHARON FALCONER'S "THANK OFFERING"
(from *Elmer Gantry*)

When she attacked the larger towns and asked for the support of the richer churches, Sharon had to create several
new methods in the trade of evangelism. The churches were suspicious of women evangelists—women might do very well in visiting the sick, knitting for the heathen, and giving strawberry
festivals, but they couldn't shout loud enough to scare the devil
out of sinners. Indeed all evangelists, men and women, were under attack. Sound churchmen here and there were asking
whether there was any peculiar spiritual value in frightening
people into groveling maniacs. They were publishing statistics
which asserted that not ten per cent of the converts at emotional
revival meetings remained church-members. They were even so
commercial as to inquire why a pastor with a salary of two thousand dollars a year—when he got it—should agonize over helping an evangelist to make ten thousand, forty thousand.

All these doubters had to be answered. Elmer persuaded
Sharon to discharge her former advance-agent—he had been a
minister and contributor to the religious press, till the unfortunate affair of the oil stock—and hire a real press-agent, trained
in newspaper work, circus advertising, and real-estate promot-
ing. It was Elmer and the press-agent who worked up the new
technique of risky but impressive defiance.

Where the former advance-man had begged the ministers

and wealthy laymen of a town to which Sharon wanted to be invited to appreciate her spirituality, and had sat nervously about hotels, the new salesman of salvation was brusque:

"I can't waste my time and the Lord's time waiting for you people to make up your minds. Sister Falconer is especially interested in this city because she has been informed that there is a subterranean quickening here such as would simply jam your churches, with a grand new outpouring of the spirit, provided some real expert like her came to set the fuse alight. But there are so many other towns begging for her services that if you can't make up your minds immediately, we'll have to accept their appeals and pass you up. Sorry. Can only wait till midnight. Tonight. Reserved my Pullman already."

There were ever so many ecclesiastical bodies who answered that they didn't see why he waited even till midnight, but if they were thus intimidated into signing the contract (an excellent contract, drawn up by a devout Christian Scientist lawyer named Finkelstein) they were the more prepared to give spiritual and financial support to Sharon's labors when she did arrive.

The new press-agent was finally so impressed by the beauties of evangelism, as contrasted with his former circuses and real estate, that he was himself converted, and sometimes when he was in town with the troupe, he sang in the choir and spoke to Y.M.C.A. classes in journalism. But even Elmer's arguments could never get him to give up a sturdy, plodding devotion to poker.

The contract signed, the advance-man remembered his former newspaper labors, and for a few days became touchingly friendly with all the reporters in town. There were late parties at his hotel; there was much sending of bell-boys for more bottles of Wilson and White Horse and Green River. The press-agent admitted that he really did think that Miss Falconer was the greatest woman since Sarah Bernhardt, and he let the boys have stories, guaranteed held exclusive, of her beauty, the glories of her family, her miraculous power of fetching sinners or rain by prayer, and the rather vaguely dated time when, as a young

girl, she had been recognized by Dwight Moody as his succes-
sor.

South of the Mason and Dixon line her grandfather was
merely Mr. Falconer, a bellicose and pious man, but far enough
north he was General Falconer of Ole Virginny—preferably
spelled that way—who had been the adviser and solace of General Robert E. Lee. The press-agent also wrote the posters for
the Ministerial Alliance, giving Satan a generous warning as to
what was to happen to him.

So when Sharon and the troupe arrived, the newspapers were
eager, the walls and shop-windows were scarlet with placards,
and the town was breathless. Sometimes a thousand people gathered at the station for her arrival.

There were always a few infidels, particularly among the reporters, who had doubted her talents, but when they saw her in
the train vestibule, in a long white coat, when she had stood
there a second with her eyes closed, lost in prayer for this new
community, when slowly she held out her white nervous hands
in greeting—then the advance-agent's work was two-thirds done
here and he could go on to whiten new fields for the harvest.

But there was still plenty of discussion before Sharon was rid
of the forces of selfishness and able to get down to the job of
spreading light.

Local committees were always stubborn, local committees
were always jealous, local committees were always lazy, and
local committees were always told these facts, with vigor. The
heart of the arguments was money.

Sharon was one of the first evangelists to depend for all her
profit not on a share of the contributions nor on a weekly offering
but on one night devoted entirely to a voluntary "thank offering" for her and her crew alone. It sounded unselfish and it
brought in more; every devotee saved up for that occasion; and it
proved easier to get one fifty-dollar donation than a dozen of a
dollar each. But to work up this lone offering to suitably thankful proportions, a great deal of loving and efficient preparation
was needed—reminders given by the chief pastors, bankers, and
other holy persons of the town, the distribution of envelopes
over which devotees were supposed to brood for the whole six

weeks of the meetings, and innumerable newspaper paragraphs about the self-sacrifice and heavy expenses of the evangelists.

It was over these innocent necessary precautions that the local committees always showed their meanness. They liked giving over only one contribution to the evangelist, but they wanted nothing said about it till they themselves had been taken care of—till the rent of the hall or the cost of building a tabernacle, the heat, the lights, the advertising, and other expenses had been paid.

Sharon would meet the committee—a score of clergymen, a score of their most respectable deacons, a few angular Sunday School superintendents, a few disapproving wives—in a church parlor, and for the occasion she always wore the gray suit and an air of metropolitan firmness, and swung a pair of pince-nez with lenses made of windowglass. While in familiar words the local chairman was explaining to her that their expenses were heavy, she would smile as though she knew something they could not guess, then let fly at them breathlessly:

"I'm afraid there is some error here! I wonder if you are quite in the mood to forget all material things and really throw your-selves into the self-abnegating glory of a hot campaign for souls? I know all you have to say—as a matter of fact, you've forgotten to mention your expenses for watchmen, extra hymn books, and hiring camp-chairs!

"But you haven't the experience to appreciate *my* expenses! I have to maintain almost as great a staff—not only workers and musicians but all my other representatives, whom you never see —as though I had a factory. Besides them, I have my charities. There is, for example, the Old Ladies' Home, which I keep up entirely—oh, I shan't say anything about it, but if you could see those poor aged women turning to me with such anxious faces—!"

(Where that Old Ladies' Home was, Elmer never learned.)

"We come here without any guarantee; we depend wholly upon the free-will offering of the last day; and I'm afraid you're going to stress the local expenses so that people will not feel like giving on the last day even enough to pay the salaries of my assistants. I'm taking—if it were not that I abominate the pitiful

and character-destroying vice of gambling, I'd say that I'm taking such a terrible gamble that it frightens me! But there it is,
and—"

While she was talking, Sharon was sizing up this new as-
sortment of clergy: the cranks, the testy male old maids, the advertising and pushing demagogues, the commonplace pulpit-
job-holders, the straddling young liberals; the real mystics, the
kindly fathers of their flocks, the lovers of righteousness. She
had picked out as her advocate the most sympathetic, and she
launched her peroration straight at him:

"Do you want to ruin me, so that never again shall I be able
to carry the message, to carry salvation, to the desperate souls
who are everywhere waiting for me, crying for my help? Is that
your purpose—you, the elect, the people chosen to help me in
the service of the dear Lord Jesus himself? Is that your purpose?
Is it? Is it?"

She began sobbing, which was Elmer's cue to jump up and
have a wonderful new idea.

He knew, did Elmer, that the dear brethren and sisters had
no such purpose. They just wanted to be practical. Well, why
wouldn't it be a good notion for the committee to go to the
well-to-do church members and explain the unparalleled situation; tell them that this was the Lord's work, and that aside
from the unquestioned spiritual benefits, the revival would do
so much good that crime would cease, and taxes thus be less-
ened; that workmen would turn from agitation to higher
things, and work more loyally at the same wages. If they got
enough pledges from the rich for current expenses, those expenses would not have to be stressed at the meetings, and people could properly be coaxed to save up for the final "thank offering"; not have to be nagged to give more than small coins at
the nightly collections.

There were other annoyances to discuss with the local committee. Why, Elmer would demand, hadn't they provided
enough dressing-rooms in the tabernacle? Sister Falconer needed
privacy. Sometimes just before the meeting she and he had to
have important conferences. Why hadn't they provided more
volunteer ushers? He must have them at once, to train them, for

it was the ushers, when properly coached, who would ease struggling souls up to the altar for the skilled finishing touches by the experts.

Had they planned to invite big delegations from the local institutions—from Smith Brothers' Catsup Factory, from the carshops, from the packing house? Oh, yes, they must plan to stir up these institutions; an evening would be dedicated to each of them, the representatives would be seated together, and they'd have such a happy time singing their favorite hymns.

By this time, a little dazed, the local committee were granting everything; and they looked almost convinced when Sharon wound up with a glad ringing:

"All of you must look forward, and joyfully, to a sacrifice of time and money in these meetings. We have come here at a great sacrifice, and we are here only to help you."

Mark Harris

Apropos of practically nothing else in Mark Harris' amusing epistolary novel, *Wake Up, Stupid*, is this mock tract in praise of female modesty.

ARE WE DRAGGING MEN TO HELL BY OUR MODERN DRESS?
(from *Wake Up, Stupid*)

CRIMES OF PASSION   DISHONORED LIVES   IMMORALITY

A good lady said, "These knee length dresses are not modest. The Holy Spirit showed me that at least half of the calf of the leg should be covered. Some feel all the calf of the leg should be covered."

Low necks, short dresses scarcely to the knees, bare arms, painted faces—in a word—everything to arouse passion and

lust is the order of the day. "Everybody does it!" I know—but
do you belong to the "everybodies" or are you a pilgrim?

In a neighboring town lives a boy who was graduated from
the State University with the highest honors. Later he had a
fine position but acquired a venereal disease, went insane, and is
now in the insane asylum part of the time. I went to Bible
school, and one day the teacher had a special meeting of the girls
and told them if they would let the Lord talk to them, they would
lengthen their dresses. When the school had a social gathering,
one boy left the party when the girls were playing games, etc.
He could see too much, he said.

(ED. NOTE. Rolled stockings and similar styles have a direct
bearing on crime incitation.)

When women come here with knee length dresses and stoop
to pick up apples, I think the men can see more than the Lord
intended them to see. I would rather wear my dresses a longer
length and please the Lord than try to please a hard-to-please
fickle world. We surely will never send men to Hell by wearing
longer dresses.

John Wesley said gay and costly apparel tends to influence
lust. During the first hundred years of her ministry, Methodism
was the greatest power for righteousness of any movement
since Pentecost. In those days of her glory, Methodism always
insisted on plainness of attire.

What does Charles Finney (one of the greatest God-used
evangelists of all time) say? "I will confess that I was formerly
myself in error. I believed that the best way for Christians to
pursue was to dress so as not to be noticed, to follow the fashions
so as not to be noticed, to follow the fashions so as not to appear singular. But I have seen my error and now wonder greatly
at my former blindness."

I am trusting the Lord to keep my three sons pure. Can the
Lord protect young people? I know He can, because He has kept
me moral. I couldn't commit adultery if you would give me the
whole world; neither can I get mixed up in an affair with some
other woman's husband.

(ED. NOTE. Adultery is common these days.)

If He can keep me moral, He can keep your son and daughter moral. The power of the Devil is great, but praise God, the Lord has more power. I don't want Jesus to say to me some day, "By the exposure of your flesh you have dragged men to Hell." Do you?

—Mrs. Dewitt Smith

(PILGRIM TRACT SOCIETY, Randleman, N. C. Supported by voluntary gifts of its readers. Tracts free as the Lord supplies the funds. Send postage for 100 samples of tracts.)

WAR AND
SERVICE LIFE

"We seldom learn moderation under any political excitement, until forty thousand square miles of territory are blown from beneath our feet."

JAMES FENIMORE COOPER, *The Monikins*

"With the fearful strain of war upon me, if I did not laugh I should die."

ABRAHAM LINCOLN

War and Service Life

S atire is a persistent camp follower. In one way or another, it
thrives on war.

In general, three main kinds of martial satire can be distinguished: that which attacks war itself, that which attacks the
enemy, and that which, whether playfully or bitterly, attacks
the military profession.

American satire has tended to be of the third sort. Only during the Revolutionary War has art been used strategically
against an enemy, and it is certain that satires, both in prose
and doggerel, including "Yankee Doodle," helped substantially
in preparing the way to victory. During the nineteenth century
satirists made bitter fun of wars—Lowell, the Mexican War;
Nasby and Kerr, the Civil War; Dunne, the Spanish-American
War—using comedy to make their antiwar messages acceptable.

Most satire of World War I and II stresses the funny absurdity of a free American male being drafted into military service and placed under the threat (usually shown as remote) of
being killed. (Mr. Roberts does get killed, but it is in a war that
is far from the scene of the story.) The satire is primarily
against authority, not war; its typical hero is the out-of-step
citizen-soldier.

Benjamin Franklin

The satirical voice was natural to Franklin. As an apprentice to his brother James in the shop of the *New-England Courant* in Boston, he studied Addison's style and first tried his own hand in the Silence Dogood Letters, which he contributed anonymously to the *Courant* by slipping them under the door of the printing shop. (Selections from the *Dogood Papers* appear on pages 234 and 257.)

But in Franklin's later satires against the policies of the English regarding their American colonies, a new strain of irony is present which suggests the manner of Swift. Like all Americans and most Europeans as well, Franklin was shocked when George III, pressed for manpower, shopped around for professional soldiers to fight Englishmen in the Colonies, and finally contracted with several German princes to supply them. Under the terms of the agreements, the suppliers were indemnified in cash for each mercenary who perished.

The following letter, purporting to be from one of these German princes, watering in Rome, to the commander of the Hessian troops in America, was first written in French while Franklin was living in Passy and soliciting France's assistance in the American cause. Circulated in pamphlet form throughout the capitals of Europe, it was an effective piece of anti-British propaganda.

THE SALE OF THE HESSIANS
(February 18, 1777)

Monsieur Le Baron:—On my return from Naples, I received at Rome your letter of the 27th December of last year. I have learned with unspeakable pleasure the courage our troops exhibited at Trenton, and you cannot imagine my joy on being told that of the 1,950 Hessians engaged in the fight, but 345 escaped. There were just 1,605 men killed, and I cannot sufficiently commend your prudence in sending an exact list of the dead to my minister in London. This precaution was the more necessary, as the report sent to the English ministry does not give but 1,455 dead. This would make 483,450 florins instead of 643,500 which I am entitled to demand under our convention. You will comprehend the prejudice which such an error would work in my finances, and I do not doubt you will take the necessary pains to prove that Lord North's list is false and yours correct.

The court of London objects that there were a hundred wounded who ought not to be included in the list, nor paid for as dead; but I trust you will not overlook my instructions to you on quitting Cassel, and that you will not have tried by human succor to recall the life of the unfortunates whose days could not be lengthened but by the loss of a leg or an arm. That would be making them a pernicious present, and I am sure they would rather die than live in a condition no longer fit for my service. I do not mean by this that you should assassinate them; we should be humane, my dear Baron, but you may insinuate to the surgeons with entire propriety that a crippled man is a reproach to their profession, and that there is no wiser course than to let every one of them die when he ceases to be fit to fight.

I am about to send to you some new recruits. Don't economize them. Remember glory before all things. Glory is true wealth. There is nothing degrades the soldier like the love of money. He must care only for honour and reputation, but this reputation must be acquired in the midst of dangers. A battle gained without costing the conqueror any blood is an inglorious success, while the conquered cover themselves with glory by perishing with their arms in their hands. Do you remember that of the 300 Lacedæmonians who defended the defile of Thermopylæ, not one returned? How happy should I be could I say the same of my brave Hessians!

It is true that their king, Leonidas, perished with them: but things have changed, and it is no longer the custom for princes of the empire to go and fight in America for a cause with which they have no concern. And besides, to whom should they pay the thirty guineas per man if I did not stay in Europe to receive them? Then, it is necessary also that I be ready to send recruits to replace the men you lose. For this purpose I must return to Hesse. It is true, grown men are becoming scarce there, but I will send you boys. Besides, the scarcer the commodity the higher the price. I am assured that the women and little girls have begun to till our lands, and they get on not badly. You did right to send back to Europe that Dr. Crumerus who was so successful in curing dysentery. Don't bother with a man who is subject to looseness of the bowels. That disease makes bad soldiers. One coward will do more mischief in an engagement than ten brave men will do good. Better that they burst in their barracks than fly in a battle, and tarnish the glory of our arms. Besides, you know that they pay me as killed for all who die from disease, and I don't get a farthing for runaways. My trip to Italy, which has cost me enormously, makes it desirable that there should be a great mortality among them. You will therefore promise promotion to all who expose themselves; you will exhort them to seek glory in the midst of dangers; you will say to Major Maundorff: that I am not at all content with his saving the 345 men who escaped the massacre of Trenton. Through the whole campaign he has not had ten men killed in consequence of his orders. Finally, let it be your principal object to prolong the war and avoid a decisive engagement on either side, for I have made arrangements for a grand Italian opera, and I do not wish to be obliged to give it up. Meantime I pray God, my dear Baron de Hohendorf, to have you in his holy and gracious keeping.

Francis Hopkinson

"This ballad was occasioned by a real incident. Certain machines, in the form of kegs, charg'd with gun powder, were sent down the river to annoy the British shipping then at Philadelphia. The danger of these machines being discovered, the British manned the wharfs and shipping, and discharged their

small arms and cannons at every thing they saw floating in the
river during the ebb tide." Author's note, from *Miscellaneous
Essays*.

THE BATTLE OF THE KEGS
(1792)

G allants attend and hear a friend,
　　 Trill forth harmonious ditty,
Strange things I'll tell which late befel
　　In Philadelphia city.

'Twas early day, as poets say,
　　Just when the sun was rising,
A soldier stood on a log of wood,
　　And saw a thing surprising.

As in amaze he stood to gaze,
　　The truth can't be denied, sir,
He spied a score of kegs or more
　　Come floating down the tide, sir.

A sailor too in jerkin blue,
　　This strange appearance viewing,
First damn'd his eyes, in great surprise,
　　Then said some mischief's brewing.

These kegs, I'm told, the rebels bold,
　　Pack'd up like pickling herring;
And they're come down t'attack the town,
　　In this new way of ferrying.

The soldier flew, the sailor too,
　　And scar'd almost to death, sir,
Wore out their shoes, to spread the news,
　　And ran till out of breath, sir.

Now up and down throughout the town,
    Most frantic scenes were acted;
And some ran here, and others there,
    Like men almost distracted.

Some fire cry'd, which some denied,
    But said the earth had quakèd;
And girls and boys, with hideous noise,
    Ran thro' the streets half naked.

Sir William he, snug as a flea,
    Lay all this time a snoring,
Nor dream'd of harm as he lay warm,
    In bed with Mrs. Loring.

Now in a fright, he starts upright,
    Awak'd by such a clatter;
He rubs both eyes, and boldly cries,
    For God's sake, what's the matter?

At his bed-side he then espy'd,
    Sir Erskine at command, sir,
Upon one foot, he had one boot,
    And th'other in his hand, sir.

"Arise, arise," Sir Erskine cries,
    "The rebels—more's the pity,
"Without a boat are all afloat,
    "And rang'd before the city.

"The motley crew, in vessels new,
    "With Satan for their guide, sir.
"Pack'd up in bags, or wooden kegs,
    "Come driving down the tide, sir.

"Therefore prepare for bloody war,
    "These kegs must all be routed,

"Or surely we despised shall be,
"And British courage doubted."

The royal band, now ready stand
   All rang'd in dread array, sir,
With stomach stout to see it out,
   And make a bloody day, sir.

The cannons roar from shore to shore,
   The small arms make a rattle;
Since wars began I'm sure no man
   E'er saw so strange a battle.

The rebel dales, the rebel vales,
   With rebel trees surrounded;
The distant wood, the hills and floods,
   With rebel echoes sounded.

The fish below swam to and fro,
   Attack'd from ev'ry quarter;
Why, sure, thought they, the devil's to pay,
   'Mongst folks above the water.

The kegs, 'tis said, tho' strongly made,
   Of rebel staves and hoops, sir,
Could not oppose their powerful foes,
   The conqu'ring British troops, sir.

From morn to night these men of might
   Display'd amazing courage;
And when the sun was fairly down,
   Retir'd to sup their porrage.

An hundred men with each a pen,
   Or more upon my word, sir,
It is most true would be too few,
   Their valour to record, sir.

Such feats did they perform that day,
    Against these wick'd kegs, sir,
That years to come, if they get home,
    They'll make their boasts and brags, sir.

Oliver Hillhouse Prince

With the single exception of "The Militia Company Drill," the humorous sketches of the Southern backwoods collected as *Georgia Scenes* were written by a lawyer named A. B. Longstreet. "The Militia Company Drill," however, was the work of a friend of Longstreet's from Connecticut, named Oliver Hillhouse Prince, who signed himself "Timothy Crabshaw."

A note by Longstreet indicates that the piece was written some twenty years earlier than the rest of *Georgia Scenes* (1835) and had been published before, presumably in a newspaper. It is an odd sidelight that, by a rather devious route, a version of this classic of the drill field found its way into Thomas Hardy's novel *The Trumpet-Major* (1880), where it appears as Chapter XXIII—which goes to prove that old soldiering stories never die, particularly when they are as amusing as "The Militia Company Drill."

THE MILITIA COMPANY DRILL
(About 1815)

I happened, not long since, to be present at the muster of a captain's company in a remote part of one of the counties; and as no general description could convey an accurate idea of the achievements of that day, I must be permitted to go a little into detail, as well as my recollection will serve me.

The men had been notified to meet at nine o'clock, "armed and equipped as the law directs"; that is to say, with a gun and cartridge box at least, but, as directed by the law of the United

States, "with a good firelock, a sufficient bayonet and belt, and a pouch with a box to contain no less than twenty-four sufficient cartridges of powder and ball."

At twelve, about one third, perhaps one half, of the men had collected, and an inspector's return of the number present, and of their arms, would have stood nearly thus: 1 captain, 1 lieutenant; ensign, none; fifers, none; privates, present, 24; ditto, absent, 40; guns, 14; gunlocks, 12; ramrods, 10; rifle pouches, 3; bayonets, none; belts, none; spare flints, none; cartridges, none; horsewhips, walking canes, and umbrellas, 10. A little before one, the captain, whom I shall distinguish by the name of Clodpole, gave directions for forming the line of parade. In obedience to this order, one of the sergeants, whose lungs had long supplied the place of a drum and fife, placed himself in front of the house, and began to bawl with great vehemence, "All Captain Clodpole's company parade here! Come, GENTLEMEN, parade here!" says he; "all you that hasn't got guns fall into the lower *eend*." He might have bawled till this time, with as little success as the sirens sung to Ulysses, had he not changed his post to a neighbouring shade. There he was immediately joined by all who were then at leisure; the others were at that time engaged as parties or spectators at a game of fives, and could not just then attend. However, in less than half an hour the game was finished, and the captain enabled to form his company, and proceed in the duties of the day.

"Look to the right and dress!"

They were soon, by the help of the non-commissioned officers, placed in a straight line; but, as every man was anxious to see how the rest stood, those on the wings pressed forward for that purpose, till the whole line assumed nearly the form of a crescent.

"Why, look at 'em," says the captain; "why, gentlemen, you are all a crooking in at both *eends*, so that you will get on to me by-and-by! Come, gentlemen, *dress, dress!*"

This was accordingly done; but, impelled by the same motives as before, they soon resumed their former figure, and so they were permitted to remain.

"Now, gentlemen," says the captain, "I am going to carry

you through the *revolutions* of the manual exercise; and I want you, gentlemen, if you please, to pay particular attention to the word of command, just exactly as I give it out to you. I hope you will have a little patience, gentlemen, if you please; and if I should be agoing wrong, I will be much obliged to any of you, gentlemen, to put me right again, for I mean all for the best, and I hope you will excuse me if you please. And one thing, gentlemen, I caution you against, in particular, and that is this: not to make any *mistakes* if you can possibly help it; and the best way to do this will be to do all the motions right at first; and that will help us to get along so much the faster; and I will try to have it over as soon as possible. Come, boys, come to a shoulder.

"*Poise, foolk!* ¹

"*Cock, foolk!* Very handsomely done.

"*Take, aim!*

"*Ram down, catridge!* No! no! *Fire!* I recollect now that firing comes next after taking aim, according to Steuben; but, with your permission, gentlemen, I'll *read* the words of command just exactly as they are printed in the book, and then I shall be sure to be right."

"Oh, yes! read it, captain, read it!" exclaimed twenty voices at once; "that will save time."

" 'Tention the whole! Please to observe, gentlemen, that at the word 'fire!' you must fire; that is, if any of your guns are *loaden'd*, you must not shoot in *yearnest*, but only make pretence like; and you, gentlemen fellow-soldiers, who's armed with nothing but sticks, riding-switches, and corn-stalks, needn't go through the firings, but stand as you are, and keep yourselves to yourselves.

"*Half cock, foolk!* Very well done.

"*S-h-e-t* (spelling) *Shet, pan!* That too would have been handsomely done, if you hadn't handled catridge instead of shetting pan; but I suppose you wasn't noticing. Now 'tention one and all, gentlemen, and do that motion again.

"*Shet, pan!* Very good, very well indeed; you did that motion equal to any old soldier; you improve astonishingly.

¹ Firelock.

"*Handle*, *catridge!* Pretty well, considering you done it wrong end foremost, as if you took the catridge out of your mouth, and bit off the twist with the catridge-box.

"*Draw, rammer!* Those who have no rammers to their guns need not draw, but only make the motion; it will do just as well, and save a great deal of time.

"*Return, rammer!* Very well again. But that would have been done, I think, with greater expertness if you had performed the motion with a little more dexterity.

"*S-h-o-u-l—Shoulder, foolk!* Very handsomely done indeed! Put your guns on the other shoulder, gentlemen.

"*Order, foolk!* Not quite so well, gentlemen; not quite altogether; but perhaps I did not speak loud enough for you to hear me all at once. Try once more, if you please. I hope you will be patient, gentlemen; we will soon be through.

"*Order, foolk!* Handsomely done, gentlemen! Very handsomely done! and all together too, except that one half of you were a *leetle* too soon, and the other half a *leetle* too late.

"In laying down your guns, gentlemen, take care to lay the locks up and the other side down.

" *'Tention the whole! Ground, foolk!* Very well.

"*Charge, bayonet!*"

(*Some of the men*)—"That can't be, captain: pray look again; for how can we charge bayonet without our guns?"

(*Captain*)—"I don't know as to that, but I know I'm right, for here 'tis printed in the book; c-h-a-r—yes, *charge, bayonet*, that's right, that's the word, if I know how to read. Come, gentlemen, do pray charge bayonet! Charge, I say! Why don't you charge! Do you think it aint so? Do you think I have lived to this time o' day, and don't know what charge bayonet is? Here, come here, you may see for yourselves; it's as plain as the nose on your fa—stop—stay—no—halt! no! Faith, I'm wrong! I turned over two leaves at once. I beg your pardon, we will not stay out long; and we'll have something to drink as soon as we have done. Come, boys, get off the stumps and logs, and take up your guns; we'll soon be done: excuse me if you please.

"*Fix, bayonet!*

"*Advance, arms!* Very well done: turn the stocks of your guns in front, gentlemen, and that will bring the barrels behind; hold them straight up and down, if you please; let go with your left, and take hold with your right hand below the guard. Steuben says the gun should be held p-e-r—*pertic'lar;* yes, you must always mind and hold your guns very pertic'lar. Now, boys, 'tention the whole!

"*Present, arms!* Very handsomely done! only hold your gun over t'other knee—t'other hand up—turn your hands round a little, and raise them up higher—draw t'other foot back—now you are nearly right—very well done.

"Gentlemen, we come now to the *revolutions*. Men, you have all got into a sort of snarl, as I may say; how did you all get into such a higglety pigglety?"

The fact was, the shade had moved considerably to the eastward, and had exposed the right wing of these hardy veterans to a galling fire of the sun. Being poorly provided with umbrellas at this end of the line, they found it convenient to follow the shade; and in huddling to the left for this purpose, they changed the figure of their line from that of a crescent to one which more nearly resembled a pair of pothooks.

"Come, gentlemen," says the captain, "spread yourselves out again into a straight line; and let us get into the wheelings and other matters as soon as possible."

But this was strenuously opposed by the soldiers. They objected to going into the *revolutions* at all, inasmuch as the weather was extremely hot, and they had already been kept in the field upward of three quarters of an hour. They reminded the captain of his repeated promise to be as short as he possibly could, and it was clear he could dispense with all this wheeling and flourishing if he chose. They were already very thirsty, and if he would not dismiss them, they declared they would go off without dismission, and get something to drink, and he might fine them if that would do him any good; they were able to pay their fine, but would not go without drink to please anybody; and they swore they would never vote for another captain who wished to be so unreasonably strict.

The captain behaved with great spirit upon the occasion, and a smart colloquy ensued; when at length becoming exasperated to the last degree, he roundly asserted that no soldier ought ever to *think hard* of the orders of his officer; and, finally, he went so far as to say, that he did not think any gentleman on that ground had any just cause to be offended with him. The dispute was finally settled by the captain sending for some grog for their present accommodation, and agreeing to omit reading the military law, and the performance of all the manœuvres, except two or three such easy and simple ones as could be performed within the compass of the shade. After they had drank their grog and had spread "themselves," they were divided into platoons.

" *'Tention the whole! To the right wheel!*"

Each man faced to the right about.

"Why, gentlemen, I did not mean for every man to stand still and turn himself *na'*trally right round; but when I told you to wheel to the right, I intended you to wheel round to the right, as it were. Please to try again, gentlemen; every right-hand man must stand fast, and only the others turn round."

In the previous part of the exercise, it had, for the purpose of sizing, been necessary to denominate every second person a "right-hand man." A very natural consequence was, that, on the present occasion, these right-hand men maintained their position, all the intermediate ones facing about as before.

"Why, look at 'em, now!" exclaimed the captain, in extreme vexation; "I'll be d—d if you understand a word I say. Excuse me, gentlemen, it *rayly* seems as if you could not come at it exactly. In wheeling to the right, the right-hand *eend* of the platoon stands fast, and the other *eend* comes round like a swingletree. Those on the outside must march faster than those on the inside. You certainly must understand me now, gentlemen; and please to try it once more."

In this they were a little more successful.

" *'Tention the whole! To the left—left, no—right—that is, the left—I mean the right—left, wheel, march!*"

In this he was strictly obeyed; some wheeling to the right, some to the left, and some to the right-left, or both ways.

"*Stop! Halt!* Let us try it again! I could not just then tell my right hand from my left! You must excuse me, if you please; experience makes perfect, as the saying is. Long as I have served, I find something new to learn every day; but all's one for that. Now, gentlemen, do that motion once more."

By the help of a non-commissioned officer in front of each platoon, they wheeled this time with considerable regularity.

"Now, boys, you must try to wheel by divisions; and there is one thing in particular which I have to request of you, gentlemen, and that is, not to make any blunder in your wheeling. You must mind and keep at a wheeling distance, and not talk in the ranks, nor get out of fix again; for I want you to do this motion well, and not to make any blunder now.

" *'Tention the whole! By divisions, to the right wheel, march!*"

In doing this it seemed as if Bedlam had broke loose: every man took the command. Not so fast on the right! Slow now! Haul down those umbrellas! Faster on the left! Keep back a little there! Don't *scrouge* so! Hold up your gun, Sam! Go faster there! faster! Who trod on my—? D—n your huffs! Keep back! Stop us, captain, do stop us! Go faster there! I've lost my shoe! Get up again, Ned! Halt! halt! halt! Stop, gentlemen! stop! stop!

By this time they had got into utter and inextricable confusion, and so I left them.

TIMOTHY CRABSHAW

Artemus Ward
(Charles Farrar Browne)

A ROMANCE—WILLIAM BARKER, THE YOUNG PATRIOT

I

No, William Barker, you cannot have my daughter's hand in marriage until you are her equal in wealth and social position."

The speaker was a haughty old man of some sixty years, and the person whom he addressed was a fine-looking young man of twenty-five.

With a sad aspect the young man withdrew from the stately mansion.

II

Six months later the young man stood in the presence of the haughty old man.

"What! *you* here again?" angrily cried the old man.

"Ay, old man," proudly exclaimed William Barker. "I am here, your daughter's equal and yours."

The old man's lips curled with scorn. A derisive smile lit up his cold features; when, casting violently upon the marble center table an enormous roll of greenbacks, William Barker cried—

"See! Look on this wealth. And I've tenfold more! Listen, old man! You spurned me from your door. But I did not despair. I secured a contract for furnishing the Army of the ———— with beef—"

"Yes, yes!" eagerly exclaimed the old man.

"—and I bought up all the disabled cavalry horses I could find—"

"I see! I see!" cried the old man. "And good beef they make, too."

"They do! they do! and the profits are immense."

"I should say so!"

"And now, sir, I claim your daughter's fair hand!"

"Boy, she is yours. But hold! Look me in the eye. Throughout all this have you been loyal?"

"To the core!" cried William Barker.

"And," continued the old man, in a voice husky with emotion, "are you in favor of a vigorous prosecution of the war?"

"I am, I am!"

"Then, boy, take her! Maria, child, come hither. Your William claims thee. Be happy, my children! and whatever our lot in life may be, *let us all support the Government!*"

Petroleum V. Nasby
(David Ross Locke)

During the Civil War period and for a few years afterward, David Ross Locke, as "Petroleum V. Nasby," was the most successful satirical humorist in America. So delighted was Abraham Lincoln by Locke's creation of the shiftless, hard-drinking, office-seeking, Negro-hating Copperhead that he told a Congressional delegation that if the humorist would come to Washington and communicate his talent to him he would "swap places with him." On another occasion the President remarked, "Nasby is worth a full division of infantry to the Union cause."

Everyone—at least everyone of Northern persuasion—read Nasby and laughed at his damning caricature of the pro-Southern, pro-slavery Ohioan, whose aims in life were plenty of whiskey, easy money, and a postmastership with no work attached. Whenever the illiterate and vulgar Nasby defended the Southern cause, or preached the inferiority of the Negro, his arguments appeared ridiculous; all that he denounced—Lincoln, the Union, the Negro—was elevated and ennobled.

Born in Broome County, New York, in 1833, Locke began as an itinerant printer but soon turned to newspapering. After a seven-year apprenticeship, he operated several small sheets in various Ohio towns, and it was in the Findlay, Ohio, *Jeffersonian* that the first Nasby letter appeared, on March 21, 1861. Later letters were reprinted in the Toledo *Blade*, of which Locke became editor in 1865, and soon they were offprinted and bound in book form, to be sold around the country.

The illiterate spelling fad of the period has proved a millstone to the Nasby letters. The fad died out and left Locke's best work with a quaint and hopelessly dated surface appearance. But many of the letters are well worth the small trouble of translating "uv" into "of," for David Ross Locke was one of the funniest men of his time as well as one most dedicated to his beliefs—a combination of qualities which made him a superlative satirist.

Of his posthumous reputation Locke said, "Wat posterity will say, I don't know; neither do I care, . . . It's this generashen I'm going for."

NASBY SHOWS WHY HE SHOULD NOT BE DRAFTED
(August 6, 1862)

I see in the papers last nite that the Government hez institooted a draft, and that in a few weeks sum hundreds uv thousands uv peeceable citizens will be dragged to the tented field.[1] I know not wat uthers may do, but ez for me, I cant go. Upon a rigid eggsaminashun uv my fizzleckle man, I find it wood be wus nor madnis for me to undertake a campane, to-wit: —

1. I'm bald-headid, and hev bin obliged to wear a wig these 22 years.

2. I hev dandruff in wat scanty hair still hangs around my venerable temples.

3. I hev a kronic katarr.

4. I hev lost, sence Stanton's order to draft, the use uv wun eye entirely, and hev kronic inflammashen in the other.

5. My teeth is all unsound, my palit aint eggsactly rite, and I hev hed bronkeetis 31 yeres last Joon. At present I hev a koff, the paroxisms uv wich is friteful to behold.

6. I'm holler-chestid, am short-winded, and hev alluz hed pains in my back and side.

7. I am afflictid with kronic diarrear and kostivniss. The money I hev paid (or promist to pay), for Jayneses karminnytiv balsam and pills wood astonish almost enny body.

8. I am rupchered in nine places, and am entirely enveloped with trusses.

---

[1] One of the most surprising results of the conscription was the amount of disease disclosed among men between "eighteen and forty-five," in districts where quotas could not be raised by volunteering.—Locke's note.

9. I hev verrykose vanes, hev a white-swellin on wun leg and a fever sore on the uther; also wun leg is shorter than tother, though I handle it so expert that nobody never noticed it.

10. I hev korns and bunyons on both feet, wich wood prevent me from marchin.

I don't suppose that my political opinions, wich are aginst the prossekooshn uv this unconstooshnel war, wood hev any wate, with a draftin orfiser; but the above reesons why I cant go, will, I make no doubt, be suffishent.

NASBY WRITES HIS FLOCK FROM A UNION JAIL
(June 20, 1863)

In a Linkin Basteel,
Columbus, Ohio,

Agen I am in durence vile. Agen I am in the hands uv Linkin's hirelin minyuns, and my church is without a paster. The sheperd is smitten and the sheep may be scattered. Were it not for two barels uv whisky that we hed in the church, I doubt wether the organnizashen wood continue. My prayer is that the cohesive flooid may hold out till I return. My capcher wuz ez follows:

Wen the Diemekrats, the peece men of Homes County, declared war, I threw off the sacredotle robes and tuk up the sword. Arrivin in at Millersberg, I jined the peace forces to onst. Ability is allus recognized, and I wus immejitly made commander-in-cheef uv the forces. A full uniform uv butiful butternut cloth and a copper-heded sword wuz presented me. I immejitly commenst drillin the men, and in two days hed them perfishent in company and battalyun drill.

We fortyfide, buildin gabeyuns, faseens, and eliptiks, and neglectid no precaushen to make victry sure. Fifteen hundred strong, we pledged ourselves to hist the black flag, and never surrender.

Finally the enemy hove in site. Ez they cum up, our men trembled with anxiety to meet em. Sum two hunderd askt permishen to withdraw from the fortyfications, make a detour over the hill, and flank em wich request, bein unwillin to restrane their arder, I ackseded to. Sum 500 jined em, and I spoze are detoorin yet, ez I hev never seem em since. This movement wuz fatle, ez all went who were sober enuff to walk. Jest afterwards cum the catastrophy. Ten uv the very men who hed bin formost in advisin resistence, cum up with the Fedrals, and advised a surrender! Hopin to gain time, I askt two hours to consider. Unfortnit errer! Before the two hours wuz up, half the men wuz sober, and, instid uv histin the black flag, they capitoolatid, deliverin up the ringleeders. I wuz taken ez a hed ringleeder, and wuz ironed and taken to Columbus, wher I now am.

In hopes uv kepin my flock together, I writ em a epistle, as follows:

To the Faithful at Wingert's Corners, Greetin:

I rite yoo in bonds. I beseech yoo, deerly beloved, to be stedfast in yoor faith, holdin on to sich truth ez I left you. Be viggelent in good works, patient in chasin enrollin offisers, and quick in tarrin and featherin on em. For, tho I am not with you, the tar-barl and what's left uv the feathers is in my study, jest behint the whisky barls. Be temprit. Ten or twenty nips per day is enuff fer any man in health; if weakly, the number may be indefinitly increest. I am alluz in bad health. Beware uv false teechers; let no Ablishnists pizen your minds. Keep up yure Sundy exercises; ef yoo hev wun among yoo that kin rede, let him next Sundy eddify yoo with Wood's speech. Neglect not the Sundy skool. That proper interest may be kept up in the minds uv the children, I wood sejest that Sundy afternoons you ketch a preacher and hev the darlins rotten-egg him. "Jest ez the twig is bent," et settry. Be ennergetik in tearin down meetin-houses, for they are injoorin us. In conclooshen, deerly beloved, remember me. Send me a eucher deck, a two-gallon jug uv corn joose; also, the weekly collekshun. Ef I survive, I will be with you again. In the faith.

Ef they send wat I want, I shal be comfortable here.

In chains, but unsubdood,

Petroleum V. Nasby

Orpheus C. Kerr
(Robert Henry Newell)

The comic pseudonym that Robert Henry Newell chose for himself was suggested by a notorious feature of Lincoln's first term as president—the swarming in Washington of the political office-seeker.

As "Orpheus C. Kerr," Newell became the outstanding satiric commentator on the military conduct of the Civil War. In the company of his "frescoed dog, Bologna," and his "gothic steed, Pegasus," Kerr writes letters to his nephew about a "war of flying turnips" seen through the bottom of a bottle. While General George B. McClellan painstakingly reorganizes the Army of the Potomac after its defeat at Bull Run, Kerr reports on the "circumspect" troops, who are "brave but not rash"; on troop commanders who forget to bring ammunition into battle and who receive news of their engagements in the newspapers; on the "patriotic women of America" winding bandages; on Lincoln "in his anecdotage," spinning interminable stories in response to urgent requests for action; and on the marvelously elaborate, if abortive, schemes of the Union "Mackerel Brigade" for the annihilation of the Southern Confederacy. As a burlesque of the Civil War, with an undercurrent of intensely antiwar satire, *The Orpheus C. Kerr Papers* contain some of the funniest and most incisive pages in the entire field of Civil War humor.

A professional journalist, Robert Henry Newell contributed to a number of papers, particularly to the New York *Sunday Mercury*. He was a poet and the author of several books, including an anti-Darwin satire called *There Was Once a Man* (1884).

THE LATEST IMPROVEMENTS IN ARTILLERY

Washington, D. C., August —, 1861.

By invitation of a well-known official, I visited the Navy-Yard yesterday, and witnessed the trial of some newly-invented rifled cannon. The trial was of short duration, and the jury brought in a verdict of "innocent of any intent to kill."

The first gun tried was similar to those used in the Revolution, except that it had a larger touch-hole, and the carriage was painted green, instead of blue. This novel and ingenious weapon was pointed at a target about sixty yards distant. It didn't hit it, and as nobody saw any ball, there was much perplexity expressed. A midshipman did say that he thought the ball must have run out of the touch-hole when they loaded up—for which he was instantly expelled from the service. After a long search without finding the ball, there was some thought of summoning the Naval Retiring Board to decide on the matter, when somebody happened to look into the mouth of the cannon, and discovered that the ball hadn't gone out at all. The inventor said this would happen sometimes, especially if you didn't put a brick over the touch-hole when you fired the gun. The Government was so pleased with this explanation, that it ordered forty of the guns on the spot, at two hundred thousand dollars apiece. The guns to be furnished as soon as the war is over.

The next weapon tried was Jink's double back-action revolving cannon for ferry-boats. It consists of a heavy bronze tube, revolving on a pivot, with both ends open, and a touch-hole in the middle. While one gunner puts a load in at one end, another puts in a load at the other end, and one touch-hole serves for both. Upon applying the match, the gun is whirled swiftly round on a pivot, and both balls fly out in circles, causing great slaughter on both sides. This terrible engine was aimed at the target with great accuracy; but as the gunner has a large family dependent on him for support, he refused to apply the match. The Government was satisfied without firing, and ordered six of the guns at a million dollars apiece. The guns to be furnished in time for our next war.

The last weapon subjected to trial was a mountain howitzer of a new pattern. The inventor explained that its great advantage was, that it required no powder. In battle it is placed on the top of a high mountain, and a ball slipped loosely into it. As the enemy passes the foot of the mountain, the gunner in charge tips over the howitzer, and the ball rolls down the side of the mountain into the midst of the doomed foe. The range of this terrible weapon depends greatly on the height of the mountain and the distance to its base. The Government ordered forty of these mountain howitzers at a hundred thousand dollars apiece, to be planted on the first mountains discovered in the enemy's country.

These are great times for gunsmiths, my boy; and if you find any old cannon around the junk-shops, just send them along.

There is much sensation in nautical circles arising from the immoral conduct of the rebel privateers; but public feeling has been somewhat easier since the invention of a craft for capturing the pirates, by an ingenious Connecticut chap. Yesterday he exhibited a small model of it at a cabinet meeting, and explained it thus:

"You will perceive," says he to the President, "that the machine itself will only be four times the size of the Great Eastern, and need not cost over a few millions of dollars. I have only got to discover one thing before I can make it perfect. You will observe that it has a steam-engine on board. This engine works a pair of immense iron clamps, which are let down into the water from the extreme end of a very lengthy horizontal spar. Upon approaching the pirate, the captain orders the engineer to put on steam. Instantly the clamps descend from the end of the spar and clutch the privateer athwartships. Then the engine is reversed, the privateer is lifted bodily out of the water, the spar swings around over the deck, and the pirate ship is let down into the hold by the run. Then shut your hatches, and you have ship and pirates safe and sound."

The President's gothic features lighted up beautifully at the words of the great inventor; but in a moment they assumed an expression of doubt, and says he:

"But how are you going to manage, if the privateer fires upon you while you are doing this?"

"My dear sir," says the inventor, "I told you I had only one thing to discover before I could make the machine perfect, and that's it."

So you see, my boy, there's a prospect of our doing something on the ocean next century, and there's only one thing in the way of our taking in pirates by the cargo.

Last evening a new brigadier-general, aged ninety-four years, made a speech to Regiment Five, Mackerel Brigade, and then furnished each man with a lead-pencil. He said that, as the Government was disappointed about receiving some provisions it had ordered for the troops, those pencils were intended to enable them to draw their rations as usual. I got a very big pencil, my boy, and have lived on a sheet of paper ever since.

Yours, pensively,

ORPHEUS C. KERR

A GREAT METAPHYSICAL VICTORY
(from *The Orpheus C. Kerr Papers*, 1862–1871)

Arriving near the celebrated Molasses Junction, where a number of Mackerels were placing a number of new cars and locomotives on the track—the object being to delude the Southern Confederacy into taking a ride in them, when, it was believed, the aforesaid Confederacy would speedily be destroyed by one of those "frightful accidents" without which a day on any American railroad would be a perfect anomaly—arriving there, I say, I took an immediate survey of the appointed field of strife.

To the inexperienced civilian eye, my boy, everything appeared to be in a state of chaotic confusion, which nothing but the military genius of our generals could make much worse. On all sides, my boy, I beheld the Mackerel chaps marching and countermarching; falling back, retiring, retreating, and making retrograde movements. Some were looking for their regiments; some were insanely looking for their officers, as though they did not know that the latter have resided permanently in Washington ever since the war commenced; some were making calls on others, and here and there might be seen squads of Confederates picking up any little thing they might happen to find.

Finding the general of the Mackerel Brigade lunching upon a bottle and tumbler near me, I saluted him, and says I:

"Tell me, my veteran, how it is that you permit the Southern Counfederacy to meander thus within your lines?"

The general looked toleratingly at me, and says he:

"I have a plan to entrap the Confederacy, and end this doomed rebellion at one stroke. Do you mark that long train of army wagons down there near my quarters?"

"Yes," says I, nervously.

"Well, then, my nice little boy," says the general, cautiously, "I'll tell you what the plan is. These wagons contain the rations of our troops. It is my purpose to induce the celebrated Confederacy to capture these wagons and attempt to eat those rations. If the Confederacy will only do that," says the general, fiercely, "it will be taken sick on the spot, and we shall capture it alive."

I could not but feel shocked at this inhuman artifice, my boy. The Southerners have indeed acted in a way to forfeit all ordinary mercy, but still, we should abstain from any retaliatory act savoring of demoniac malignity. Our foes are at least human beings.

Suppressing my horror, however, I assumed a practical aspect, and says I:

"But how are the Mackerel warriors to subsist, my Napoleon, if you allow the rations to go?"

"Thunder!" says the general, handing me a paper from his pocket. "They are to subsist exclusively on the enemy. Just peruse this document, which I have just fulminated."

Taking the paper, I found it to be the following

PROCLAMATION.

Whereas, The matter of provisions is a great expense to the United States of America, besides offering inducements for unexpected raids on the part of the famishing foeman; the Mackerel Brigade is hereby directed to live entirely upon the Southern Confederacy, eating him alive wherever found, and partaking of no other food.

The Brigade will not be permitted to take any clothing with it on the march, being required henceforth to dress exclusively in the habiliments of captured Confederacies.

We have done with retrograde movements. No more lines of retreat will be kept open, and henceforth the Mackerel Brigade is to make nothing but great captures.

By order of
THE GENERAL OF THE MACKEREL BRIGADE
[Green Seal.]

This able document, my boy, pleased me greatly as an evidence that the war had indeed commenced in earnest; and though at that moment, I beheld some half a dozen Confederacies ransacking the tent where the general kept his mortgages, his bank account, and other Government property, I felt that our foes were about to be summarily dealt with at last.

An orderly having finally given notice to the Confederacies rummaging within our lines to get to their proper places, in order that the battle might begin, the Anatomical Cavalry, under Captain Samyule Sa-mith, made a headlong charge upon a body of foes who were destroying a bridge near the middle of the field, and succeeded in obliging them to remain there. This brilliant movement was the signal for a general engagement, and a regiment of Confederacies at once advanced within our lines and inquired the way to Washington.

Having given them the desired information, and allowed a number of other similar regiments to take a position between the Mackerels and the capital, the general gave orders for the Conic Section and the Orange County Howitzers to fall cautiously back, in order that the remaining Confederacies might get between us and Richmond.

You will perceive that by this movement, my boy, we cut the enemy's force completely in two, thus compelling him to attack us either in the front or in the rear, and giving him no choice of any other operation save flank movements. Our plans being thus perfected, Captain Villiam Brown, with Company 3, Regiment 5, was ordered to charge into a wood near at hand, with a view to induce some recently-arrived reserve Confederacies to take position in our centre, while still others would be likely to flank us on the right and left.

You may remember, my boy, that it has heretofore been our misfortune to fight on the circumference of a circle, while the Confederacy had the inside, and this great strategic scheme was intended to produce a result *vice versa*.

It was a great success, my boy—a great success; and our troops presently found themselves inside the most complete circle on record. Villiam Brown not only charged into the wood, but staid there; and when one of the Orange County Howitzers was discharged with great precision at a reporter who was caught sneaking into our lines, the report was heard by the Venerable Gammon at Washington, causing that revered man to telegraph to all the papers, that no one need feel alarmed, as he was perfectly safe, and that our victory was very complete.

What particular danger the Venerable Gammon had incurred, I can't say, my boy; nor what he knew about the battle; but his dispatch caused renewed confidence all over the country, and was a great comfort to his friends.

Having got the Confederacies just where he wanted them, the General of the Mackerel Brigade now dispatched ten veterans under Sergeant O'Pake to attack a few hundred foes who had intrenched themselves in an unseemly manner right among our wagons. The Mackerels were well received as prisoners of war, and paroled on the spot; a proceeding which so greatly pleased the idolized general, that he at once issued this second

PROCLAMATION.

It must be understood, that in his recent proclamation directing the Mackerel Brigade to dine exclusively upon Southern Confederacies, the general commanding did not intend that such dining should take place without the free consent of aforesaid Confederacies.

It must not be understood that the order concerning the confiscation of Confederate garments is intended to authorize a forcible confiscation of such costume, in opposition to the free will of the wearers.

By "no lines of retreat being kept open," is meant: no lines of which the general commanding was at that time cognizant.

THE GENERAL OF THE MACKEREL BRIGADE.

This admirable order, my boy, produced great enthusiasm in the ranks, as no Confederacies had yet been caught, and there was some danger of starvation in the *corps*.

And now, my boy, occurred that magnificent piece of generalship which is destined to live forever on the annals of fame, and convince the world that our military leaders possess a genius eminently fitting every one of them for the next Presidency, or any other peaceful office. By skillful manœuvring, the gifted General of the Mackerel Brigade had succeeded in cutting the enemy's force to pieces, the pieces being mixed up with our own army. Then came the words: "Forward, double-quick!"

Facing toward Washington, our vanguard forced the Confederacies before them to move right ahead. Swiftly following the vanguard, and evidently fancying that it was flying before them, came a regiment of Confederacies. Pursuing the latter, as though in triumph, appeared the Conic Section, Mackerel Brigade; closely succeeded in its turn by a regiment of Confederacies in charge of our baggage-wagons, racing after whom was a regiment of Mackerels; and so on to the end of the line.

You may ask me, my boy, with which side rested the victory in this remarkable movement?

That question, my boy, cannot be decided yet, as the whole procession has scarcely reached Washington; but the answer may be said to depend very much upon whether the last regiment coming in is Mackerel or Confederate.

The contest, my boy, has assumed a profound metaphysical aspect, and the development of a little more military genius on our own side will tend to utterly confound our enemies and— everybody else.

Yours, ponderingly,
ORPHEUS C. KERR

James Thurber

I am indebted to Nathaniel Benchley for the information that a California newspaper once reported *as fact* that Grant was drinking and wrestling with his aides on the eve of Appomattox.

The paper's source was none other than the following unimpeachable document by the late and deeply regretted military historian, James Thurber.

IF GRANT HAD BEEN DRINKING AT APPOMATTOX

The morning of the ninth of April, 1865, dawned beautifully. General Meade was up with the first streaks of crimson in the eastern sky. General Hooker and General Burnside were up, and had breakfasted, by a quarter after eight. The day continued beautiful. It drew on toward eleven o'clock. General Ulysses S. Grant was still not up. He was asleep in his famous old navy hammock, swung high above the floor of his headquarters' bedroom. Headquarters was distressingly disarranged: papers were strewn on the floor; confidential notes from spies scurried here and there in the breeze from an open window; the dregs of an overturned bottle of wine flowed pinkly across an important military map.

Corporal Shultz, of the Sixty-fifth Ohio Volunteer Infantry, aide to General Grant, came into the outer room, looked around him, and sighed. He entered the bedroom and shook the General's hammock roughly. General Ulysses S. Grant opened one eye.

"Pardon, sir," said Corporal Shultz, "but this is the day of surrender. You ought to be up, sir."

"Don't swing me," said Grant, sharply, for his aide was making the hammock sway gently. "I feel terrible," he added, and he turned over and closed his eye again.

"General Lee will be here any minute now," said the Corporal firmly, swinging the hammock again.

"Will you cut that out?" roared Grant. "D'ya want to make me sick, or what?" Shultz clicked his heels and saluted. "What's he coming here for?" asked the General.

"This is the day of surrender, sir," said Shultz. Grant grunted bitterly.

"Three hundred and fifty generals in the Northern armies," said Grant, "and he has to come to *me* about this. What time is it?"

"You're the Commander-in-Chief, that's why," said Corporal Shultz. "It's eleven twenty-five, sir."

"Don't be crazy," said Grant. "Lincoln is the Commander-in-Chief. Nobody in the history of the world ever surrendered before lunch. Doesn't he know that an army surrenders on its stomach?" He pulled a blanket up over his head and settled himself again.

"The generals of the Confederacy will be here any minute now," said the Corporal. "You really ought to be up, sir."

Grant stretched his arms above his head and yawned.

"All right, all right," he said. He rose to a sitting position and stared about the room. "This place looks awful," he growled.

"You must have had quite a time of it last night, sir," ventured Shultz.

"Yeh," said General Grant, looking around for his clothes. "I was wrassling some general. Some general with a beard."

Shultz helped the commander of the Northern armies in the field to find his clothes.

"Where's my other sock?" demanded Grant. Shultz began to look around for it. The General walked uncertainly to a table and poured a drink from a bottle.

"I don't think it wise to drink, sir," said Shultz.

"Nev' mind about me," said Grant, helping himself to a second, "I can take it or let it alone. Didn' ya ever hear the story about the fella went to Lincoln to complain about me drinking too much? 'So-and-So says Grant drinks too much,' this fella said. 'So-and-So is a fool,' said Lincoln. So this fella went to What's-His-Name and told him what Lincoln said and he came roarin' to Lincoln about it. 'Did you tell So-and-So I was a fool?' he said. 'No,' said Lincoln, 'I thought he knew it.'" The General smiled, reminiscently, and had another drink. "*That's* how I stand with Lincoln," he said, proudly.

The soft thudding sound of horses' hooves came through the open window. Shultz hurriedly walked over and looked out.

"Hoof steps," said Grant, with a curious chortle.

"It is General Lee and his staff," said Shultz.

"Show him in," said the General, taking another drink. "And see what the boys in the back room will have."

Shultz walked smartly over to the door, opened it, saluted, and stood aside. General Lee, dignified against the blue of the April sky, magnificent in his dress uniform, stood for a moment framed in the doorway. He walked in, followed by his staff. They bowed, and stood silent. General Grant stared at them. He only had one boot on and his jacket was unbuttoned.

"I know who you are," said Grant. "You're Robert Browning, the poet."

"This is General Robert E. Lee," said one of his staff, coldly.

"Oh," said Grant. "I thought he was Robert Browning. He certainly looks like Robert Browning. There was a poet for you, Lee: Browning. Did ja ever read 'How They Brought the Good News from Ghent to Aix'? 'Up Derek, to saddle, up Derek, away; up Dunder, up Blitzen, up Prancer, up Dancer, up Bouncer, up Vixen, up—' "

"Shall we proceed at once to the matter in hand?" asked General Lee, his eyes disdainfully taking in the disordered room.

"Some of the boys was wrassling here last night," explained Grant. "I threw Sherman, or some general a whole lot like Sherman. It was pretty dark." He handed a bottle of Scotch to the commanding officer of the Southern armies, who stood holding it, in amazement and discomfiture. "Get a glass, somebody," said Grant, looking straight at General Longstreet. "Didn't I meet you at Cold Harbor?" he asked. General Longstreet did not answer.

"I should like to have this over with as soon as possible," said Lee. Grant looked vaguely at Shultz, who walked up close to him, frowning.

"The surrender, sir, the surrender," said Corporal Shultz in a whisper.

"Oh, sure, sure," said Grant. He took another drink. "All right," he said. "Here we go." Slowly, sadly, he unbuckled his sword. Then he handed it to the astonished Lee. "There you are,

General," said Grant. "We dam' near licked you. If I'd been feeling better we *would* of licked you."

Finley Peter Dunne

Mr. Dooley stands foremost among America's folk philosophers. From Jack Downing to Will Rogers, no other commentator on the national scene achieved the same harmony of humor and critical perspicuity that was the natural voice of Finley Peter Dunne's Irish saloon-keeper.

When Dunne's dialect pieces first began to be published in Chicago in 1892, the country was ready for a Mr. Dooley. The deceptively genial sage of "Archey Road" (Archer Avenue) appeared at a time when Americans were awakening, like so many Rip Van Winkles, into a new, industrialized and power-conscious United States. It was a strange and unfamiliar time; after the fabulous growth period of the Gilded Age the country seemed to have become too vast and bewildering to make sense to the common man. In the 1890s people worried as they had never worried during the boom days of the late sixties and seventies. They worried whether the Bible was the literal truth and whether man was really related to the monkeys; they worried over the consequences of America's new aggressive role in world politics, and over the consequences of the social injustices which were shockingly apparent. Most people felt a hunger for reform but an even greater fear of being poisoned by radicalism.

Blandly, devastatingly, Dooley took all of these deep concerns in stride.

Our expansionist policies and particularly the Spanish-American War provided Dunne with material for some of Dooley's best pieces. This dialogue with Dooley's friend Mr. Hennessy shows the barkeeper commenting on the Philippine situation. Dewey's highly publicized victory over a few rusty Spanish warships in Manila Bay in May, 1898, brought the Philippines prominently into the news, but many Americans— including President McKinley—had only the haziest idea of where, or what, the Islands were.

MR. DOOLEY ON THE PHILIPPINES
(1898)

I know what I'd do if I was Mack," said Mr. Hennessy. "I'd hist a flag over th' Ph'lippeens, an' I'd take in th' whole lot iv thim."

"An' yet," said Mr. Dooley, "tis not more thin two months since ye larned whether they were islands or canned goods. Ye'er back yard is so small that ye'er cow can't turn r-round without buttin' th' woodshed off th' premises, an' ye wudden't go out to th' stock yards without takin' out a policy on yer life. Suppose ye was standin' at th' corner iv State Sthreet an' Archey R-road, wud ye know what car to take to get to th' Ph'lippeens? If yer son Packy was to ask ye where th' Ph'lippeens is, cud ye give him anny good idea whether they was in Rooshia or jus' west iv th' thracks?"

"Mebbe I cudden't," said Mr. Hennessy, haughtily, "but I'm f'r takin' thim in, annyhow."

"So might I be," said Mr. Dooley, "if I cud on'y get me mind on it. Wan iv the worst things about this here war is th' way it's makin' puzzles f'r our poor, tired heads. Whin I wint into it, I thought all I'd have to do was to set up here behind th' bar with a good tin-cint see-gar in me teeth, an' toss dinnymite bombs into th' hated city iv Havana. But look at me now. Th' war is still goin' on; an' ivry night, whin I'm countin' up the cash, I'm askin' mesilf will I annex Cubia or lave it to the Cubians? Will I take Porther Ricky or put it by? An' what shud I do with the Ph'lippeens? Oh, what shud I do with thim? I can't annex thim because I don't know where they ar-re. I can't let go iv thim because some wan else'll take thim if I do. They are eight thousan' iv thim islands, with a popylation iv wan hundherd millyon naked savages; an' me bedroom's crowded now with me an' th' bed. How can I take thim in, an' how on earth am I goin' to cover th' nakedness iv thim savages with me wan shoot iv clothes? An' yet 'twud break me heart to think iv givin' people I niver see or heerd tell iv back to other people I don't know. An', if I don't take thim, Schwartzmeister down th' sthreet, that has half me thrade already, will grab thim sure.

"It ain't that I'm afraid iv not doin' th' r-right thing in th' end, Hinnissy. Some mornin' I'll wake up an' know jus' what to do, an' that I'll do. But 'tis th' annoyance in th' mane time. I've been r-readin' about th' counthry. 'Tis over beyant ye'er left shoulder whin ye're facin' east. Jus' throw ye'er thumb back, an' ye have it as ac'rate as anny man in town. 'Tis farther thin Boohlgahrya an' not so far as Blewchoochoo. It's near Chiny, an' it's not so near; an', if a man was to bore a well through fr'm Goshen, Indianny, he might sthrike it, an' thin again he might not. It's a poverty-sthricken counthry, full iv goold an' precious stones, where th' people can pick dinner off th' threes an' ar-re starvin' because they have no step-ladders. Th' inhabitants is mostly naygurs an' Chinnymen, peaceful, industhrus, an' law-abidin', but savage an' bloodthirsty in their methods. They wear no clothes except what they have on, an' each woman has five husbands an' each man has five wives. Th' r-rest goes into th' discard, th' same as here. Th' islands has been ownded be Spain since befure th' fire; an' she's threated thim so well they're now up in ar-rms again her, except a majority iv thim which is thurly loyal. Th' natives seldom fight, but whin they get mad at wan another they r-run-a-muck. Whin a man r-runs-a-muck, sometimes they hang him an' sometimes they discharge him an' hire a new motorman. Th' women ar-re beautiful, with languishin' black eyes, an' they smoke see-gars, but ar-re hurried an' incomplete in their dhress. I see a pitcher iv wan th' other day with nawthin' on her but a basket of cocoanuts an' a hoop-skirt. They're no prudes. We import juke, hemp, cigar wrappers, sugar, an' fairy tales fr'm th' Ph'lippeens, an' export six-inch shells an' th' like. Iv late th' Ph'lippeens has awaked to th' fact that they're behind th' times, an' has received much American amminition in their midst. They say th' Spanyards is all tore up about it.

"I larned all this fr'm th' papers, an' I know 'tis sthraight. An' yet, Hinnissy, I dinnaw what to do about th' Ph'lippeens. An' I'm all alone in th' wurruld. Ivrybody else has made up his mind. Ye ask anny con-ducthor on Ar-rchy R-road, an' he'll tell ye. Ye can find out fr'm the papers; an', if ye really want to know, all ye have to do is to ask a prom'nent citizen who can mow all th' lawn he owns with a safety razor. But I don't know."

"Hang on to thim," said Mr. Hennessy, stoutly. "What we've got we must hold."

"Well," said Mr. Dooley, "if I was Mack, I'd lave it to George. I'd say: 'George,' I'd say, 'if ye're f'r hangin' on, hang on it is. If ye say, lave go, I dhrop thim.' 'Twas George won thim with th' shells, an' th' question's up to him."

Mark Twain

As he grew older Mark Twain's jocose skepticism often turned to somber disillusion. The "Unspoken War Prayer" is a starkly ironic passage in the manner of Swift at his darkest, the sort of satire, totally unrelieved by comedy, that Twain discovered his contemporary American audiences could not or would not understand.

UNSPOKEN WAR PRAYER
(from *Europe and Elsewhere*, 1904–1905)

Oh, Lord our Father, our young patriots, idols of our hearts, go forth to battle. Be Thou near them! With them—in spirit—we also go from the sweet peace of our beloved firesides to smite the foe.

Oh, Lord, our God, help us to tear their soldiers to bloody shreds with our shells; help us to cover their smiling fields with the pale forms of their patriot dead; help us to drown the thunder of the guns with the wounded, writhing in pain; help us to lay waste their humble homes with the hurricane of fire; help us to wring the hearts of their unoffending widows with unavailing grief; help us to turn them out roofless with their little children to wander unfriended over wastes of their desolated land in rags and hunger and thirst, sport of the sun-flames of summer and the icy winds of winter, broken in spirit, worn with travail, imploring Thee for the refuge of the grave and denied it—for our sakes, who adore Thee, Lord, blast their hopes, blight their lives, protract their bitter pilgrimage, make heavy their steps, water their way with their tears, stain the white snow with the blood of their wounded feet! We ask of One who is the spirit of Love and Who is the everfaithful refuge and friend of all that are sore beset, and seek His aid with humble and contrite hearts. Grant our prayer, oh Lord, and Thine shall be the praise and honor and glory, now and ever.

Amen.

Edward Streeter

Back home, Americans were patriotically buying Liberty Bonds, braving meatless days and proudly doing their all for victory, while in the trenches overseas the doughboys were fighting mud, sore feet, cooties and Germans. The citizen-soldiers were soon to find that their war bore little resemblance to the glorious crusade of democracy against the Hun which was being fought in the press, and to realize that a breach wider than the Atlantic now separated them from the folks back in the States.

This letter from Edward Streeter's *Dere Mable* and the following one by the Indiana humorist Kin Hubbard (Frank McKinney Hubbard, 1868–1930) satirize the absurdities of soldiering and wryly deglamorize the war.

"I DONT LIKE THE SARGENT"
(from *Dere Mable*)

*D*ere Mable:
    I havnt rote for some time I had such sore feet lately. When they broke up our regiment and sent me over to

the artillery I thought I was goin to quit usin my feet. That was
just another roomor.

Thanks for the box of stuff you sent me. I guess the brake-
man must have used it for a chair all the way. It was pretty
well baled but that dont matter. And thanks for the fudge too.
That was fudge wasnt it, Mable? And the sox. They dont fit
but I can use them for somethin. A good soldier never throws
nothin away. An thank your mother for the half pair of gloves
she sent me. I put them away. Maybe sometime shell get a
chance to nit the other half. Or if I ever get all my fingers
shot off theyll come in very handy.

The artillerys a little different from the infantry. They make
us work harder. At least theres more work on the skedule. I
know now what they mean when they say that the "artillerys
active on the western front."

They got a drill over here called the standin gun drill. The
names misleadin. I guess it was invented by a troop of Jap
akrobats. They make you get up and sit on the gun. Before you
can get settled comfortable they make you get down again. It
looks like they didnt know just what they did want you to do.

I dont like the sargent. I dont like any sargent but this one
particular. The first day out he kept sayin "Prepare to mount"
and then "Mount." Finally I went up to him and told him that
as far as I was concerned he could cut that stuff for I was always prepared to do what I was told even though it was the
middle of the night. He said, Fine, then I was probably prepared to scrub pans all day Sunday.

I dont care much for horses. I think they feels the same way
about me. Most of them are so big that the only thing there
good for is the view of the camp you get when you climb up.
They are what they call hors de combat in French. My horse
died the other day. I guess it wasnt much effort for him. If it
had been he wouldnt have done it.

They got a book they call Drill Regulations Field and Light.
Thats about as censible as it is all the way through. For instance they say that when the command for action is given one
man jumps for the wheel and another springs for the trail an
another leaps for the muzzle. I guess the fellow that rote the
regulations thought we was a bunch of grass hoppers.

Well I got to quit now an rite a bunch of other girls. Thanks again for the box although it was so busted that it wasnt much good but that dont matter.

Yours till you here otherwise,

Bill

Kin Hubbard
(Frank McKinney Hubbard)

A LETTER FROM TH' FRONT
(from *Abe Martin on the War and Other Things*)

Mrs. Min Nugent, cook o' th' New Palace hotel, has received th' follerin' interestin' letter from her son Stew, who is somewhere in France with th' American expeditionary forces:

DEAR MAW:

Well, here I am. I hope you are well. We had some trip comin' over. Cigarettes galore. A piece of shrapnel jest now broke th' last pane o' glass in my window as I write. I have enough terbacker t' last a week. Unless some has been sent since I left I'll probably be without some days before some comes. I'm billeted on th' parlor floor of an ole historic chateau with a mantle piece that goes back t' th' renaissance. My shoes are dryin' on th' mantle. Cigarettes should be mailed at intervals o' two days apart t' assure a steady, unbroken flow. Eatin' t'backer, too, only cigarettes is th' most important. . . . I'm writin' now with a pencil as a piece of flyin' shrapnel jest busted my fountain pen th' sheriff give me when I enlisted. Tell him I'm out o' fountain pens agin, but would rather have cigarettes. It's wonderful how indifferent you git t' danger over here. I'm not spendin' any o' my pay as I want t' loaf a couple o' years when I git home, so any cigarettes or t'backer you send me is jest that much saved. I wouldn' give much fer this historic chateau after th' shrapnel gits thro' with it. . . . I'm finishin' this letter this mornin' as a piece of shrapnel put

my candle out last night an' no matches wuz t' be had. Th'
French people wuz certainly glad t' see me but they have
scarcely enough cigarettes fer 'emselves, an' are tired out an'
poor after fightin' so long, so I hate t' ask 'em fer 'em when
friends kin send 'em t' me so easily any time. It don't look
right t' take 'em from 'em an' I know you would not want me
t' do so. It's different with eggs, which are plentiful. I can't
talk any French an' I can't tell what ther sayin, but I wouldn'
ask 'em fer cigarettes, an' you wouldn' either if you could see
what they've been up against. Are there any cigarette clubs at
home? Some o' the boys say ther's clubs in ther towns that
gather money with which t' buy them an' send them t' them.
Girls send them th' same as socks, an' believe me, th' boys are
glad t' git 'em. I hope you are well an' strong an' able t' work
fer many years t' come. You should be glad you've got a good,
easy cookin' job when you think o' th' poor ole women over
here plowin'. Ther haint nothin' in loafin'. I'm goin' to work
some when I git back. I'm goin' over t' th' mantle an' git my
shoes as soon as th' shellin' lets up a little. Mark your packages
care A. E. F. You cant carry a pipe over here very handy.
Shrapnel knocks 'em out o' your mouth. You bet I've got my
three cigarette cases distributed where they'll stop th' most
schrapnel. It don't look like I'd ever git my shoes as ther's a
constant hail o' schrapnel. Don't worry about me.

Your lovin' son,
STEW.

A.E.F. France.
(Put this on all cigarette packages sure.)

Ralph Barton

THE CAUSES OF THE WAR MADE PLAIN
(from *God's Country*)

While the people of America were wallowing in the out-
put of the national cornucopia, a great war—by far
the greatest war that had ever been fought in the history of
the universe—broke out in Europe.

So suddenly had the war broken out that the Americans, who had forgotten that Europe existed, found it difficult to realize what had happened. They had simply come down to breakfast one morning and there it was in their newspapers. The big story ran all the way across the top of page one, down the right-hand five columns, and over to page two. As soon as they had ascertained who had won the ball games and fixed the changes in the standings of the teams in their minds, the Americans read of the doings of uhlans and cuirassiers, cossacks and dragoons, hussars and lancers, of fortresses and frontiers, howitzers and shrapnel, of flanking movements and frontal assaults, and the magic words thrilled them to the marrow. They could hear the rattle of musketry as they crushed their corn flakes, and when they dashed their spoons against their teeth they heard sabers clattering against the flagstones of conquered villages.

Since the foundation of the Public Thing, the Americans had spent twenty years, or an average of one day a week, at war, and they had gladly handed over $8 in taxes for war to every $1 for all other government activities during their national life; but, as the wars had all been forced upon them, and had all been waged in behalf of humanity, justice and civilization, the Americans could hardly be counted as a warlike people. It was, therefore, as amateurs that they followed, with breathless interest, the push of the German army to the heart of France, its repulse at the Marne, and its final stand at the Aisne.

At last, when the armies had "dug in" and the more spectacular manœuvres were over, the Americans looked up from their newspapers and began to ask each other—timidly, at first, lest they expose their ignorance—what the war was all about. Presently, when it was discovered that nobody knew, they stopped asking each other, and began telling each other. Small, private wars broke out all over America and the magazines, in the interests of peace, engaged experts to write articles explaining the true causes of the European conflict.

"The war," the articles said, in substance, "is the inevitable outcome of deep-seated causes."

That was enough for the majority of the people. They accepted the explanation, adopted it as their own, and announced

that they were ready to break anybody's face who disagreed
with it.

But a professional spiritualistic medium in Jefferson City,
Missouri, who held séances Monday, Wednesday and Friday
evenings and spent the rest of his time writing letters to the
magazines and newspapers, took exception to the explanation
and addressed an epistle to the editor of the magazine in which
he had read it. It ran:

> *dere Sir, i receve your valude magazine regalery and cannot*
> *live without it which is the best of its kind in the world but i*
> *shoud like to ast the riter of the artical about the war in the dec.*
> *number* what Causes? *thanking you in advanse and asuring you*
> *of my devosion to your valude publication i am sincerly yours.*
>   *yours truly.*
>   PRO BONO PUBLICO.
> *P. S.—i bet you havn't got the* "guts" *to publish this leter.*

Now, editors pay a great deal of attention to letters of this
kind, for they feel that they represent the Average Reader's
point of view instead of the Average Letter Writer's. Consequently, it was turned over to the author of the war article with
the request that he elaborate his statements in a fresh article.

"This frightful war," clicked out the expert's typewriter, almost of its own accord, "is the unavoidable consequence of the
international hatred and rivalry born of and fostered by secret diplomatic machinations during the past fifty years in Europe."

The majority of the people again accepted this explanation as
final; but Pro Bono Publico dispatched another letter from
Jefferson City.

> *dere Sir, your magazine is the first to be wore out in my*
> *wateing room it makes such a hit with my clints but what your*
> *war riter says is the* Cause *of the war cannot be for are we not*
> *taut in our schools as children that hatered and rivaltry between*
> *the nations is* just *and* good? *acording to him if hatered and*
> *rivaltry brings on war then they would be nothing for us to do*
> *but go on fiteing untill the best nation on erth (that is the*

*good old U.S.A. of coarse) has fot and licked all the other na-
tions off the face of the erth and go on fiteing untill the best
state has won and then go on keeping it up untill the best man
has won and is left alone all by his lonesome in the world. because everybody hates his next dore naybor like poison and is
his rival the same as the nations are the same but that dont
make war but it makes pride and go getiveness. if you dont
beleve what i say ast any Busness man worthy of the name if
rivaltry and hatered is not the cause of bigger and better Busness and Progres and not the cause of war.*

"The true cause of the war," then put forward the magazine
writers, "lies in the vast and intricate network of offensive and
defensive alliances and treaties that existed between the gov-
ernments of Europe and of which the Triple Alliance and the
Triple Entente were the chief."

After the usual complimentary phrases addressed to the
magazine, Pro Bono Publico wrote:

*what country ever paid the slitest bit of attention to a treety
it dident want to pay attention to? what about the treety italy
had with germany and austary? and what about germanys
treety with the belgiums?*

"Then it is militarism," said the sweating authors. "Militarism, pure and simple, is the cause of the war. The war was
created merely to put to some use the vast armies and navies
the European nations had been organizing."

*fiddlesticks!!! (wrote Pro Bono Publico) have we not been
told on good awtharity that keeping up the Army and the
Navy is the best inssurence against war? and besides i hope
you dont think us taxpayers pays our taxes to have a Army and
Navy to fite wars with not at all as we hate the very idea of
war. it is to have prades with and carry Old Glorry down Main
street to the tune of fife and drum.*

"Well, then," wrote the writers, "the war is being waged
against the Kaiser, personally, because he is an arrogant and a
dangerous lunatic and a menace to world peace."

Jefferson City was heard from as follows:

that arguyment wont hold no watter. it apears to me the kaiser has got his wish if what you say is true for where is world peece at Now? *in concludeing i would say as of yours proximo was* Alexander the grate *and* julis Ceser *and* ST. GEORGE *dangerous lunatiks?!!? and* Napolyon??!!!?!?

The magazine writers removed their coats and rolled up their sleeves.

"This war," they wrote, "is being fought to curb Germany's gluttonous thirst for colonial expansion which menaces . . ."

Before they had had time to finish this explanation, the British Foreign Office sent up such a hue and cry about the German atrocities in gallant little Belgium that the writers were obliged to devote their energies to pieces about humanity and international law. This gave them a breathing space, and when the indignation over German barbarity had calmed down a little, they returned to the task of explaining the war with a more cynical air.

"The causes of the war lie deeper than we have thus far looked for them. It is, at bottom, a war between Liverpool and Hamburg, between Havre and Bremen. It is a war for industrial supremacy. It is a business war."

Ha Ha Ha (wrote Pro Bono Publico) *your riter makes me laugf. even if they* are *forenners these here uropeen Busness men has got better sence than to bust up there markets and ruinate there stock exchange and money just because they is* sore *at each other. they no as well as we do that the fat pickings in a war is on the side of the newtril countrys and they woud not have alloud no war in there own countrys excep mayby a little one to go out and lick a small coliny of niggers somewheres to take there gold mines away from them or something of the kind.*

"Very well, then," screamed the magazine writers, who were now quite frantic, "this war is being fought by the Central Powers uniquely to avenge the murder of the Austrian Archduke Franz Ferdinand at the hands of what they call a young Serbian citizen. The Allies are defending their honor, for they know that the assassin was not a Serbian, but a Bosnian, and a member of the loathsome Black Hand Society."

When Pro Bono Publico read this, he was silenced. Thoughts of the old days filled his mind and stirred his soul. The clash of metal upon metal reached his ears from the battlefields of Europe and he saw a feudal baron, mounted on a milk-white charger, brandishing his sword and leading his vassals against the neighboring castle to avenge the murder of a kinsman. He saw the other side swoop down from their hilltop, shouting, "Death to the others and long live us!" He heard the crunch of hauberks under horses' hoofs and the ripping of wood as lances doubled against breasts. He smelt the blood oozing from fissures in the armor of loyal vassals dying in the service of their lords, using their last gasps to declare that *their* castles, *their* colors, *their* hilltops and *their* seigneurs were undoubtedly the finest in the world.

As he dreamed this splendid dream, Pro Bono Publico came slowly to the realization that, without question, the noblest occupation to which man could possibly turn his hand here below is the cracking open of an enemy's skull with some blunt instrument. At the Wednesday evening séance, he caused the materialization of the spirits of Alexander the Great, Julius Cæsar, Napoleon and St. George, who told his clients that the murder of the Austrian Archduke Franz Ferdinand was the true and only cause of the war, and that a more magnificent war for a nobler cause had never been fought. The clients vowed that these great captains of the past could not speak other than the truth and they agreed that the war was, indeed, a magnificent one. From that time forward, people spoke no more of the "European War" but of the "Magnificent War," and so it has been known ever since.

Thomas Heggen

World War II was the inspiration for a number of amusing novels about service life; *See Here, Private Hargrove* and *No*

Time for Sergeants were two of the best. But no service story to come out of the war surpasses *Mr. Roberts*, the comedy of the noncombatant ship *Reluctant*. There is broad humor in the intrigues of Lieutenant Roberts, Ensign Pulver and the rest of the ship's officers and men against their "chicken" captain; yet just below the comic surface of the story is a telling indictment of the human wastes of war.

The following selection is the Introduction to *Mr. Roberts*, a guided tour of the *Reluctant*.

THE "RELUCTANT"
(The Introduction to *Mr. Roberts*)

Now, in the waning days of the second World War, this ship lies at anchor in the glassy bay of one of the back islands of the Pacific. It is a Navy cargo ship. You know it as a cargo ship by the five yawning hatches, by the house amidships, by the booms that bristle from the masts like mechanical arms. You know it as a Navy ship by the color (dark, dull blue), by the white numbers painted on the bow, and unfailingly by the thin ribbon of the commission pennant flying from the mainmast. In the Navy Register, this ship is listed as the *Reluctant*. Its crew never refer to it by name: to them it is always "this bucket."

In an approximate way it is possible to fix this ship in time. The local civil time is 0614 and the day is one in the spring of 1945. Sunrise was three minutes ago and the officer-of-the-deck is not quite alert, for the red truck lights atop the masts are still burning. It is a breathless time, quiet and fresh and lovely. The water inside the bay is planed to perfect smoothness, and in the emergent light it is bronze-colored, and not yet blue. The sky, which will be an intense blue, is also dulled a little by the film of night. The inflamed sun floats an inch or so above the horizon, and the wine-red light it spreads does not hurt the eyes at all. Over on the island there begin to be signs of life. An arm of blue smoke climbs straight and clean from the palm groves. Down on the dock people are moving about. A jeep goes by on the beach road and leaves a puff of dust behind. But on this ship there seems to be no one stirring. Just off the bow, a school of flying fish breaks the water suddenly. In the quiet the effect is as startling as an explosion.

In Germany right now it would be seven o'clock at night. It would be quite dark, and perhaps there is a cold rain falling. In this darkness and in this rain the Allied armies are slogging on toward Berlin. Some stand as close as one hundred and fifty miles. Aachen and Cologne have fallen, inside of days Hanover will fall. Far around the girdle of the world, at Okinawa Gunto it is now three in the morning. Flares would be dripping their slow, wet light as the United States Tenth Army finishes its job. These are contemporary moments of that in which our ship lies stagnant in the bay.

Surely, then, since this is One World, the tranquil ship is only an appearance, this somnolence an illusion. Surely an artillery shell fired at Hanover ripples the air here. Surely a bomb dropped on Okinawa trembles these bulkheads. This is an American Man o' War, manned by American Fighting Men: who would know better than they that this is One World? Who indeed? Of course, then, this indolence is only seeming, this lethargy a façade: in actuality this ship must be throbbing with grim purposefulness, intense activity, and a high awareness of its destiny. Of course.

Let us go aboard this Man o' War.

Step carefully there over little Red McLaughlin, sleeping on the hatch cover. Red is remarkable for being able to sleep anywhere: probably he was on his way down to the compartment when he dropped in his tracks, sound asleep. There do not, in truth, seem to be many people up yet—but then it is still a few minutes to reveille. Reveille is at six-thirty. In the Chief's quarters there is one man up: it is Johnson, the chief master-at-arms. He is the one who makes reveille. Johnson is drinking coffee and he seems preoccupied: perhaps, as you suggest, his mind is thousands of miles away, following the battle-line in Germany. But no—to tell the truth—it is not. Johnson is thinking of a can of beer, and he is angry. Last night he hid the can carefully beneath a pile of dirty scivvies in his locker: now it is gone. Johnson is reasonably certain that Yarby, the chief yeoman, took it; but he cannot prove this. He is turning over in his mind ways of getting back at Yarby. Let us move on.

Down in the armory a group of six men sits tensely around a wooden box. You say they are discussing fortifications?—you distinctly heard the word "sandbag" spoken? Yes, you did: but it is feared that you heard it out of context. What Olson, the first-class gunner's mate, said was: "Now watch the son-of-a-bitch sandbag me!" Used like that, it is a common colloquialism of poker: this is an all-night poker game.

We find our way now to the crew's compartment. You are surprised to see so many men sleeping, and so soundly? Perhaps it would be revelatory to peer into their dreams. No doubt, as you say, we will find them haunted by battles fought and battles imminent. This man who snores so noisily is Stefanowski, machinist's mate second class. His dream? . . . well . . . there is a girl . . . she is inadequately clothed . . . she is smiling at Stefanowski . . . let us not intrude.

You are doubtless right: certainly an officer will be more sensitive. In this stateroom, with his hand dangling over the side of the bunk, is Ensign Pulver. He is one of the engineering officers. And you *are* right; his dream *is* conditioned by the war. In his dream he is all alone in a lifeboat. He is lying there on a leather couch and there are cases of Schlitz beer stacked all about him. On the horizon he sees the ship go down at last; it goes down slowly, stern first. A swimming figure reaches the boat and clutches the gunwales. Without rising from his couch, Ensign Pulver takes the ball-bat at his side and smashes the man's hands. Every time the man gets his hands on the gunwales, Pulver pounds them with the bat. Finally the man sinks in a froth of bubbles. Who is this man—a Jap? No, it is the Captain. Ensign Pulver smiles happily and opens a can of beer.

What manner of ship is this? What does it do? What is its combat record? Well, those are fair questions, if difficult ones. The *Reluctant*, as was said, is a naval auxiliary. It operates in the back areas of the Pacific. In its holds it carries food and trucks and dungarees and toothpaste and toilet paper. For the most part it stays on its regular run, from Tedium to Apathy and back; about five days each way. It makes an occasional trip to Monotony, and once it made a run all the way to Ennui, a distance of two thousand nautical miles from Tedium. It performs its dreary and unthanked job, and performs it, if not inspiredly, then at least adequately.

It has shot down no enemy planes, nor has it fired upon any, nor has it seen any. It has sunk with its guns no enemy subs, but there *was* this once that it fired. This periscope, the lookout sighted it way off on the port beam, and the Captain, who was scared almost out of his mind, gave the order: "Commence firing!" The five-inch and the two port three-inch guns fired for perhaps ten minutes, and the showing was really rather embarrassing. The closest shell was three hundred yards off, and all the time the unimpressed periscope stayed right there. At one thousand yards it was identified as the protruding branch of a floating tree. The branch had a big bend in it and didn't even look much like a periscope.

So now you know: that is the kind of ship the *Reluctant* is. Admittedly it is not an heroic ship. Whether, though, you can also denounce its men as unheroic is another matter. Before that is summarily done, a few obvious facts about heroism should perhaps be pleaded; the first of them being that there are *kinds* of it. On this ship, for instance, you might want to consider Lieutenant Roberts as a hero. Lieutenant Roberts is a young man of sensitivity, perceptiveness, and idealism; attributes which are worthless and even inimical to such a community as this. He wants to be in the war; he is powerfully drawn to the war and to the general desolation of the time, but he is held off, frustrated, defeated by the rather magnificently non-conductive character of his station. He is the high-strung instrument assuming the low-strung rôle. He has geared himself to the tempo of the ship and made the adjustment with— the words are not believed misplaced—gallantry, courage, and fortitude. Perhaps he is a kind of hero.

And then in simple justice to the undecorated men of the *Reluctant* it should also be pointed out that heroism—physical heroism—is very much a matter of opportunity. On the physical level heroism is not so much an act, implying volition, as it is a reflex. Apply the rubber hammer to the patella tendon and, commonly, you produce the knee jerk. Apply the situation permitting bravery to one hundred young males with actively functioning adrenal glands and, reasonably, you would produce seventy-five instances of clear-cut heroism. Would, that is, but for one thing: that after the fifty-first the word would dissolve into meaninglessness. Like the knee jerk, physical courage is perhaps latent and even implicit in the individual, needing only the application of situation, of opportunity, to reveal it. A case in point: Ensign Pulver.

Ensign Pulver is a healthy, highly normal young man who sleeps a great deal, is amiable, well-liked, and generally regarded by his shipmates as being rather worthless. At the instigation of forces well beyond his control, he joined the Naval Reserve and by the same forces was assigned to this ship, where he spends his time sleeping, discoursing, and plotting ingenious offensives against the Captain which he never executes. Alter the accidents, apply the situation, locate Pulver in the ball turret of a B-29 over Japan, and what do you have? You have Pulver, the Congressional Medal man, who single-handedly and successively shot down twenty-three attacking Zekes, fought the fire raging in his own ship, with his bare hands held together the severed wing struts and with his bare feet successfully landed the grievously wounded plane on its home field.

These, then—if the point is taken—are unheroic men only because they are non-combatant; whether unwillingly or merely unavoidably is not important. They fight no battles: *ergo* in a certain literal and narrow sense they are non-combatant. But in the larger vision these men are very definitely embattled, and rather curiously so. The enemy is not the unseen Jap, not the German, nor the abstract villainy of fascism: it is that credible and tangible villain, the Captain. The warfare is declared and continual, and the lines have long been drawn. On one side is the Captain, alone; opposing him are the other one hundred and seventy-eight members, officers and men, of the ship's company. It is quite an even match.

The Captain of a naval vessel is a curious affair. Personally he may be short, scrawny, unprepossessing; but a Captain is not a person and cannot be viewed as such. He is an embodiment. He is given stature, substance, and sometimes a new dimension by the massive, cumulative authority of the Navy Department which looms behind him like a shadow. With some Captains this shadow is a great, terrifying cloud; with others, it is scarcely apparent at all: but with none can it go unnoticed. Now to this the necessary exception: Captain Morton. With Captain Morton it could and does up to a point go unnoticed. The crew knows instinctively that the Captain is vulnerable, that he is unaware of the full dimensions of his authority; and, thus stripped of his substance, they find him detestable and not at all terrifying. He is not hated, for in hate there is something of fear and something of respect, neither of which is present here. And you could not say loathed, for loathing is passive and this is an active feeling. Best say detested; vigorously disliked. As the chosen enemy he is the object of an incessant guerilla warfare, which is, for the Navy, a most irregular business. Flat declarations like "Captain Morton is an old fart" appear in chalk from time to time on gun mounts; cigarette butts, an obsession of the Captain's, are mysteriously inserted into his cabin; his telephone rings at odd hours of the night; once when he was standing on the quarterdeck a helmet dropped from the flying bridge missed him by perhaps a yard—the margin of a warning. Childishness? Pettiness? Perhaps: but remember that these are the only weapons the men have. Remember that they are really hopelessly outmatched. Remember that the shadow, acknowledged or not, is there all the time.

Captain Morton is a tall bulging middle-aged man with a weak chin and a ragged mustache. He is bowlegged and broad-beamed (for which the crew would substitute "lard-assed"), and he walks with the absurd roll of an animated Popeye. If you ask, any crew member will give you the bill of particulars against the Captain, but he will be surprised that you find it necessary to ask. He will tell you that the man is stupid, incompetent, petty, vicious, treacherous. The signalmen or yeomen will insist that he is unable to understand the simplest message or letter. Anyone in the deck divisions will tell you that he is far more concerned with keeping the decks cleared of cigarette butts than with discharging cargo, his nominal mission. All of the crew will tell you of the petty persecution he directs against them: the preposterous insistence (for an auxiliary operating in the rear areas) that men topside wear hats and shirts at all times; the shouting and grumbling and name-calling; the stubborn refusal to permit recreation parties ashore; the absurd and constantly increasing prohibitions against leaning on the rail, sleeping on deck, gum-chewing, heavy-soled shoes, that and this and that. And you will be told with damning finality that the man is vulgar, foul-mouthed. In an indelicate community this charge may appear surprising, but of all it is clearly the most strongly laid.

These are the ostensible reasons for the feeling against the Captain; and possibly, possibly not, they are the real ones. It is for a student of causative psychology to determine whether the Captain created his own situation, or whether it was born, sired by boredom and dammed by apathy, of the need for such an obsessional pastime. The only thing abundantly certain is that it is there.

Now on this slumbrous ship, this battle-ground, this bucket, there is sudden movement. Chief Johnson leans back in his chair, yawns, stretches, and gets up. He looks at his watch—0629—time to make reveille. He picks up his whistle, yawns again, and shuffles forward to the crew's compartment. Now there will be action on this torrid ship. Now the day will spring to life; now men will swarm the decks and the sounds of purposeful activity fill the air. Now at least, at reveille, this Man o' War will look the part.

Chief Johnson blows his whistle fiercely in the compartment. He starts forward and works aft among the bunks croaking in a raw, sing-song voice: "Reveille . . . Hit the deck! . . . Rise and shine! . . . Get out of them goddam sacks! . . . What the hell you trying to do, sleep your life away? . . . Reveille . . . Hit the deck! . . ." He is like a raucous minstrel, the way he chants and wanders through the compartment. Here and there an eye cocks open and looks tolerantly upon the Chief; now and then a forgiving voice mumbles sleepily, "Okay chief okay . . ." but not a body moves, not a muscle stirs.

Chief Johnson reaches the after door. He turns around for a moment and surveys the sagging bunks. He has done his job: he has observed the rules. Some of these men, he knows, will get up in half an hour to eat breakfast. Most of the rest, the ones who don't eat breakfast, will probably get up at eight. Chief Johnson walks sleepily aft and turns in in his own bunk to sleep until eight. Eight o'clock is a reasonable hour for a man's arising; and this is, above all else, a reasonable ship.

Joseph Heller

Though it draws something from each, *Catch-22* is a departure from both the comic service-life story and the large-scale, realistic portrayal of the military profession and war. Published in 1961, *Catch-22* is an explosive antiwar satire, at once funny and terrifying; grotesque and yet a true reflection of the nuclear age nightmare of war and annihilation.

The officers and men of the island-based bomber squadron in the story are, to put it mildly, broadly caricatured: Colonel Cathcart keeps raising the number of missions his men must fly in an effort to attract the attention of the editors of the *Saturday Evening Post;* Milo Minderbinder, the arch war-profiteer, eventually bombs his own squadron because the Germans offered him a favorable contract; Clevinger is crazy because he thinks the war is normal; and Yossarian is motivated only by an "insane" desire to continue living.

An important contemporary novel, *Catch-22* is an outstanding example of recent American satire.

CLEVINGER
(from *Catch-22*)

Outside the hospital the war was still going on. Men went mad and were rewarded with medals. All over the world, boys on every side of the bomb line were laying down their lives for what they had been told was their country, and no one seemed to mind, least of all the boys who were laying down their young lives. There was no end in sight. The only end in sight was Yossarian's own, and he might have remained in the hospital until doomsday had it not been for that patriotic Texan with his infundibuliform jowls and his lumpy, rumpleheaded, indestructible smile cracked forever across the front of his face like the brim of a black ten-gallon hat. The Texan wanted everybody in the ward to be happy but Yossarian and Dunbar. He was really very sick.

But Yossarian couldn't be happy, even though the Texan didn't want him to be, because outside the hospital there was still nothing funny going on. The only thing going on was a war, and no one seemed to notice but Yossarian and Dunbar. And when Yossarian tried to remind people, they drew away from him and thought *he* was crazy. Even Clevinger, who should have known better but didn't, had told him he was crazy the last time they had seen each other, which was just before Yossarian had fled into the hospital.

Clevinger had stared at him with apoplectic rage and indignation and, clawing the table with both hands, had shouted, "You're crazy!"

"Clevinger, what do you want from people?" Dunbar had replied wearily above the noises of the officers' club.

"I'm not joking," Clevinger persisted.

"They're trying to kill me," Yossarian told him calmly.

"No one's trying to kill you," Clevinger cried.

"Then why are they shooting at me?" Yossarian asked.

"They're shooting at *everyone*," Clevinger answered. "They're trying to kill everyone."

"And what difference does that make?"

Clevinger was already on the way, half out of his chair with emotion, his eyes moist and his lips quivering and pale. As always occurred when he quarreled over principles in which he believed passionately, he would end up gasping furiously for air and blinking back bitter tears of conviction. There were many principles in which Clevinger believed passionately. He was crazy.

"Who's they?" he wanted to know. "Who, specifically, do you think is trying to murder you?"

"Every one of them," Yossarian told him.

"Every one of whom?"

"Every one of whom do you think?"

"I haven't any idea."

"Then how do you know they aren't?"

"Because . . . " Clevinger sputtered, and turned speechless with frustration.

Clevinger really thought he was right, but Yossarian had proof, because strangers he didn't know shot at him with cannons every time he flew up into the air to drop bombs on them, and it wasn't funny at all. And if that wasn't funny, there were lots of things that weren't even funnier. There was nothing funny about living like a bum in a tent in Pianosa between fat mountains behind him and a placid blue sea in front that could gulp down a person with a cramp in the twinkling of an eye and ship him back to shore three days later, all charges paid, bloated, blue and putrescent, water draining out through both cold nostrils.

The tent he lived in stood right smack up against the wall of the shallow, dull-colored forest separating his own squadron from Dunbar's. Immediately alongside was the abandoned railroad ditch that carried the pipe that carried the aviation gasoline down to the fuel trucks at the airfield. Thanks to Orr, his roommate, it was the most luxurious tent in the squadron. Each time Yossarian returned from one of his holidays in the hospital or rest leaves in Rome, he was surprised by some new comfort Orr had installed in his absence—running water, wood-burning fireplace, cement floor. Yossarian had chosen the site, and he and Orr had raised the tent together. Orr, who was a grinning pygmy with pilot's wings and thick, wavy brown hair parted in the middle, furnished all the knowledge, while Yossarian, who was taller, stronger, broader and faster, did most of the work. Just the two of them lived there, although the tent was big enough for six. When summer came, Orr rolled up the side flaps to allow a breeze that never blew to flush away the air baking inside.

Immediately next door to Yossarian was Havermeyer, who liked peanut brittle and lived all by himself in the two-man tent in which he shot tiny field mice every night with huge bullets from the .45 he had stolen from the dead man in Yossarian's tent. On the other side of Havermeyer stood the tent McWatt no longer shared with Clevinger, who had still not returned when Yossarian came out of the hospital. McWatt shared his tent now with Nately, who was away in Rome courting the sleepy whore he had fallen so deeply in love with there who was bored with her work and bored with him too. McWatt was crazy. He was a pilot and flew his plane as low as he dared over Yossarian's tent as often as he could, just to see how much he could frighten him, and loved to go buzzing with a wild, close roar over the wooden raft floating on empty oil drums out past the sand bar at the immaculate white beach where the men went swimming naked. Sharing a tent with a man who was crazy wasn't easy, but Nately didn't care. He was crazy, too, and had gone every free day to work on the officers' club that Yossarian had not helped build.

Actually, there were many officers' clubs that Yossarian had not helped build, but he was proudest of the one on Pianosa. It was a sturdy and complex monument to his powers of determination. Yossarian never went there to help until it was finished; then he went there often, so pleased was he with the large, fine, rambling shingled building. It was truly a splendid structure, and Yossarian throbbed with a mighty sense of accomplishment each time he gazed at it and reflected that none of the work that had gone into it was his.

There were four of them seated together at a table in the officers' club the last time he and Clevinger had called each other crazy. They were seated in back near the crap table on which Appleby always managed to win. Appleby was as good at shooting crap as he was at playing ping-pong, and he was as good at playing ping-pong as he was at everything else. Everything Appleby did, he did well. Appleby was a fair-haired boy from Iowa who believed in God, Motherhood and the American Way of Life, without ever thinking about any of them, and everybody who knew him liked him.

"I hate that son of a bitch," Yossarian growled.

The argument with Clevinger had begun a few minutes

earlier when Yossarian had been unable to find a machine gun. It was a busy night. The bar was busy, the crap table was busy, the ping-pong table was busy. The people Yossarian wanted to machine-gun were busy at the bar singing sentimental old favorites that nobody else ever tired of. Instead of machine-gunning them, he brought his heel down hard on the ping-pong ball that came rolling toward him off the paddle of one of the two officers playing.

"That Yossarian," the two officers laughed, shaking their heads, and got another ball from the box on the shelf.

"That Yossarian," Yossarian answered them.

"Yossarian," Nately whispered cautioningly.

"You see what I mean?" asked Clevinger.

The officers laughed again when they heard Yossarian mimicking them. "That Yossarian," they said more loudly.

"That Yossarian," Yossarian echoed.

"Yossarian, please," Nately pleaded.

"You see what I mean?" asked Clevinger. "He has antisocial aggressions."

"Oh, shut up," Dunbar told Clevinger. Dunbar liked Clevinger because Clevinger annoyed him and made the time go slow.

"Appleby isn't even here," Clevinger pointed out triumphantly to Yossarian.

"Who said anything about Appleby?" Yossarian wanted to know.

"Colonel Cathcart isn't here, either."

"Who said anything about Colonel Cathcart?"

"What son of a bitch *do* you hate, then?"

"What son of a bitch *is* here?"

"I'm not going to argue with you," Clevinger decided. "You don't know who you hate."

"Whoever's trying to poison me," Yossarian told him.

"Nobody's trying to poison you."

"They poisoned my food twice, didn't they? Didn't they put poison in my food during Ferrara and during the Great Big Siege of Bologna?"

"They put poison in *everybody's* food," Clevinger explained.

"And what difference does *that* make?"

"And it wasn't even poison!" Clevinger cried heatedly, growing more emphatic as he grew more confused.

As far back as Yossarian could recall, he explained to Clevinger with a patient smile, somebody was always hatching a plot to kill him. There were people who cared for him and people who didn't, and those who didn't hated him and were out to get him. They hated him because he was Assyrian. But they couldn't touch him, he told Clevinger, because he had a sound mind in a pure body and was as strong as an ox. They couldn't touch him because he was Tarzan, Mandrake, Flash Gordon. He was Bill Shakespeare. He was Cain, Ulysses, the Flying Dutchman; he was Lot in Sodom, Deirdre of the Sorrows, Sweeney in the nightingales among trees. He was miracle ingredient Z-247. He was—

"Crazy!" Clevinger interrupted, shrieking. "That's what you are! Crazy!"

"—immense. I'm a real, slam-bang, honest-to-goodness, three-fisted humdinger. I'm a bona fide supraman."

"Superman?" Clevinger cried. "Superman?"

"Supraman," Yossarian corrected.

"Hey, fellas, cut it out," Nately begged with embarrassment. "Everybody's looking at us."

"You're crazy," Clevinger shouted vehemently, his eyes filling with tears. "You've got a Jehovah complex."

"I think everyone is Nathaniel."

Clevinger arrested himself in mid-declamation, suspiciously. "Who's Nathaniel?"

"Nathaniel who?" inquired Yossarian innocently.

Clevinger skirted the trap neatly. "You think everybody is Jehovah. You're no better than Raskolnikov—"

"Who?"

"—yes, Raskolnikov, who—"

"Raskolnikov!"

"—who—I mean it—who felt he could justify killing an old woman—"

"No better than?"

"—yes, justify, that's right—with an ax! And I can prove it to you!" Gasping furiously for air, Clevinger enumerated Yossarian's symptoms: an unreasonable belief that everybody around him was crazy, a homicidal impulse to machine-gun strangers, retrospective falsification, an unfounded suspicion that people hated him and were conspiring to kill him.

But Yossarian knew he was right, because, as he explained to Clevinger, to the best of his knowledge he had never been wrong. Everywhere he looked was a nut, and it was all a sensible young gentleman like himself could do to maintain his perspective amid so much madness. And it was urgent that he did, for he knew his life was in peril.

Yossarian eyed everyone he saw warily when he returned to the squadron from the hospital. Milo was away, too, in Smyrna for the fig harvest. The mess hall ran smoothly in Milo's absence. Yossarian had responded ravenously to the pungent aroma of spicy lamb while he was still in the cab of the ambulance bouncing down along the knotted road that lay like a broken suspender between the hospital and the squadron. There was shish-kabob for lunch, huge, savory hunks of spitted meat sizzling like the devil over charcoal after marinating seventy-two hours in a secret mixture Milo had stolen from a crooked trader in the Levant, served with Iranian rice and asparagus tips Parmesan, followed by cherries jubilee for dessert and then steaming cups of fresh coffee with Benedictine and brandy. The meal was served in enormous helpings on damask tablecloths by the skilled Italian waiters Major —— de Coverley had kidnaped from the mainland and given to Milo.

Yossarian gorged himself in the mess hall until he thought he would explode and then sagged back in a contented stupor, his mouth filmy with a succulent residue. None of the officers in the squadron had ever eaten so well as they ate regularly in Milo's mess hall, and Yossarian wondered awhile if it wasn't perhaps all worth it. But then he burped and remembered that they were trying to kill him, and he sprinted out of the mess hall wildly and ran looking for Doc Daneeka to have himself taken off combat duty and sent home. He found Doc Daneeka in sunlight, sitting on a high stool outside his tent.

"Fifty missions," Doc Daneeka told him, shaking his head. "The colonel wants fifty missions."

"But I've only got forty-four!"

Doc Daneeka was unmoved. He was a sad, birdlike man with the spatulate face and scrubbed, tapering features of a well-groomed rat.

"Fifty missions," he repeated, still shaking his head. "The colonel wants fifty missions."

THE BLACK AND
THE WHITE

". . . it appeared to me that the greatest and best feelings of the human heart were paralyzed by the relative positions of the slave and owner."

MRS. FRANCES TROLLOPE, *Domestic Manners of the Americans*

The Black and the White

*I*t is hard to imagine what kind of a country the United States would have become had not the "peculiar institution" of Negro slavery taken root in the South.

Huck Finn would be forever rafting down the Mississippi alone, without Nigger Jim.

Abraham Lincoln would not have issued the Emancipation Proclamation declaring the slave ". . . thenceforward, and forever free," or spoken the Gettysburg Address.

Hollywood would not have searched for anyone to play Scarlett O'Hara.

Most of our music would sound strange to our ears.

Until recently, most satire relating to the American Negro has been written by white writers for white audiences, and, with some exceptions, has been of the "respectable" kind that doesn't mean any harm—or any good either. However, during the Abolition-movement period and the Civil War, the Negro figures in satires for and against the idea of white supremacy.

In the past, formal literature by Negro writers, intended for an interracial audience, has avoided the satiric voice, with its implication of complicity between the writer and his audience. Today, however, some Negro writers (as well as such perform-

ers as Dick Gregory) *address satire to a general audience. Their
work is of particular value, for such satire is an effective short-
cut to understanding.*

James Russell Lowell

The Biglow Papers (from which "The Candidate's Letter"
[page 84] was taken) provide an outstanding example of the
use of comic satire as propaganda. As a young man, Lowell
was a fervent abolitionist and, like most New Englanders,
opposed to the Mexican War, which promised to increase the
area of slavery territory. Through his characterizations of
Hosea Biglow, his father Ezekiel and the Reverend Homer
Wilber, Lowell ridiculed pro-slavery politics and the expansionist movement.

Chief among slavery's apologists was John C. Calhoun, who
stood firmly on the Constitution's specific toleration of human
bondage (particularly in providing that the states should
participate in the return of fugitive slaves) and defended the
"Peculiar Institution" as a positive good.

The following verses were suggested to Lowell by an actual
debate following an Abolitionist attempt to arouse sympathy in
Congress for the cause of two men, Drayton and Sayres, who
unsuccessfully had tried to free some seventy-seven slaves. The
reactions from the states'-rights forces, led by Calhoun, were
violent and immediate.

The other senators in the dispute are: Henry Stuart Foote of
Mississippi, who denounced any attempt of Congress to inter-
fere on the slavery issue as "a nefarious attempt to commit
grand larceny"; Willie P. Mangum of North Carolina; Lewis
Cass, formerly Jackson's Secretary of War, then Senator from
Michigan and Democratic nominee for the Presidency; Jefferson Davis, then, with Foote, a Senator from Mississippi; Edward A. Hannegan of Indiana, an aggressive champion of expansion; Spencer Jarnagin of Tennessee; Charles G. Atherton
of New Hampshire; W. T. Colquitt of Georgia; Reverdy Johnson from Maryland; James D. Wescott of Florida; Dixon H.
Lewis of Alabama.

JOHN C. CALHOUN STANDS ON THE CONSTITUTION
(from *The Biglow Papers*, 1846–1848)

Here we stan' on the Constitution, by thunder!
 It's a fact o' wich ther's bushils o' proofs;
Fer how could we trample on't so, I wonder,
 Ef 't worn't thet it's ollers under our hoofs?"
  Sez John C. Calhoun, sez he;
  "Human rights hain't no more
  Right to come on this floor,
 No more'n the man in the moon," sez he.

"The North hain't no kind o' bisness with nothin',
 An' you've no idee how much bother it saves;
We ain't none riled by their frettin' an' frothin',
 We're *used* to layin' the string on our slaves,"
  Sez John C. Calhoun, sez he;—
  Sez Mister Foote,
  "I should like to shoot
 The holl gang, by the gret horn spoon!" sez he.

"Freedom's Keystone is Slavery, thet ther's no doubt
   on,
 It's sutthin' thet's—wha' d' ye call it?—divine,—
An' the slaves thet we ollers *make* the most out on
 Air them north o' Mason an' Dixon's line,"
  Sez John C. Calhoun, sez he;—
  "Fer all thet," sez Mangum,
  " 'T would be better to hang 'em,
 An' so git red on 'em soon," sez he.

"The mass ough' to labor an' we lay on soffies,
 Thet's the reason I want to spread Freedom's aree;

It puts all the cunninest on us in office,
    An' reelises our Maker's orig'nal idee,"
Sez John C. Calhoun, sez he;—
    "Thet's ez plain," sez Cass,
    "Ez thet some one's an ass,
    It's ez clear ez the sun is at noon," sez he.

"Now don't go to say I'm the friend of oppression,
    But keep all your spare breath fer coolin' your
        broth,
Fer I ollers hev strove (at least thet's my impression)
    To make cussed free with the rights o' the North,"
Sez John C. Calhoun, sez he;—
    "Yes," sez Davis o' Miss.,
    "The perfection o' bliss
    Is in skinnin' thet same old coon," sez he.

"Slavery's a thing thet depends on complexion,
    It's God's law thet fetters on black skins don't
        chafe;
Ef brains wuz to settle it (horrid reflection!)
    Wich of our onnable body'd be safe?"
Sez John C. Calhoun, sez he;—
    Sez Mister Hannegan,
    Afore he began agin,
    "Thet exception is quite oppertoon," sez he.

"Gen'nle Cass, Sir, you need n't be twitchin' your
        collar,
    Your merit's quite clear by the dut on your knees,
At the North we don't make no distinctions o' color;
    You can all take a lick at our shoes wen you
        please,"
Sez John C. Calhoun, sez he;—
    Sez Mister Jarnagin,
    "They wun't hev to larn agin,
    They all on 'em know the old toon," sez he.

"The slavery question ain't no ways bewilderin',
    North an' South hev one int'rest, it's plain to a
        glance;
No'thern men, like us patriarchs, don't sell their
        childrin,
    But they *du* sell themselves, ef they git a good
        chance,"
      Sez John C. Calhoun, sez he;—
        Sez Atherton here,
        "This is gittin' severe,
    I wish I could dive like a loon," sez he.

"It'll break up the Union, this talk about freedom,
    An' your fact'ry gals (soon ez we split) 'll make
        head,
An' gittin' some Miss chief or other to lead 'em,
    'll go to work raisin' permiscoous Ned,"
      Sez John C. Calhoun, sez he;—
      "Yes, the North," sez Colquitt,
      "Ef we Southeners all quit,
    Would go down like a busted balloon," sez he.

"Jest look wut is doin', wut annyky's brewin'
    In the beautiful clime o' the olive an' vine,
All the wise aristoxy's a tumblin' to ruin,
    An' the sankylots drorin' an' drinkin' their wine,"
      Sez John C. Calhoun, sez he;—
      "Yes," sez Johnson, "in France
      They're beginnin' to dance
    Beëlzebub's own rigadoon," sez he.

"The South's safe enough, it don't feel a mite skeery,
    Our slaves in their darkness an' dut air tu blest
Not to welcome with proud hallylugers the ery
    Wen our eagle kicks yourn from the naytional
        nest,"
      Sez John C. Calhoun, sez he;—

"Oh," sez Westcott o' Florida,
"Wut treason is horrider
Then our priv'leges tryin' to proon?" sez he.

"It's 'coz they're so happy, thet, wen crazy sarpints
Stick their nose in our bizness, we git so darned
riled;
We think it's our dooty to give pooty sharp hints,
Thet the last crumb of Edin on airth shan't be
spiled,"
Sez John C. Calhoun, sez he;—
"Ah," sez Dixon H. Lewis,
"It perfectly true is
Thet slavery's airth's grettest boon," sez he.

Orpheus C. Kerr
(Robert Henry Newell)

Among the various solutions proposed to solve the "Negro
Question" was deportation of the Negroes. Depending on the
turn of mind of the proponent of the plan, deportation was to be
voluntary or involuntary; the Negroes were to be returned to
Africa, whence they had come, or sent elsewhere. The following
portion of Letter LXII, dated August 15, 1862, from the
Orpheus C. Kerr Papers, is a memorable satire on white benevo-
lence.

SCHEME FOR THE BENEFIT OF THE BLACK RACE
(from *The Orpheus C. Kerr Papers*, 1862–1871)

The other day, I went down to Accomac again, to see the
General of the Mackerel Brigade, who had invited me to be
present while he made an offer of bliss to a delegation from that
oppressed race which has been the sole cause of this unnatural
war, and is, therefore, exempted from all concern in it.

The General, my boy, was seated in his temporary room of audience when I arrived, examining a map of the Border States through a powerful magnifying-glass, and occasionally looking into a tumbler, as though he expected to find something there.

"Well, old Honesty," says I, affably, "what is our next scheme for the benefit of the human race?"

He smiled paternally upon me, and says he:

"It is my purpose to settle the Negro Question in accordance with the principles laid down in the Book of Exodus. Thunder!" says the General, with magisterial emphasis, "if we do not secure the pursuit of happiness to the slave, even, we violate the Constitution and become obnoxious to the Border communities."

I was reflecting upon this remark, my boy, and wondering what the Constitution had to do with the Book of Exodus, when the delegation made its appearance, and caused the room to darken perceptibly. Not to lose time, the General waved his hand for the visitors to be seated, and, says he:

"You and we are different races, and for this reason it must be evident to you, as well as to myself, that it is better you should be voluntarily compelled to colonize some distant but salubrious shore. There is a wide difference between our races; much wider, perhaps, than that which exists between any other two races. Your race suffers very greatly, and our race suffers in suffering your race to suffer. In a word, we both suffer, which establishes a reason why our race should not suffer your race to remain here any longer. You who are here are all present, I suppose."

A voice—"Yes, sah."

"Perhaps you have not been here all your lives. Your race is suffering the greatest wrong that ever was; but when you cease to suffer, your sufferings are still far from an equality with our sufferings. Our white men are now changing their base of operations daily, and often taking Malvern Hills. This is on your account. You are the cause of it. How you have caused it I will not attempt to explain, for I do not know; but it is better for us both to be separated, and it is vilely selfish in you (I do not speak unkindly) to wish to remain here in preference to going to Nova Zembla. The fact that we have always oppressed you

renders you still more blameable, especially when we reflect
upon the fact that you have never shown resistance. A trip on
your part to Nova Zembla will benefit both races. I cannot
promise you much bliss right away. You may starve at first, or
die on the passage; but in the Revolutionary War General
Washington lived exclusively on the future. He was benefit-
ting his race; and though I do not see much similarity between
his case and yours, you had better go to Nova Zembla. You
may think that you could live in Washington, perhaps more so
than you could on a foreign shore. This is a mistake. None but
white army contractors and brigadiers on furlough can live
here.

"The festive isle of Nova Zembla has been in existence for
some time, and is larger than any smaller place I know of.
Many of the original settlers have died, and their offspring
would still be living had they lived long enough to become
accustomed to the climate. You may object to go on account of
your affection for our race, but it does not strike me that there
is any cogent reason for such affection. So you had better go
to Nova Zembla. The particular place I have in view for your
colonization is the great highway between the North Pole and Sir
John Franklin's supposed grave. It is a popular route of travel,
being much frequented by the facetious penguin and the flowing seal. It has great resources for ice-water, and you will be
able to have ice cream every day, provided you supply yourselves with the essence of lemon and patent freezers. As to
other food, I can promise you nothing. There are fine harbors
on all sides of this place, and though you may see no ships there,
it will be still some satisfaction to know that you have such
admirable harbors. Again, there is evidence of very rich bear-
hunting. When you take your wives and families to a place
where there is no food, nor any ground to be cultivated, nor any
place to live in, then the human mind would as naturally turn
to bear-hunting as to anything else. But if you should die of
starvation at the outset, even bear-hunting may dwindle into
insignificance. Why I attach so much importance to bear-
hunting is, it will afford you an opportunity to die more easily

than by famine and exposure. Bear-hunting is the best thing
I know of under such circumstances.

"You are intelligent, and know that human life depends as
much upon those who possess it as upon anybody else. And
much will depend upon yourselves if you go to Nova Zembla.
As to the bear-hunting, I think I see the means available for
engaging you in that very soon without injury to ourselves. I
wish to spend a little money to get you there, and may possibly
lose it all; but we cannot expect to succeed in anything if we
are not successful in it.

"The political affairs of Nova Zembla are not in quite such a
condition as I could wish, the bears having occasional fights
there, over the body of the last Esquimaux governor; but these
bears are more generous than we are. They have no objection to
dining upon the colored race.

"Besides, I would endeavor to have you made equals, and have
the best assurance that you should be equals of the best. The
practical thing I want to ascertain is, whether I can get a certain
number of able-bodied men to send to a place offering such encouragement and attractions. Could I get a hundred tolerably
intelligent men, with their wives and children, to partake of all
this bliss? Can I have fifty? If I had twenty-five able-bodied men,
properly seasoned with women and children, I could make a
commencement.

"These are subjects of very great importance, and worthy of a
month's study of the paternal offer I have made you. If you
have no consideration for yourselves, at least consider the bears,
and endeavor to reconcile yourselves to the beautiful and pleasing little hymn of childhood, commencing:

> 'I would not live always;
> I ask not to stay.' "

At the termination of this flattering and paternal address, my
boy, the delegation took their hats and commenced to leave in
very deep silence; thereby proving that persons of African
descent are utterly insensible of kindness and much inferior to
the race at present practising strategy on this continent.

Colonization, my boy, involves a scheme of human happiness so entirely beyond the human power of conception, that the conception of it will almost pass for something inhuman.

Yours, utopianically,

ORPHEUS C. KERR

Petroleum V. Nasby
(David Ross Locke)

The Fourteenth Constitutional Amendment, proposed by the Northern "Radicals," provided that former slaves were citizens and that as citizens they had equal rights under the laws of the land. Petroleum Nasby, in characteristic fashion, reflects the reactions to the Amendment on the part of unreconstructed Copperhead forces in Ohio.

The "succession of Wade" refers to the fact that had President Johnson been removed by impeachment, the Presidency would have fallen to the president of the Senate, Ben Wade of Ohio, a leading Radical. "Vallandygum" is Clement L. Vallandigham, leader of the Copperheads (Northern Democrats sympathetic to the Confederacy), who was imprisoned under Lincoln's proclamation of 1862, which denied the protection of habeas corpus to persons "guilty of any disloyal practice affording aid and comfort to rebels." Naturally, Vallandigham is one of Nasby's "heroes."

MR. NASBY ASSISTS IN THE OHIO ELECTION
(1867)

POST OFFIS, CONFEDRIT X ROADS
(Wich is in the Stait uv Kentucky),
October 12, 1867.

Feelin that the time hed arrived which wuz to decide whether 7,000 degradid niggers wuz to grind 500,000 proud Caucashens into the dust, I felt that ef I shood fail in my dooty now,

I shood be forever disgraced. Accordingly, I put in on elekshun day at a Dimocratic town in Ohio—the battlefield—the identikle place into wich I made a speech doorin the campane.

I arrived ther on the mornin uv the elekshun, and found that comperhensive arrangements hed bin made for defeatin this most nefarus and dangerous proposishen. Paradin the streets ez early ez 7 A.M. wuz a wagon containin 25 virgins, runnin from 27 to 31, the most uv em ruther wiry in texture, and over their heads wuz banners, with the followin techin inscriptions: "Fathers, save us from Nigger Ekality!" "White Husbans or nun!" It wood hev bin better, I thot, hed they bin somewhat younger. Ther wuz suthin preposterous in the ijea uv females uv that age callin upon fathers to save em from anythin, when in the course of nacher their fathers must hev bin a lyin in the silent tomb for several consecutive years, onless, indeed, they marrid young. Ef still livin (I judged from the aged appearance uv the damsels), their parents must be too far advanced in yeers to take an activ part in biznis. In anuther wagon wuz a collekshun uv men wich hed bin hired from the railrode, twelve miles distant, whose banners read, "Shel ignerent Niggers vote beside intelligint Wite men?" and the follerin verse:—

> "Shel niggers black this land possess,
> And rool us whites up here?
> O, no, my friends; we ruther guess
> We'll never stand that ere."

It okkurd to me that it wood hev done better hed their spellin bin more akkerit; but upon inquiry I found that it didn't make no diffrence. That wuz the pervailin way of spellin things in that vicinity. Hangin over the polls wuz a broad peece uv white muslin, onto wich was painted, in large letters, "Caucashuns, Respeck yer Noses—the nigger stinks!" Then I knowed it wuz safe. That odor hez never yet bin resisted by the Democrasy, and it hez its inflooence over Republikins.

I never saw sich enthoosiasm, or more cheerin indicasuns uv the pride uv race. Ez evidence uv the deep feeling that pervaded that community, I state that nine paupers in the poorhouse demanded to be taken to the polls, that they might enter their protest agin bringin the nigger up to a ekality with em, wich wuz nine gain with no offsets, ez ther wuzn't an Ablishnist in the institooshun. Two men, in the county jale for petty larceny, wuz, at their own rekest, taken out of doorance vile by the Sheriff uv the county, that they mite, by the ballot, protest agin bein degraded by bein compelled, when their time wuz out, to acknowledge the nigger ez their ekal. One enthoosiastic Dimekrat, who cost us $5, hed to be carried to the polls. He hed commenced early at one uv the groseries, and hed succumbd afore votin. We found him sleepin peacefully in a barn. We lifted the patriotic man, and in percession marched to the polls. We stood him on his feet, two men supportin him—one on either side. I put a straight ticket into his fingers, and takin his wrist with one hand, held his fingers together with tother, and guided his hand to the box. Ez it neared the winder, he started ez ef a electric shock hed struck him, and, straightenin up, asked, "Is it the sthrate ticket? Is Constooshnel Amindmint No! onto it?"

Ashoorin him that it wuz all rite, he suffered me to hold his hand out to the Judge uv Eleckshun, who took the ballot and deposited it in the box. "Thank Hivin!" sed he, "the nagur is not yet my ayquil!" and doublin up at the thigh and knee-joints, he sank, limber-like, and gently, onto the ground. Ez he hed discharged the dooty uv an Amerikin freeman, we rolled him out to one side uv the house, wher the drippin uv the rain from the roof wood do suthin toward soberin him off, and left him alone in his glory.

The Amendment got but a very few votes in that locality. The Republikins jined us in repudiatin it, mostly upon ethno-logikle grounds. One asserted that he hed bin in favor uv emancipashen in time uv war, becoz the Afrikin cood thereby be indoost to fite agin their Southern masters, and it wood hev the effeck uv makin the drafts come lighter in his township. He wuz a humanitarian likewise. He opposed crooelty toward em. He wept when he heerd uv the massacre at Fort Piller, becoz in the army the nigger wuz ez much a man ez anybody, and sich wholesale slaughters tendid to make calls for "500,- 000 more" more frekent. But when it come to givin uv em the privilege uv votin beside him, it coodent be thot uv. He cood never consent that a race whose heels wuz longer than hizzen shood rool Ameriky. "My God!" sed this ardent Republikin, "ef you give em the ballot, wat kin prevent em from bein Congrismen, Senators, Vice-Presidents, and even Presidents? I shudder when I think uv it;" and he hurried in his vote.

I didn't quite see the force uv his objecshen, for it never okkurred to me that bein sent to Congris wuz the nateral consekence uv votin. I hev voted for thirty years, at many elections four or five times, but I hev never bin to Congris. Wher is the constitooency wich wood elect me? But it wuzn't my biznis to controvert his posishen. It made no diffrence to me wat his reason wuz for votin ez I desired him to vote.

The nigger-lovers beat up one man to vote for the Amendment, wich, I saw by his dissatisfied look, hed bin overperswadid. "Sir!" sed I, "do yoo consider a Afrikin suffishently intelligent to be trustid with so potent a weapon ez the ballot?"

Bustin away from them wich hed him in charge, he exclaimed, "No, I don't! I can't vote for it. They ain't intelligent enuff. Sir, scratch off the 'Yes' from my ballot, and put onto it 'No!'"

"Here is a pensil," sed I.

"Do it yerself," sed he; "I can't write."

And I did it. Sich is the effeck uv a word in season. Words fitly spoken is apples uv gold, set in picters uv silver.

One man woodent listen to me, but votid the Amendment. He hed bin a soljer, and for eleven months pertook uv the hospitality uv the Confedrits at Andersonville. Escapin, he wuz helped to the Fedrel lines by a nigger, who wuz flogged almost to death, in his site, for not betrayin wher he wuz hid. I mite ez well hev talked to a lamp-post. Ez he shoved in his ballot, he remarkt suthin about he'd ruther see a nigger vote than a d—d rebel, any time. From the direckshun uv his eye-site, I persoom he referred to me.

I left for home ez soon ez the votes wuz counted, and the result wuz made known, only waitin till the poll-books wuz made out, and the judges uv eleckshun hed got ther names written by the clerks, and hed made their marks to em. On my

way home I wuz gratified to see how the nateral antipathy to
the nigger hed revived. At Cincinati, the nite uv the eleckshn,
they wuz bangin uv em about, the patriotic Democrisy goin for
em wherever they cood find em, and the next day, ez I saw em at
the ralerode stashens, they hed, generally speekin, ther heds
bandaged. It wuz cheerin to me, and I gloated over it.

Full of gladnis, I entered Kentucky, and joyfully I wendid
my way to the Corners. I wuz the bearer uv tidins uv great joy,
and my feet wuz pleasant onto the mountains. Ez I walked into
Bascom's, they all saw in my face suthin uv importance.

"Wat is it?" sed Deekin Pogram. "Is it weal or woe?"

"Is the proud Caucashen still in the ascendant in Ohio, or
hez the grovelin Afrikin ground him into the dust?" askt Issaker
Gavitt.

"My friend," sed I, takin up the Deekin's whisky, wich, in
the eggscitement uv the moment, he didn't observe, "the Con-
stitooshnel Amendment, givin the nigger ekal rites, hez bin
voted down by the liberty-lovin freemen uv Ohio. Three cheers
for Ohio."

They wuz given with a will. The wildest enthoosiasm wuz
awakened. Bascom put a spigot in a fresh barl, and the church
bells wuz set a ringin. The niggers wore a dismayed look, and
got out uv the way ez soon ez possible. A meetin wuz towunst
organized. Deekin Pogram spoke. He felt that this wuz a proud
day. Light wuz breakin. The dark clouds uv fanaticism wuz
breakin away. We hed now the Afrikin under our feet. We
hev got him in his normal posishen in Ohio, and, please
God, we will soon hev him likewise in Kentucky. He moved
the adopshen uv the follerin resolooshens: —

"Wareas, Noer cust Canan, and condemned him to be a
servant unto his brethren, thereby cleerly indikatin the status
uv the race for all time to come to be one uv inferiority; and,

"Wareas, To further show to the eyes uv the most obtoose
that a diffrence wuz intended, the Almighty gave the nigger a
diffrent anatomicle struckter, for full partikelars uv wich see
the speeches uv the Demokratic stumpers doorin the late campaign; and,

"WAREAS, The attempt to place the nigger on an ekality with the white in votin ez well ez taxashun, we consider the sappin uv the very foundashun uv civil liberty, ez well ez uv the Crischen religion; therefore,

"*Resolved*, That the Constooshnel and Biblikle Democracy uv Kentucky send greetin to their brethren uv Ohio, with thanks for their prompt and effectooal squelchin uv the idea uv nigger superiority.

"*Resolved*, That to the Republikins uv Ohio, who, risin above party considerashuns, voted agin suffrage, our thanks is due, and we congratulate em that now they, ez well ez us, are saved from the danger uv marryin niggers; and likewise do we asshoor em, that in a spirit uv mutual forbearance, we care not wat particular creed they perfess, so long ez they vote our principles.

"*Resolved*, That the will uv the people havin bin cleerly indikated, we demand the insershun uv the word 'white' in the Coonstitooshun uv the Yoonited States.

"*Resolved*, That we ask the colored voters uv Tennessee, and other States where colored men hev votes, to observe how they are treated in Ohio, where the Ablishnists don't need em. In them States we extend to em a corjel invitashun to act with us.

"*Resolved*, That a copy uv these resolooshens be sent to President Johnson, with an ashoorance uv our unabated confidence in his integrity, patriotism, and modisty."

The meetin broke up with three cheers for the Dimocracy uv Ohio, nine for the Republikins uv that State, and one for the State at large.

The Fakulty uv the Institoot met next mornin, for the purpus uv revisin the Scripters. It wuz desided that the word "white" should be insertid wherever necessary, and that that edishen only be yoosed by the Dimocracy and Conservativ Republikins. We made progress, the follerin bein a few uv the changes: —

" 'So God creatid a *white* man in his own image.'

" 'Whosoever, therefore, shell confess me before *white* men,' &c.

" 'Suffer little *white* children to come unto me, for uv sich is the kingdom uv Heaven.' "

Wich last is comfortin, ez it shows that the distincshen is kept up through all eternity. I give these merely ez samples. We shel hev it finisht in a few days, and, ef funds kin be raised, shel publish it. Sich a vershun uv the Skripters is needid.

I find the Demekratic mind is exercised over the question uv the succession to Wade. My voice is for Vallandygum. Never wuz there sich a saint, never wuz ther a man so abused by the tyranikel minions of irresponsible power. He hez suffered for us, and now he must hev his reward. It hez bin urged that the ten cent colleckshun in 1863 was suffishent pay for his marter-dom. I deny it. I know all about it. He got nothin uv it. Every Demekrat in Ohio who hed taxes to pay, or who wanted a new pare uv pants, or whose boots needed half solin, took up a col-leckshun for Vallandygum. I know that's so, for I wuz a Deme-krat in Ohio, laborin under pekooniary embarasments in them days myself. Let Vallandygum hev the place he so well earned.

PETROLEUM V. NASBY, P. M.

(Wich is Postmaster).

Ralph Ellison

INVISIBLE MAN
(from *Invisible Man*)

I am an invisible man. No, I am not a spook like those who haunted Edgar Allan Poe; nor am I one of your Hollywood-movie ectoplasms. I am a man of substance, of flesh and bone, fiber and liquids—and I might even be said to possess a mind. I am invisible, understand, simply because people refuse to see me. Like the bodiless heads you see sometimes in circus side-shows, it is as though I have been surrounded by mirrors of

hard, distorting glass. When they approach me they see only
my surroundings, themselves, or figments of their imagination
—indeed, everything and anything except me.

Nor is my invisibility exactly a matter of a bio-chemical
accident to my epidermis. That invisibility to which I refer
occurs because of a peculiar disposition of the eyes of those with
whom I come in contact. A matter of the construction of their
inner eyes, those eyes with which they look through their physical eyes upon reality. I am not complaining, nor am I protesting
either. It is sometimes advantageous to be unseen, although it is
most often rather wearing on the nerves. Then too, you're constantly being bumped against by those of poor vision. Or again,
you often doubt if you really exist. You wonder whether you
aren't simply a phantom in other people's minds. Say, a figure in
a nightmare which the sleeper tries with all his strength to
destroy. It's when you feel like this that, out of resentment, you
begin to bump people back. And, let me confess, you feel that
way most of the time. You ache with the need to convince yourself that you do exist in the real world, that you're a part of all
the sound and anguish, and you strike out with your fists, you
curse and you swear to make them recognize you. And, alas,
it's seldom successful.

One night I accidentally bumped into a man, and perhaps
because of the near darkness he saw me and called me an insulting name. I sprang at him, seized his coat lapels and demanded that he apologize. He was a tall blond man, and as my
face came close to his he looked insolently out of his blue eyes
and cursed me, his breath hot in my face as he struggled. I
pulled his chin down sharp upon the crown of my head, butting
him as I had seen the West Indians do, and I felt his flesh
tear and the blood gush out, and I yelled, "Apologize! Apologize!" But he continued to curse and struggle, and I butted him
again and again until he went down heavily, on his knees,
profusely bleeding. I kicked him repeatedly, in a frenzy because he still uttered insults though his lips were frothy with
blood. Oh yes, I kicked him! And in my outrage I got out my
knife and prepared to slit his throat, right there beneath the
lamplight in the deserted street, holding him by the collar with

one hand, and opening the knife with my teeth—when it occurred to me that the man had not *seen* me, actually; that he, as far as he knew, was in the midst of a walking nightmare! And I stopped the blade, slicing the air as I pushed him away, letting him fall back to the street. I stared at him hard as the lights of a car stabbed through the darkness. He lay there, moaning on the asphalt; a man almost killed by a phantom. It unnerved me. I was both disgusted and ashamed. I was like a drunken man myself, wavering about on weakened legs. Then I was amused. Something in this man's thick head had sprung out and beaten him within an inch of his life. I began to laugh at this crazy discovery. Would he have awakened at the point of death? Would Death himself have freed him for wakeful living? But I didn't linger. I ran away into the dark, laughing so hard I feared I might rupture myself. The next day I saw his picture in the *Daily News*, beneath a caption stating that he had been "mugged." Poor fool, poor blind fool, I thought with sincere compassion, mugged by an invisible man!

Most of the time (although I do not choose as I once did to deny the violence of my days by ignoring it) I am not so overtly violent. I remember that I am invisible and walk softly so as not to awaken the sleeping ones. Sometimes it is best not to awaken them; there are few things in the world as dangerous as sleepwalkers. I learned in time though that it is possible to carry on a fight against them without their realizing it. For instance, I have been carrying on a fight with Monopolated Light & Power for some time now. I use their service and pay them nothing at all, and they don't know it. Oh, they suspect that power is being drained off, but they don't know where. All they know is that according to the master meter back there in their power station a hell of a lot of free current is disappearing somewhere into the jungle of Harlem. The joke, of course, is that I don't live in Harlem but in a border area. Several years ago (before I discovered the advantage of being invisible) I went through the routine process of buying service and paying their outrageous rates. But no more. I gave up all that, along with my apartment, and my old way of life: That way based upon the fallacious assumption that I, like other men, was visible. Now, aware of my invisibility, I live rent-free in a building rented strictly to whites, in a section of the basement that was shut off and forgotten during the nineteenth century, which I discovered when I was trying to escape in the night from Ras the Destroyer. But that's getting too far ahead of the story, almost to the end, although the end is in the beginning and lies far ahead.

The point now is that I found a home—or a hole in the ground, as you will. Now don't jump to the conclusion that because I call my home a "hole" it is damp and cold like a grave; there are cold holes and warm holes. Mine is a warm hole. And remember, a bear retires to his hole for the winter and lives until spring; then he comes strolling out like the Easter chick breaking from its shell. I say all this to assure you that it is incorrect to assume that, because I'm invisible and live in a hole, I am dead. I am neither dead nor in a state of suspended animation. Call me Jack-the-Bear, for I am in a state of hibernation.

My hole is warm and full of light. Yes, *full* of light. I doubt if there is a brighter spot in all New York than this hole of mine, and I do not exclude Broadway. Or the Empire State Building on a photographer's dream night. But that is taking advantage of you. Those two spots are among the darkest of our whole civilization—pardon me, our whole *culture* (an important distinction, I've heard)—which might sound like a hoax, or a contradiction, but that (by contradiction, I mean) is how the world moves: Not like an arrow, but a boomerang. (Beware of those who speak of the *spiral* of history; they are preparing a boomerang. Keep a steel helmet handy.) I know; I have been boomeranged across my head so much that I now can see the darkness of lightness. And I love light. Perhaps you'll think it strange that an invisible man should need light, desire light, love light. But maybe it is exactly because I *am* invisible. Light confirms my reality, gives birth to my form. A beautiful girl once told me of a recurring nightmare in which she lay in the center of a large dark room and felt her face expand until it filled the whole room, becoming a formless mass while her eyes ran in bilious jelly up the chimney. And so it is with me. Without light I am not only invisible, but formless as well; and to be unaware of one's form is to live a death. I myself, after existing some twenty years, did not become alive until I discovered my invisibility.

That is why I fight my battle with Monopolated Light & Power. The deeper reason, I mean: It allows me to feel my vital aliveness. I also fight them for taking so much of my money before I learned to protect myself. In my hole in the basement there are exactly 1,369 lights. I've wired the entire ceiling, every inch of it. And not with fluorescent bulbs, but with the older, more-expensive-to-operate kind, the filament type. An act of sabotage, you know. I've already begun to wire the wall. A junk man I know, a man of vision, has supplied me with wire and sockets. Nothing, storm or flood, must get in the way of our need for light and ever more and brighter light. The truth is the light and light is the truth. When I finish all four walls, then I'll start on the floor. Just how that will go, I don't know. Yet when you have lived invisible as long as I have you develop a certain ingenuity. I'll solve the problem. And maybe I'll invent a gadget to place my coffeepot on the fire while I lie in bed, and even invent a gadget to warm my bed—like the fellow I saw in one of the picture magazines who made himself a gadget to warm his shoes! Though invisible, I am in the great American tradition of tinkers. That makes me kin to Ford, Edison and Franklin. Call me, since I have a theory and a concept, a "thinker-tinker." Yes, I'll warm my shoes; they need it, they're usually full of holes. I'll do that and more.

Harry Golden

As is well known to the millions who have read his books—
Only in America and *For 2¢ Plain*—Harry Golden publishes
the *Carolina Isrealite*, a monthly newspaper written entirely
by Mr. Golden without the aid of syndicated features, comic
strips, or news wire services. Mr. Golden simply says what he
has on his mind, entertainingly and—when the occasion demands—satirically. The famous Golden Vertical Negro Plan is

an example of an almost extinct breed of newspaper satire, the trick of which is to make the reader open his eyes before he cancels his subscription.

THE VERTICAL NEGRO PLAN
(from *Only in America*)

Those who love North Carolina will jump at the chance to share in the great responsibility confronting our Governor and the State Legislature. A special session of the Legislature (July 25–28, 1956) passed a series of amendments to the State Constitution. These proposals submitted by the Governor and his Advisory Education Committee included the following:

(A) The elimination of the compulsory attendance law, "to prevent any child from being forced to attend a school with a child of another race."

(B) The establishment of "Education Expense Grants" for education in a private school, "in the case of a child assigned to a public school attended by a child of another race."

(C) A "uniform system of local option" whereby a majority of the folks in a school district may suspend or close a school if the situation becomes "intolerable."

But suppose a Negro child applies for this "Education Expense Grant" and says he wants to go to the private school too? There are fourteen Supreme Court decisions involving the use of public funds; there are only two "decisions" involving the elimination of racial discrimination in the public schools.

The Governor has said that critics of these proposals have not offered any constructive advice or alternatives. Permit me, therefore, to offer an idea for the consideration of the members of the regular sessions. A careful study of my plan, I believe, will show that it will save millions of dollars in tax funds and eliminate forever the danger to our public education system. Before I outline my plan, I would like to give you a little background.

One of the factors involved in our tremendous industrial

growth and economic prosperity is the fact that the South, voluntarily, has all but eliminated VERTICAL SEGREGATION. The tremendous buying power of the twelve million Negroes in the
South has been based wholly on the absence of racial segregation. The white and Negro stand at the same grocery and su-
permarket counters; deposit money at the same bank teller's
window; pay phone and light bills to the same clerk; walk
through the same dime and department stores, and stand at
the same drugstore counters.

It is only when the Negro "sets" that the fur begins to fly.

Now, since we are not even thinking about restoring VERTI-
CAL SEGREGATION, I think my plan would not only comply with
the Supreme Court decisions, but would maintain "sitting-
down" segregation. Now here is the GOLDEN VERTICAL NEGRO
PLAN. Instead of all those complicated proposals, all the next session needs to do is pass one small amendment which would provide *only* desks in all the public schools of our state—*no seats*.

The desks should be those standing-up jobs, like the old-
fashioned bookkeeping desk. Since no one in the South pays the
slightest attention to a VERTICAL NEGRO, this will completely
solve our problem. And it is not such a terrible inconvenience for
young people to stand up during their classroom studies. In fact,
this may be a blessing in disguise. They are not learning to
read sitting down, anyway; maybe standing up will help. This
will save more millions of dollars in the cost of our remedial
English course when the kids enter college. In whatever direction you look, with the GOLDEN VERTICAL NEGRO PLAN you
save millions of dollars, to say nothing of eliminating forever
any danger to our public education system upon which rests the
destiny, hopes, and happiness of this society.

MY WHITE BABY PLAN offers another possible solution to
the segregation problem—this time in a field other than education.

Here is an actual case history of the "White Baby Plan to
End Racial Segregation":

Some months ago there was a revival of the Laurence Olivier
movie, *Hamlet*, and several Negro schoolteachers were eager to

see it. One Saturday afternoon they asked some white friends to lend them two of their little children, a three-year-old girl and a six-year-old boy, and, holding these white children by the hands, they obtained tickets from the movie-house cashier without a moment's hesitation. They were in like Flynn.

This would also solve the baby-sitting problem for thousands and thousands of white working mothers. There can be a mutual exchange of references, then the people can sort of pool their children at a central point in each neighborhood, and every time a Negro wants to go to the movies all she need do is pick up a white child—and go.

Eventually the Negro community can set up a factory and manufacture white babies made of plastic, and when they want to go to the opera or to a concert, all they need do is carry that plastic doll in their arms. The dolls, of course, should all have blond curls and blue eyes, which would go even further; it woud give the Negro woman and her husband priority over the whites for the very best seats in the house.

While I still have faith in the White Baby Plan, my final proposal may prove to be the most practical of all.

Only after a successful test was I ready to announce formally the Golden "Out-of-Order" Plan.

I tried my plan in a city of North Carolina, where the Negroes represent 39 per cent of the population.

I prevailed upon the manager of a department store to shut the water off in his "white" water fountain and put up a sign, "Out-of-Order." For the first day or two the whites were hesitant, but little by little they began to drink out of the water fountain belonging to the "coloreds"—and by the end of the third week everybody was drinking the "segregated" water; with not a single solitary complaint to date.

I believe the test is of such sociological significance that the Governor should appoint a special committee of two members of the House and two Senators to investigate the Golden "Out-of-Order" Plan. We kept daily reports on the use of the unsegregated water fountain which should be of great value to this committee. This may be the answer to the necessary uplifting of

the white morale. It is possible that the whites may accept deseg-
regation if they are assured that the facilities are still "separate,"
albeit "Out-of-Order."

As I see it now, the key to my Plan is to keep the "Out-of-
Order" sign up for at least two years. We must do this thing
gradually.

HIGHER
EDUCATION

"Next to the clerk in holy orders, the fellow with the foulest job in the world is the schoolmaster."

> H. L. MENCKEN, "The Educational Process," from Education, *Prejudices: Third Series*

". . . academies promote good fellowship in knowledge and good fellowship in knowledge promotes F.U.D.G.E.'s and H.O.A.X.'s."

> JAMES FENIMORE COOPER, *The Monikins*

Higher Education

The American college and university are hotbeds of satire. Campus humor magazines are filled with non campus mentis burlesques of the broadest gauge, and no faculty member is safe from the danger that he or she will wind up in a colleague's novel in a most unflattering light. As for the institution itself, where once it was criticized for being an ivory tower aloof from the real world, today the university is blamed for losing sight of the meaning of education in its eagerness to equip its students for practical affairs. It is not surprising that a university which offers its students courses both in Sanskrit and Hotel Management should be vulnerable to imaginative criticism.

Benjamin Franklin

Between April and September of 1722, Benjamin Franklin slipped fourteen Silence Dogood letters under the door of his brother's printing shop, where the *New-England Courant* was published. His Mrs. Dogood is witty, dignified and enlightened —all that Franklin believed Cotton Mather, author of *Essays to Do Good*, was not—and her natural manner is at once humorous and crisply moral.

The following letter describes Mrs. Dogood's allegorical vision of a college very like one called Harvard. In 1722 Harvard was freeing itself from churchly authority but was still regarded by young Franklin, who reflected the opinion of many other New England "Leather Aprons," as a breeding ground of snobbery, reaction and ignorance.

MRS. SILENCE DOGOOD DREAMS ABOUT A COLLEGE
(1722)

Dogood Papers, No. IV
 From Monday May 7, to Monday May 14, 1722
 An sum etiam nunc vel Græcè loqui vel Latinè docendus?
             —CICERO.
To the Author of *The New-England Courant.*
Sir,
 Discoursing the other day at dinner with my reverend boarder, formerly mentioned (whom for distinction sake we will call by the name of *Clericus*), concerning the education of children, I asked his advice about my young son William, whether or no I had best bestow upon him academical learning, or (as our phrase is) *bring him up at our college:* He persuaded me to do it by all means, using many weighty arguments with me, and answering all the objections that I could form against it; telling me, withal, that he did not doubt but that the lad would take his learning very well, and not idle away his time as too many there nowadays do. These words of Clericus gave me a curiosity to inquire a little more strictly into the present circumstances of that famous seminary of learning; but the information which he gave me was neither pleasant nor such as I expected.
 As soon as dinner was over, I took a solitary walk into my orchard, still ruminating on Clericus's discourse with much consideration, until I came to my usual place of retirement under the great apple-tree; where, having seated myself, and carelessly laid my head on a verdant bank, I fell by degrees into a

soft and undisturbed slumber. My waking thoughts remained with me in my sleep, and before I awakened again, I dreamt the following Dream.

I fancied I was traveling over pleasant and delightful fields and meadows, and through many small country towns and villages; and as I passed along, all places resounded with the fame of the Temple of Learning: Every peasant, who had wherewithal, was preparing to send one of his children at least to this famous place; and in this case most of them consulted their own purses instead of their children's capacities: So that I observed, a great many, yea, the most part of those who were traveling thither, were little better than dunces and blockheads. Alas! Alas!

At length I entered upon a spacious plain, in the midst of which was erected a large and stately edifice: It was to this that a great company of youths from all parts of the country were going; so, stepping in among the crowd, I passed on with them, and presently arrived at the gate.

The passage was kept by two sturdy porters named *Riches* and *Poverty*, and the latter obstinately refused to give entrance to any who had not first gained the favor of the former; so that, I observed, many who came even to the very gate were obliged to travel back again as ignorant as they came, for want of this necessary qualification. However, as a spectator I gained admittance, and with the rest entered directly into the temple.

In the middle of the great hall stood a stately and magnificent throne, which was ascended to by two high and difficult steps. On the top of it sat Learning in awful state; she was apparelled wholly in black, and surrounded almost on every side with innumerable volumes in all languages. She seemed very busily employed in writing something on half a sheet of paper, and upon Enquiry, I understood she was preparing a paper called, *The New-England Courant*. On her right hand sat English, with a pleasant smiling countenance, and handsomely attired; and on her left were seated several antique figures with their faces veiled. I was considerably puzzled to guess who they were, until one informed me (who stood beside me) that those figures on her left hand were *Latin*, *Greek*, *Hebrew*, etc., and that they were

very much reserved, and seldom or never unveiled their faces
here, and then to few or none, though most of those who have in
this place acquired so much learning as to distinguish them from
English, pretended to an intimate acquaintance with them. I
then inquired of him, what could be the reason why they continued veiled, in this place especially: He pointed to the foot of
the throne, where I saw *Idleness*, attended with *Ignorance*, and
these (he informed me) were they who first veiled them, and still
kept them so.

Now I observed that the whole tribe who entered into the temple with me began to climb the throne; but the work proving
troublesome and difficult to most of them, they withdrew their
hands from the plow, and contented themselves to sit at the foot,
with Madam *Idleness* and her maid *Ignorance*, until those who
were assisted by diligence and a docible temper, had wellnigh
got up the first step: But the time drawing nigh in which they
could no way avoid ascending, they were fain to crave the assistance of those who had got up before them, and who, for the reward perhaps of a pint of milk, or a piece of plum-cake, lent
the lubbers a helping hand, and sat them in the eye of the world,
upon a level with themselves.

The other step being in the same manner ascended, and the
usual ceremonies at an end, every beetle-scull seemed well satisfied with his own portion of learning, though perhaps he was
e'en just as ignorant as ever. And now the time of their departure being come, they marched out of doors to make room for
another company, who waited for entrance: And I, having seen
all that was to be seen, quitted the hall likewise, and went to
make my observations on those who were just gone out before me.

Some I perceived took to merchandising, others to traveling,
some to one thing, some to another, and some to nothing; and
many of them from henceforth, for want of patrimony, lived as
poor as churchmice, being unable to dig, and ashamed to beg,
and to live by their wits it was impossible. But the most part of
the crowd went along a large beaten path, which led to a temple
at the further end of the plain, called, *the Temple of Theology*.
The business of those who were employed in this temple being

laborious and painful, I wondered exceedingly to see so many go toward it; but while I was pondering this matter in my mind, I spied Pecunia behind a curtain, beckoning to them with her hand, which sight immediately satisfied me for whose sake it was that a great part of them (I will not say all) traveled that road. In this temple I saw nothing worth mentioning, except the ambitious and fraudulent contrivances of *Plagius*, who (notwithstanding he had been severely reprehended for such practices before) was diligently transcribing some eloquent paragraphs out of Tillotson's works, etc., to embellish his own.

Now I bethought myself in my sleep that it was time to be at home, and as I fancied I was traveling back thither, I reflected in my mind on the extreme folly of those parents who, blind to their children's dullness, and insensible of the solidity of their skulls, because they think their purses can afford it, will needs send them to the Temple of Learning, where, for want of a suitable genius, they learn little more than how to carry themselves handsomely, and enter a room genteelly (which might as well be acquired at a dancing school), and from whence they return, after abundance of trouble and charge, as great blockheads as ever, only more proud and self-conceited.

While I was in the midst of these unpleasant reflections, Clericus (who with a book in his hand was walking under the trees) accidentally awakened me; to him I related my dream with all its particulars, and he, without much study, presently interpreted it, assuring me, that it was a lively representation of HARVARD COLLEGE, Etcetera.

I remain, Sir, Your humble Servant,

Silence Dogood

John Trumbull

John Trumbull (see page 238) was a tutor at Yale when he wrote his long Hudibrastic satire on education called *The Progress of Dulness*. Here are some lines from the poem: a teacher's portrait of the college student.

A COLLEGE EDUCATION
(from *The Progress of Dulness*, 1772–1773)

Two years thus spent in gathering knowledge,
The lad sets forth t'unlade at college,
While down his sire and priest attend him,
To introduce and recommend him;
Or if detain'd, a letter's sent
Of much apocryphal content,
To set him forth, how dull soever,
As very learn'd and very clever;
A genius of first emission,
With burning love for erudition;
So studious he'll outwatch the moon
And think the planets set too soon.
He had but little time to fit in;
Examination too must frighten.
Depend upon't he must do well,
He knows much more than he can tell;
Admit him, and in little space
He'll beat his rivals in the race;
His father's incomes are but small,
He comes now, if he comes at all.
    So said, so done, at college now
He enters well, no matter how;
New scenes awhile his fancy please,
But all must yield to love of ease.
In the same round condemn'd each day,
To study, read, recite and pray;
To make his hours of business double—
He can't endure th' increasing trouble;
And finds at length, as times grow pressing,
All plagues are easier than his lesson.
With sleepy eyes and count'nance heavy,
With much excuse of *non paravi*,
Much absence, *tardes* and *egresses*,
The college-evil on him seizes.

Then ev'ry book, which ought to please,
Stirs up the seeds of dire disease;
Greek spoils his eyes, the print's so fine,
Grown dim with study, or with wine;
Of Tully's Latin much afraid,
Each page, he calls the doctor's aid;
While geometry, with lines so crooked,
Sprains all his wits to overlook it.
His sickness puts on every name
Its cause and uses still the same;
'Tis tooth-ache, cholic, gout or stone,
With phases various as the moon;
But though through all the body spread,
Still makes its cap'tal seat, the head.
In all diseases, 'tis expected,
The weakest parts be most infected.

Washington Irving

Irving, failing in his search for a link between America and his romantic ideal of nobility and antiquity, turned the American past to ridicule. This diverting burlesque is characteristic of Irving's comic chronicle of New York's Dutch, *A History of New York . . . by Diedrich Knickerbocker*, a delightful jumble of parody and caricature.

A SCIENTIFIC DEMONSTRATION
(from *A History of New York . . . by Diedrich Knickerbocker*, 1809)

Professor Von Poddingcoft (or Puddinghead, as the name may be rendered into English,) was long celebrated in the university of Leyden, for profound gravity of deportment, and a talent at going to sleep in the midst of examinations, to the infinite relief of his hopeful students, who thereby worked their way through college with great ease and little study. In the

course of one of his lectures, the learned professor, seizing a
bucket of water, swung it around his head at arm's length. The
impulse with which he threw the vessel from him, being a cen-
trifugal force, the retention of his arm operating as a centripetal
power, and the bucket, which was a substitute for the earth, describing a circular orbit round about the globular head and ruby
visage of Professor Von Poddingcoft, which formed no bad representation of the sun. All of these particulars were duly explained to the class of gaping students around him. He ap-
prised them, moreover, that the same principle of gravitation,
which retained the water in the bucket, restrains the ocean from
flying from the earth in its rapid revolutions; and he farther informed them that should the motion of the earth be suddenly
checked, it would incontinently fall into the sun, through the
centripetal force of gravitation, a most ruinous event to this
planet, and one which would also obscure, though it most probably would not extinguish, the solar luminary. An unlucky strip-
ling, one of those vagrant geniuses, who seem sent into the
world merely to annoy worthy men of the puddinghead order,
desirous of ascertaining the correctness of the experiment, suddenly arrested the arm of the professor, just at the moment that
the bucket was in its zenith, which immediately descended with
astonishing precision upon the philosophic head of the instruc-
tor of youth. A hollow sound, and a red-hot hiss, attended the
contact; but the theory was in the amplest manner illustrated, for
the unfortunate bucket perished in the conflict; but the blazing
countenance of Professor Von Poddingcoft emerged from
amidst the waters, glowing fiercer than ever with unutterable indignation, whereby the students were marvelously edified, and
departed considerably wiser than before.

Don Marquis

Not all higher education is confined within ivy-covered
walls: the advanced cerebrations of Hermione and Her Little
Group of Serious Thinkers is a spoof of the spontaneous col-

lectivization of enfranchised American flappers into the most
frightening weapon against cultural darkness the world has
ever known.

ARE'NT THE RUSSIANS WONDERFUL?
(from *Hermione and Her Little Group of Serious Thinkers*)

Aren't the Russians marvelous people!
We've been taking up Diaghileff in a serious way—our
little group, you know—and, really, he's wonderful!

Who else but Diaghileff could give those lovely Russian
things the proper accent?

And accent—if you know what I mean—accent is everything!
Accent! Accent! What would art be without accent?

Accent is coming in—if you get what I mean—and what they
call "punch" is going out. I always thought it was a frightfully
vulgar sort of thing, anyhow—punch!

The thing I love about the Russians is their Orientalism.

You know, there's an old saying that if you find a Russian
you catch a Tartar . . . or something like that.

I'm sure that is wrong. . . . I get so *mixed* on quotations.
But I always know where I can find them, if you know what I
mean.

But the Russian *verve* isn't Oriental, is it?

Don't you just dote on *verve?*

That's what makes Bakst so fascinating, don't you think?—
his *verve!*

Though they do say that the Russian operas don't analyze as
well as the German or the Italian ones—if you get what I mean.

Though for that matter, who analyzes them?

One may not know how to an analyze an opera, and yet one
may know what one likes!

I suppose there will be a frightful lot of imitations of Russian
music and ballet now. Don't you just hate imitators?

One finds it everywhere—imitation! It's the sincerest flattery,
they say. But that doesn't excuse it, do you think?

There's a girl—one of my friends, she says she is—who is always trying to imitate me. My expressions, you know, and the way I talk and walk, and all that sort of thing.

She gets some of my superficial mannerisms . . . but she can't quite do my things as if they were her own, you know . . . there is where the accent comes in again!

HOW SUFFERING PURIFIES ONE!

(from *Hermione and Her Little Group of Serious Thinkers*)

Oh, to go through fire and come out purified!

Suffering is wonderful, isn't it? Simply *wonderful!*

The loveliest man talked to us the other night—to our Little Group of Serious Thinkers, you know—about social ideals and suffering.

The reason so many attempts to improve things fail, you know, is because the people who try them out haven't suffered personally.

He had the loveliest eyes, this man.

He made me think. I said to myself, "After all, have I suffered? Have I been purified by fire?"

And I decided that I had—that is spiritually, you know.

The suffering—the spiritual suffering—that I undergo through being misunderstood is something *frightful!*

Mamma discourages every Cause I take up. So does Papa. I get no sympathy in my devotion to my ideals. Only opposition!

And from a child I have had such a high-strung, sensitive nervous organization that opposition of any sort has made me ill.

There are some temperaments like that.

Once when I was quite small and Mamma threatened to spank me, I had convulsions.

And nothing but opposition, opposition, opposition now!

Only we advanced thinkers know what it is to suffer! To go through fire for our ideals!

And what is physical suffering by the side of spiritual suffering?

I so often think of that when I am engaged in sociological

work. Only the other night—it was raining and chilly, you know—some of us went down in the auto to one of the missions and looked at the sufferers who were being cared for.

And the thought came to me all of a sudden:

"Yes, physical suffering may be relieved—but what is there to relieve spiritual suffering like mine?"

Though, of course, it improves one.

I think it is beginning to show in my eyes.

I looked at them for nearly two hours in the mirror last evening, trying to be quite certain.

And, you know, there's a kind of look in them that's never been there until recently. A kind of a—a—

Well, it's an *intangible* look, if you get what I mean.

Not exactly a *hungry* look, more of a *yearning* look!

Thank heaven, though, I can control it—one should always be the captain of one's soul, shouldn't one?

I hide it at times. Because one must hide one's suffering from the world, mustn't one?

Randall Jarrell

Poet, critic, novelist, teacher, Randall Jarrell could make his way around the inside of a university blindfolded. He has taught at Kenyon College, the University of Texas, Sarah Lawrence, Princeton, the University of Illinois, and the University of North Carolina. The portrait of the young university president in *Pictures from an Institution* is authoritative.

PRESIDENT ROBBINS OF BENTON
(from *Pictures from an Institution*)

President Robbins, judge him as you please, was not human. He had not had time to be; besides, his own gift was for seeming human. He had taught sociology only a year, and during the last three months of that year he had already been selected to be Dean of Men at ————; two years later he was appointed Dean of the College of Arts and Sciences at ————; in six years he was President of Benton. *They* had selected him. But how had *they* known whom to select? Would someone else have done as well? Why had they selected *just him?*

If you ask this, you have never selected or been selected; you would know, then. Such questions are as ridiculous as asking how stigmata know whom to select—as asking, "Wouldn't somebody else have done just as well as St. Francis?" A *vocation,* a *calling*—these words apply quite as well in secular affairs as in religious: Luther knew. Have you yourself never known one of these *idiots savants* of success, of Getting Ahead in the World? About other things they may know something or they may not, but about the World they have forgotten—in previous existences for which, perhaps, they are being punished?—far more than you or I will ever learn.

President Robbins was, of course, one of these men. He "did not have his Ph.D."—but had that bothered one administrator upon this earth? All had been as refreshingly unprejudiced about his lack of one as the President of Benton now was about anybody's possession of one. But at Benton all of them were like this: they looked up your degrees so they could tell you that, whatever the things were, they didn't mind. President Robbins had an M.A. from Oxford—he had been a Rhodes Scholar— and an LL.D. granted, in 1947, by Menuire. (It's a college in Florida.) To make the President dislike you for the rest of his life, say to him with a resigned anthropological smile: "I've just been reading that in 1948 Menuire College gave the degree of Doctor of Humor to Milton Berle."

President Robbins had brought seven former Rhodes Scholars to Benton during his first two years there. Benton thought him in most ways an ideal President, but about this they felt as the constituents of a Republican senator do when he appoints seven former U.N. officials to postmasterships. An ounce of Rhodes Scholars was worth a pound of Rhodes Scholars, in Benton's opinion.

But when the President spoke to them they could have forgiven him a wilderness of Rhodes Scholars. Benton had a day for parents and alumnae which was, or was not, called Founder's Day—I have forgotten. Yet surely it was not: who could have founded Benton? Benton is a Category like Time or Space or Causality.

I have forgotten the name of the day, but I remember its lunch. The day before, a third of our luncheon had been a salad of uncooked spinach, a midnight-green salad with, here and there among the leaves, an eye of beet: a yew-tree's notion of a salad: a salad that was exactly like a still-life by Soutine—had I not been poor I should have had it varnished and framed. But on parents' day we had, among other things, lobster and shrimp in little crumbling shells—no, *big* crumbling shells—of pastry. The girl with whom I used to play tennis was waiting on our table; she mumbled to me, "Gee, what's up?" I flickered my eyes toward the longest table: the President sat there among matrons. Had I been hatted, had I been gowned, had I been shod as were those matrons, I should have sold myself and made my fortune; but alas! they had had the idea before me.

That night we came together to hear President Robbins: the matrons, the girls, the teachers, Constance, Dr. Rosenbaum, Gertrude Johnson, I. "Good God," Gertrude whispered to me when she had looked around her; for once she was wordless. We suffered our way through a long program, and then President Robbins began to speak.

After two sentences one realized once more that President Robbins was an extraordinary speaker, a speaker of a—one says *an almost extinct school*, but how does one say the opposite? *a not-yet-evolved school?* He did something so logical that it is impossible that no one else should have thought of it, and yet no one has. President Robbins *crooned* his speeches.

His voice not only took you into his confidence, it laid a fire for you and put out your slippers by it and then went into the other room to get into something more comfortable. It was a Compromising voice. President Robbins was, in Shaw's phrase, "a man of good character where women are concerned," and he had never touched a Benton girl except in a game of water-polo; yet as you heard him speak something muttered inside you, "To a nunnery, go!"

He would say to you in private in his office, about the teachers of Benton: "We like to feel that we educate [there was a slow, chaste separation between the next two words: they seemed youths and maidens who have become strong and sublimated through remaining apart] each . . . other." If his voice was tender then, consider what it became in public: for that voice did not sell itself to the highest bidder, it just gave itself away to everybody.

President Robbins made a speech that—that—as Gertrude said, you had to hear it not to believe it. When he finished (and not a minute too late; the audience wolfed that speech down the way the Afghans ate their horsemeat) he finished by thanking the students, parents, and faculty of Benton for the experience of working with, of learning from, and of growing to . . . love . . . such generous and intelligent, such tolerant and understanding, such—and here he paused quite a long time—such . . . good . . . people. As he said . . . *good* . . . there was in his voice so radiant a freshness, so yearning a transfiguration of all created things—how *chromatic* it was!—that the audience rose from their seats and sang, like Sieglinde: *Thou art the Spring!* No, they didn't actually, insensate things, but they wanted to: you could look at them and see that they were Changed.

Gertrude said softly, "Let's go in and wring the dew out of our stockings; mine are soaked." I thought, "Good old Gertrude"; but as soon as I realized what I was thinking, I stopped.

At our nation's capital, hidden away by legislators, there is a colossal statue of George Washington—seated, antique, naked to the waist; he looks as awful as Ingres' Zeus, but good. I sometimes thought that this statue, rather than the Smith shrike-tree, should have been put at the center of Benton as a representation of President Robbins Being the Spirit of Benton. But the shrike-tree was good too.

People really did think of the President in a costume somewhat similar to the statue's: *Time* and *Life* and *Newsweek*, just after his appointment, had all carried pictures of him taken in the days when he had not yet thought of becoming an educator, but was only a diver at the Olympic Games. People would say, "Did you see where they appointed this diver a college-president?"—plenty of presidents had been football-players, but a diver was something new. (The picture in *Life* showed him standing between Johnny Weismuller and Eleanor Holm; and I heard a little boy say about it, in the most disgusted voice I've ever heard: "They've made *Tarzan* the president of an old girls' college!") When the President went on money-raising tours among his alumnae and his students' parents and grandparents and guardians—

Poor man! he spent half his time on these, and half making speeches, and half writing articles for magazines and appearing on radio forums and testifying before Congressional committees that it would be unwise, in time of war, to draft the girls of Benton into the Women's Army Auxiliary Corps, and half . . . as you see, he had learned the secret of busy and successful men: that there are thirty-six hours in every day, if you only know where to look for them. If he had known where to find one more, an hour for himself, a kind of Children's Hour for the boy Dwight Robbins, who can say what might have become of him? But he had never known.

His appeals for funds were nowhere more successful than in Hollywood. Several Benton alumnae were stars, socially-conscious script-writers, wives or daughters of producers. President Robbins appealed to them sitting in somewhat Hawaiian swimming-shorts at the grassy verge of swimming-pools: as he looked thoughtfully into the thoughtless water he seemed to the alumnae some boyish star who, playing Tom Sawyer, fancies for the moment that he is Narcissus. Not to have given him what he asked, they felt, would have been to mine the bridge that bears the train that carries the supply of this year's Norman Rockwell Boy Scout Calendars. They felt this; it seems far-fetched to me.

He was, in sober truth, in awful truth, a dedicated man (the really damned not only like Hell, they feel loyal to it); and if his dedication was to the things of this world, to this world, should we scorn him for it any more than we scorn some holy *faquir*, some yellow-robed disciple sitting cross-legged among those whom the Buddha addressed as *Bhikkus?* If it were not for men like President Robbins, how could this world go on? *Every-thing* would be different.

And yet one must admit that such men are in long supply.

Mary McCarthy

JOCELYN COLLEGE
(from *The Groves of Academe*)

Jocelyn College . . . had a faculty of forty-one persons and a student-body of two hundred and eighty-three—a ratio of one teacher to every 6.9 students, which made possible the practice of "individual instruction" as carried on at Bennington (6:1), Sarah Lawrence (6.4:1), Bard (6.9:1), and St. John's (7.7:1). It had been founded in the late Thirties by an experimental educator and lecturer, backed by a group of society-women in Cleveland, Pittsburgh, and Cincinnati who wished to strike a middle course between the existing extremes, between Aquinas and Dewey, the modern dance and the labor movement. Its students were neither to till the soil as at Antioch nor weave on looms as at Black Mountain; they were to be grounded neither in the grass-roots present as at Sarah Lawrence nor in the great-books past as at St. John's or Chicago; they were to specialize neither in verse-writing, nor in the poetic theatre, nor in the tech-niques of co-operative living—they were simply to be free, spon-taneous, and coeducational.

What the founder had had in mind was a utopian experiment in so-called "scientific" education; by the use of aptitude tests, psychological questionnaires, even blood-sampling and cranial measurements, he hoped to discover a method of gauging stu-dent-potential and directing it into the proper channels for maxi-mum self-realization—he saw himself as an engineer and the college as a reclamation project along the lines of the Grand Coulee or the TVA. The women behind him, however, regarded the matter more simply, in the usual fashion of trustees. What they wanted to introduce into their region was a center of "personalized" education, with courses tailored to the individual need, like their own foundation-garments, and a staff of experts and consultants, each with a little "name" in his field, like the Michels and Antoines of Fifth Avenue, to interpret the student's personality. In the long run, these views, seemingly so harmonious, were found to be far apart. The founder had the sincere idea of running his college as a laboratory; failure in an individual case he found as interesting as success. Under his permissive system, the students were free to study or not as they chose; he believed that the healthy organism would elect, like an animal, what was best for it. If the student failed to go in the direction indicated by the results of his testing, or in any direction at all, this was noted down and in time communicated to his parents, merely as a matter of interest—to push him in any way would be a violation of the neutrality of the experiment. The high percentage of failure was taken to be significant of the failures of secondary education; any serious reform in methodology must reach down to the kindergarten and the nursery school, through the whole preparatory system, and it was noteworthy, in this connection, that the progressive schools were doing their job no better than the old-fashioned classical ones. Indeed, comparative studies showed the graduates of progressive schools to be *more* dependent on outside initiative, on an authoritarian leader-pattern, than any other group in the community.

This finding convinced the trustees, who included the heads of two progressive schools, that the founder was ahead of his time, a stimulating man in the tradition of Pasteur and the early vivisectionists, whom history would give his due. He left the college the legacy of a strong scientific bent and a reputation for enthusiasm and crankishness that reflected itself in budgetary difficulties and in the prevalence of an "undesirable" type of student. Despite a high tuition and other screening devices (a geographical quota, interviews with the applicant and with the applicant's parents, submission of a photograph when this was not practicable, solicitation of private schools), despite a picturesque campus—a group of long, thick-walled, mansarded, white-shuttered stone dwellings arranged around a cupolaed chapel with a planting of hemlocks, the remains of a small, old German Reformed denominational college that had imparted to the secluded ridge a Calvinistic sweetness of worship and election—something, perhaps the coeducational factor, perhaps the once-advertised freedom, had worked to give the college a peculiarly plebeian and subversive tone, like that of a big-city high-school.

It was the mixture of the sexes, some thought, that had introduced a crude and predatory bravado into the campus life; the glamour was rubbed off sex by the daily jostle in soda-shop and barroom and the nightly necking in the social rooms, and this, in its turn, had its effect on all ideals and absolutes. Differences were leveled; courses were regarded with a cynical, practical eye; students of both sexes had the wary disillusionment and aimlessness of battle-hardened Marines. After six months at Jocelyn, they felt that they had "seen through" life, through all attempts to educate and improve them, through love, poetry, philosophy, fame, and were here, it would seem, through some sort of coercion, like a drafted army. Thronging into store or classroom, in jeans, old sweaters, caps, visors, strewing cigarette-butts and candy-wrappers, they gave a mass impression that transcended their individual personalities, which were often soft, perturbed, uncertain, innocent; yet the very sight of an individual face, plunged deep in its own introspection, as in a blanket, heightened the crowd-sense they communicated, like soldiers in a truck, subway riders on their straps, serried but isolated, each in his stubborn dream, resistant to waking fully—at whatever time of day, the Jocelyn students were always sleepy, yawning, and rather gummy-eyed, as though it were seven in the morning and they unwillingly on the street.

Yet this very rawness and formlessness in the students made them interesting to teach. Badly prepared, sleepy, and evasive, they *could* nevertheless be stirred to wonder and pent admiration at the discovery of form and pattern in history or a work of art or a laboratory experiment, though ceding this admiration grudgingly and by degrees, like primitive peoples who must see an act performed over and over again before they can be convinced that some magic is not behind it, that they are not the dupes of an illusionist. To teachers with some experience of the ordinary class-bound private college student, of the quiet lecture-hall with the fair duteous heads bent over the notebooks, Joce-lyn's hard-eyed watchers signified the real. Seeing them come year after year, the stiff-spined, angry only children with inhibi-tions about the opposite sex, being entrained here remedially by their parents, as they had been routed to the dentist for braces, the wild-haired progressive-school rejects, offspring of broken homes, the sexually adventurous youths looking to meet their opposite numbers in the women's dormitories, without the social complications of fraternities and sororities or the restraints of grades, examinations, compulsory athletics, R.O.T.C., the single well-dressed Adonis from Sewickley with a private plane and a neurosis, the fourteen-year-old mathematical Russian Jewish boys on scholarships, with their violin cases and timorous, old-country parents, hovering humbly outside the Registrar's door as at a consular office, the cold peroxided beauties who had once done modeling for Powers and were here while waiting for a screen-test, the girls from Honolulu or Taos who could "sit on" their hair and wore it down their backs, Godiva-style, and were named Rina or Blanca or Snow-White, the conventional Ally-sons and Pattys whose favorite book was *Winnie-the-Pooh*—see-ing them, the old-timers shook their heads and marveled at how the college could continue but in the same style that they mar-veled at the survival of the race itself. Among these students, they knew, there would be a large percentage of trouble-makers and a handful of gifted creatures who would redeem the whole; four out of five of these would be, predictably, the scholarship students, and the fifth a riddle and an anomaly, coming for-ward at the last moment, from the ranks of Allysons or Blancas, like the tortoise in the fable, or the sleeper in the horse-race, a term which at Jocelyn had a peculiar nicety of meaning.

And over the management of these students, the faculty, equally heterogeneous, would, within the year, become em-broiled, with each other, with the student-body, or with the President or trustees. A scandal could be counted on that would cause a liberal lady somewhere to strike the college from her will: a pregnant girl, the pilfering of reserve books from the library, the usual plagiarism case, alleged racial discrimination, charges of alcoholism or homosexuality, a strike against the food in the dining-room, the prices in the college store, suppression of the student paper, alleged use of a course in myth to proselytize for religion, a student demand that a rule be laid down, in the handbook, governing sexual intercourse, if disciplinary action was to be taken against those who made love *off* the college premises and were observed by faculty-snoopers. No truly great question had ever agitated the campus since the original days of the founder, but the ordinary trivia of college life were here blown up, according to critics, out of all proportion. There had been no loyalty oath, no violation of academic freedom, but problems of freedom and fealty were discovered in the smallest issue, in whether, for example, students in the dining-hall, when surrendering their plates to the waiters, should pass them to the right or the left, clockwise or counter-clockwise; at an all-college meeting, held in December of this year, compulsory for all students, faculty, and administrative staff, President Maynard Hoar had come within an ace of resigning when his appeal for moderation in the discussion had met with open cat-calls from the counterclockwise faction.

Thus the college faced every year an insurrectionary situation; in the course of twelve years it had had five presidents, including the founder, who was unseated after only eleven months of service. During the War, it had nearly foundered and been saved by the influx of veterans studying under the GI bill and by the new plutocracy of five-percenters, car-dealers, black-market slaughterers, tire-salesmen, and retail merchants who seemed to Jocelyn's presidents to have been specially enriched by Providence, working mysteriously, with the interest of the small college in mind. These new recruits to the capitalist classes had no educational prejudices, were extremely respectful of the faculty, to whom they sent bulky presents of liquor or perfume, as to valuable clients at Christmas-time; they came to the college seldom, sometimes only once, for Commencement, passed out cigars and invitations to use the shack at Miami or Coral Gables *any time at all*—this benign and preoccupied gratitude, tactfully conscious of services rendered, extended also to friends and roommates of the poorer sort. Several years after graduation, little shoals of Jocelyn students would still be found living together co-operatively, in Malibu or St. Augustine—occasionally with an ex-teacher—sharing a single allowance under the bamboo tree.

THE ARTS

"Art, *n*. This word has no definition."

AMBROSE BIERCE, The Devil's Dictionary

"The American feeling, or lack of feeling, for art has been immemorially easy to satirize, whether at the one extreme of Babbittry or at the other of Bohemia . . . the American bent, the American genius, has honestly moved in other directions."

LOUIS KRONENBERGER, Company Manners

Benjamin Franklin

In the early eighteenth century, James Franklin's *New-England Courant* endeavored to reflect London in Boston much as *The New Yorker* now reflects New York in Denver. The *Courant's* editorial tone was sophisticated, critical and humorous, and the Dogood letters, which appeared in 1722, suited the sheet perfectly. They caught some of the spirit of relaxed enlightenment of Ben Franklin's model, Addison. In this letter, a murderous piece of literary criticism, young Franklin shows his cosmopolitan disdain of bad provincial poesy.

HOW TO WRITE A FUNERAL ELEGY
(1722)

Dogood Papers, No. VII
> *Give me the Muse, whose generous Force,*
> *Impatient of the Reins,*
> *Pursues an unattempted Course,*
> *Breaks all the Criticks Iron Chains.*
>
> WATTS

To the Author of the New-England Courant.
SIR,

It has been the Complaint of many Ingenious Foreigners, who have travell'd amongst us, *That good Poetry is not to be expected in* New-England. I am apt to Fancy, the Reason is, not because our Countrymen are altogether void of a Poetical Genius, not yet because we have not those Advantages of Education which other Countries have, but purely because we do not afford that Praise and Encouragement which is merited, when any thing extraordinary of this Kind is produc'd among us: Upon which Consideration I have determined, when I meet with a Good Piece of *New-England* poetry, to give it a suitable Encomium, and thereby endeavor to discover to the World some of its Beautys, in order to encourage the Author to go on, and bless the World with more, and more Excellent Productions.

There has lately appear'd among us a most Excellent Piece of Poetry, entitled, *An Elegy upon the much Lamented Death of Mrs.* Mehitebell Kitel, *Wife of Mr.* John Kitel *of* Salem, *Etc.* It may justly be said in its Praise, without flattery to the Author, that it is the most *Extraordinary* Piece that was ever wrote in *New-England.* The Language is so soft and Easy, the Expression so moving and pathetick, but above all, the Verse and Numbers so Charming and Natural, that it is almost beyond Comparison.

The Muse *disdains*
Those Links and Chains,
Measures and Rules of Vulgar Strains,
And o'er the Laws of Harmony a Sovereign Queen she reigns.

I find no English Author, Ancient or Modern, whose Elegies may be compar'd with this, in respect to the Elegance of Stile, or Smoothness of Rhime; and for the affecting Part, I will leave your Readers to judge, if ever they read any Lines, that would sooner make them *draw their Breath* and Sigh, if not shed Tears, than these following.

Come let us mourn, for we have lost a
Wife, a Daughter, and a Sister,
Who has lately taken Flight, and
greatly we have mist her.

In another place,

Some little Time before she yielded up her Breath,
She said, I ne'er shall hear one Sermon more on Earth.
She kist her Husband some little Time before she expir'd,
Then lean'd her Head the Pillow on, just out of Breath and
tir'd.

But the Threefold Appellation in the first Line

—a Wife, a Daughter, and a Sister,

must not pass unobserved. That Line in the celebrated *Watts,*

GUNSTON, *the Just, the Generous, and the Young,*

is nothing Comparable to it. The latter only mentions three Qualifications of *one* person who was deceased, which therefore could raise Grief and Compassion but for *One.* Thereas the former, (*our most excellent Poet*) gives his Reader a Sort of an Idea of the Death of *Three Persons,* viz.

—a Wife, a Daughter, and a Sister,

which is *Three Times* as great a Loss as the Death of *One,* and consequently must raise *Three Times* as much grief and Compassion in the Reader.

I should be very much straitened for Room, if I should attempt to discover even half the Excellencies of this Elegy which are obvious to me. Yet I cannot omit one Observation, which is, that the Author has (to his Honour) invented a new Species of Poetry, which wants a Name, and was never before known. His muse scorns to be confin'd to the old Measures and Limits, or to observe the dull Rules of Criticks;

Nor Rapin *gives her Rules to fly, nor* Purcell *Notes to Sing.*
                                                            Watts.

Now 'tis Pity that such an Excellent Piece should not be dignify'd with a particular Name; and seeing it cannot justly be called either *Epic, Sapphic, Lyric,* or *Pindaric,* nor any other Name yet invented, I presume it may, (in Honour and Remembrance of the Dead) be called the KITELIC. Thus much in the Praise of *Kitelic Poetry.*

It is certain, that those Elegies which are of our own Growth, (and our Soil seldom produces any other sort of Poetry) are by far the greatest part, wretchedly Dull and Ridiculous. Now since it is imagin'd by many, that our Poets are honest, well-meaning Fellows, who do their best, and that if they had but some Instructions how to govern Fancy with Judgment, they would make indifferent good Elegies; I shall here subjoin a Receipt for that purpose, which was left me as a Legacy, (among other valuable Rarities) by my Reverend Husband. It is as follows,

A RECEIPT to make a New-England Funeral ELEGY

For the Title of your Elegy. *Of these you may have enough ready made to your Hands; but if you should chuse to make it your self, you must be sure not to omit the words Ætatis Suæ, which will Beautify it exceedingly.*

For the Subject of your Elegy. *Take one of your Neighbors who has lately departed this Life; it is no great matter at what Age the Party dy'd, but it will be best if he went away suddenly, being Kill'd, Drown'd, or Frose to Death.*

Having chose the Person, take all his Virtues, Excellencies, &c. and if he have not enough, you may borrow some to make up a sufficient Quantity: To these add his last Words, dying Expressions, &c. if they are to be had; mix all these together, and be sure you strain them well. Then season all *with a Handful or two of Melancholly Expressions, such as,* Dreadful, Deadly, cruel cold Death, unhappy Fate, weeping Eyes, &c. *Have mixed all these Ingredients well, put them into the empty Scull of some* young Harvard; (*but in Case you have ne'er One at Hand, you may use your own,*) *there let them Ferment for the Space of a Fortnight, and by that Time they will be incorporated into a Body, which take out, and having prepared a sufficient Quantity of double Rhimes, such as* Power, Flower; Quiver, Shiver; Grieve us, Leave us; tell you, excel you; Expeditions, Physicians; Fatigue him, Intrigue him; &c. *you must spread all upon Paper, and if you can procure a Scrap of Latin to put at* the End, *it will garnish it mightily; then having affixed your Name at the Bottom, with* a Mœstus Composuit, *you will have an Excellent Elegy.*

N. B. *This Receipt will serve when a Female is the Subject of your Elegy, provided you borrow a greater quantity of Virtues, Excellencies, &c.*

Sir,

Your Servant,
Silence Dogood

Fitz-Greene Halleck
and
Joseph Rodman Drake

The painter John Trumbull (a second cousin of his namesake, the author of *M'Fingal*) was nearing the end of his noteworthy career—first as soldier of the Revolution, then as its foremost commemorative artist—when Congress decided to dress the Capitol Rotunda with a group of his historical subjects. The principal work was to be the "Declaration of Independence," which Trumbull had done in a small-sized version years before, using portraits of the Founding Fathers taken from life. Unfortunately, as it turned out, President Madison insisted that the painting be monumentally enlarged for the Rotunda; he decreed that the figures be life-sized. Trumbull, who had only one good eye and who had probably worked himself out on this particular painting, produced a stiff and unnatural enlargement, which was unfavorably received.

As further ill luck would have it, the unveiling of the "National Painting" took place at a moment when two of the cleverest occasional satirists America has ever known were active in New York. These were young Fitz-Greene Halleck and Joseph Rodman Drake, who wrote as "Croaker" in the *Evening Post* and the *National Advertiser* during the year 1819. Today, the *Croaker Papers* are difficult to read because of their density of allusions to long-forgotten personalities and incidents, and particularly to contemporary theatrical performances, but their deft and witty versification and their ex-

ceptional critical acuity are easily apparent. Halleck himself—
who became a distinguished leader of national letters (Drake
died of tuberculosis in 1820 at the age of twenty-five)—called
the *Croaker Papers* "harmless pleasantries luckily suited to the
hour of their appearance." But some years ago the historian
Allan Nevins placed them as ". . . the most famous series of
satirical poems, the *Biglow Papers* excepted, in American
literature."

THE NATIONAL PAINTING
(from *Croaker Papers*, 1819)

Awake! ye forms of verse divine—
    Painting! descend on canvass wing,
And hover o'er my head Design!
    Your son, your glorious son I sing!
At Trumbull's name, I break my sloth,
    To load him with poetic riches;
The Titian of a table cloth!
    The Guido of a pair of breeches!

Come star-eyed maid—Equality!
    In thine adorer's praise I revel;
Who brings, so fierce his love to thee—
    All forms and faces to a level:
Old, young—great, small—the grave, the gay;
    Each man might swear the next his brother,
And there they stand in dread array,
    To fire their votes at one another.

How bright their buttons shine! how straight
    Their coat-flaps fall in plaited grace;
How smooth the hair on every pate;
    How vacant each immortal face!
And then thy tints—the shade—the flush—
    (I wrong them with a strain too humble)

Not mighty Sherred's strength of brush
   Can match thy glowing hues, my Trumbull.

Go on, great painter! dare be dull;
   No longer after nature dangle;
Call rectilinear beautiful;
   Find grace and freedom in an angle:
Pour on the red—the green—the yellow—
   "Paint 'till a horse may mire upon it,"
And while I've strength to write or bellow,
   I'll sound your praises in a sonnet.

CROAKER

Mark Twain

In 1878 Mark Twain toured Europe in the company of his family and a friend, Joseph Twitchell. The high point of the journey was a walking trip Twain and Twitchell made through the Black Forest and the Alps, which Twain recounted in *A Tramp Abroad* (in which Twitchell appears as "Harris").

In the fall of that year, Twitchell returned to the States while Twain, his wife Olivia and the rest of his party (including a friend from Elmira, Miss Clara Spaulding) continued their travels into Italy. From Venice, Twain wrote to Twitchell: "Livy and Clara Spaulding are having a royal time worshipping the old Masters, and I as good a time gritting my ineffectual teeth over them." Ineffectual? The fact is that these museum visits inspired what is possibly the funniest piece of demolition in the history of art criticism.

The scene is the Doges' Palace in Venice. We may imagine the ladies of Twain's party reverently admiring the imposing masterpieces, while Twain moves from "Tintoretto's three-acre picture in the Great Council Chamber" into the presence of the Hair Trunk.

THE IMMORTAL HAIR TRUNK
(from *A Tramp Abroad*, 1880)

The other great work which fascinated me was Bassano's immortal Hair Trunk. This is in the Chamber of the Council of Ten. It is in one of the three forty-foot pictures which decorate the walls of the room. The composition of this picture is beyond praise. The Hair Trunk is not hurled at the stranger's head—so to speak—as the chief feature of an immortal work so often is; no, it is carefully guarded from prominence, it is subordinated, it is restrained, it is most deftly and cleverly held in reserve, it is most cautiously and ingeniously led up to, by the master, and consequently when the spectator reaches it at last, he is taken unawares, he is unprepared, and it bursts upon him with a stupefying surprise.

One is lost in wonder at all the thought and care which this elaborate planning must have cost. A general glance at the picture could never suggest that there was a hair trunk in it; the Hair Trunk is not mentioned in the title even—which is, "Pope Alexander III. and the Doge Ziani, the Conqueror of the Emperor Frederick Barbarossa"; you see, the title is actually utilized to help divert attention from the Trunk; thus, as I say, nothing suggests the presence of the Trunk, by any hint, yet everything studiedly leads up to it, step by step. Let us examine into this, and observe the exquisitely artful artlessness of the plan.

At the extreme left end of the picture are a couple of women, one of them with a child looking over her shoulder at a wounded man sitting with bandaged head on the ground. These people seem needless, but no, they are there for a purpose; one cannot look at them without seeing the gorgeous procession of grandees, bishops, halberdiers, and banner-bearers which is passing along behind them; one cannot see the procession without feeling a curiosity to follow it and learn whither it is going; it leads him to the Pope, in the center of the picture, who is talking with the bonnetless Doge—talking tranquilly, too, although within twelve feet of them a man is beating a drum, and

not far from the drummer two persons are blowing horns, and
many horsemen are plunging and rioting about—indeed,
twenty-two feet of this great work is all a deep and happy holiday serenity and Sunday-school procession, and then we come
suddenly upon eleven and one-half feet of turmoil and racket
and insubordination. This latter state of things is not an accident, it has its purpose. But for it, one would linger upon the
Pope and the Doge, thinking them to be the motive and supreme
feature of the picture; whereas one is drawn along, almost unconsciously, to see what the trouble is about. Now at the very
end of this riot, within four feet of the end of the picture, and
full thirty-six feet from the beginning of it, the Hair Trunk
bursts with an electrifying suddenness upon the spectator, in all
its matchless perfection, and the great master's triumph is
sweeping and complete. From that moment no other thing in
those forty feet of canvas has any charm; one sees the Hair
Trunk, and the Hair Trunk only—and to see it is to worship it.
Bassano even placed objects in the immediate vicinity of the
Supreme Feature whose pretended purpose was to divert attention from it yet a little longer and thus delay and augment the
surprise; for instance, to the right of it he has placed a stooping
man with a cap so red that it is sure to hold the eye for a moment—to the left of it, some six feet away, he has placed a red-
coated man on an inflated horse, and that coat plucks your eye
to that locality the next moment—then, between the Trunk and
the red horseman he has intruded a man, naked to his waist,
who is carrying a fancy flour-sack on the middle of his back
instead of on his shoulder—this admirable feat interests you, of
course—keeps you at bay a little longer, like a sock or a jacket
thrown to the pursuing wolf—but at last, in spite of all dis-
tractions and detentions, the eye of even the most dull and heed-
less spectator is sure to fall upon the World's Masterpiece, and
in that moment he totters to his chair or leans upon his guide
for support.

Descriptions of such a work as this must necessarily be imperfect, yet they are of value. The top of the Trunk is arched;
the arch is a perfect half-circle, in the Roman style of archi-
tecture, for in the then rapid decadence of Greek art, the rising

influence of Rome was already beginning to be felt in the art of the Republic. The Trunk is bound or bordered with leather all around where the lid joins the main body. Many critics consider this leather too cold in tone; but I consider this its highest merit, since it was evidently made so to emphasize by contrast the impassioned fervor of the hasp. The high lights in this part of the work are cleverly managed, the *motif* is admirably subordinated to the ground tints, and the technique is very fine. The brass nail-heads are in the purest style of the early Renaissance. The strokes, here, are very firm and bold—every nail-head is a portrait. The handle on the end of the Trunk has evidently been retouched—I think, with a piece of chalk—but one can still see the inspiration of the Old Master in the tranquil, almost too tranquil, hang of it. The hair of this Trunk is *real* hair—so to speak—white in patches, brown in patches. The details are finely worked out; the repose proper to hair in a recumbent and inactive attitude is charmingly expressed. There is a feeling about this part of the work which lifts it to the highest altitudes of art; the sense of sordid realism vanishes away—one recognizes that there is *soul* here.

View this Trunk as you will, it is a gem, it is a marvel, it is a miracle. Some of the effects are very daring, approaching even to the boldest flights of the rococo, the sirocco, and the Byzantine schools—yet the master's hand never falters—it moves on, calm, majestic, confident—and, with that art which conceals art, it finally casts over the *tout ensemble*, by mysterious methods of its own, a subtle something which refines, subdues, etherealizes the arid components and endues them with the deep charm and gracious witchery of poesy.

Among the art treasures of Europe there are pictures which approach the Hair Trunk—there are two which may be said to equal it, possibly—but there is none that surpasses it. So perfect is the Hair Trunk that it moves persons who ordinarily have no feeling for art. When an Erie baggagemaster saw it two years ago, he could hardly keep from checking it; and once when a customs inspector was brought into its presence, he gazed upon it in silent rapture for some moments, then slowly and unconsciously placed one hand behind him with the palm uppermost, and got out his chalk with the other. These facts speak for themselves.

Mark Twain

Pity the poor Indian—driven from his ancestral hunting grounds into the novels of Fenimore Cooper! In *A Fable for Critics*, James Russell Lowell described the Cooper Redskin as follows:

> His Indians, with proper respect be it said,
> Are just Natty Bumppo, daubed over with red . . .

"Fenimore Cooper's Literary Offenses"—Twain's reaction against the academic critics who praised the Leather-Stocking novels as "pure works of art"—is an extremely entertaining piece of destructive criticism. But it is more than that. The essay is a manifesto of the school of realism.

Among the countless writers, editors and critics who responded to Twain's antiromantic respect for fact was Harold Ross. During his roving days as a tramp reporter, Ross read and reread "Fenimore Cooper's Literary Offenses"; its satire and its plea for factual accuracy in writing profoundly impressed the future founder and editor of *The New Yorker*.

In the following passage, the Cooper Indian bites the dust —or rather, as will be seen, misses the boat.

COOPER INDIANS
(from *Fenimore Cooper's Literary Offenses*, 1895)

The Pathfinder *and* The Deerslayer *stand at the head of Cooper's novels as artistic creations. There are others of his works which contain parts as perfect as are to be found in these, and scenes even more thrilling. Not one can be compared with either of them as a finished whole.*

The defects in both of these tales are comparatively slight. They were pure works of art. Prof. Lounsbury.

*The five tales reveal an extraordinary fullness of invention.
. . . One of the very greatest characters in fiction, Natty
Bumppo. . . .
The craft of the woodsman, the tricks of the trapper, all the
delicate art of the forest, were familiar to Cooper from his youth
up.* Prof. Brander Matthews.

*Cooper is the greatest artist in the domain of romantic fiction
yet produced by America.* Wilkie Collins.

It seems to me that it was far from right for the Professor of
English Literature in Yale, the Professor of English Literature in Columbia, and Wilkie Collins to deliver opinions on
Cooper's literature without having read some of it. It would
have been much more decorous to keep silent and let persons
talk who have read Cooper.

Cooper's art has some defects. In one place in *Deerslayer*,
and in the restricted space of two-thirds of a page, Cooper has
scored 114 offenses against literary art out of a possible 115. It
breaks the record.

There are nineteen rules governing literary art in the domain
of romantic fiction—some say twenty-two. In *Deerslayer*
Cooper violated eighteen of them. These eighteen require:

1. That a tale shall accomplish something and arrive somewhere. But the *Deerslayer* tale accomplishes nothing and arrives
in the air.

2. They require that the episodes of a tale shall be necessary
parts of the tale, and shall help to develop it. But as the *Deerslayer* tale is not a tale, and accomplishes nothing and arrives
nowhere, the episodes have no rightful place in the work, since
there was nothing for them to develop.

3. They require that the personages in a tale shall be alive,
except in the case of corpses, and that always the reader shall be
able to tell the corpses from the others. But this detail has often
been overlooked in the *Deerslayer* tale.

4. They require that the personages in a tale, both dead and

alive, shall exhibit a sufficient excuse for being there. But this detail also has been overlooked in the *Deerslayer* tale.

5. They require that when the personages of a tale deal in conversation, the talk shall sound like human talk, and be talk such as human beings would be likely to talk in the given circumstances, and have a discoverable meaning, also a discoverable purpose, and a show of relevancy, and remain in the neighborhood of the subject in hand, and be interesting to the reader, and help out the tale, and stop when the people cannot think of anything more to say. But this requirement has been ignored from the beginning of the *Deerslayer* tale to the end of it.

6. They require that when the author describes the character of a personage in his tale, the conduct and conversation of that personage shall justify said description. But this law gets little or no attention in the *Deerslayer* tale, as Natty Bumppo's case will amply prove.

7. They require that when a personage talks like an illustrated, gilt-edged, tree-calf, hand-tooled, seven-dollar Friendship's Offering in the beginning of a paragraph, he shall not talk like a negro minstrel in the end of it. But this rule is flung down and danced upon in the *Deerslayer* tale.

8. They require that crass stupidities shall not be played upon the reader as "the craft of the woodsman, the delicate art of the forest," by either the author or the people in the tale. But this rule is persistently violated in the *Deerslayer* tale.

9. They require that the personages of a tale shall confine themselves to possibilities and let miracles alone; or, if they venture a miracle, the author must so plausibly set it forth as to make it look possible and reasonable. But these rules are not respected in the *Deerslayer* tale.

10. They require that the author shall make the reader feel a deep interest in the personages of his tale and in their fate; and that he shall make the reader love the good people in the tale and hate the bad ones. But the reader of the *Deerslayer* tale dislikes the good people in it, is indifferent to the others, and wishes they would all get drowned together.

11. They require that the characters in a tale shall be so clearly defined that the reader can tell beforehand what each will do in a given emergency. But in the *Deerslayer* tale this rule is vacated.

In addition to these large rules there are some little ones. These require that the author shall

12. *Say* what he is proposing to say, not merely come near it.

13. Use the right word, not its second cousin.

14. Eschew surplusage.

15. Not omit necessary details.

16. Avoid slovenliness of form.

17. Use good grammar.

18. Employ a simple and straightforward style.

Even these seven are coldly and persistently violated in the *Deerslayer* tale.

Cooper's gift in the way of invention was not a rich endowment; but such as it was he liked to work it, he was pleased with the effects, and indeed he did some quite sweet things with it. In his little box of stage-properties he kept six or eight cunning devices, tricks, artifices for his savages and woodsmen to deceive and circumvent each other with, and he was never so happy as when he was working these innocent things and seeing them go. A favorite one was to make a moccasined person tread in the tracks of the moccasined enemy, and thus hide his own trail. Cooper wore out barrels and barrels of moccasins in working that trick. Another stage-property that he pulled out of his box pretty frequently was his broken twig. He prized his broken twig above all the rest of his effects, and worked it the hardest. It is a restful chapter in any book of his when somebody doesn't step on a dry twig and alarm all the reds and whites for two hundred yards around. Every time a Cooper person is in peril, and absolute silence is worth four dollars a minute, he is sure to step on a dry twig. There may be a hundred handier things to step on, but that wouldn't satisfy Cooper. Cooper requires him to turn out and find a dry twig; and if he can't do it, go and borrow one. In fact, the Leatherstocking Series ought to have been called the Broken Twig Series.

I am sorry there is not room to put in a few dozen instances of the delicate art of the forest, as practiced by Natty Bumppo and some of the other Cooperian experts. Perhaps we may venture two or three samples. Cooper was a sailor—a naval officer; yet he gravely tells us how a vessel, driving toward a lee shore in a gale, is steered for a particular spot by her skipper because he knows of an *undertow* there which will hold her back against the gale and save her. For just pure woodcraft, or sailor-craft, or whatever it is, isn't that neat? For several years Cooper was daily in the society of artillery, and he ought to have noticed that when a cannon-ball strikes the ground it either buries itself or skips a hundred feet or so; skips again a hundred feet or so—and so on, till finally it gets tired and rolls. Now in one place he loses some "females"—as he always calls women— in the edge of a wood near a plain at night in a fog, on purpose to give Bumppo a chance to show off the delicate art of the forest before the reader. These mislaid people are hunting for a fort. They hear a cannon-blast, and a cannon-ball presently comes rolling into the wood and stops at their feet. To the females this suggests nothing. The case is very different with the admirable Bumppo. I wish I may never know peace again if he doesn't strike out promptly and *follow the track* of that cannon-ball across the plain through the dense fog and find the fort. Isn't it a daisy? If Cooper had any real knowledge of Nature's ways of doing things, he had a most delicate art in concealing the fact. For instance: one of his acute Indian experts, Chingachgook (pronounced Chicago, I think), has lost the trail of a person he is tracking through the forest. Apparently that trail is hopelessly lost. Neither you nor I could ever have guessed out the way to find it. It was very different with Chicago. Chicago was not stumped for long. He turned a running stream out of its course, and there, in the slush in its old bed, were that person's moccasin tracks. The current did not wash them away, as it would have done in all other like cases—no, even the eternal laws of Nature have to vacate when Cooper wants to put up a delicate job of woodcraft on the reader.

We must be a little wary when Brander Matthews tells us that Cooper's books "reveal an extraordinary fullness of invention." As a rule, I am quite willing to accept Brander Matthews's literary judgments and applaud his lucid and graceful phrasing of them; but that particular statement needs to be taken with a few tons of salt. Bless your heart, Cooper hadn't any more invention than a horse; and I don't mean a high-class horse, either; I mean a clothes-horse. It would be very difficult to find a really clever "situation" in Cooper's books, and still more difficult to find one of any kind which he has failed to render absurd by his handling of it. Look at the episodes of "the caves"; and at the celebrated scuffle between Magua and those others on the table-land a few days later; and at Hurry Harry's queer water-transit from the castle to the ark; and at Deerslayer's half-hour with his first corpse; and at the quarrel between Hurry Harry and Deerslayer later; and at—but choose for yourself; you can't go amiss.

If Cooper had been an observer his inventive faculty would have worked better; not more interestingly, but more rationally, more plausibly. Cooper's proudest creations in the way of "situations" suffer noticeably from the absence of the observer's protecting gift. Cooper's eye was splendidly inaccurate. Cooper seldom saw anything correctly. He saw nearly all things as through a glass eye, darkly. Of course a man who cannot see the commonest little every-day matters accurately is working at a disadvantage when he is constructing a "situation." In the *Deerslayer* tale Cooper has a stream which is fifty feet wide where it flows out of a lake; it presently narrows to twenty as it meanders along for no given reason, and yet when a stream acts like that it ought to be required to explain itself. Fourteen pages later the width of the brook's outlet from the lake has suddenly shrunk thirty feet, and become "the narrowest part of the stream." This shrinkage is not accounted for. The stream has bends in it, a sure indication that it has alluvial banks and cuts them; yet these bends are only thirty and fifty feet long. If Cooper had been a nice and punctilious observer he would have noticed that the bends were oftener nine hundred feet long than short of it.

Cooper made the exit of that stream fifty feet wide, in the first place, for no particular reason; in the second place, he narrowed it to less than twenty to accommodate some Indians. He bends a "sapling" to the form of an arch over this narrow passage, and conceals six Indians in its foliage. They are "laying" for a settler's scow or ark which is coming up the stream on its way to the lake; it is being hauled against the stiff current by a rope whose stationary end is anchored in the lake; its rate of progress cannot be more than a mile an hour. Cooper describes the ark, but pretty obscurely. In the matter of dimensions "it was little more than a modern canal-boat." Let us guess, then, that it was about one hundred and forty feet long. It was of "greater breadth than common." Let us guess, then, that it was about sixteen feet wide. This leviathan had been prowling down bends which were but a third as long as itself, and scraping between banks where it had only two feet of space to spare on each side. We cannot too much admire this miracle. A low-roofed log dwelling occupies "two-thirds of the ark's length"— a dwelling ninety feet long and sixteen feet wide, let us say—a kind of vestibule train. The dwelling has two rooms—each forty-five feet long and sixteen feet wide, let us guess. One of them is the bedroom of the Hutter girls, Judith and Hetty; the other is the parlor in the daytime, at night it is papa's bed-chamber. The ark is arriving at the stream's exit now, whose width has been reduced to less than twenty feet to accommodate the Indians—say to eighteen. There is a foot to spare on each side of the boat. Did the Indians notice that there was going to be a tight squeeze there? Did they notice that they could make money by climbing down out of that arched sapling and just stepping aboard when the ark scraped by? No, other Indians would have noticed these things, but Cooper's Indians never notice anything. Cooper thinks they are marvelous creatures for noticing, but he was almost always in error about his Indians. There was seldom a sane one among them.

The ark is one hundred and forty-feet long; the dwelling is ninety feet long. The idea of the Indians is to drop softly and secretly from the arched sapling to the dwelling as the ark creeps along under it at the rate of a mile an hour, and butcher the family. It will take the ark a minute and a half to pass under. It will take the ninety-foot dwelling a minute to pass under.

Now, then, what did the six Indians do? It would take you thirty years to guess, and even then you would have to give it up, I believe. Therefore, I will tell you what the Indians did. Their chief, a person of quite extraordinary intellect for a Cooper Indian, warily watched the canal-boat as it squeezed along under him, and when he had got his calculations fined down to exactly the right shade, as he judged, he let go and dropped. And *missed the house!* That is actually what he did. He missed the house, and landed in the stern of the scow. It was not much of a fall, yet it knocked him silly. He lay there unconscious. If the house had been ninety-seven feet long he would have made the trip. The fault was Cooper's not his. The error lay in the construction of the house. Cooper was no architect.

There still remained in the roost five Indians. The boat has passed under and is now out of their reach. Let me explain what the five did—you would not be able to reason it out for yourself. No. 1 jumped for the boat, but fell in the water astern of it. Then No. 2 jumped for the boat, but fell in the water still farther astern of it. Then No. 3 jumped for the boat, and fell a good way astern of it. Then No. 4 jumped for the boat, and fell in the water *away* astern. Then even No. 5 made a jump for the boat—for he was a Cooper Indian. In the matter of intellect, the difference between a Cooper Indian and the Indian that stands in front of a cigar-shop is not spacious. The scow episode is really a sublime burst of invention; but it does not thrill, because the inaccuracy of the details throws a sort of air of factitiousness and general improbability over it. This comes of Cooper's inadequacy as an observer.

George Ade

All the capital letters Don Marquis left out of archy and mehitabel can be found in the Fables in Slang of George Ade. Twelve years older than Marquis, George Ade wrote his first Fable in 1897, while he was a top-ranking reporter and popular

columnist on the Chicago *Record*. With two columns to fill
daily, he had sought a fresh slant to his feature, "Stories of the
Streets and of the Town," and found it in a kind of ragtime
version of Aesop. In the Adean fable Americans are substituted
for talking animals, the language is heavily overstuffed with
colloquialism, and the "morals" are all variations on the theme
of Nobody Wins.

The first of many collections of Fables in Slang appeared in
1899. They were nationally popular within a short time, and
Ade continued to turn them out for more than twenty years. In
the style of a fable by Ade himself: They made him Rich,
which allowed him to Follow a Lucrative but Undistinguished
Career as a Playwright, which in turn allowed him to stop writing Fables.

It is easy for us to forget, reading Ade today, that he started
writing Fables in Slang long before the American vernacular
was anything more than a casual acquaintance of literature.
The humorous use of what Ade called "slang" was something
new at the turn of the century, although we would now apply
some other phrase to the very special thing Ade did. "Fables in
Cliché" might be more appropriate, particularly in the case of
the earlier Fables. Ade knew more about clichés than any other
writer of his period in America. His ear was always cocked for
the newly born set phrase, for the word that wears its social
connotations like an Easter bonnet, for the cant of lunch room,
bridge table and bar.

THE *FABLE* OF *WHAT HAPPENED* THE *NIGHT THE MEN CAME* TO THE *WOMEN'S CLUB*

In a Progressive Little City claiming about twice the Population that the Census Enumerators could uncover, there was a
Literary Club. It was one of these Clubs guaranteed to fix you
out with Culture while you wait. Two or three Matrons, who
were too Heavy for Light Amusements, but not old enough to
remain at Home and Knit, organized the Club. Nearly every
Woman in town rushed to get in, for fear somebody would say
she hadn't been Asked.

The Club used to Round Up once a week at the Homes of

Members. There would be a Paper, followed by a Discussion, after which somebody would Pour.

The Organization seemed to be a Winner. One Thing the Lady Clubbers were Dead Set On. They were going to have Harmony with an Upper Case H. They were out to cut a seven-foot Swath through English Literature from Beowulf to Bangs, inclusive, and no petty Jealousies or Bickerings would stand in the Way.

So while they were at the Club they would pull Kittenish Smiles at each other, and Applaud so as not to split the Gloves. Some times they would Kiss, too, but they always kept their Fingers crossed.

Of course, when they got off in Twos and Threes they would pull the little Meat-Axes out of the Reticules and hack a few Monograms, but that was to have been expected.

Everything considered, the Club was a Tremendous Go. At each Session the Lady President would announce the Subject for the next Meeting. For instance, she would say that Next Week they would take up Wyclif. Then every one would romp home to look in the Encyclopedia of Authors and find out who in the world Wyclif was. On the following Thursday they would have Wyclif down Pat, and be primed for a Discussion. They would talk about Wyclif as if he had been down to the House for Tea every evening that Week.

After the Club had been running for Six Months it was beginning to be Strong on Quotations and Dates. The Members knew that Mrs. Browning was the wife of Mr. Browning, that Milton had Trouble with his Eyes, and that Lord Byron wasn't all that he should have been, to say the Least. They began to feel their Intellectual Oats. In the meantime the Jeweler's Wife had designed a Club Badge.

The Club was doing such Notable Work that some of the Members thought they ought to have a Special Meeting and invite the Men. They wanted to put the Cap-Sheaf on a Profitable Season, and at the same time hand the Merited Rebuke to some of the Husbands and Brothers who had been making Funny Cracks.

It was decided to give the Star Programme at the Beadle

Home, and after the Papers had been read then all the Men and
Five Women who did not hold office could file through the
Front Room and shake Hands with the President, the Vice-
President, the Recording Secretary, the Corresponding Secre-
tary, the Treasurer, and the members of the various Com-
mittees, all of whom were to line up and Receive.

The reason the Club decided to have the Brain Barbecue at
the Beadle Home was that the Beadles had such beautiful big
Rooms and Double Doors. There was more or less quiet Har-
poon Work when the Announcement was made. Several of
the Elderly Ones said that Josephine Beadle was not a Representative Member of the Club. She was Fair to look upon, but
she was not pulling very hard for the Uplifting of the Sex. It
was suspected that she came to the Meetings just to Kill Time
and see what the Others were Wearing. She refused to buckle
down to Literary Work, for she was a good deal more interested
in the Bachelors who filled the Windows of the new Men's
Club than she was in the Butler who wrote "Hudibras." So why
should she have the Honor of entertaining the Club at the Annual Meeting? Unfortunately, the Members who had the most
Doing under their Bonnets were not the ones who could come to
the Front with large Rooms that could be Thrown together, so
the Beadle Home got the Great Event.

Every one in Town who carried a Pound of Social Influence
showed up in his or her Other Clothes. Extra Chairs had to be
brought in, and what with the Smilax and Club Colors it was
very Swell, and the Maiden in the Lace Mitts who was going to
write about it for the Weekly threw a couple of Spasms.

The Men were led in pulling at the Halters and with their
Ears laid back. After they got into the Dressing Room they
Stuck there until they had to be Shooed out. They did not know
what they were going against, but they had their Suspicions.
They managed to get Rear Seats or stand along the Wall so
that they could execute the Quiet Sneak if Things got too
Literary. The Women were too Flushed and Proud to Notice.

At 8:30 P.M. the Lady President stood out and began to
read a few Pink Thoughts on "Woman's Destiny—Why Not?"
Along toward 9:15, about the time the Lady President was be-

ginning to show up Good and Earnest, Josephine Beadle, who
was Circulating around on the Outskirts of the Throng to make
sure that everybody was Happy, made a Discovery. She noticed that the Men standing along the Wall and in the Doorways
were not more than sixty per cent En Rapport with the Long
Piece about Woman's Destiny. Now Josephine was right there
to see that Everybody had a Nice Time, and she did not
like to see the Prominent Business Men of the Town dying of
Thirst or Leg Cramp or anything like that, so she gave two or
three of them the Quiet Wink, and they tiptoed after her out to
the Dining Room, where she offered Refreshments, and said
they could slip out on the Side Porch and Smoke if they
wanted to.

Probably they preferred to go back in the Front Room and
hear some more about Woman's Destiny not.

As soon as they could master their Emotions and get control
of their Voices, they told Josephine what they thought of her.
They said she made the Good Samaritan look like a Cheap
Criminal, and if she would only say the Word they would begin
to put Ground Glass into the Food at Home. Then Josephine
called them "Boys," which probably does not make a Hit with
one who is on the sloping side of 48. More of the Men seemed
to awake to the Fact that they were Overlooking something, so
they came on the Velvet Foot back to the Dining Room and
declared themselves In, and flocked around Josephine and
called her "Josie" and "Joe." They didn't care. They were having a Pleasant Visit.

Josephine gave them Allopathic Slugs of the Size that they
feed you in the Navy and then lower you into the Dingey and
send you Ashore. Then she let them go out on the Porch to
smoke. By the time the Lady President came to the last Page
there were only two Men left in the Front Room. One was
Asleep and the other was Penned In.

The Women were Huffy. They went out to make the Men
come in, and found them Bunched on the Porch listening to a
Story that a Traveling Man had just brought to Town that
Day.

Now the Plan was that during the Reception the Company

would stand about in little Groups, and ask each other what
Books they liked, and make it something on the order of a
Salon. This Plan miscarried, because all the Men wanted to
hear Rag Time played by Josephine, the Life-Saver. Josephine
had to yield, and the Men all clustered around her to give their
Moral Support. After one or two Selections, they felt sufficiently Keyed to begin to hit up those low-down Songs about
Baby and Chickens and Razors. No one paid any Attention to
the Lady President, who was off in a Corner holding an Indignation Meeting with the Secretary and the Vice-President.

When the Women began to sort out the Men and order them
to start Home and all the Officers of the Club were giving
Josephine the frosty Good Night, any one could see that there
was Trouble ahead.

Next Day the Club held a Special Session and expelled
Josephine for Conduct Unbecoming a Member, and Josephine
sent Word to them as follows: "Rats."

Then the Men quietly got together and bought Josephine
about a Thousand Dollars' Worth of American Beauty Roses
to show that they were With her, and then Homes began to
break up, and somebody started the Report that anyway it was
the Lady President's Fault for having such a long and pokey
Essay that wasn't hers at all, but had been Copied out of a Club
Paper published in Detroit.

Before the next Meeting there were two Factions. The Lady
President had gone to a Rest Cure, and the Meeting resolved
itself into a Good Cry and a general Smash-Up.

MORAL: *The only Literary Men are those who have to Work
at it.*

Don Marquis

"The roach and the cat," wrote Christopher Morley of archy
and mehitabel, "by their humble station in life and the lowli-
ness of their associates, provided an admirable vantage for
merciless joshing of everything biggity." To Morley's appraisal,
the editor can only add that Marquis' style is as infectious as
his irreverence:

for instance when archy meets
pete the parrot several
hundred years of apotheosis
of the immortal bard and a few
library walls of shakespeare
criticism go drifting gently down
the avon and art
like everything else has lost
its capital letter

pete the parrot and shakespeare

(from *archy and mehitabel*)

i got acquainted with
a parrot named pete recently
who is an interesting bird
pete says he used
to belong to the fellow
that ran the mermaid tavern
in london then i said
you must have known
shakespeare know him said pete
poor mutt i knew him well
he called me pete and i called him
bill but why do you say poor mutt
well said pete bill was a
disappointed man and was always
boring his friends about what
he might have been and done
if he only had a fair break
two or three pints of sack
and sherris and the tears
would trickle down into his
beard and his beard would get
soppy and wilt his collar
i remember one night when
bill and ben jonson and
frankie beaumont

were sopping it up
here i am ben says bill
nothing but a lousy playwright
and with anything like luck
in the breaks i might have been
a fairly decent sonnet writer
i might have been a poet
if i had kept away from the theatre

yes says ben i ve often
thought of that bill
but one consolation is
you are making pretty good money
out of the theatre

money money says bill what the hell
is money what i want is to be
a poet not a business man
these damned cheap shows
i turn out to keep the
theatre running break my heart
slap stick comedies and
blood and thunder tragedies
and melodramas say i wonder
if that boy heard you order
another bottle frankie
the only compensation is that i get
a chance now and then
to stick in a little poetry
when nobody is looking
but hells bells that isn t
what i want to do
i want to write sonnets and
songs and spenserian stanzas
and i might have done it too
if i hadn t got
into this frightful show game
business business business

grind grind grind
what a life for a man
that might have been a poet

well says frankie beaumont
why don t you cut it bill
i can t says bill
i need the money i ve got
a family to support down in
the country well says frankie
anyhow you write pretty good
plays bill any mutt can write
plays for this london public
says bill if he puts enough
murder in them what they want
is kings talking like kings
never had sense enough to talk
and stabbings and stranglings
and fat men making love
and clowns basting each
other with clubs and cheap puns
and off color allusions to all
the smut of the day oh i know
what the low brows want
and i give it to them

well says ben jonson
don t blubber into the drink
brace up like a man
and quit the rotten business
i can t i can t says bill
i ve been at it too long i ve got to
the place now where i can t
write anything else
but this cheap stuff
i m ashamed to look an honest
young sonneteer in the face
i live a hell of a life i do

the manager hands me some mouldy old
manuscript and says
bill here s a plot for you
this is the third of the month
by the tenth i want a good
script out of this that we
can start rehearsals on
not too big a cast
and not too much of your
damned poetry either
you know your old
familiar line of hokum
they eat up that falstaff stuff
of yours ring him in again
and give them a good ghost
or two and remember we gotta
have something dick burbage can get
his teeth into and be sure
and stick in a speech
somewhere the queen will take
for a personal compliment and if
you get in a line or two somewhere
about the honest english yeoman
it s always good stuff
and it s a pretty good stunt
bill to have the heavy villain
a moor or a dago or a jew
or something like that and say
i want another
comic welshman in this
but i don t need to tell
you bill you know this game
just some of your ordinary
hokum and maybe you could
kill a little kid or two a prince
or something they like
a little pathos along with
the dirt now you better see burbage

tonight and see what he wants
in that part oh says bill
to think i am
debasing my talents with junk
like that oh god what i wanted
was to be a poet
and write sonnet serials
like a gentleman should

well says i pete
bill s plays are highly
esteemed to this day
is that so says pete
poor mutt little he would
care what poor bill wanted
was to be a poet

archy

F.P.A.

(Franklin Pierce Adams)

THE LANDING OF THE PILGRIM FATHERS

PILGRIM DADS
LAND ON MASS.
COAST TOWN

INTREPID BAND OF BRITONS, SEEKING FAITH'S PURE SHRINE, REACH ROCK-BOUND COAST, SINGING AMID STORM

PROVINCETOWN, MASS., Dec. 21—Poking her nose through the fog, the ship *Mayflower*, of Southampton, Jones, Master, limped into port tonight.

On board were men with hoary hair and women with fear-less eyes, 109 in all.

Asked why they made the journey, they alleged that religious freedom was the goal they sought here.

The *Mayflower* carried a cargo of antique furniture.

Among those on board were William Bradford, M. Standish, Jno. Alden, Peregrine White, John Carver and others.

Steps are being taken to organize a society of Mayflower Descendants.

Dorothy Parker

A PIG'S-EYE VIEW OF LITERATURE

THE LIVES AND TIMES OF JOHN KEATS, PERCY BYSSHE SHELLEY, AND GEORGE GORDON NOEL, LORD BYRON

Byron and Shelley and Keats
   Were a trio of lyrical treats.
The forehead of Shelley was cluttered with curls,
And Keats never was a descendant of earls,
And Byron walked out with a number of girls,
   But it didn't impair the poetical feats
     Of Byron and Shelley,
     Of Byron and Shelley,
   Of Byron and Shelley and Keats.

OSCAR WILDE

If, with the literate, I am
Impelled to try an epigram,
I never seek to take the credit;
We all assume that Oscar said it.

HARRIET BEECHER STOWE

The pure and worthy Mrs. Stowe
Is one we all are proud to know
As mother, wife, and authoress—
Thank God, I am content with less!

D. G. ROSSETTI

Dante Gabriel Rossetti
Buried all of his *libretti*,
Thought the matter over—then
Went and dug them up again.

THOMAS CARLYLE

Carlyle combined the lit'ry life
With throwing teacups at his wife,
Remarking, rather testily,
"Oh, stop your dodging, Mrs. C.!"

CHARLES DICKENS

Who call him spurious and shoddy
Shall do it o'er my lifeless body.
I heartily invite such birds
To come outside and say those words!

ALEXANDRE DUMAS AND HIS SON

Although I work, and seldom cease,
At Dumas *père* and Dumas *fils*,
Alas, I cannot make me care
For Dumas *fils* and Dumas *père*

ALFRED, LORD TENNYSON

Should Heaven send me any son,
I hope he's not like Tennyson.
I'd rather have him play a fiddle
Than rise and bow and speak an idyll.

GEORGE GISSING

When I admit neglect of Gissing,
They say I don't know what I'm missing.
Until their arguments are subtler,
I think I'll stick to Samuel Butler.

WALTER SAVAGE LANDOR

Upon the work of Walter Landor
I am unfit to write with candor.
If you can read it, well and good;
But as for me, I never could.

GEORGE SAND

What time the gifted lady took
Away from paper, pen, and book,
She spent in amorous dalliance
(They do those things so well in France).

Wolcott Gibbs

Grand Master of parody and satire, Wolcott Gibbs was for
many years a jack-of-all-trades at *The New Yorker*, having contributed to every department except two, women's fashion and
horse racing, "two fields in which my information was generally felt to be inadequate, though not by me."

The two pieces included here will illustrate the fact that,
until his death a few years ago, Wolcott Gibbs was among his
other competencies one of *The New Yorker*'s most entertaining
critics of the arts.

RING OUT, WILD BELLS

When I finally got around to seeing Max Reinhardt's
cinema version of "A Midsummer-Night's Dream," and
saw a child called Mickey Rooney playing Puck, I remembered
suddenly that long ago I had taken the same part.

Our production was given on the open-air stage at the Riverdale Country School, shortly before the war. The scenery was only the natural scenery of that suburban dell, and the cast was exclusively male, ranging in age from eleven to perhaps seventeen. While we had thus preserved the pure, Elizabethan note of the original, it must be admitted that our version had its drawbacks. The costumes were probably the worst things we had to bear, and even Penrod, tragically arrayed as Launcelot in his sister's stockings and his father's drawers, might have been embarrassed for us. Like Penrod, we were costumed by our parents, and like the Schofields, they seemed on the whole a little weak historically. Half of the ladies were inclined to favor the Elizabethan, and they had constructed rather bunchy ruffs and farthingales for their offspring; others, who had read as far as the stage directions and learned that the action took place in an Athenian wood, had produced something vaguely Athenian, usually beginning with a sheet. Only the fairies had a certain uniformity. For some reason their parents had all decided on cheesecloth, with here and there a little ill-advised trimming with tinsel.

My own costume was mysterious, but spectacular. As nearly as I have ever been able to figure things out, my mother found her inspiration for it in a Maxfield Parrish picture of a court jester. Beginning at the top, there was a cap with three stuffed horns; then, for the main part, a pair of tights that covered me to my wrists and ankles; and finally slippers with stuffed toes that curled up at the ends. The whole thing was made out of silk in alternate green and red stripes, and (unquestionably my poor mother's most demented stroke) it was covered from head to foot with a thousand tiny bells. Because all our costumes were obviously perishable, we never wore them in rehearsal, and naturally nobody knew that I was invested with these peculiar sound effects until I made my entrance at the beginning of the second act.

Our director was a man who had strong opinions about how Shakespeare should be played, and Puck was one of his favorite characters. It was his theory that Puck, being "the incarnation of mischief," never ought to be still a minute, so I had been coached to bound onto the stage, and once there to dance up and down, cocking my head and waving my arms.

"I want you to be a little whirlwind," this man said.

Even as I prepared to bound onto the stage, I had my own misgivings about those dangerously abundant gestures, and their probable effect on my bells. It was too late, however, to invent another technique for playing Puck, even if there had been room for anything but horror in my mind. I bounded onto the stage.

The effect, in its way, must have been superb. With every leap I rang like a thousand children's sleighs, my melodies foretelling God knows what worlds of merriment to the enchanted spectators. It was even worse when I came to the middle of the stage and went into my gestures. The other ringing had been loud but sporadic. This was persistent, varying only slightly in volume and pitch with the vehemence of my gestures. To a blind man, it must have sounded as though I had recklessly decided to accompany myself on a xylophone. A maturer actor would probably have made up his mind that an emergency existed, and abandoned his gestures as impracticable under the circumstances. I was thirteen, and incapable of innovations. I had been told by responsible authorities that gestures went with this part, and I continued to make them. I also continued to ring—a silvery music, festive and horrible.

If the bells were hard on my nerves, they were even worse for the rest of the cast, who were totally unprepared for my new interpretation. Puck's first remark is addressed to one of the fairies, and it is mercifully brief.

I said, " 'How now, spirit! Whither wander you?' "

This unhappy child, already embarrassed by a public appearance in cheesecloth and tinsel, was also burdened with an opening speech of sixteen lines in verse. He began bravely:

> "Over hill, over dale,
>   Through brush, through brier,
> Over park, over pale,
>   Through flood, through fire . . ."

At the word "fire," my instructions were to bring my hands up from the ground in a long, wavery sweep, intended to represent fire. The bells pealed. To my startled ears, it sounded more as if they exploded. The fairy stopped in his lines and looked at me sharply. The jingling, however, had diminished; it was no more than as if a faint wind stirred my bells, and he went on:

> "I do wander everywhere,
> Swifter than the moone's sphere . . ."

Here again I had another cue, for a sort of swoop and dip indicating the swiftness of the moone's sphere. Again the bells rang out, and again the performance stopped in its tracks. The fairy was clearly troubled by these interruptions. He had, however, a child's strange acceptance of the inscrutable, and was even able to regard my bells as a last-minute adult addition to the program, nerve-racking but not to be questioned. I'm sure it was only this that got him through that first speech.

My turn, when it came, was even worse. By this time the audience had succumbed to a helpless gaiety. Every time my bells rang, laughter swept the spectators, and this mounted and mingled with the bells until everything else was practically inaudible. I began my speech, another long one, and full of incomprehensible references to Titania's changeling.

"Louder!" said somebody in the wings. "You'll have to talk louder."

It was the director, and he seemed to be in a dangerous state.

"And for heaven's sake, stop that jingling!" he said.

I talked louder, and I tried to stop the jingling, but it was no use. By the time I got to the end of my speech, I was shouting and so was the audience. It appeared that I had very little control over the bells, which continued to jingle in spite of my passionate efforts to keep them quiet.

All this had a very bad effect on the fairy, who by this time had many symptoms of a complete nervous collapse. However, he began his next speech:

> "Either I mistake your shape and making quite,
> Or else you are that shrewd and knavish sprite

Called Robin Goodfellow: are you not he
That . . ."

At this point I forgot that the rules had been changed and I was supposed to leave out the gestures. There was a furious jingling, and the fairy gulped.

"Are you not he that, that . . ."

He looked miserably at the wings, and the director supplied the next line, but the tumult was too much for him. The unhappy child simply shook his head.

"Say anything!" shouted the director desperately. "Anything at all!"

The fairy only shut his eyes and shuddered.

"All right!" shouted the director. "All right, Puck. *You* begin *your* next speech."

By some miracle, I actually did remember my next lines, and had opened my mouth to begin on them when suddenly the fairy spoke. His voice was a high, thin monotone, and there seemed to be madness in it, but it was perfectly clear.

" 'Fourscore and seven years ago,' " he began, " 'our fathers brought forth on this continent a new nation, conceived . . .' "

He said it right through to the end, and it was certainly the most successful speech ever made on that stage, and probably one of the most successful speeches ever made on any stage. I don't remember, if I ever knew, how the rest of us ever picked up the dull, normal thread of the play after that extraordinary performance, but we must have, because I know it went on. I only remember that in the next intermission the director cut off my bells with his penknife, and after that things quieted down and got dull.

ADULTERY MAKES DULL BEDFELLOWS

Sinister chaps, these gods that be, Michael," says Diana, and away we go. The scene is a living room in the home of Mrs. Reggie Williams Browne, the time is a breathing space or vacuum in the history of the world, and the remark is occasioned almost entirely by the circumstance that it has been de-

cided by somebody, though certainly not by me, that what New
York really needs at the moment is another comedy by Frederick
Lonsdale. I don't know exactly what to tell you about the
evening that may be lying in wait for you at the Fulton. There
is, of course, an abundant supply of those epigrams with which
Mr. Lonsdale has been titillating the Morgan-Harjes set since
1908. The quality of these quips is uneven. Sometimes a cliché
has been so ingeniously rearranged that it comes out sounding
almost like wit, sometimes the author's gay perversity is such
that wicked old dowagers in the audience nudge one another almost out from under their hair, but most of the time, I'm afraid,
his record of stylish conversations is just stupefying. At one
point, for instance, Diana, a moderately sinister chap herself,
offers us a rather involved thought about the double standard.
"To a woman," she says, taking a deep breath, "a man's past
only means that, thank God, he's had experience, while, to a
man, a woman's past only means—that she's had a past." Don't
bother to unwrap it. It's just a sample.

The real complexity of life among Mr. Lonsdale's powerfully sexed grammarians can be indicated in a sentence, though
a tough one: Michael, engaged to Molly, is really in love with
Diana, whom he seduced once in Paris; George can't decide
whether to marry Celia or Maggie, both of whom he has seduced here and there at various times; and Elsie, though married to Reggie, is still strongly attracted to her first husband,
John, who has seduced practically everybody and likes to talk
about it. Anyway, all these people, along with a drunken butler
and an old family lawyer, both standard models, are visible on
the stage, sometimes all at once. It is a rich and sophisticated
dish, though not precisely, you might say, the Blue Plate Gibbs.
How Mr. Lonsdale gets everything straightened out in the end,
I won't try to tell you in this fortunately limited space. An im-
pacted wisdom tooth, the drunken butler, and a good many
dubious coincidences are involved, but the whole business isn't
very clear to me even now, and I think you'd better just accept
my word that everybody winds up in the right bed. Come to
think of it, George (see synopsis) really doesn't, but the hell
with him.

Moving on to the cast, the chief attraction is probably Roland Young, a good actor but not, apparently, a very acute judge of scripts. It is Mr. Young's task to portray a small, neat, harried character, who has had eleven mistresses in the past and is now mixed up with two more. "I am a dull man," he says gloomily, "with just one way of expressing myself." Mr. Young indicates this unhappy state largely by popping his eyes and sniffing his mustache, but he is funny enough and has my respectful sympathy. His co-star, Margaret Lindsay, a handsome recruit from the films, with an impressive voice, has been entrusted with Diana and some of the most staggering lines since *Lady Windermere's Fan*. Here is strictly a triumph of beauty over syntax. Arthur Margetson, as a cynical man of the world, contributes a cryptic smile and a fashionable presence and is, I'm sure, exactly what the author had in mind. Of the others— Doris Dalton, Philip Ober, Henry Mowbray, Augusta Dabney— I can only say that they don't seem exactly right for Lonsdale types, something, praise God, that might happen to anybody. Raymond Sovey's boudoir setting is obviously just the place for a roll in the ermine and the living room is very pretty, too. The name of this piece, by the way, is *Another Love Story*.

Robert Benchley

OPERA SYNOPSES

SOME SAMPLE OUTLINES OF GRAND OPERA PLOTS FOR HOME STUDY

I

DIE MEISTER-GENOSSENSCHAFT

SCENE: *The Forests of Germany.*
TIME: *Antiquity.*

CAST

STRUDEL, *God of Rain* ....Basso
SCHMALZ, *God of Slight Drizzle* ....Tenor
IMMERGLÜCK, *Goddess of the Six Primary Colors* ....Soprano
LUDWIG DAS EIWEISS, *the Knight of the Iron Duck* ...Baritone
THE WOODPECKER ....Soprano

ARGUMENT

The basis of "Die Meister-Genossenschaft" is an old legend of Germany which tells how the Whale got his Stomach.

ACT 1

The Rhine at Low Tide Just Below Weldschnoffen.—Immerglück has grown weary of always sitting on the same rock with the same fishes swimming by every day, and sends for Schwül to suggest something to do. Schwül asks her how she would like to have pass before her all the wonders of the world fashioned by the hand of man. She says, rotten. He then suggests that Ringblattz, son of Pflucht, be made to appear before her and fight a mortal combat with the Iron Duck. This pleases Immerglück and she summons to her the four dwarfs: Hot Water, Cold Water, Cool, and Cloudy. She bids them bring Ringblattz to her. They refuse, because Pflucht has at one time rescued them from being buried alive by acorns, and, in a rage, Immerglück strikes them all dead with a thunderbolt.

ACT 2

A Mountain Pass.—Repenting of her deed, Immerglück has sought advice of the giants, Offen and Besitz, and they tell her that she must procure the magic zither which confers upon its owner the power to go to sleep while apparently carrying on a conversation. This magic zither has been hidden for three hundred centuries in an old bureau drawer, guarded by the Iron Duck, and, although many have attempted to rescue it, all have died of a strange ailment just as success was within their grasp.

But Immerglück calls to her side Dampfboot, the tinsmith of the gods, and bids him make for her a tarnhelm or invisible cap which will enable her to talk to people without their understanding a word she says. For a dollar and a half extra Dampfboot throws in a magic ring which renders its wearer insensible. Thus armed, Immerglück starts out for Walhalla, humming to herself.

ACT 3

The Forest Before the Iron Duck's Bureau Drawer.—Merglitz, who has up till this time held his peace, now descends from a balloon and demands the release of Betty. It has been the will of Wotan that Merglitz and Betty should meet on earth and hate each other like poison, but Zweiback, the druggist of the gods, has disobeyed and concocted a love-potion which has rendered the young couple very unpleasant company. Wotan, enraged, destroys them with a protracted heat spell.

Encouraged by this sudden turn of affairs, Immerglück comes to earth in a boat drawn by four white Holsteins, and, seated alone on a rock, remembers aloud to herself the days when she was a girl. Pilgrims from Augenblick, on their way to worship at the shrine of Schmürr, hear the sound of reminiscence coming from the rock and stop in their march to sing a hymn of praise for the drying-up of the crops. They do not recognize Immerglück, as she has her hair done differently, and think that she is a beggar girl selling pencils.

In the meantime, Ragel, the papercutter of the gods, has fashioned himself a sword on the forge of Schmalz, and has called the weapon "Assistance-in-Emergency." Armed with "Assistance-in-Emergency" he comes to earth, determined to slay the Iron Duck and carry off the beautiful Irma.

But Frimsel overhears the plan and has a drink brewed which is given to Ragel in a golden goblet and which, when drunk, makes him forget his past and causes him to believe that he is Schnorr, the God of Fun. While laboring under this spell, Ragel has a funeral pyre built on the summit of a high mountain and, after lighting it, climbs on top of it with a mandolin which he plays until he is consumed.

Immerglück never marries.

II

IL MINNESTRONE

(PEASANT LOVE)

SCENE: *Venice and Old Point Comfort.*
TIME: *Early 16th Century.*

CAST

ALFONSO, *Duke of Minnestrone* ....Baritone
PARTOLA, *a Peasant Girl* ....Soprano

CLEANSO		Tenor
TURINO	*Young Noblemen of Venice*	Tenor
BOMBO		Basso
LUDOVICO	*Assassins in the Service of*	Basso
ASTOLFO	*Cafeteria Rusticana*	Methodist

Townspeople, Cabbies and Sparrows

ARGUMENT

"Il Minnestrone" is an allegory of the two sides of a man's nature (good and bad), ending at last in an awfully comical mess with everyone dead.

ACT 1

A Public Square, Ferrara.—During a peasant festival held to celebrate the sixth consecutive day of rain, Rudolpho, a young nobleman, sees Lilliano, daughter of the village bell-ringer, dancing along throwing artificial roses at herself. He asks of his secretary who the young woman is, and his secretary, in order to confuse Rudolpho and thereby win the hand of his ward, tells him that it is his (Rudolpho's) own mother, disguised for the festival. Rudolpho is astounded. He orders her arrest.

ACT 2

Banquet Hall in Gorgio's Palace.—Lilliano has not forgotten Breda, her old nurse, in spite of her troubles, and determines to avenge herself for the many insults she received in her youth by poisoning her (Breda). She therefore invites the old nurse to a banquet and poisons her. Presently a knock is heard. It is Ugolfo. He has come to carry away the body of Michelo and to leave an extra quart of pasteurized. Lilliano tells him that she no longer loves him, at which he goes away, dragging his feet sulkily.

Act 3

In Front of Emilo's House.—Still thinking of the old man's curse, Borsa has an interview with Cleanso, believing him to be the Duke's wife. He tells him things can't go on as they are, and Cleanso stabs him. Just at this moment Betty comes rushing in from school and falls in a faint. Her worst fears have been realized. She has been insulted by Sigmundo, and presently dies of old age. In a fury, Ugolfo rushes out to kill Sigmundo and, as he does so, the dying Rosenblatt rises on one elbow and curses his mother.

III

LUCY DE LIMA

SCENE: *Wales.*
TIME: *1700 (Greenwich).*

Cast

WILLIAM WONT, *Lord of Glennnn* ....Basso
LUCY WAGSTAFF, *his daughter* ....Soprano
BERTRAM, *her lover* ....Tenor
LORD ROGER, *friend of Bertram* ....Soprano
IRMA, *attendant to Lucy* ....Basso

Friends, Retainers, and Members of the local Lodge of Elks.

ARGUMENT

"Lucy de Lima" is founded on the well-known story by Boccaccio of the same name and address.

ACT 1

Gypsy Camp Near Waterbury.—The gypsies, led by Edith, go singing through the camp on the way to the fair. Following them comes Despard, the gypsy leader, carrying Ethel, whom he has just kidnapped from her father, who had previously just kidnapped her from her mother. Despard places Ethel on the ground and tells Mona, the old hag, to watch over her. Mona nurses a secret grudge against Despard for having once cut off her leg, and decides to change Ethel for Nettie, another kidnapped child. Ethel pleads with Mona to let her stay with Despard, for she has fallen in love with him on the ride over. But Mona is obdurate.

ACT 2

The Fair.—A crowd of sightseers and villagers is present. Roger appears, looking for Laura. He can not find her. Laura appears, looking for Roger. She can not find him. The gypsy queen approaches Roger and thrusts into his hand the locket stolen from Lord Brym. Roger looks at it and is frozen with astonishment, for it contains the portrait of his mother when she was in high school. He then realizes that Laura must be his sister, and starts out to find her.

ACT 3

Hall in the Castle.—Lucy is seen surrounded by every luxury, but her heart is sad. She has just been shown a forged letter from Stewart saying that he no longer loves her, and she remembers her old free life in the mountains and longs for another romp with Ravensbane and Wolfshead, her old pair of rompers. The guests begin to assemble for the wedding, each bringing a roast ox. They chide Lucy for not having her dress changed. Just at this moment the gypsy band bursts in and Cleon tells the wedding party that Elsie and not Edith is the child who was stolen from the summerhouse, showing the blood-stained derby as proof. At this, Lord Brym repents and gives his blessing on the pair, while the fishermen and their wives celebrate in the courtyard.

A SPRIG OF
HOLLYWOOD

"Strip away the phony tinsel and you can find the real
tinsel underneath."

Oscar Levant (on Hollywood)

Nathanael West

A sort of half-mythical Camelot-by-the-Pacific, Hollywood is a rich and intriguing field for satire. Of all the novels which have caricatured the dream industry and its spiritual environs, probably the best to date is Nathanael West's *The Day of the Locust*. This comic yet unforgiving satire against illusion-seekers is not a "Hollywood novel" in the usual sense at all; not a single successful producer or hopeful starlet appears in it; the story deals with ordinary people trapped in a nightmare of make-believe.

The selection which follows describes a chilling mob scene which takes place at the premiere of a new Hollywood extravaganza.

THE PREMIERE
(from *The Day of the Locust*)

When Tod reached the street, he saw a dozen great violet shafts of light moving across the evening sky in wide crazy sweeps. Whenever one of the fiery columns reached the lowest point of its arc, it hit for a moment the rose-colored domes and delicate minarets of Kahn's Persian Palace Theatre. The purpose of this display was to signal the world premiere of a new picture.

Turning his back on the searchlights, he started in the opposite direction, toward Homer's place. Before he had gone very far, he saw a clock that read a quarter past six and changed his mind about going back just yet. He might as well let the poor fellow sleep for another hour and kill some time by looking at the crowds.

When still a block from the theatre, he saw an enormous electric sign that hung over the middle of the street. In letters ten feet high he read that—

"MR. KAHN A PLEASURE DOME DECREED"

Although it was still several hours before the celebrities would arrive, thousands of people had already gathered. They stood facing the theatre with their backs toward the gutter in a thick line hundreds of feet long. A big squad of policemen was trying to keep a lane open between the front rank of the crowd and the façade of the theatre.

Tod entered the lane while the policeman guarding it was busy with a woman whose parcel had torn open, dropping oranges all over the place. Another policeman shouted for him to get the hell across the street, but he took a chance and kept going. They had enough to do without chasing him. He noticed how worried they looked and how careful they tried to be. If they had to arrest someone, they joked good-naturedly with the culprit, making light of it until they got him around the corner, then they whaled him with their clubs. Only so long as the man was actually part of the crowd did they have to be gentle.

Tod had walked only a short distance along the narrow lane when he began to get frightened. People shouted, commenting on his hat, his carriage, and his clothing. There was a continuous roar of catcalls, laughter and yells, pierced occasionally by a scream. The scream was usually followed by a sudden movement in the dense mass and part of it would surge forward wherever the police line was weakest. As soon as that part was rammed back, the bulge would pop out somewhere else.

The police force would have to be doubled when the stars started to arrive. At the sight of their heroes and heroines, the crowd would turn demoniac. Some little gesture, either too pleasing or too offensive, would start it moving and then nothing but machine guns would stop it. Individually the purpose of its members might simply be to get a souvenir, but collectively it would grab and rend.

A young man with a portable microphone was describing the scene. His rapid, hysterical voice was like that of a revivalist preacher whipping his congregation toward the ecstasy of fits.

"What a crowd, folks! What a crowd! There must be ten thousand excited, screaming fans outside Kahn's Persian tonight. The police can't hold them. Here, listen to them roar."

He held the microphone out and those near it obligingly roared for him.

"Did you hear it? It's a bedlam, folks. A veritable bedlam! What excitement! Of all the premieres I've attended, this is the most . . . the most . . . stupendous, folks, Can the police hold them? Can they? It doesn't look so, folks . . ."

Another squad of police came charging up. The sergeant pleaded with the announcer to stand further back so the people couldn't hear him. His men threw themselves at the crowd. It allowed itself to be hustled and shoved out of habit and because it lacked an objective. It tolerated the police, just as a bull elephant does when he allows a small boy to drive him with a light stick.

Tod could see very few people who looked tough, nor could he see any working men. The crowd was made up of the lower middle classes, every other person one of his torchbearers.

Just as he came near the end of the lane, it closed in front of him with a heave, and he had to fight his way through. Someone knocked his hat off and when he stooped to pick it up, someone kicked him. He whirled around angrily and found himself surrounded by people who were laughing at him. He knew enough to laugh with them. The crowd became sympathetic. A stout woman slapped him on the back, while a man handed him his hat, first brushing it carefully with his sleeve. Still another man shouted for a way to be cleared.

By a great deal of pushing and squirming, always trying to look as though he were enjoying himself, Tod finally managed to break into the open. After rearranging his clothes, he went over to a parking lot and sat down on the low retaining wall that ran along the front of it.

New groups, whole families, kept arriving. He could see a change come over them as soon as they had become part of the crowd. Until they reached the line, they looked diffident, almost furtive, but the moment they had become part of it, they turned arrogant and pugnacious. It was a mistake to think them harmless curiosity seekers. They were savage and bitter, especially the middle-aged and the old, and had been made so by boredom and disappointment.

All their lives they had slaved at some kind of dull, heavy labor, behind desks and counters, in the fields and at tedious machines of all sorts, saving their pennies and dreaming of the leisure that would be theirs when they had enough. Finally that day came. They could draw a weekly income of ten or fifteen dollars. Where else should they go but California, the land of sunshine and oranges?

Once there, they discovered that sunshine isn't enough. They get tired of oranges, even of avocado pears and passion fruit. Nothing happens. They don't know what to do with their time. They haven't the mental equipment for leisure, the money nor the physical equipment for pleasure. Did they slave so long just to go on an occasional Iowa picnic? What else is there? They watch the waves come in at Venice. There wasn't any ocean where most of them came from, but after you've seen one wave, you've seen them all. The same is true of the airplanes at Glendale. If only a plane would crash once in a while so that they could watch the passengers being consumed in a "holocaust of flame," as the newspapers put it. But the planes never crash.

Their boredom becomes more and more terrible. They realize that they've been tricked and burn with resentment. Every day of their lives they read the newspapers and went to the movies. Both fed them on lynchings, murder, sex crimes, explosions, wrecks, love nests, fires, miracles, revolutions, wars. This daily diet made sophisticates of them. The sun is a joke. Oranges can't titillate their jaded palates. Nothing can ever be violent enough to make taut their slack minds and bodies. They have been cheated and betrayed. They have slaved and saved for nothing.

S. J. Perelman

If, sifting through the rubble, some anthropologist of the future should stumble upon the works of S. J. Perelman, he would probably cast his treasure aside as meaningless. Perelman's Rosetta Stone of nifties, puns, and clichés within clichés would be indecipherable to anyone oblivious of his sources of inspiration, notably the madcap *lieux* of Madison Avenue and Hollywood.

Since his early Marx Brothers scripts, Perelman has been successful in elevating the ragged and ridiculous in the American idiom to pinnacles of absurdity. In another clime such an entertainer might have sought out less yielding targets for his aim and written in other forms as well as those employable by *The New Yorker*, Hollywood and Broadway; but in another clime there would not have been an S. J. Perelman. No other country is vast enough to contain a pun like *Lox vobiscum*, for one thing.

PHYSICIAN, STEEL THYSELF

Do you happen to know how many tassels a Restoration coxcomb wore at the knee? Or the kind of chafing dish a bunch of Skidmore girls would have used in a dormitory revel in 1911? Or the exact method of quarrying peat out of a bog at the time of the Irish Corn Laws? In fact, do you know anything at all that nobody else knows or, for that matter, gives a damn about? If you do, then sit tight, because one of these days you're going to Hollywood as a technical supervisor on a million-dollar movie. You may be a bore to your own family, but you're worth your weight in piastres to the picture business.

Yes, Hollywood dearly loves a technical expert, however recondite or esoteric his field. It is a pretty picayune film that cannot afford at least one of them; sometimes they well-nigh outnumber the actors. The Sherlock Holmes series, for instance, employs three servants on a full-time basis—one who has made a lifelong study of the décor at 221-B Baker Street, a second deeply versed in the great detective's psychology and mannerisms, and a third who spots anachronisms in the script which may distress Holmesians, like penicillin and the atomic bomb. An ideal existence, you might think, and yet there have been exceptions. I once knew a French artillery officer at M-G-M, imported at bloodcurdling expense from overseas as adviser on a romance about Indo-China, who languished for two years in an office under the Music Department. Over the noon yoghurt, his voice trembled as he spoke of his yearning to return to Saigon, where they were waiting to shoot him, but the director of *Blistered Bugles* felt him indispensable. At last he departed, with close to forty thousand rutabagas in his money belt, a broken man. His sole contribution was that he had succeeded in having "*pouf*" altered to "*sacré bloo.*" Another expert I met during the same epoch was a jovial, gnarled little party named Settembrini, conceded to be the foremost wrought-iron craftsman in the country. He had been flown three thousand miles to authenticate several flambeaux shown briefly in a night shot of Versailles. We subsequently chanced to be on the same train going East, and except for the fact that he wore a gold derby and was lighting his cigar with a first-mortgage bond, he seemed untouched. "Fine place," he commented, flicking ashes into the corsage of a blonde he had brought along for the purpose. "Sunshine, pretty girls, grapefruit ten for a quarter." I asked him whether the flambeaux had met the test. "One hundred per cent," he replied, "but they threw 'em out. In the scene where Marie Antoinette comes down the steps, a lackey holds a flashlight so she don't trip over her feet."

The latest group of specialists to be smiled upon by the cinema industry, it would appear, are the psychoanalysts. The vogue of psychological films started by *Lady in the Dark* has resulted in flush times for the profession, and anyone who can tell a frazzled id from a father fixation had better be booted and spurred for an impending summons to the Coast. The credit title of *Spellbound*, Alfred Hitchcock's recent thriller, for example, carried the acknowledgment "Psychiatric sequences supervised by Dr. May Romm," and Sidney Skolsky, reporting on a picture called *Obsessed* (formerly *One Man's Secret* and before that *One Woman's Secret*), states, "Joan Crawford is huddling with an eminent psychiatrist who will psych her forthcoming role in *The Secret* for her." A psychiatrist suddenly pitchforked into Hollywood, the ultimate nightmare, must feel rather like a small boy let loose in a toy store, but I wonder how long he can maintain a spirit of strict scientific objectivity. The ensuing vignette, a hasty attempt to adumbrate this new trend, is purely fanciful. There are, naturally, no such places as the Brown Derby, Vine Street, and Hollywood Boulevard, and if there should turn out to be, I couldn't be sorrier.

Sherman Wormser, M.D., Ph.D., came out of the Hollywood Plaza Hotel, somewhat lethargic after a heavy Sunday brunch, and paused indecisively on the sidewalk. The idea of taking a walk, which had seemed so inspired a moment ago in his room, now depressed him immeasurably. To the south, Vine Street stretched away interminably—unending blocks of bankrupt night clubs, used-car lots, open-air markets, and bazaars full of unpainted furniture and garden pottery. To the north, it rose abruptly in a steep hill crowned by a cluster of funeral homes and massage parlors in tan stucco. Over all of it hung a warm miasma vaguely suggestive of a steam laundry. Sherman moved aimlessly toward the Boulevard and paused for a brief self-inventory in the window of the Broadway-Hollywood department store.

Most of Dr. Wormser's patients in New York, accustomed to his neat morning coat and pencil-striped trousers, would have had some difficulty in recognizing their father confessor at the moment. He wore a pea-green playsuit with deep, flaring lapels, tailored of rough, towel-like material, arbitrarily checked and striated in front but mysteriously turned to suède in back. Over a gauzy, salmon-colored polo shirt he had knotted a yellow foulard handkerchief in a bow reminiscent of George Primrose's Minstrels, and on his head was sportily perched an

Alpinist's hat modeled after those worn by the tyrant Gessler.
Eight weeks before, when he had arrived to check on the
dream sequences of R.K.O.'s *Befuddled*, he would not have been
caught dead in these vestments, but his sack suits had seemed so
conspicuous that, chameleon-like, he soon developed a sense of
protective coloration.

He had settled his hat at a jauntier angle and was turning
away from the window when he became aware that a passer-by
was staring fixedly at him. The man wore an off-white polo
coat which hung open, its belt trailing on the pavement. Underneath were visible pleated lavender slacks and a mono-
grammed yachting jacket trimmed with brass buttons. The
face under the scarlet beret was oddly familiar.

"I beg pardon," hesitated the stranger, "I think we—you're
not Sherman Wormser, are you?" At the sound of his voice,
Sherman's mouth opened in delight. He flung his arm about
the man's shoulders.

"Why, Randy Kalbfus, you old son of a gun!" he crowed.
"Two years ago! The Mental Hygiene Convention in Cleveland!"

"Bull's-eye," chuckled Kalbfus. "I thought it was you, but
—well, you look different, somehow."

"Why—er—I used to have a Vandyke." Wormser felt his
cheeks growing pink. "I shaved it off out here. The studio, you
know. Say, you had one, too, for that matter. What became of
yours?"

"Same thing," Kalbfus admitted sheepishly. "My producer
said it was corny. He's got a block about psychiatrists wearing
goatees."

"Yes, involuntary goatee rejection," nodded Wormser.
"Stekel speaks of it. Well, well. I heard you were in town.
Where you working?"

"Over at Twentieth. I'm straightening out a couple of
traumas in *Delirious*."

"You don't say!" Despite himself, Sherman's tone was faintly
patronizing. "I turned down that assignment, you know. Didn't
feel I could justify the symbolism of the scene where Don
Ameche disembowels the horse."

"Oh, that's all out now," said Kalbfus amiably. "That was the early version."

"Well," said Sherman quickly, eager to retrieve himself, "it's the early version that catches the Wormser, what?" Kalbfus laughed uproariously, less at the witticism than because this was the first time anyone had addressed him in three days.

"Look," he suggested, linking arms with Sherman, "let's hop over to the Bamboo Room and have a couple of Zombolas." On their way across to the Brown Derby, he explained the nature of the drink to Wormser, who was still a bit staid and Eastern in his choice of beverages. "It's just a tall glass of rum mixed with a jigger of gin, some camphor ice, and a twist of avocado," he said reassuringly.

"Isn't that a little potent?" asked Wormser dubiously.

"You're cooking with grass it's potent," returned his companion pertly, if inaccurately. "That's why they won't serve more than six to a customer." Seated in the cool darkness of the bar, with three Zombolas coursing through their vitals, the colleagues felt drawn to each other. No trace of professional hostility or envy lingered by the time they had finished reviewing the Cleveland convention, the rapacity of their fellow-practitioners, and their own stanch integrity.

"How do you like it out here, Randy?" Wormser inquired. "I get a slight sense of confusion. Perhaps I'm not adjusted yet."

"You're inhibited," said Kalbfus, signaling the waiter to repeat. "You won't let yourself go. Infantile denial of your environment."

"I know," said Wormser plaintively, "but a few weeks ago I saw Jack Benny in a sleigh on Sunset Boulevard—with real reindeer. And last night an old hermit in a pillowcase stopped me and claimed the world was coming to an end. When I objected, he sold me a box of figs."

"You'll get used to it," the other replied. "I've been here five months, and to me it's God's country. I never eat oranges, but hell, can you imagine three dozen for a quarter?"

"I guess you're right," admitted Wormser. "Where are you staying?"

"At the Sunburst Auto Motel on Cahuenga," said Kalbfus, draining his glass. "I'm sharing a room with two extra girls from Paramount."

"Oh, I'm sorry. I—I didn't know you and Mrs. Kalbfus were separated."

"Don't be archaic. She's living there, too." Kalbfus snapped his fingers at the waiter. "Once in a while I fall into the wrong bed, but Beryl's made her emotional adjustment; she's carrying on with a Greek in Malibu. Interesting sublimation of libido under stress, isn't it? I'm doing a paper on it." Wormser raised his hand ineffectually to ward off the fifth Zombola, but Kalbfus would not be overborne.

"None of that," he said sharply. "Come on, drink up. Yes, sir, it's a great town, but I'll tell you something, Sherm. We're in the wrong end of this business. Original stories—that's the caper." He looked around and lowered his voice. "I'll let you in on a secret, if you promise not to blab. I've been collaborating with the head barber over at Fox, and we've got a ten-strike. It's about a simple, unaffected manicurist who inherits fifty million smackers."

"A fantasy, eh?" Wormser pondered. "That's a good idea."

"What the hell do you mean, fantasy?" demanded Kalbfus heatedly. "It happens every day. Wait till you hear the twisteroo, though. This babe, who has everything—houses, yachts, cars, three men in love with her—suddenly turns around and gives back the dough."

"Why?" asked Wormser, sensing that he was expected to.

"Well, we haven't worked that out yet," said Kalbfus confidentially. "Probably a subconscious wealth phobia. Anyway, Zanuck's offered us a hundred and thirty G's for it, and it isn't even on paper."

"Holy cow!" breathed Wormser. "What'll you do with all that money?"

"I've got my eye on a place in Beverly," Kalbfus confessed. "It's only eighteen rooms, but a jewel box—indoor plunge, indoor rifle range, the whole place is indoors. Even the barbecue."

"That can't be," protested Wormser. "The barbecue's always outdoors."

"Not this one," beamed Kalbfus. "That's what makes it so unusual. Then, of course, I'll have to give Beryl her settlement when the divorce comes through."

"You—you just said everything was fine between you," faltered Wormser.

"Oh, sure, but I've really outgrown her," shrugged Kalbfus. "Listen, old man, I wouldn't want this to get into the columns. You see, I'm going to marry Ingrid Bergman."

A strange, tingling numbness, like that induced by novocain, spread downward from the tips of Wormser's ears. "I didn't know you knew her," he murmured.

"I don't," said Kalbfus, "but I saw her the other night at the Mocambo, and she gave me a look that meant only one thing." He laughed and swallowed his sixth Zombola. "It's understandable, in a way. She must have known instinctively."

"Known what?" Wormser's eyes, trained to withstand the unusual, stood out in high relief.

"Oh, just that I happen to be the strongest man in the world," said Kalbfus modestly. He rose, drew a deep breath, and picked up the table. "Watch," he ordered, and flung it crisply across the bar. Two pyramids of bottles dissolved and crashed to the floor, taking with them a Filipino busboy and several hundred cocktail glasses. Before the fixtures had ceased quivering, a task force of bartenders and waiters was spearing down on Kalbfus. There was an obscure interval of scuffling, during which Wormser unaccountably found himself creeping about on all fours and being kicked by a fat lady. Then the shouts and recriminations blurred, and suddenly he felt the harsh impact of the pavement. In a parking lot, eons later, the mist cleared and he was seated on the running board of a sedan, palpating a robin's egg on his jaw. Kalbfus, his face puffier than he last remembered it, was shakily imploring him to forgive and dine at his motel. Wormser slowly shook his head.

"No, thanks." Though his tongue was a bolt of flannel, Sherman strove to give his words dignity. "I like you, Kalbfuth, but you're a little unthtable." Then he got to his feet, bowed formally, and went into the Pig'n Whistle for an atomburger and a frosted mango.

Lillian Ross

The truth about Hollywood does not travel well. Jar it ever so slightly and the bouquet is lost, the aroma spoiled. Only by the deftest handling is it preserved intact.

The following selection is from Lillian Ross's *Picture*, a detailed chronicle of how John Huston filmed *The Red Badge of Courage*. It is a rare piece of journalism in which the full flavor of The Industry has been conserved by the simple device of letting it speak for itself.

"THROW THE LITTLE OLD LADY DOWN THE STAIRS"
(from *Picture*)

The maze of paths followed by all the individuals at M-G-M who work together to make a motion picture led inexorably to the office of Louis B. Mayer, and I found him there one day, behind a series of doors, talking to Arthur Freed, a producer of musicals for the studio. Mayer's office was about half as large as the lounge of the Music Hall, and he sat behind a huge cream-colored desk overlooking a vast expanse of peach-colored carpet. The walls of the office were panelled in cream-colored leather, and there was a cream-colored bar, a cream-colored fireplace with cream-colored fire irons, cream-colored leather chairs and couches, and a cream-colored grand piano. Behind Mayer's desk stood an American flag and a marble statue of the M-G-M lion. The desk was covered with four cream-colored telephones, a prayer book, several photographs of lions, a tintype of Mayer's mother, and a statuette of the Republican Party's elephant. The big desk hid most of Mayer, but I could see his powerful shoulders, decked in navy blue, and a gay, polka-dot bow tie that almost touched his chin. His large head seems set upon the shoulders, without an intervening neck. His hair is thick and snow-white, his face is ruddy, and his eyes, behind glasses with amber-colored frames, stared with a sort of fierce blankness at Freed, who was showing him a report on the box-office receipts of his latest musical, then playing at the Radio City Music Hall.

"Great! I saw it!" Mayer said, sweeping Freed back with his arm. "I said to you the picture would be a wonderful hit. In here!" he cried, poking his index finger at his chest. "It wins the audience in here!" He lifted his snowy head and looked at the cream-colored wall before him as though he were watching the Music Hall screen. "Entertainment!" he cried, transfixed by what he seemed to see on the screen, and he made the face of a man who was emotionally stirred by what he was watching. "It's good enough for you and I and the box office," he said, turning back to Freed. "Not for the smart alecks. It's not good enough any more," he went on, whining coyly, in imitation of someone saying that winning the heart of the audience was not good enough. He pounded a commanding fist on his desk and looked at me. "Let me tell you something!" he said. "Prizes! Awards! Ribbons! We had two pictures here. An Andy Hardy picture, with little Mickey Rooney, and 'Ninotchka,' with Greta Garbo. 'Ninotchka' got the prizes. *Blue* ribbons! *Purple* ribbons! Nine bells and seven stars! Which picture made the money? 'Andy Hardy' made the money. Why? Because it won praise from the heart. No ribbons!"

"Hah!" Mr. Freed said.

"Twenty-six years with the studio!" Mayer went on. "They used to listen to me. Never would Irving Thalberg make a picture I was opposed to. I had a worship for that boy. He worked. Now they want cocktail parties and their names in the papers. Irving listened to me. Never satisfied with his own work. That was Irving. Years later, after Irving passed away, they still listened. They make an Andy Hardy picture." He turned his powerful shoulders toward me. "Andy's mother is dying, and

they make the picture showing Andy standing outside the door.
Standing. I told them, 'Don't you know that an American boy
like that will get down on his hands and knees and *pray?*' They
listened. They brought Mickey Rooney down on his hands and
knees." Mayer leaped from his chair and crouched on the peach-
colored carpet and showed how Andy Hardy had prayed. "The
biggest thing in the picture!" He got up and returned to his
chair. "Not good enough," he said, whining coyly again. "Don't
show the good, wholesome, American mother in the home.
Kind. Sweet. Sacrifices. Love." Mayer paused and by his expression demonstrated, in turn, maternal kindness, sweetness,
sacrifice, and love, and then glared at Freed and me. "No!" he
cried. "Knock the mother on the jaw!" He gave himself an
uppercut to the chin. "Throw the little old lady down the
stairs!" He threw himself in the direction of the American flag.
"Throw the mother's good, homemade chicken soup in the
mother's face!" He threw an imaginary plate of soup in Freed's
face. "*Step* on the mother! *Kick* her! That is *art*, they say.
Art!" He raised and lowered his white eyebrows, wiggled his
shoulders like a hula dancer, and moved his hands in a mysterious pattern in the air. "Art!" he repeated, and gave an angry
growl.

"You said it," said Freed.

" 'Andy Hardy'! I saw the picture and the tears were in my
eyes," Mayer said. "I'm not ashamed. I'll see it again. Every
time, I'll cry."

"In musicals, we don't have any of those phony artistic pretensions," Freed said.

Mayer gave no sign that he had heard Freed. "Between you
and I and the lamppost," he said, straightening his bow tie,
"the smart alecks around here don't know the difference between the heart and the gutter. They don't want to listen to you.
Marie Dressler! Who thought you could take a fat old lady and
make her a star? I did it. And Wally Beery. And Lionel Barry-
more." He leaned back in his chair, one hand tucked into his
shirt, his eyes squinting, his voice turning into the querulous
rasp of Dr. Gillespie informing Dr. Kildare of his diagnosis of
the disease. Then, resuming his natural manner, he said, "The

audience knows. Look at the receipts. Give the audience what they want? No. Not *good* enough." He paused.

"Thoreau said most of us lead lives of quiet desperation," Freed said quickly. "Pictures should make you feel better, not worse."

Again Mayer did not seem to hear. " 'The Red Badge of Courage,' " he said. "A million and a half. Maybe more. What for? There's no story. I was against it. They wanted to make it. I don't say no. John Huston. He was going to do 'Quo Vadis.' What he wanted to do to the picture! No heart. His idea was he'd throw the Christians to the lions. That's all. I begged him to change his ideas. I got down on my hands and knees to him. I sang 'Mammy' to him. I showed him the meaning of heart. I crawled to him on hands and knees. 'Ma-a-ammy!' With tears. No! No heart! He *thanked* me for taking him off the picture. Now he wants 'The Red Badge of Courage.' Dore Schary wants it. All right. I'll watch. I don't say no, but I wouldn't make that picture with Sam *Gold*wyn's money."

Thomas Meehan

EARLY MORNING OF A MOTION-PICTURE EXECUTIVE

One of the smallest minorities in Hollywood nowadays is the group that believes James Joyce's "Ulysses" will be made into a superior movie . . . behind the entire hoopla is Jerry Wald, the producer . . . he prepared a memorandum . . . that included the following: "The way I would like to see this story on the screen is to oversimplify it. It has three levels: Stephen Dedalus, the intellectual; Leopold Bloom, the passive, ill-informed victim of habitual feelings, and Mrs. Bloom, sensual, carnal, wholly natural. Thus, the three leading characters represent Pride, Love, and The Flesh. My feeling is that this project is really in its purest form: father searching for his son

and son searching for his father. It is a highly controversial
book and out of it could be created a motion picture as exciting
as 'Peyton Place' but on a higher level."—The Times.

. . . Yes a quarter after what an unearthly hour I suppose
theyre just getting out on the lot at Fox now Mari-
lyn Monroe combing out her hair for the day let me see if I can
doze off 1 2 3 4 5 where was it in Jerrys memorandum yes oversimplify O I love great books Id love to have the whole of Hollywood filming nothing but great books God in heaven theres nothing like literature pre sold to the public the treatment and the
working script by Dalton Trumbo and the finished picture in
color and Todd A O as for them saying theres no audience interest in pictures based on great books I wouldnt give a snap of my
two fingers for all their motivational research indie exhibs whatever they call themselves why dont they go out and make a
picture I ask them and do a socko 21 Gs in Philly and a wow 41
in Chi ah that they cant answer yes in its purest form father
searching for his son and son searching for his father chance
for myriad boffolas there old man staggers out one door of pub
where the beer and the boffola foam while kid goes in other O I
love a good laugh Stephen Dedalus the intellectual we might try
to get Paul Newman for the part hes a strong BO draw in
Exodus certainly hed do very nicely too better soft pedal the
egghead bit though make him a newspaper reporter have to
shoot a lot of location stuff in Dublin by the waters of the Liffey
by the rivering waters of we might fake it on the back lot and
bring it in under three million or else knock up the budget and
spot celebs the way Columbia did with Pepe it coined a huge
forty five thou in its first week on Bway gives the property a
touch of class I wonder could we get Bobby Darin on a percentage deal to sing Galway Bay I better have Sammy check in the
morning where the hell Galway Bay is its somewhere around
Dublin surely long color process shot of the bay at dusk cut
to faces of old women in black shawls and the women in the uplands making hay speak a language that the strangers do not

know a scene which it will knock them out of the back of the house in Terre Haute

the alarmclock in the maids room clattering the brains out of itself better take another seconal and try to sleep again so as I can get up early Ill call a title conference at ten wait now who was it yes Kirk Douglas already made Ulysses the old story though this ones on three levels we might call it Pride Love and The Flesh that has a nice sound to it Ill have Sammy get ahold of Central Registry and see if the titles reserved Leopold Bloom the passive ill informed victim of habitual feelings problem on the religion bit though dont want Bnai Brith down on our necks well give him an Irish name in any case Leopold Malone and his loving wife Molly sensual carnal wholly natural she wheels her wheelbarrow through streets wide and narrow personally Id like to build the script around Molly and get MM for the role so why am I after worrying we cant go wrong with Maureen O Hara flashback to Gibraltar where she was a girl a flower of the mountain yes so are those bimbos all flowers of the mountain lap dissolve he kisses her under the Moorish wall we might send down a second unit to get some outdoor Gibraltar stuff cut in a flamenco dream sequence shoot it there and dub it on the soundtrack later yes chance too for widescreen color background O the sea the sea there crimson sometimes like fire and the glorious sunsets and the figtrees in the Alameda gardens yes well have Louella bawling like a goddam baby baaaawwaaaaaww at the world preem

ah well theres no talking around it were one of the smallest minorities in Hollywood nowadays us thinking that James Joyces Ulysses will be made into a superior movie TJ saying to me Harry youre one hundred per cent crazy him with his two dollar cigars and his Irving Thalberg award chasing those little chits of starlets and he not long married Mouth Almighty I call him and his squinty eyes of all the big stuppoe studio heads I ever met God help the world if everyone out here was like him yes always and ever making the same pictures showdownatshotguncreek whatever he calls the new one ah God send him more sense and me more money O he does look the fool sitting at the head of the conference table as big as you please he can go smother for all the fat lot I care Im unabashedly intellectual and Ill make this movie or Im walking off the lot this day week Ive still got my integrity after all how long is it Ive been out here wait yes since 1923 O I love lying in bed God here we are as bad as ever after yes thirty eight years how many studios have I worked at RKO and Fox and Metro and Paramount where I was a young man and the day I talked to deMille when he was making the original of The Ten Commandments and yes he wouldnt answer at first only looked out over the set and the thousands of extras I was thinking of so many things he didnt know of yes how someday Id have my own swimming pool and go to Vilma Bankys parties and all the long years since Joan Crawford in Our Dancing Daughters and Richard Dix and yes the year Metro missed the boat on Dinner at Eight and Fred Astaire and Ginger Rogers and Asta rrrrrffffffrrrrr fffff and the andyhardy series and The Best Years of Our Lives and O all the Academy Award dinners yes Disney going about smug with his Oscars the Levant what year was it Gert and I took the cruise there I never miss his TV show and Rhonda Fleming with her hair all red and flaming and Sandra Dee and Vista Vision and stereophonic sound cleaning up in the foreign market and Ben Hur and the night TJ asked me what my next project would be when was it yes the night they screened Psycho in Santa Monica eeeeeeeekkk its an Irish story I told him like The Quiet Man or shall we get Rock Hudson I was just thinking of it for the first time yes and I had Sammy give me a five page synopsis and the day in Romanoffs I asked Jerry Wald about it yes Ulysses by James Joyce which it is a highly controversial book and I asked him yes could out of it be created a picture as exciting as Peyton Place and yes he said yes it could yes but on a higher level Yes.

HIGH SOCIETY,
FASHION
AND CELEBRITY

"F'river an' iver people have been growin' rich, goin'
down to some kind iv a Newport, makin' monkeys iv
thimsilves an' goin' back to the jungle."

FINLEY PETER DUNNE, *Observations
by Mr. Dooley* (1902)

George William Curtis

As a rule, posterity shows little consideration to idealists, reformers, orators, world travelers, or distinguished editors—and George William Curtis was all of these. For many years, between the 1850s and the 1880s, Curtis was a moral force in public affairs. By his essays and speeches and throughout his twenty-nine-year tenure as editor of *Harper's Weekly*, he was influential as an independent who supported in turn all the important liberal causes of his era: abolition, Civil Service reform, woman's suffrage, and improved relations between capital and labor.

Yet today, if Curtis is mentioned at all, more than likely it is as the author of *The Potiphar Papers*, a suite of satires of New York's upper class. When they first appeared in *Putnam's Monthly* in 1853, the caricatures of the rich and fatuous Mrs. Potiphar, the Reverend Cream Cheese, the fashionable Mrs. Croesus, and their friends and hangers-on were immediately popular. Today they are a quaint but still entertaining period piece—a young man's view (Curtis was then twenty-nine) of the "best society" of New York around 1850.

MRS. POTIPHAR'S BALL
(from "Our Best Society" in *The Potiphar Papers*, 1854)

If gilt were only gold, or sugar-candy common sense, what a fine thing our society would be! If to lavish money upon *objets de vertu*, to wear the most costly dresses, and always to have them cut in the height of the fashion; to build houses thirty feet broad, as if they were palaces; to furnish them with all the luxurious devices of Parisian genius; to give superb banquets, at which your guests laugh, and which make you miserable; to drive a fine carriage and ape European liveries, and crests, and coats-of-arms; to resent the friendly advances of your baker's wife, and the lady of your butcher (you being yourself a

cobbler's daughter); to talk much of the "old families" and of
your aristocratic foreign friends; to despise labour; to prate of
"good society;" to travesty and parody, in every conceivable way,
a society which we know only in books and by the superficial
observation of foreign travel, which arises out of a social organization entirely unknown to us, and which is opposed to our
fundamental and essential principles; if all this were fine, what a
prodigiously fine society would ours be!

This occurred to us upon lately receiving a card of invitation
to a brilliant ball. We were quietly ruminating over our evening
fire, with Disraeli's Wellington speech, "all tears," in our
hands, with the account of a great man's burial, and a little
man's triumph across the channel. So many great men gone, we
mused, and such great crises impending! This democratic movement in Europe; Kossuth and Mazzini waiting for the moment
to give the word; the Russian bear watchfully sucking his paws;
the Napoleonic empire redivivus; Cuba, and annexation, and
slavery; California and Australia, and the consequent considera-
tions of political economy; dear me! exclaimed we, putting on a
fresh hodful of coal, we must look a little into the state of
parties.

As we put down the coal-scuttle there was a knock at the
door. We said, "come in," and in came a neat Alhambra-
watered envelope, containing the announcement that the queen
of fashion was "at home" that evening week. Later in the evening, came a friend to smoke a cigar. The card was lying upon
the table, and he read it with eagerness. "You'll go, of course,"
said he, "for you will meet all the 'best society.' "

Shall we, truly? Shall we really see the "best society of the
city," the picked flower of its genius, character, and beauty?
What makes the "best society" of men and women? The
noblest specimens of each, of course. The men who mould the
time, who refresh our faith in heroism and virtue, who make
Plato, and Zeno, and Shakspeare, and all Shakspeare's gentlemen, possible again. The women, whose beauty, and sweetness, and dignity, and high accomplishment, and grace, make
us understand the Greek Mythology, and weaken our desire to
have some glimpse of the most famous women of history. The

"best society" is that in which the virtues are most shining, which is the most charitable, forgiving, long-suffering, modest, and innocent. The "best society" is, in its very name, that in which there is the least hypocrisy and insincerity of all kinds, which recoils from, and blasts, artificiality, which is anxious to be all that it is possible to be, and which sternly reprobates all shallow pretence, all coxcombry and foppery, and insists upon simplicity as the infallible characteristic of true worth. That is the "best society," which comprises the best men and women.

Had we recently arrived from the moon, we might, upon hearing that we were to meet the "best society," have fancied that we were about to enjoy an opportunity not to be overvalued. But unfortunately we were not so freshly arrived. We had received other cards, and had perfected our toilette many times, to meet this same society, so magnificently described, and had found it the least "best" of all. Who compose it? Whom shall we meet if we go to this ball? We shall meet three classes of persons: first, those who are rich, and who have all that money can buy; second, those who belong to what are technically called "the good old families," because some ancestor was a man of mark in the state or country, or was very rich, and has kept the fortune in the family; and, thirdly, a swarm of youths who can dance dexterously, and who are invited for that purpose. Now these are all arbitrary and factitious distinctions upon which to found so profound a social difference as that which exists in American, or, at least, in New York society. First, as a general rule, the rich men of every community who make their own money are not the most generally intelligent and cultivated. They have a shrewd talent which secures a fortune, and which keeps them closely at the work of amassing from their youngest years until they are old. They are sturdy men of simple tastes often. Sometimes, though rarely, very generous, but necessarily with an altogether false and exaggerated idea of the importance of money. They are a rather rough, unsympathetic, and, perhaps, selfish class, who, themselves, despise purple and fine linen, and still prefer a cot-bed and a bare room, although they may be worth millions. But they are married to scheming, or ambitious, or disappointed women, whose life is a prolonged pageant, and they are dragged hither and thither in it, are bled of their golden blood, and forced into a position they do not covet and which they despise. Then there are the inheritors of wealth. How many of them inherit the valiant genius and hard frugality which built up their fortunes; how many acknowledge the stern and heavy responsibility of their opportunities; how many refuse to dream their lives away in a Sybarite luxury; how many are smitten with the lofty ambition of achieving an enduring name by works of a permanent value; how many do not dwindle into dainty dilettanti, and dilute their manhood with factitious sentimentality instead of a hearty, human sympathy; how many are not satisfied with having the fastest horses and the "crackest" carriages, and an unlimited wardrobe, and a weak affectation and puerile imitation of foreign life?

And who are these of our secondly, these "old families"? The spirit of our time and of our country knows no such thing, but the habitué of "society" hears constantly of "a good family." It means simply, the collective mass of children, grandchildren, nephews, nieces, and descendants of some man who deserved well of his country, and whom his country honors. But sad is the heritage of a great name! The son of Burke will inevitably be measured by Burke. The niece of Pope must show some superiority to other women (so to speak), or her equality is inferiority. The feeling of men attributes some magical charm to blood, and we look to see the daughter of Helen as fair as her mother, and the son of Shakspeare musical as his sire. If they are not so, if they are merely names, and common persons— if there is no Burke, nor Shakspeare, nor Washington, nor Bacon, in their words, or actions, or lives, then we must pity them, and pass gently on, not upbraiding them, but regretting that it is one of the laws of greatness that it dwindles all things in its vicinity, which would otherwise show large enough. Nay, in our regard for the great man, we may even admit to a compassionate honor, as pensioners upon our charity, those who bear and transmit his name. But if these heirs should presume upon that fame, and claim any precedence of living men and women because their dead grandfather was a hero,—they must be shown the door directly. We should dread to be born a Percy, or a Colonna, or a Bonaparte. We should not like to be the second Duke of Wellington, nor Charles Dickens, jr. It is a terrible thing, one would say, to a mind of honorable feeling, to be pointed out as somebody's son, or uncle, or granddaughter, as if the excellence were all derived. It must be a little humiliating to reflect that if your great uncle had not been somebody, you would be nobody,—that, in fact, you are only a name, and that, if you should consent to change it for the sake of a fortune, as is sometimes done, you would cease to be any thing but a rich man. "My father was President, or Governor of the State," some pompous man may say. But, by Jupiter! king of gods and men, what are *you?* is the instinctive response. Do you not see, our pompous friend, that you are only pointing your own unimportance? If your father was Governor of the State, what right have you to use that fact only to fatten your self-conceit? Take care, good care; for whether you say it by your lips or by your life, that withering response awaits you,—"then what are *you?*" If your ancestor was great, you are under bonds to greatness. If you are small, make haste to learn it betimes, and, thanking Heaven that your name has been made illustrious, retire into a corner and keep it, at least, untarnished.

Our thirdly, is a class made by sundry French tailors, bootmakers, dancing-masters, and Mr. Brown. They are a corps-de-ballet, for the use of private entertainments. They are fostered by society for the use of young debutantes, and hardier damsels, who have dared two or three years of the "tight" polka. They are cultivated for their heels, not their heads. Their life begins at ten o'clock in the evening, and lasts until four in the morning. They go home and sleep until nine; then they reel, sleepy, to counting-houses and offices, and doze on desks until dinner-time. Or, unable to do that, they are actively at work all day, and their cheeks grow pale, and their lips thin, and their eyes bloodshot and hollow, and they drag themselves home at evening to catch a nap until the ball begins, or to dine and smoke at their club, and be very manly with punches and coarse stories; and then to rush into hot and glittering rooms, and seize very *décolleté* girls closely around the waist, and dash with them around an area of stretched linen, saying in the panting pauses, "How very hot it is!" "How very pretty Miss Podge looks!" "What a good redowa!" "Are you going to Mrs. Potiphar's?"

Is this the assembled flower of manhood and womanhood, called "best society," and to see which is so envied a privilege? If such are the elements, can we be long in arriving at the present state, and necessary future condition of parties?

.   .   .   .

We went to the brilliant ball. There was too much of every thing. Too much light, and eating, and drinking, and dancing, and flirting, and dressing, and feigning, and smirking, and much too many people. Good taste insists first upon fitness. But why had Mrs. Potiphar given this ball? We inquired industriously, and learned it was because she did not give one last year. Is it then essential to do this thing biennially? inquired we with some trepidation. "Certainly," was the bland reply, "or society will forget you." Every body was unhappy at Mrs. Potiphar's, save a few girls and boys, who danced violently all the evening. Those who did not dance walked up and down the rooms as well as they could, squeezing by non-dancing ladies, causing them to swear in their hearts as the brusque broadcloth carried away the light outworks of gauze and gossamer. The dowagers, ranged in solid phalanx, occupied all the chairs and sofas against the wall, and fanned themselves until suppertime, looking at each other's diamonds, and criticising the toilettes of the younger ladies, each narrowly watching her peculiar Polly Jane, that she did not betray too much interest in any man who was not of a certain fortune. It is the cold, vulgar truth, madam, nor are we in the slightest degree exaggerating. Elderly gentlemen, twisting single gloves in a very wretched manner, came up and bowed to the dowagers, and smirked, and said it was a pleasant party, and a handsome house, and then clutched their hands behind them, and walked miserably away, looking as affable as possible. And the dowagers made a little fun of the elderly gentlemen, among themselves, as they walked away.

Then came the younger non-dancing men—a class of the

community who wear black cravats and waistcoats, and thrust their thumbs and forefingers in their waistcoat pockets, and are called "talking men." Some of them are literary, and affect the philosopher; have, perhaps, written a book or two, and are a small species of lion to very young ladies. Some are of the *blasé* kind; men who affect the extremest elegance, and are reputed "so aristocratic," and who care for nothing in particular, but wish they had not been born gentlemen, in which case they might have escaped ennui. These gentlemen stand with hat in hand, and coats and trowsers most unexceptionable. They are the "so gentlemanly" persons of whom one hears a great deal, but which seems to mean nothing but cleanliness. Vivian Grey and Pelham are the models of their ambition, and they succeed in being Pendennis. They enjoy the reputation of being "very clever," and "very talented fellows," "smart chaps," &c., but they refrain from proving what is so generously conceded. They are often men of a certain cultivation. They have travelled, many of them,—spending a year or two in Paris, and a month or two in the rest of Europe. Consequently they endure society at home, with a smile, and a shrug, and a graceful superciliousness, which is very engaging. They are perfectly at home, and they rather despise Young America, which, in the next room, is diligently earning its invitation. They prefer to hover about the ladies who did not come out this season, but are a little used to the world, with whom they are upon most friendly terms, and who criticise together very freely all the great events in the great world of fashion.

These elegant Pendennises we saw at Mrs. Potiphar's, but not without a sadness which can hardly be explained. They had been boys once, all of them, fresh and frank-hearted, and full of a noble ambition. They had read and pondered the histories of great men; how they resolved, and struggled, and achieved. In the pure portraiture of genius, they had loved and honoured noble women, and each young heart was sworn to truth and the service of beauty. Those feelings were chivalric and fair. Those boyish instincts clung to whatever was lovely, and rejected the specious snare, however graceful and elegant. They sailed, new knights, upon that old and endless crusade against hypocrisy and the devil, and they were lost in the luxury of Corinth, nor longer seek the difficult shores beyond. A present smile was worth a future laurel. The ease of the moment was worth immortal tranquillity. They renounced the stern worship of the unknown God, and acknowledged the deities of Athens. But the seal of their shame is their own smile at their early dreams, and the high hopes of their boyhood, their sneering infidelity of simplicity, their skepticism of motives and of men. Youths, whose younger years were fervid with the resolution to strike and win, to deserve, at least, a gentle remembrance, if not a dazzling fame, are content to eat, and drink, and sleep well; to go to the opera and all the balls; to be known as "gentlemanly," and "aristocratic," and "dangerous," and "elegant;" to cherish a luxurious and enervating indolence, and to "succeed," upon the cheap reputation of having been "fast" in Paris. The end of such men is evident enough from the beginning. They are snuffed out by a "great match," and become an appendage to a rich woman; or they dwindle off into old roués, men of the world in sad earnest, and not with elegant affectation, *blasé;* and as they began Arthur Pendennises, so they end the Major. But, believe it, that old fossil heart is wrung sometimes by a mortal pang, as it remembers those squandered opportunities and that lost life.

From these groups we passed into the dancing-room. We have seen dancing in other countries, and dressing. We have certainly never seen gentlemen dance so easily, gracefully and well as the American. But the *style* of dancing, in its whirl, its rush, its fury, is only equalled by that of the masked balls at the French opera, and the balls at the *Salle Valentino*, the *Jardin Mabille*, the *Chateau Rouge*, and other favourite resorts of Parisian Grisettes and Lorettes. We saw a few young men looking upon the dance very soberly, and, upon inquiry, learned that they were engaged to certain ladies of the corps-de-ballet. Nor did we wonder that the spectacle of a young woman whirling in a *décolleté* state, and in the embrace of a warm youth, around a heated room, induced a little sobriety upon her lover's face, if not a sadness in his heart. Amusement, recreation, enjoyment! There are no more beautiful things. But this proceed-

ing falls under another head. We watched the various toilettes
of these bounding belles. They were rich and tasteful. But a man
at our elbow, of experience and shrewd observation, said, with
a sneer, for which we called him to account, "I observe that
American ladies are so rich in charms that they are not at all
chary of them. It is certainly generous to us miserable black
coats. But, do you know, it strikes me as a generosity of display
that must necessarily leave the donor poorer in maidenly feeling." We thought ourselves cynical, but this was intolerable;
and in a very crisp manner we demanded an apology.

"Why," responded our friend with more of sadness than of
satire in his tone, "why are you so exasperated? Look at this
scene! Consider that this is, really, the life of these girls. This
is what they 'come out' for. This is the end of their ambition.
They think of it, dream of it, long for it. Is it amusement? Yes,
to a few, possibly. But listen, and gather, if you can, from their
remarks (when they make any) that they have any thought beyond this, and going to church very rigidly on Sunday. The
vigor of polking and church-going are proportioned; as is the
one so is the other. My young friend, I am no ascetic, and do not
suppose a man is damned because he dances. But Life is not a
ball (more's the pity, truly, for these butterflies), nor is its sole
duty and delight, dancing. When I consider this spectacle,—
when I remember what a noble and beautiful woman is, what a
manly man,—when I reel, dazzled by this glare, drunken with
these perfumes, confused by this alluring music, and reflect
upon the enormous sums wasted in a pompous profusion that
delights no one,—when I look around upon all this rampant
vulgarity in tinsel and Brussels lace, and think how fortunes
go, how men struggle and lose the bloom of their honesty, how
women hide in a smiling pretence, and eye with caustic glances
their neighbor's newer house, diamonds, or porcelain, and observe their daughters, such as these,—why, I tremble and tremble, and this scene to-night, every 'crack' ball this winter will
be, not the pleasant society of men and women, but—even in
this young country—an orgie such as rotting Corinth saw, a
frenzied festival of Rome in its decadence."

There was a sober truth in this bitterness, and we turned

away to escape the sombre thought of the moment. Addressing
one of the panting Houris who stood melting in a window, we
spoke (and confess how absurdly) of the Düsseldorf Gallery. It
was merely to avoid saying how warm the room was, and how
pleasant the party was; facts upon which we had already sufficiently enlarged. "Yes, they are pretty pictures; but la! how long
it must have taken Mr. Düsseldorf to paint them all;" was the
reply.

William Allen Butler

In its day "Nothing to Wear" was a literary sensation. Soon
after it appeared in *Harper's Weekly* in 1857, this verse caricature of the shallow and undressable Miss Flora McFlimsey was
widely reprinted and avidly read throughout this country and
in England. It struck a universal chord. Men read the poem as
a satire against women; women read it as a satire against other
women; the old guard appreciated it as a blast against the
nouveaux riches; and the younger generation (then delighting
in the audacity of *Vanity Fair*) found it the last word in
modernism. Even today it is difficult to realize that William
Butler's romping (and frequently unscannable) verses were
written as long ago as 1857. Only the moral finale, which the
author added as an afterthought, clearly dates the poem;
unfortunately, writers don't write lines like "Where the glare
and the glitter and tinsel of Time" any more.

"NOTHING TO WEAR"
(1857)

AN EPISODE OF CITY LIFE

Miss Flora McFlimsey, of Madison Square,
Has made three separate journeys to Paris,
And her father assures me, each time she was there,
That she and her friend Mrs. Harris

(Not the lady whose name is so famous in history,
But plain Mrs. H., without romance or mystery)
Spent six consecutive weeks without stopping
In one continuous round of shopping,—
Shopping alone, and shopping together,
At all hours of the day, and in all sorts of weather,—
For all manner of things that a woman can put
On the crown of her head or the sole of her foot,
Or wrap round her shoulders, or fit round her waist,
Or that can be sewed on, or pinned on, or laced,
Or tied on with a string, or stitched on with a bow,
In front or behind, above or below;
For bonnets, mantillas, capes, collars, and shawls;
Dresses for breakfasts and dinners and balls;
Dresses to sit in and stand in and walk in;
Dresses to dance in and flirt in and talk in;
Dresses in which to do nothing at all;
Dresses for winter, spring, summer, and fall;
All of them different in color and pattern,
Silk, muslin, and lace, crape, velvet, and satin,
Brocade, and broadcloth, and other material,
Quite as expensive and much more ethereal;
In short, for all things that could ever be thought of,
Or milliner, *modiste*, or tradesman be bought of,
    From ten-thousand-francs robes to twenty-sous frills;
In all quarters of Paris, and to every store,
While McFlimsey in vain stormed, scolded, and swore,
    They footed the streets, and he footed the bills.

The last trip, their goods shipped by the steamer *Arago*,
Formed, McFlimsey declares, the bulk of her cargo,
Not to mention a quantity kept from the rest,
Sufficient to fill the largest-sized chest,
Which did not appear on the ship's manifest,
But for which the ladies themselves manifested
Such particular interest, that they invested
Their own proper persons in layers and rows
Of muslins, embroideries, worked underclothes,

Gloves, handkerchiefs, scarfs, and such trifles as those;
Then, wrapped in great shawls, like Circassian beauties,
Gave *good-by* to the ship, and *go-by* to the duties.
Her relations at home all marveled, no doubt
Miss Flora had grown so enormously stout
　　For an actual belle and a possible bride;
But the miracle ceased when she turned inside out,
　　And the truth came to light, and the dry-goods beside,
Which, in spite of collector and custom-house sentry,
Had entered the port without any entry.

And yet, though scarce three months have passed since the day
This merchandise went, on twelve carts, up Broadway,
This same Miss McFlimsey, of Madison Square,
The last time we met was in utter despair,
Because she had nothing whatever to wear!

Nothing to Wear! Now, as this is a true ditty,
　　I do not assert—this, you know, is between us—
That she's in a state of absolute nudity,
　　Like Powers' Greek Slave, or the Medici Venus;
But I do mean to say, I have heard her declare,
　　When, at the same moment, she had on a dress
　　Which cost five hundred dollars, and not a cent less
　　And jewelry worth ten times more, I should guess,
That she had not a thing in the wide world to wear!

·　·　·　·　·　·　·　·　·　·　·

Oh, ladies, dear ladies, the next sunny day
Please trundle your hoops just out of Broadway,
From its whirl and its bustle, its fashion and pride,
And the temples of Trade which tower on each side,
To the alleys and lanes, where Misfortune and Guilt
Their children have gathered, their city have built;
Where Hunger and Vice, like twin beasts of prey,
　　Have hunted their victims to gloom and despair;
Raise the rich, dainty dress, and the fine broidered skirt,

Pick your delicate way through the dampness and dirt,
  Grope through the dark dens, climb the rickety stair
To the garret, where wretches, the young and the old,
Half-starved and half-naked, lie crouched from the cold.
  See those skeleton limbs, those frost-bitten feet,
All bleeding and bruised by the stones of the street;
Hear the sharp cry of childhood, the deep groans that swell
  From the poor dying creature who writhes on the floor,
Hear the curses that sound like the echoes of Hell,
  As you sicken and shudder and fly from the door;
Then home to your wardrobes, and say, if you dare,—
Spoiled children of Fashion,—you've nothing to wear!

And oh, if perchance there should be a sphere
Where all is made right which so puzzles us here,
Where the glare and the glitter and tinsel of Time
Fade and die in the light of that region sublime,
Where the soul, disenchanted of flesh and of sense,
Unscreened by its trappings and shows and pretense,
Must be clothed for the life and the service above,
With purity, truth, faith, meekness, and love;
O daughters of Earth! foolish virgins, beware!
Lest in that upper realm you have nothing to wear!

George Ade

As he continued year after year to supply the market with
Fables in Slang, George Ade often let his entertainment turn
pointedly satirical. Yet, like Sinclair Lewis, he was far too
deeply engrossed in the American scene to stand at any great
critical distance from it. Mencken, commenting on some of
Ade's more acerbic Fables, described the phenomenon as follows: "Up to a certain point it is all laughter, but after that
there is a flash of the knife, a show of teeth. Here a national
limitation often closes in upon the satirist. He cannot quite

separate the unaccustomed from the abominable; he is unable
to avoid rattling his philistine trappings a bit proudly; he must
prove that he, too, is a right-thinking American, a solid citizen
and a patriot, unshaken in his lofty rectitude by such poisons as
aristocracy, adultery, *hors d'oeuvres* and the sonata form."

Here is one of Ade's later Fables which shows the flash of
the knife: a satire against those who count and those who count
them.

THE FABLE OF THE SPOTLIGHTERS AND THE SPOTTER

Once a Traveller arrived at a Cure where the Water of the
Healing Springs smelled so awful that the Management
felt justified in asking $10 a Day.

This Traveller was a City Yap, which is worse than being a
Begosher, because the R. F. D. Boob usually knows that he is
below Par.

The City Yap is a Vertebrate with Shiny Hair, living under
the dominion of the Traffic Cops.

He will stand in front of a Window, with others of his Kind,
for an Hour at a time, watching a powerful Blonde demonstrate
a Fireless Cooker.

When $100,000,000 gets married to a Title, it is the City
Yap who has to be clubbed back by the Police so that the Bride
can get her Purchase into the Sanctuary.

When Jack Dempsey or Prince Blozotski arrives by Special
Train, the City Yap is the poor Google-Eye that you see standing in the Rain.

He believes that Greatness means having one's Name on the
Front Page; consequently it is better to jump off the Williams-
burg Bridge than to be an Emeritus Professor at Johns Hop-
kins.

Perhaps the Reader will ask: "Could a City Yap afford to
put up at one of these Ten-a-Day Resorts?"

Listen!

Some of the City Yaps have been to Harvard. They have tailor-made Underwear, Gold Service for Company, De Luxe Editions, Divorce Papers—Everything.

This particular Species of Metropolitan Mokus used to Boast that he could walk into any Hotel and the Clerks would hoist the Flag.

Such a Claim might not seem Portentous to one residing in Grand Island or Waupaca, but there are Favoured Spots within the Republic at which being known by the Boys behind the Desk is the very Essence of Fame.

Sure enough, the Lad who gives out the Keys recognized the Traveller and called him by Name and let on as though the Tavern had just opened and here was the first Customer.

After the newly arrived Delegate from the Asphalt Jungles had read a Telegram saying that Frazzingham Preferred had advanced from ¾ to ⅞ on a Report that the King of Rumania had received a Letter from the King of Greece, he brushed up a little and then sauntered back to the Bureau of Information and asked the Room Clerk if any one was stopping in the House.

Of course he knew that some 500 Transients of fair Business Standing and the usual Family connections were scattered about the Premises.

When he said "Any One," he meant did they have any one who would get Attention from the Head Waiter Himself.

A true Worshipper of the Exalted Few regards the common Run of Humanity as mere Whitebait. If you wish to hand him a Thrill, you must show him a Tarpon.

"We have so many Stars here that even the Manager is trembling," replied Cuthbert, the refined Room Clerk. "Do you see that Bunch out on the Piazza, taking the Sun? Leave me call them off to you. First, there is Jimmy Hooper, supposed to be the nerviest Plunger on the Exchange. He can lose or win a Million without disturbing the Ash on his Cigarette. He makes all the other High Rollers in the world look like Marble Players. He is King of the Gilt-Edge Gams."

"I have read all about him in the Papers," said the Roof-Garden Rufus.

"Then there is Mr. Hiram Cherrib, who has closed out all

his big Interests and puts in his Time endowing Hospitals and slipping Coin to Presbyterian Colleges. He allows that he will shoot every Bean in the old Tin Box and die Poor if he can do good to those that he formerly Did so successfully."

"For years I have yearned to get a peek at Mr. Cherrib," said the Café Habitué.

"And lookie! There is Mrs. Beverly Margrave, often called the uncrowned Empress of the American Hote Mond. You've heard of her!"

"HAVE I?" exclaimed the Bumpkin from the Boulevards. His Nostrils were quivering.

"She was a Terwhilligus from Baltimore, you may recall. I know People who would give their Eye-Teeth just to have her Insult them. Then they could say they had Met her. Right next to her Nobs is the famous preacher, Rev. Ormsby Toncell. They say he pulls down the biggest Salary and has the swellest lot of Box-Holders of any Parson in this whole Country. Even the English think he's English. He must be a talented Guy, all right!"

"Hardly a week passes but I see an Interview with him," said the Subway Simp.

"As I live and breathe, she's out there, too!" ejaculated the highly intelligent Room Clerk.

"Who?" asked the eager Cosmopolite.

"Lottie Limmet, the big Hit in that new Piece called 'Oh, Lizzie!' You remember—the Police made them change it. She had a Song that caused a Strike in the Orchestra. Some of the Musicians said they had Families."

"I tried to buy Seats"—in a Choking Whisper—"but they were sold out Eight Weeks in advance, and the Speculators asked Ten for Two on the Aisle."

"She is Some Gal. It is reported that they are going to put up a Statue of her at Yale. The Female Party right near her is supposed to be the Richest Woman in the Western Hemisphere."

"You don't mean Jane Plummer, the Widow that gets a Full Page in the Sunday Issue every two or three weeks?" asked the City Chap, his Cup of Joy just about ready to slop over.

"None other. I remember reading how much her Income would weigh if she changed it into Nickels. By the way, there's another Big Gun out there. I didn't notice him at first. Probably you've read the Editorial Attacks on Steve Gurney, the Political Boss."

"You don't mean the head of the Venal State Machine, who sits in a Back Room and gives orders to the Legislature and dictates Appointments and pulls all that Coarse Stuff, do you?"

"That's the Bird! I can see that you're well read. They've been trying for Years to get something on him and take his Measure, but he is still riding the Tractor."

"Me to put myself next," said Mr. H. Polloi. "I don't often get a Close-Up of these Immortals, and I'm sure going to Periscope."

So he edged out into the Sunlight and stalked his Prey.

There was one empty Chair right in the thick of the Who's Who, and he nailed it.

Oh, Joy! Oh, Bliss! And a couple of Raptures!

He found himself within smelling-distance of Lottie Limmet, the Forty-Second Street Parisienne.

There was no mistaking the much talked-of Cutie.

If Colours could be converted into Sounds her Costume would have been a Siren Whistle.

She had her Limbs crossed in such a way as to prove that she spared no Expense, but, nevertheless, her Knee-Caps were modestly concealed.

He knew it was She or Her because alongside of the Gay Creature and very Chummy was the famous Wall Street Blokie, Jimmy Hooper, dressed up like a Horse.

Yes, indeed! Shepherd's Plaid, Stripes on the Shirt, and a Bow Tie that looked like a Clot of Blood.

He had "Gambler" placarded all over him.

Our Hero knew that every Soubrette has a Gentleman Broker Friend who gives her Tips on the Market, so that ofttimes she will clean up as much as $300,000 at a Crack and then send her Mother a Watch.

He knew, because that was the part of the Paper he devoured.

It is easy to get acquainted with an Actress, so in a few

minutes George W. Fresh was carrying on with the Footlight Favourite and exchanging Hot Ones with Jimmy the Sport.

Presently the one who had been identified as Steve Gurney, Malefactor and Enemy of the People, edged over with his Rocking Chair and joined in the gay chatter of the Bohemians.

After giving Steve the Up-and-Down, it was easy to believe all that had been printed about him in the Righteous Press.

He was undershot and had Fuzz on the Back of his Hands.

He looked like a Vessel Unloader who had put on a Mail Order Suit in order to attend a Clam Bake.

The sort of Person you wouldn't care to meet in a Lonesome Street on a Rainy Night.

While the Investigator was letting himself go, in the company of these Abandoned Characters, and wondering what the Boys at the Lunch Club would say when he pulled it on them, he sized the other Notables close at hand.

Mrs. Beverly Margrave was perceptibly annoyed by the immediate presence of the *Canaille*, meaning Ordinary Skates.

Her prim but high-priced Suit of Quaker Gray, the chiselled suggestion of Patrician Reserve on her cold features, the wince of Pain and the lifted Eyebrow when Steve Gurney guffawed loudly, and the fact that she was reading George Moore—all these Items meant much to the Observant Traveller.

Why deny Class Distinction when even a Stranger can single out a True Genevieve with Pink Corpuscles?

Near the Queen of the Swagger Set, a pale Gentleman in somber Attire seemed quite lost in contemplation of the hazy Landscape.

He gave no heed to the gabby Groundlings only a few feet away.

He held daintily between the Forefinger and Thumb a White Rose with slender Stem.

At intervals he would lift the gorgeous Bloom to the Olfactory Orifices and inhale in a conservative manner, closing his Eyes and seeming to pass into a pleasant Trance.

It was a Cinch to place this Party as the Rev. Ormsby Toncell.

The absence of Jewellery, the Ascetic Pallor, the simple

adoration of Purity's Emblem—all these bespoke a Nature more Spiritual than Broadway.

Out by the Veranda Rail, seemingly lost in Meditation as he propped his Chin with a Newspaper made into a Roll, sat Horace Cherrib, the foremost Benefactor of his Time.

The City Fellow knew him by the Side Whiskers.

In every Good Show, the Elderly Person with Money who is trying to save some one else from Ruin and bring Happiness to the Deserving carries quite a mess of Ivy in front of each Listener.

Even if there had been no Trade-Marks, it would have been a Pipe to make the eminent Philanthropist.

The Light of Goodness twinkled in his Baby Blue Eyes and a Smile of infinite Kindliness illumined his Handsome Diagram.

He seemed oblivious, detached, quite unaware that others were watching him.

He was planning, dreaming—what? Possibly new Hospitals for the Crippled Children, more Colleges for the Farm Hands.

It was worth a Day's Journey just to sit and look at the great Cherrib.

You may be sure that the Lynx also improved this Golden Opportunity to get a line on Jane Plummer, the good old Standby of the Sunday Editor.

He knew her by the Ear-Bobs, which were Pearls about the size of Ripe Olives.

He had put in a lot of time studying Price Tags and he judged the Pearls would fetch close to $50,000 apiece, or $100,000 for the Two.

But, of course, she could afford it, so it was none of his Business.

Mrs. Plummer, whose Vast Fortune if converted into $1 Bills and placed End to End would reach from Boston to Omaha, was engaged in some sort of Fancy Work on a Tambourine Frame.

She chatted in a care-free way as her jewelled Fingers plied the busy Needle.

Her remarks were addressed to a timid little Woman in

rusty Black, who seemed more or less Cowed, which proved that she must be the hired Companion.

The Boy from the City had learned by a careful course of Reading, while lying in Bed, that every Woman of tremendous Wealth is trailed by a Female Friday who is addressed by her last Name.

He tried to pick out a Label for this Worm and decided that it might be Wiggins or Tubbs.

While he was wallowing in blissful Juxtaposition to the Prominent, some one touched him on the Shoulder.

It was the Room Clerk.

"I am off Watch," said the Employee, "and will take you on for Nine Holes."

Excusing himself from the Musical Comedy Star and the bold Speculator and the unprincipled Corrupter, he started for the Locker Room with Cuthbert, who had put him next to the King Pins.

"You are unquestionably the Child of Fortune," said the Room Clerk. "I take it that Mixer is your Middle Name. You work fast."

"One is always safe in flagging a theatrical Fairy," was the modest Reply. "I had no hesitancy about busting in as soon as I heard my friend Jimmy Hooper kidding her along."

"Why, you poor Fish! You have been getting gay for a Half Hour with Mrs. Beverly Margrave, acknowledged Leader of the Young Married Set."

"You must be mistaken. Mrs. Margrave was dressed in Gray and reading one of them High-Brow Books, and she got peeved because we made so much Racket."

"The Lady in Gray who won't speak to any one is Lottie Limmet. She won't even sign Autograph Albums."

"Back up! Do you mean to tell me that Mrs. Beverly Margrave, who comes of the most Aristocratic Family in Maryland, would stand for all that Joshing from a Rounder like Hooper?"

"Are you talking about that Buddie with the Loud Checks and the Crimson Cravat?"

"Sure."

"That was the Rev. Ormsby Toncell, and, take it from me, he's a regular Human Being."

"I think you're Twisted."

"No chance. Room Clerks know everything."

"I'm almost positive that the Reverend Toncell sat over to my right. He was dressed something like an Undertaker and kept smelling a Rose."

"You just got them reversed, that's all. The one with the Rose was Jimmy Hooper. He's Nuts about Flowers and keeps a fresh Bouquet on his Desk all the time."

"Have you got the unblushing Face to tell me that the Jolly Party with the Make-Up was the exclusive Matron and that a celebrated Preacher wore any such Stripes on his Shirt?"

"That's what I'm trying to Convey."

"Well, I'll prove that you're off. Do you think Mrs. Beverly Margrave and the Rev. Ormsby Toncell would hobnob with Steve Gurney after what all the newspapers have printed about him?"

"They didn't hobnob with Steve. They couldn't. He never goes near a Silk Stocking unless he wants to use him, and then he sends for him."

"Didn't I see it with my own Eyes?"

"Oh, you mean the big, square-jawed Burly that never buttons his Vest! That was Horace Cherrib, whom I told you about— the one that's going to save the World by feeding it $10 Bills."

"I don't think you took a good Look."

"Cert'nly I did. Steve wasn't near you Folks. He sat over there by himself and never chirped. 'Silent Steve,' his Friends call him."

"I refuse to believe that a kind-faced and gentle Soul like that is really the Boss of a disreputable Machine."

"No other kind could be. He wins out by making Friends."

"Well, anyway, I made no miscue on the Rich Widow. I marked her by the Expensive Pearls."

"Where do you get that Noise? Her Bill for Jewellery last year was 85 cents. She bought a jet Hat-Pin."

"Oh, come off! You don't mean to say—"

"Yes; the scared little Dame in the Black Gown, purchased direct from one of our largest Department Stores, has more Currency than you and I could shovel with two Shovels in two Weeks."

"How about the one with the enormous Pearls and the seven Rings?"

"Oh, that's her French Maid—from Wisconsin."

Moral: The recognized Types never run true to Form during the Vacation Period.

Will Rogers

Will Rogers was the last of the homely humorists. A professional entertainer in rodeos, the Ziegfeld Follies, radio, motion pictures, personal appearances, and in his syndicated newspaper columns, the homespun wit from Claremore, Oklahoma, never lost his instinctive distrust of everything biggity or phony.

Characteristically, the satire in Will Rogers' columns and occasional pieces is broadly political, suggested by what he read in the daily newspaper. His favorite butt was Congress, which he said was putting the professional humorist out of business. But he could let fly on any subject that happened to arouse or tickle him.

HOW TO TELL A BUTLER, AND OTHER ETIQUETTE

Somebody must have seen me out in Public; I think it was Emily Post, for she sent me a book on ETIQUETTE that she had written herself.

It has 700 pages in it. You wouldn't think there was that much Etiquette, would you! Well, I hadn't read far when I found that I was wrong on most every line of the whole Book.

Now, you wouldn't think a Person could live under fairly civilized conditions (as I imagined I was doing) and be so dumb as to not have at least one of these forms of Etiquette right. Well, when I got through reading it, I felt like I had been a heathen all my life. But after I got to noticing other people I met I didn't feel so bad. Some of them didn't know much more about it than I did.

So I predict that her Book and all the other things you read now on Etiquette are going to fall on fertile soil. Now take, for instance, being introduced, or introducing someone; that is the first thing in the Book. I didn't know up to then that inflection of the voice was such a big factor in introductions.

She says that the prominence of the party being introduced determines the sound of the voice, as she says for instance, "Are you there?" and then on finding out you are there she says, "Is it raining?"

Now the inflection that you use on asking any one if they are there, is the same inflection that you are to use on introducing Mr. Gothis, if he is the more prominent of the two. Then for the other person, who Mr. Gothis probably got his from, why, you use the "Is it raining?" inflection.

You see, a fellow has to know a whole lot more than you think he does before he can properly introduce people to each other. First he has to be up on his Dun and Bradstreet to tell which of the two is the more prominent. Second, he has to be an Elocutionist so he will know just where to bestow the inflection.

Well, I studied on that introduction Chapter till I thought I had it down pat. So I finally got a chance to try it out. My wife had invited a few friends for Dinner, and as she hadn't finished cooking it before they come, I had to meet them and introduce them to each other.

Well, I studied for half an hour before they come, trying to figure out which one was the most prominent so I could give her the "Are you there?" inflection. It was hard to figure out because any one of them couldn't be very prominent and be coming to our House for Dinner. So I thought, well, I will just give them both the "Is it raining?" inflection.

Then I happened to remember that the Husband of one of them had just bought a Drug Store, so I figured that I better give her the benefit of the "Are you there?" inflection, for if Prohibition stays in effect it's only a matter of days till her Husband will be prominent.

So, when they arrived I was remembering my opening Chapter of my Etiquette on Introductions. When the first one come I was all right; I didn't have to introduce her to anyone. I just opened our front door in answer to the Bell which didn't work. But I was peeping through the Curtains, and as I opened the door to let her in 2 of our Dogs and 4 Cats come in.

Well, while I was shooing them out, apologizing, and trying to make her believe it was unusual for them to do such a thing, now there I was! This Emily Post wrote 700 pages on Etiquette, but not a line on what to do in an emergency to remove Dogs and Cats and still be Nonchalant.

The second Lady arrived just as this Dog and Cat Pound of ours was emptying. She was the new Prescription Store Owner's Wife and was to get the "Are you there?" inflection. Her name was (I will call her Smith, but that was not her name). She don't want it to get out that she knows us.

Well, I had studied that Book thoroughly but those animals entering our Parlor had kinder upset me. So I said, "Mrs. Smith, Are you there? I want you to meet Mrs. Jones. Is it raining?"

Well, these Women looked at me like I was crazy. It was a silly thing to say. Mrs. Smith was there of course, or I couldn't have introduced her, and asking Mrs. Jones if it was raining was most uncalled for, because I had just looked out myself and, besides, any one that ever lived in California knows it won't rain again till next year.

But that didn't discourage me. I kept right on learning and from now on I am just mangy with Etiquette.

Why, just the other day, I heard what I had always considered up to then a well behaved Woman, introduce one Gentleman friend to another and she said, "Allow me to present."

Now anybody that's ever read the first 5 lines in the book knows that the word Present is never used only on formal occasions. You should always say "May I introduce" on all informal occasions. There was a Woman who, to look at her, you would never have thought she could possibly be so rude and uncultured as to have made a mistake like that.

It just spoiled her for me. I don't care how many nice things she may do in the future, she just don't belong.

Rule 2, Chapter 5—: "No Gentleman under any circumstances chews Gum in Public." Now that kinder knocked me for a Goal, for I had been Chewing Gum before some of the best families in this Country. But from now on it is out. I am going to live according to the Book.

Chapter 6—: "Gentlemen should not walk along the Street with their Cane or Stick striking the picket fence. Such habits should be curbed in the nursery."

Now that rule didn't hit me so hard for I am not lame and I don't carry a Cane yet, and furthermore, there is no Picket fences in California. If they had enough pickets to make a fence they would take them and build another Bungalow and rent it.

Outside of eating with a sharp knife, there is no rule in the Book that lays you liable to as much criticism as the following: "Whether in a private Car, a Taxi, or a carriage, a lady must never sit on a Gentleman's left, because according to European Etiquette a Lady 'on the left' is no lady."

I thought at first when I read that it was a misprint, and meant a Lady should never sit on a Gentleman's Lap, instead of Left. But now I find that it really was Left. So I guess you can go ahead and sit on the lap. It don't say not to. But don't sit on his Left, or you can never hope to enter smart society.

Then it says "the Owner of the car should always occupy the right hand side of the rear seat." No matter how many payments he has to make on it, that is considered his seat.

Chapter 7 is given over entirely to The Opera. What to wear, when to applaud—it tells everything but how to enjoy the thing. The fellow that figures out how to enjoy the Opera in a foreign tongue, without kidding himself or fourflushing, has a fortune in store for him.

Chapter 12 tells how the Butler should dress. You don't

know what a relief it was to me to find that news. I never had one, but if I do I will know what to costume him in.

The Book says: "At six o'clock the Butler puts on his dress Suit. The Butler's suit differs from that of a Gentleman by having no braid on his trousers."

Now all you Birds that never could tell the Servants from the Guests, except somebody called one of them a Butler and the other a Gentleman, you can't tell them that way. More than likely the Butler is the Gentleman of the two.

But I can tell the Butler. He has no braid on his trousers.

Now, all I got to do is find out how to tell the Gentleman.

If you see people walking around looking down at your trousers, in the future, you will know they are looking to see if the braid is left off.

Donald Ogden Stewart

FORMAL AND INFORMAL DRINKING
(from *Perfect Behavior*)

Drinking has, of course, always been a popular sport among the members of the better classes of society, but never has the enthusiasm for this pastime been so great in America as since the advent of "prohibition." Gentlemen and ladies who never before cared much for "drinking" have now given up almost all other amusements in favor of this fascinating sport; young men and débutantes have become, in the last few years, fully as expert in the game as their parents. In many cities, "drinking" has become more popular than "bridge" or dancing and it is predicted that, with a few more years of "prohibition," "drinking" will supersede golf and baseball as the great American pastime.

The effect of this has been to change radically many of the fundamental rules of the sport, and the influence on the etiquette of the game has been no less marked. What was considered "good form" in this pastime among our forefathers is now decidedly *démodé*, and the correct drinker of 1910 is as obsolete and out of date in the present decade as the "frock-coat."

The game today is divided into (a) formal and (b) informal drinking. "Formal drinking" is usually played after dinner and is more and more coming to take the place of charades, sleight-of-hand performances, magic lantern shows, "dumb crambo," et cetera, as the parlor amusement *par excellence*. "Formal drinking" can be played by from one to fifteen people in a house of ordinary dimensions; for a larger number it is generally better to provide a garage, a large yard, and special police, fire and plate glass insurance. The game is played with glasses, ice, and a dozen bottles of either whisky or gin.

The sport is begun by the host's wife, who says, "How would you all like to play a little bridge?" This is followed by silence. Another wife then says, "I think it would be awfully nice to play a little bridge." One of the men players then steps forward and says, "I think it would be awfully nice to have a little drink."

An "It" is then selected—always, by courtesy, the host. The "It" then says, "How would you all like to have a little drink?" The men players then answer in the affirmative, and the "It's" wife says, "Now, Henry dear, please—remember what happened last time." The "It" replies, "Yes, dear," and goes into the cellar, while the "It's" wife, after providing each guest with a glass, puts away the Dresden china clock, the porcelain parrot, and the gold fish globe.

Sides are chosen—usually with the husbands on one "team" and the wives on the other. The purpose of the game is for the "husbands' team" to try to drink up all the "It's" liquor before the "wives' team" can get them to go home.

When the "It" returns with the liquor he pours out a portion for each player and at a given signal all drink steadily for several minutes. The "It's" wife then says, "Now—how about a few rubbers of bridge?" She is immediately elected "team captain" for the rest of the evening. It is the duty of the "team captain" to provide cracked ice and water, to get ready the two spare bedrooms, to hold Wallie Spencer's hand, to keep Eddie

Armstrong from putting his lighted cigaret ends on the piano, and to break up the party as soon as possible. The game generally ends when (1) the liquor is all gone, (2) the "It" (or three guests) have passed "out," (3) Wallie Spencer starts telling about his war experiences. "Informal" drinking needs, of course, no such elaborate preparations and can be played anywhere and any time there is anything to drink. The person who is caught with the liquor is "It," and the object of the game is to take all the liquor away from the "It" as soon as possible. In order to avoid being "It," many players sometimes resort to various low subterfuges, such as sneaking down alone to the club locker-room during a dance, but this practice is generally looked upon with great disfavor—especially by that increasingly large group of citizens who are unselfishly devoting their lives to the cause of a "dry America" by consuming all of the present rapidly diminishing visible supply.

F.P.A.
(Franklin Pierce Adams)

As is well known, there are no classes of society in the United States and everyone is born with an equal opportunity of rising into a higher one.

This paradox is the starting point of American social satire.

PALM BEACH

Mr. and Mrs. Martin Foss,
Catherine Fox and Eleanor Goss,
Mr. and Mrs. James W. Cox,
Mr. and Mrs. Lyttleton Fox,
Mr. and Mrs. E. F. Hutton,

Mr. and Mrs. Arthur Cutten,
Mrs. Finley Peter Dunne,
Grover A. Whalen and Gurnee Munn,
Mr. and Mrs. Alfred Hearn,
Mr. and Mrs. Jerome D. Kern,
Gerald Brooks and Gerhard M. Dahl,
Mr. and Mrs. Lessing Rosenthal,
Leopold Stokowski and James T. Pope,
Mr. and Mrs. H. B. Swope,
Edward T. Stotesbury and Mrs. Frank Case,
Barclay Warburton, Eleanor Chase,
Mr. Dudley Field Malone,
Mr. Percy Mendelsohn,
Milton Florsheim and Percy Pyne,
Mr. and Mrs. Arthur Hammerstein,
Addison Mizner and Elsie Cripps,
Mr. and Mrs. Henry Phipps,
Mrs. Thomas Chadbourne and Frank X. Shields,
Robert Schaffner and the Rosenfields,
The Harvey Shaffers and the Westport Helds,
The Ziegfelds, the Felds, and the Rosenfelds,
Francis T. Hunter and Bruno Huhn,
Mrs. Vincent Astor and Heywood Broun,
Mr. and Mrs. McAneeny,
Mrs. Bruce Powell and Miss Marion Sweeney,
James P. Donahue and T. L. Jones,
The Pittsburgh Kaufmanns and the Syracuse Kohns,
Mr. and Mrs. William Norris,
Mr. Ira Nelson Morris,
Mr. and Mrs. Edgerton Freeman,
R. L. Goldberg and William Seeman,
Mr. and Mrs. Harrison Stoach,
Mr. and Mrs. Arthur Somers Roche,
The Mitchells, the Hardings, the Snowdens, and the Peaveys,
The Baches, the Beaches, the Kahns, and the Levys,
Evangeline Johnson and Alice De Lamar,
Mr. Josef Urban and S. T. Carr,
The Riddles, the Biddles, and the Henry Reas,

The Parks, the Clarkes, and the Alfred Kays,
The Mayers, the Thayers, the Marstons, and the Dillmans,
The Seligmans, the Slaters, the Stehlis, and the Stillmans
Lie on the beach to get an umber tint
With nothing to do but get their names in print.

Dorothy Parker

FROM THE DIARY OF A NEW YORK LADY

DURING DAYS OF HORROR, DESPAIR, AND WORLD CHANGE

Monday. Breakfast tray about eleven; didn't want it. The champagne at the Amorys' last night was *too* revolting, but what *can* you do? You can't stay until five o'clock on just *nothing*. They had those *divine* Hungarian musicians in the green coats, and Stewie Hunter took off one of his shoes and led them with it, and it *couldn't* have been funnier. He is *the* wittiest number in the *entire* world; he *couldn't* be more perfect. Ollie Martin brought me home and we both fell asleep in the car—*too* screaming. Miss Rose came about noon to do my nails, simply *covered* with *the* most divine gossip. The Morrises are going to separate *any minute*, and Freddie Warren *definitely* has ulcers, and Gertie Leonard simply *won't* let Bill Crawford out of her sight even with Jack Leonard *right there in the room*, and it's all *true* about Sheila Phillips and Babs Deering. It *couldn't* have been more thrilling. Miss Rose is *too* marvelous; I really think that a lot of times people like that are a lot more intelligent than a lot of people. Didn't notice until after she had gone that the damn fool had put that *revolting* tangerine-colored polish on my nails; *couldn't* have been more furious. Started to read a book, but too nervous. Called up and found I could get two tickets for the opening of "Run like a Rabbit" tonight for forty-eight dollars. Told them they had *the* nerve of the world, but what *can* you do? Think Joe said he was dining out, so telephoned some *divine* numbers to get someone to go

to the theater with me, but they were all tied up. Finally got
Ollie Martin. He *couldn't* have more poise, and what do *I* care
if he *is* one? *Can't* decide whether to wear the green crepe or
the red wool. Every time I look at my finger nails, I could *spit*.
Damn Miss Rose.

Tuesday. Joe came barging in my room this morning at
practically nine o'clock. Couldn't have been more furious.
Started to fight, but *too* dead. Know he said he wouldn't be
home to dinner. Absolutely *cold* all day; couldn't *move*. Last
night *couldn't* have been more perfect. Ollie and I dined at
Thirty-Eight East, absolutely *poisonous* food, and not one *living* soul that you'd be seen *dead* with, and "Run like a Rabbit"
was *the* world's worst. Took Ollie up to the Barlows' party and
it *couldn't* have been more attractive—*couldn't* have been more
people absolutely *stinking*. They had those Hungarians in the
green coats, and Stewie Hunter was leading them with a fork
—everybody simply *died*. He had *yards* of green toilet paper
hung around his neck like a lei; he *couldn't* have been in better
form. Met a *really new number*, very tall, *too* marvelous, and
one of those people that you can *really* talk to them. I told him
sometimes I get so *nauseated* I could *yip*, and I felt I absolutely
had to do something like write or paint. He said why didn't I
write or paint. Came home alone; Ollie passed out *stiff*. Called
up the new number three times today to get him to come to
dinner and go with me to the opening of "Never Say Good
Morning," but first he was out and then he was all tied up with
his mother. Finally got Ollie Martin. Tried to read a book, but
couldn't sit still. *Can't* decide whether to wear the red lace or the
pink with the feathers. Feel *too* exhausted, but what *can* you do?

Wednesday. The most terrible thing happened *just this minute*. Broke one of my finger nails *right off short*. Absolutely *the*
most horrible thing I ever had happen to me in my life.
Called up Miss Rose to come over and shape it for me, but she
was out for the day. I do have *the* worst luck in the *entire*
world. Now I'll have to go around like this all day and all night,
but what *can* you do? *Damn* Miss Rose. Last night *too* hectic.

"Never Say Good Morning" *too* foul, *never* saw more poisonous clothes on the stage. Took Ollie up to the Ballards' party; *couldn't* have been better. They had those Hungarians in the green coats and Stewie Hunter was leading them with a freesia —*too* perfect. He had on Peggy Cooper's ermine coat and Phyllis Minton's silver turban; *simply* unbelievable. Asked simply *sheaves* of *divine* people to come here Friday night; got the address of those Hungarians in the green coats from Betty Ballard. She says just engage them until four, and then whoever gives them another three hundred dollars, they'll stay till five. *Couldn't* be cheaper. Started home with Ollie, but had to drop him at his house; he *couldn't* have been sicker. Called up the new number today to get him to come to dinner and go to the opening of "Everybody Up" with me tonight, but he was tied up. Joe's going to be out; he didn't *condescend* to say *where, of course*. Started to read the papers, but nothing in them except that Mona Wheatley is in Reno charging *intolerable cruelty*. Called up Jim Wheatley to see if he had anything to do tonight, but he was tied up. Finally got Ollie Martin. *Can't* decide whether to wear the white satin or the black chiffon or the yellow pebble crepe. Simply *wrecked* to the *core* about my finger nail. Can't *bear* it. *Never* knew *anybody* to have such *unbelievable* things happen to them.

Thursday. Simply *collapsing* on my *feet*. Last night *too* marvelous. "Everybody Up" *too* divine, *couldn't* be filthier, and the new number was there, *too* celestial, only he didn't see me. He was with Florence Keeler in that *loathsome* gold Schiaparelli model of hers that every *shopgirl* has had since *God* knows. He must be out of his *mind;* she wouldn't *look* at a man. Took Ollie to the Watsons' party; *couldn't* have been more thrilling. Everybody simply *blind*. They had those Hungarians in the green coats and Stewie Hunter was leading them with a lamp, and, after the lamp got broken, he and Tommy Thomas did adagio dances—*too* wonderful. Somebody told me Tommy's doctor told him he had to absolutely get *right out of town*, he has *the* world's worst stomach, but you'd *never* know it. Came home alone, couldn't find Ollie *anywhere*. Miss Rose came at noon to

shape my nail, *couldn't* have been more fascinating. Sylvia
Eaton can't go *out the door* unless she's had a hypodermic, and
Doris Mason *knows every single word* about Douggie Mason
and that girl up in Harlem, and Evelyn North won't be *induced*
to keep away from those three acrobats, and they don't *dare* tell
Stuyvie Raymond *what* he's got the matter with him. *Never*
knew anyone that had a more simply *fascinating* life than Miss
Rose. Made her take that *vile* tangerine polish off my nails and
put on dark red. Didn't notice until after she had gone that it's
practically *black* in electric light; *couldn't* be in a worse state.
Damn Miss Rose. Joe left a note saying he was going to
dine out, so telephoned the new number to get him to come to
dinner and go with me to that new movie tonight, but he didn't
answer. Sent him three telegrams to *absolutely surely* come tomorrow night. Finally got Ollie Martin for tonight. Looked at
the papers, but nothing in them except that the Harry Motts
are throwing a tea with Hungarian music on Sunday. Think
will ask the new number to go to it with me; they must have
meant to invite me. Began to read a book, but too exhausted.
Can't decide whether to wear the new blue with the white
jacket or save it till tomorrow night and wear the ivory moire.
Simply *heartsick* every time I think of my nails. *Couldn't* be
wilder. Could *kill* Miss Rose, but what *can* you do?

Friday. Absolutely *sunk; couldn't* be worse. Last night *too*
divine, movie *simply* deadly. Took Ollie to the Kingslands'
party, *too* unbelievable, everybody absolutely *rolling*. They had
those Hungarians in the green coats, but Stewie Hunter wasn't
there. He's got a *complete* nervous breakdown. Worried *sick*
for fear he won't be well by tonight; will absolutely *never* forgive him if he doesn't come. Started home with Ollie, but
dropped him at his house because he *couldn't* stop crying. Joe
left word with the butler he's going to the country this afternoon for the week-end; *of course* he wouldn't *stoop* to say *what*
country. Called up *streams* of marvelous numbers to get someone to come dine and go with me to the opening of "White
Man's Folly," and then go somewhere after to dance for a while;
can't *bear* to be the first one there at your own party. Everybody

was tied up. Finally got Ollie Martin. *Couldn't* feel more depressed; never should have gone *anywhere near* champagne and Scotch together. Started to read a book, but too restless. Called up Anne Lyman to ask about the new baby and *couldn't* remember if it was a boy or girl—*must* get a secretary *next week.* Anne *couldn't* have been more of a help; she said she didn't know whether to name it Patricia or Gloria, so then of course I knew it was a girl *right away.* Suggested calling it Barbara; forgot she already had one. Absolutely *walking the floor* like a *panther* all day. Could *spit* about Stewie Hunter. Can't *face* deciding whether to wear the blue with the white jacket or the purple with the beige roses. Every time I look at those *revolting* black nails, I want to absolutely *yip.* I really have *the* most horrible things happen to me of anybody in the *entire* world. *Damn* Miss Rose.

Frank Sullivan

GLORIA SWANSON DEFENDS HER TITLE

Valentina, the designer, is reported to be running up a Vesuvius hat for Gloria Swanson. A concealed smoke-pot will send tiny clouds of perfumed vapors from its crown for several hours at a time.—Lucius Beebe in the "Herald Tribune."

Gloria Swanson arrived at the Colony for lunch, and Gene ushered her ceremoniously to a table. The other women in the restaurant, knowing that Miss Swanson dressed with taste, imagination, and daring, appraised her with swift glances. Detecting no breath-taking innovation in Miss Swanson's toilette, they returned to their Melba toast with feelings of relief.

But not for long. No sooner had Miss Swanson settled herself at her table than a puff of smoke escaped from her hat and wreathed upward. Gene blanched and his eyes popped for the merest fraction of a second. Then, inured as he was to fashionable ladies' hats, he recovered his *savoir-faire*.

The second puff from Miss Swanson's hat followed quickly on the first and was observed by Mrs. Gilbert Miller, Mrs. Harrison Williams, and Mrs. Gloria Morgan Vanderbilt, the three best-dressed women in New York. They exchanged alarmed glances.

The next puff galvanized Marcel, a green bus boy who had not yet acquired the Colony *savoir-faire*. He turned pale, seized a water carafe, and was about to put out Miss Swanson's hat when a curt command from Gene sent him to the kitchen in confusion.

The fourth puff was observed not only by Mrs. Woolworth Donahue, Mrs. William Rhinelander Stewart, Mrs. Byron Foy, Mrs. William S. Paley, Mrs. Orson Munn, and Mrs. Thomas Shevlin, the six best-dressed women in New York, but also by the one hundred and twelve other best-dressed women present.

An electric something filled the room. The ladies realized that once again the shrewd and daring Gloria had outgeneraled them, but after the first sharp pang of baffled rage they steeled themselves to a pretended indifference to her new hat.

"Gloria's hat puffs," one fashionable lady remarked languidly.

"Yes, I notice. But can it blow rings?" replied her companion in an equally languid tone.

Miss Swanson continued her luncheon in regal calm, her hat meanwhile huffing and puffing away. She exchanged smiling bows with the other best-dressed ladies, all of whom, she knew, cherished the secret hope that she would run out of smoke in the middle of the luncheon.

A distinguished-looking gentleman at a table across the room seemed particularly fascinated. He could not take his eyes from Miss Swanson's hat. Pretty soon he tore the cellophane from a package of cigarettes, built a fire on his plate, and, by deft maneuvering of a damp napkin, began sending smoke signals across the room.

"Tony," said Mabel Dodge Luhan to her Indian consort (for it was none other), "stop flirting and eat your maize!"

Miss Swanson finished her luncheon and left in a shower of pretty compliments from her colleagues—the Gloria-darling-your-new-hat-is-too-divine sort of thing. She smilingly acknowledged them. She was not fooled.

That afternoon well-dressed circles on Fifth and Park Avenues hummed with excitement. The fashionable women of New York are inured to hardship and prepared to make any sacrifice for the Cause. They could not afford to take Gloria's new hat lying down, for it was a challenge—a glove, so to speak—flung in the face of every woman at the Colony that afternoon. It must be topped at luncheon the following day or the best-dressed women of New York would Lose Face! The fashion designers of the metropolis sprang into action; lights burned late in the ateliers of New York's master hat creators.

War stimulates invention. Valentina's rash *défi* had its effect. Overnight the hat made greater strides than it would ordinarily in a year's time. And at luncheon hour the following day there began to trickle into the Colony a collection of hats which was remarkable even for that place.

There were hats that crackled, and sizzled, and spouted, and made odd noises. There were hats that disappeared and then reappeared. There were invisible hats, and hats within hats. But there were no hats that smoked, for the law of fashion forbade infringement on Gloria's model.

One best-dressed lady wore a hat of off-salmon straw that spouted jets of flame to match. Another lady wore a rather cute number which sent up a geyser of champagne every five minutes.

There were hats that exploded at stated intervals and hats that circled about the wearer's head on a trolley. One hat was trimmed with a moving electric bulletin board, in the manner of Times Square, which flashed late fashion news from Paris. Another hat played "Oh, Johnny, How You Can Love" and other tunes whenever its wearer inserted a nickel in a slot in the crown. (Carmel Snow, the fashion expert, estimated later that at least 50 per cent of the hats were electrically driven.)

An adventurous woman had the happy inspiration to wear a live homing pigeon trimmed with off-white velvet bows. At least it would have been a happy idea had not another adventurous woman had the same idea, unfortunately choosing as her hat a dove of the opposite sex. The two hats got a crush on each other before their owners had finished half a Martini and, taking off from their moorings, attempted to set up housekeeping in a third hat, which they mistook for a nest.

The prize, had there been one, would perhaps have gone to a woman who had been inspired by the idea of the magnetic mine. In her hat an electric magnet had been concealed which attracted other hats. The magnetic hat had lifted at least a dozen other hats from their anchorages before an "accidental" shove from an infuriated victim short-circuited it.

There might have been more sabotage in the excitement had not the rival best-dressed women for once been united in a common cause. "Get Gloria" was their slogan. Maintain the balance of power in hats; let no lady run amok. That way chaos lay.

But where was Gloria? A rumor spread that she had got cold feet and wouldn't appear. Then suddenly a whisper like the sound of a breeze moving through pines swept through the restaurant. It was the old Colony grapevine spreading word that Gloria had arrived—in a new hat!

A moment later she appeared. She was wearing—an old-fashioned bonnet of straw, trimmed with nothing and tied under her chin in a sedate bow.

The girls, not to be taken off guard again, waited for the innocent-looking contraption to start whatever monkeyshines Valentina and Gloria had contrived for it. But it did nothing. Gloria seated herself, ordered and consumed her luncheon, seemingly unaware that she was the center of interest. All about her, hats were bursting into flame or song, making uncanny sounds, flying about the room, or cutting other fantastic didos. Her hat just bobbed demurely as she pecked away at her frugal meal.

Miss Swanson finished her luncheon and started to leave. On her way out, she stopped at several tables and complimented the girls on their new hats. "My dear, your hat is too stunning for words!" But her own little number somehow, in a curious way one couldn't quite put one's finger on, made them all seem overdressed. Every woman in the Colony realized that once again Gloria Swanson had outwitted them; that once again the doughty little screen star had successfully defended her title as Best-Dressed Woman in New York.

E. B. White

Around the *New Yorker* offices on West Forty-third Street it is considered bad form to single out the contributions of any one writer-editor of the magazine, but exception is readily made in the case of E. B. White. "It was White," said Marc Connelly, "who brought the steel and music to the magazine."

An essayist of distinction, White has written many funny and effective satires on progress-worship and other shabby devotions of Americans. In the following piece he ridicules a fashionable magazine's pipe dream of ultimate elegance.

DUSK IN FIERCE PAJAMAS

Ravaged by pink eye, I lay for a week scarce caring whether I lived or died. Only Wamba, my toothless old black nurse, bothered to bring me food and quinine. Then one day my strength began to return, and with it came Wamba to my bedside with a copy of *Harper's Bazaar* and a copy of *Vogue*. "Ah brought you couple magazines," she said proudly, her red gums clashing.

In the days that followed (happy days of renewed vigor and reawakened interest), I studied the magazines and lived, in their pages, the gracious lives of the characters in the ever-moving drama of society and fashion. In them I found surcease from the world's ugliness, from disarray, from all unattractive things. Through them I escaped into a world in which there was no awkwardness of gesture, no unsuitability of line, no people of no importance. It was an enriching experience. I realize now that my own life is by contrast an unlovely thing, with its disease, its banalities, its uncertainties, its toil, its single-breasted suits, and its wine from lesser years. I am aware of a life all around me of graciousness and beauty, in which every moment is a tiny pearl of good taste, and in which every acquaintance has the common decency to possess a good background.

Lying here in these fierce pajamas, I dream of the *Harper's Bazaar* world, the *Vogue* life; dream of being a part of it. In fancy I am in Mrs. Cecil Baker's pine-panelled drawing-room. It is dusk. (It is almost always dusk in the fashion magazines.) I have on a Gantner & Mattern knit jersey bathing suit with a flat-striped bow and an all-white buck shoe with a floppy tongue. No, that's wrong. I am in chiffon, for it is the magic hour after bridge. Suddenly a Chippendale mahogany hors-d'œuvre table is brought in. In its original old blue-and-white Spode compartments there sparkle olives, celery, hard-boiled eggs, radishes— evidently put there by somebody in the employ of Mrs. Baker. Or perhaps my fancy wanders away from the drawing-room: I am in Mrs. Baker's dining-room, mingling unostentatiously with the other guests, my elbows resting lightly on the dark polished oak of the Jacobean table, my fingers twiddling with the early Georgian silver. Or perhaps I am not at Mrs. Baker's oak table in chiffon at all—perhaps instead I am at Mrs. Jay Gould's teakwood table in a hand-knitted Anny Blatt ensemble in diluted tri-colors and an off-the-face hat.

It is dusk. I am dining with Rose Hobart at the Waldorf. We have lifted our champagne glasses. "To sentiment!" I say. And the haunting dusk is shattered by the clean glint of jewels by Cartier.

It is dusk. I am seated on a Bruce Buttfield pouf, for it is dusk.

Ah, magazine dreams! How dear to me now are the four evenings in the life of Mrs. Allan Ryan, Junior. I have studied them one by one, and I feel that I know them. They are perfect little crystals of being—static, precious. There is the evening when she stands, motionless, in a magnificent sable cape, her left arm hanging gracefully at her side. She is ready to go out to dinner. What will this, her first of four evenings, bring of romance, or even of food? Then there is the evening when she just sits on the edge of a settee from the Modernage Galleries, the hard bright gleam of gold lamé topping a slim, straight, almost Empire skirt. I see her there (the smoke from a cigarette rising), sitting, sitting, waiting. Or the third evening—the evening with books. Mrs. Ryan is in chiffon; the books are in morocco. Or the fourth evening, standing with her dachshund, herself in profile, the dog in full face.

So I live the lives of other people in my fancy: the life of the daughter of Lord Curzon of Kedleston, who has been visiting the Harold Talbotts on Long Island. All I know of her is that she appeared one night at dinner, her beauty set off by the lustre of artificial satin and the watery fire of aquamarine. It is all I know, yet it is enough; for it is her one perfect moment in time and space, and I know about it, and it is mine.

It is dusk. I am with Owen Johnson over his chafing dish. It is dusk. I am with Prince Matchabelli over his vodka. Or I am with the Countess de Forceville over her bridge tables. She and I have just pushed the tables against the wall and taken a big bite of gaspacho. Or I am with the Marquis de Polignac over his Pommery.

How barren my actual life seems, when fancy fails me, here with Wamba over my quinine. Why am I not to be found at dusk, slicing black bread very thin, as William Powell does, to toast it and sprinkle it with salt? Why does not twilight find me (as it finds Mrs. Chester Burden) covering a table with salmon-pink linens on which I place only white objects, even to a white salt shaker? Why don't I learn to simplify my entertaining, like the young pinch-penny in *Vogue*, who has all his friends in before the theatre and simply gives them champagne cocktails, caviar, and one hot dish, then takes them to the show? Why do I never give parties after the opera, as Mr. Paul Cravath does, at which I have the prettiest women in New York? Come to think of it, why don't the prettiest women in New York ever come down to my place, other than that pretty little Mrs. Fazaenzi, whom Wamba won't let in? Why haven't I a butler named Fish, who makes a cocktail of three parts gin to one part lime juice, honey, vermouth, and apricot brandy in equal portions—a cock-

tail so delicious that people like Mrs. Harrison Williams and
Mrs. Goodhue Livingston seek him out to get the formula? And
if I *did* have a butler named Fish, wouldn't I kid the pants off
him?

All over the world it is dusk! It is dusk at Armando's on East
Fifty-fifth Street. Armando has taken up his accordion; he is
dreaming over the keys. A girl comes in, attracted by the accordion, which she mistakes for Cecil Beaton's camera. She is in
stiff green satin, and over it she wears a silver fox cape which
she can pull around her shoulders later in the evening if she gets
feeling like pulling a cape around her shoulders. It is dusk on
the Harold Castles' ranch in Hawaii. I have risen early to shoot a
goat, which is the smart thing to do in Hawaii. And now I am
walking silently through hedges of gardenias, past the flaming
ginger flowers, for I have just shot a goat. I have on nothing but
red sandals and a Martex bath towel. It is dusk in the Lauren-
tians. I am in ski togs. I feel warm and safe, knowing that the
most dangerous pitfall for skiers is *color*, knowing that although
a touch of brilliance against the snow is effective, too much of it
is the sure sign of the amateur. It is the magic hour before cocktails. I am in the modern penthouse of Monsieur Charles de
Beistegui. The staircase is entirely of cement, spreading at the
hemline and trimmed with padded satin tubing caught at the
neck with a bar of milk chocolate. It is dusk in Chicago. I am
standing beside Mrs. Howard Linn, formerly Consuelo Vanderbilt, formerly Sophie M. Gay, formerly Ellen Glendinning, formerly Saks-Fifth Avenue. It is dusk! A pheasant has Julian
Street down and is pouring a magnificent old red Burgundy
down his neck. Dreams, I'm afraid. It is really dusk in my own
apartment. I am down on my knees in front of an airbound
radiator, trying to fix it by sticking pins in the vent. Dusk in
these fierce pajamas. Kneeling here, I can't help wondering
where Nancy Yuille is, in her blue wool pants and reefer and
her bright red mittens. For it is dusk. I said *dusk*, Wamba!
Bring the quinine!

COURTSHIP AND MARRIAGE

"Almoste every boddy gits married, and it iz a good joke."

JOSH BILLINGS (Henry W. Shaw)

Washington Irving

Diedrich Knickerbocker has just concluded an eloquent denunciation of the tyranny over minority opinions which he finds prevalent in the United States. But he observes that in spite of wholesale persecutions of "unbelievers" the Yankee race has somehow managed to multiply at an astonishing rate.

BUNDLING
(from *A History of New York* . . . *by Diedrich Knickerbocker*, 1809)

This amazing increase may, indeed, be partly ascribed to a singular custom prevalent among them, commonly known by the name of *bundling*—a superstitious rite observed by the young people of both sexes, with which they usually terminated their festivities; and which was kept up with religious strictness by the more bigoted part of the community. This ceremony was likewise, in those primitive times, considered as an indispensable preliminary to matrimony; their courtships commencing where ours usually finish—by which means they acquired that intimate acquaintance with each other's good qualities before marriage, which has been pronounced by philosophers the sure basis of a happy union. Thus early did this cunning and ingenious people display a shrewdness of making a bargain, which has ever since distinguished them—and a strict adherence to the good old vulgar maxim about "buying a pig in a poke."

To this sagacious custom, therefore, do I chiefly attribute the unparalleled increase of the Yanokie or Yankee race; for it is a certain fact, well authenticated by court records and parish registers, that wherever the practice of bundling prevailed, there was an amazing number of sturdy brats annually born unto the State, without the license of the law, or the benefit of clergy. Neither did the irregularity of their birth operate in the least to their disparagement. On the contrary, they grew up a long-sided, raw-boned, hardy race of whoreson whalers, wood-cutters, fishermen, and pedlers, and strapping corn-fed wenches; who by their united efforts tended marvelously towards peopling those notable tracts of country called Nantucket, Piscataway, and Cape Cod.

Eugene Field

When Grover Cleveland took possession of the White House he was a bachelor and, if that wasn't bad enough, the acknowledged father of an illegitimate child. "Ma, Ma! Where's my Pa?" the Republicans had taunted, and the victorious Democrats, making the best of it, had replied "Gone to the White House, Ha, Ha, Ha!" But no one was happy that the President was wifeless.

At the start of his first term, Cleveland entrusted the running of the White House to his sister Rose, a large, authoritative lady who managed it with a sure but heavy hand. Then, in the spring of 1886, the country was delighted to discover that a new chatelaine would be coming to Pennsylvania Avenue. Cleveland had been secretly engaged to his young and pretty friend Frances Folsom, and they were to be married in June. No nuptials in American history were to arouse more clamor and festivity than Cleveland's.

Eugene Field in Chicago added to the holiday spirit with these mildly satirical epithalamiums. In the verses, Rose Elizabeth is Cleveland's sister, the displaced mistress of the White House. "Dan'l" is Daniel S. Lamont, Cleveland's indispensable man Friday, first his confidential secretary, eventually his Secretary of War. The Mugwumps referred to were the reformers within the Republican Party who had refused to vote with the party and thereby inadvertently helped Cleveland. "Sir Lamar" is a Senator from Mississippi who bore the imposing name of Lucius Quintus Cincinnatus Lamar.

THE WHITE HOUSE BALLADS
(1886)

SISTER ROSE'S SUSPICIONS

What of these tidings, Grover dear,
  That are reported far and near
Upon suspicion's breath?
And is it true, as eke 'tis said,
That you have made your mind to wed?"
  Quoth Rose Elizabeth.

With that his conscience smote him sore—
He cast his eyes upon the floor,
  But not a word he saith.
Then did she guess his secret flame;
In sooth she was a crafty dame,
  Was Rose Elizabeth.

She flaunted out into the hall
In grievous wrath and tears withal,
  Did Rose Elizabeth;
And when he saw her grewsome rage
That no entreaties could assuage,
  He fiercely muttered, " 'S death!"

THE WEDDING DAY

Oh, hand me down my spike-tail coat
  And reef my waistband in,
And tie this necktie round my throat
  And fix my bosom-pin;
I feel so weak and flustered like,
  I don't know what to say—
For I'm to be wedded to-day, Dan'l,
  I'm to be wedded to-day!

Put double sentries at the doors
  And pull the curtains down,
And tell the Democratic bores
  That I am out of town:
It's funny folks hain't decency
  Enough to stay away
When I'm to be wedded today, Dan'l,
  I'm to be wedded to-day!

The bride, you say, is calm and cool
  In satin robes of white.
Well, I am stolid, as a rule,
  But now I'm flustered quite;
Upon a surging sea of bliss
  My soul is borne away,
For I'm to be wedded to-day, Dan'l,
  I'm to be wedded to-day!

THE TYING OF THE TIE

Now was Sir Grover passing wroth.
"A murrain seize the man," he quoth,
  "Who first invented ties!
Egad, they are a grievous bore,
And tying of them vexeth sore
  A person of my size!"

Lo, at his feet upon the floor
Were sprent the neckties by the score,
  And collars all a-wreck;
And good Sir Grover's cheeks were flame,
And good Sir Grover's arms were lame
  With wrestling at his neck.

But much it joyed him when he heard
Sir Daniel say: "I fain will gird
  Your necktie on for you,
As 't will not cause you constant fear
Of bobbing round beneath your ear
  Or setting you askew."

Sir Daniel grasped one paltry tie
And, with a calm, heroic eye
   And confidential air
(As who should say, "Odds bobs, I vow
There's nothing like the knowing how")
   He mounted on a chair.

And whilst Sir Grover raised his chin
(For much he did respect the pin)
   Sir Daniel tied the tie,
The which, when good Sir Grover viewed—
Albeit it belike a dude—
   He heaved a grateful sigh.

THE KISSING OF THE BRIDE

And when at last, with priestly pray'r
And music mingling in the air,
   The nuptial knot was tied,
Sir Grover, flaming crimson red,
"Soothly, it is my mind," he said,
   "That I salute the bride!"

Whereat upon her virgin cheek,
So smooth, so plump, and comely eke,
   He did implant a smack
So lusty that the walls around
Gave such an echo to the sound
   As they had like to crack.

No modern salutation this,
No mincing, maudlin Mugwump kiss,
   To chill a bride's felicity;
Exploding on her blushing cheek,
Its virile clamor did bespeak
   Arcadian simplicity.

THE CUTTING OF THE CAKE

Sir Grover quoth: "Let each one here
Of soups and wine and sumptuous cheer
   Most heartily partake;

And whilst you are thus well employed,
I ween my consort will be joyed
    To cut the bridal cake!"

Then saith the bride, as courtesying low:
"There is no sweeter task, I trow,
    Than which is now my life,
To do thy will, my liege; so I
Would fain with thy request comply
    If I but had a knife."

Thereat of shining blades a score
Leaped from their knightly sheaths before
    You could have counted two;
As each brave knight right humbly prayed
The lady to accept his blade
    Wherewith her will to do.

But Lady Frances shook her head
And with sweet dignity she said:
    "None other's blade I'll take
Save his who hath my rev'rence won—
My pole-star and my central sun—
    And his shall cut the cake!"

Then did Sir Grover bend him to
His trouser pockets, whence he drew
    A jack-knife, big and fat,
The which he gave into her hand,
Whereat the others murmured, and
    They marvelled much thereat.

But when the cake was cut, the rest
Made proper hurry to attest
    In knightly phrase emphatic
How that the cake was passing nice,
And how the blade that cleft each slice
    Was truly democratic.

THE PASSING OF THE COMPLIMENT

Eftsoons the priest had made his say,
The courtly knights and ladies gay
    Did haste from every side,
With honeyed words and hackneyed phrase
And dainty smiles withal, to praise
    Sir Grover's blushing bride.

Out spake the courtly Sir Lamar:
"Of all fair brides, you, lady, are
    The fairest I have seen;
Not only of this castle grand,
But of all hearts throughout the land,
    Are you acknowledged queen!"

Whereat the Lady Frances bowed;
And rapturous murmurs in the crowd
    Did presently attest
That of the chestnuts uttered there
This chestnut was without compare—
    Foredating all the rest.

Donald Ogden Stewart

WEDDING ETIQUETTE
(from *Perfect Behavior*)

INVITATIONS AND WEDDING PRESENTS

The proper time to send out invitations to a wedding is between two and three weeks before the day set for the ceremony, although the out-of-town invitations should be mailed in plenty of time to allow the recipient to purchase and forward a suitable present. As the gifts are received, a check mark should be placed after the name of the donor, together with a short description of the present and an estimate as to its probable cost. This list is to be used later, at the wedding reception, in determining the manner in which the bride is to greet the various guests. It has been found helpful by many brides to devise some sort of memory system whereby certain names immediately suggest certain responses, thus:

"Mr. Snodgrass—copy of *Highways and Byways in Old France*—c. $6.50"—"how do you do, Mr. Snodgrass, have you met my mother?"

"Mr. Brackett—solid silver candlesticks—$68.50"—"hello, Bob, you old peach. How about a kiss?"

The real festivities of a wedding start about three days before the ceremony, with the arrival of the "wedding party," in which party the most responsible position is that of best man. Let us suppose that you are to be the best man at the Roe-Doe nuptials. What are your duties?

In the first place, you must prepare yourself for the wedding by a course of training extending for over a month or more prior to the actual event. It should be your aim to work yourself into such a condition that you can go for three nights without sleep, talk for hours to the most impossibly stupid of young women, and consume an unending amount of alcohol. You are then prepared for the bachelor dinner, the bridal dinner, the bridesmaids, the wedding, and the wedding reception.

DUTIES OF THE BEST MAN

UPON your arrival in the city where the wedding is to take place you will be met by the bridegroom, who will take you to the home of the bride where you are to stay. There you are met by the bride's father. "This is my best man," says the groom. "The best man?" replies her father. "Well, may the best man win." At once you reply, "Ha! Ha! Ha!" He then says, "Is this your first visit to Chicago?" to which the correct answer is, "Yes, sir, but I hope it isn't my last."

The bride's mother then appears. "This is my best man," says the groom. "Well," says she, "remember—the best man doesn't always win." "Ha! Ha! Ha!" you at once reply. "Is this your first visit to Chicago?" says she, to which you answer, "Yes—but I hope it isn't my last."

You are then conducted to your room, where you are left alone to unpack. In a few minutes the door will open and a small boy enter. This is the brother of the bride. You smile at him pleasantly and remark, "Is this your first visit to Chicago?" "What are you doing?" is his answer. "Unpacking," you reply. "What's that?" says he. "A cutaway," you reply. "What's that?" says he. "A collar bag." "What's that?" "A dress shirt." "What's that?" says he. "Another dress shirt." "What's that?" says he. "Say, listen," you reply, "don't I hear some one calling you?" "No," says he, "what's that?" "That," you reply, with a sigh of relief, "is a razor. Here—take it and play with it." In three minutes, if you have any luck at all, the bride's brother will have cut himself severely in several places which will cause him to run crying from the room. You can then finish unpacking.

THE BRIDE'S TEA

THE first function of the pre-nuptial festivities is generally a tea at the bride's home, where the ushers and bridesmaids meet to become "acquainted." It is your duty, as best man, to go to the hotel where the ushers are stopping and bring them to this tea. Just as you will leave on this mission the groom will whisper in your ear, "For God's sake, remember to tell them that her father and mother are terribly opposed to drinking in any form." This is an awfully good joke on her father and mother.

As you step out of the hotel elevator you hear at the end of the hall a chorus shouting, "Mademoiselle from Armentières—*parlez vous!*" Those are your ushers.

Opening the door of the room you step forward and announce, "Fellows, we have got to go to a tea right away. Come on—let's go." At this, ten young men in cutaways will stand up and shout, "Yeaaa—the best man—give the best man a drink!" From then on, at twelve minute intervals, it is your duty to say, "Fellows, we have got to go to a tea right away. Come on—let's go." Each time you will be handed another drink, which you may take with either your right or left hand.

After an hour the telephone will ring. It will be the groom. He will say, "Everybody is waiting for you and the ushers," to which you reply, "We are just leaving." He then says, "And don't forget to tell them what I told you about her father and mother."

You then hang up the receiver, take a drink in one hand and say, "Fellows, I have a very solemn message for you. It's a message which is of deep importance to each one of us. Fellows— her father and mother object to the use of alcohol in any form."

This statement will be greeted with applause and cheers. You will all then take one more drink, put on your silk hats and gray gloves, and leave the room singing, "Her father and mother object to drink—*parlez vous.*"

The tea given by the bride's parents is generally a small affair to which only the members of the wedding party are invited. When you and the ushers arrive, you will find the bride, the maid of honor and the bridesmaids waiting for you. As you enter the room, make a polite bow to the bride's father and mother, and be sure to apologize for your lateness. Nothing so betrays the social "oil can" as a failure to make a plausible excuse for tardiness. Whenever you are late for a party you must always have ready some good reason for your fault, such as, "Excuse me, Mrs. Doe, I'm afraid I am a little late, but you see, just as I was dressing, this filling dropped out of my tooth and I had to have it put back in." If the host and hostess seem to doubt your statement, it would be well to show them the recalcitrant filling in question, although if they are "well-bred" they will probably in most cases take you at your word.

THE MAID OF HONOR

You and the ushers will then be introduced to the bridesmaids and the maid of honor. As you meet this latter young lady, who is the bride's older sister and, of course, your partner for the remainder of the wedding festivities, she will say, "The best man? Well, they say that the best man wins . . . Ha! Ha! Ha!" This puts her in class G 6 without further examination, and your only hope of prolonging your life throughout the next two days lies in the frequent and periodic administration of stimulants.

THE BACHELOR DINNER AND AFTER

THAT evening the groom gives for the best man and the ushers what is known as a "bachelor dinner." It is his farewell to his men friends as he passes out of the state of bachelorhood. The formal passing out generally occurs toward the end of the dinner, and is a quaint ceremony participated in by most of those present.

It is customary for the best man to wake up about noon of the following day. You will not have the slightest idea as to where you are or how you got there. You will be wearing your dress trousers, your stiff or pleated bosom dress shirt, black socks and pumps, and the coat of your pajamas. In one hand you will be clutching a chrysanthemum. After a few minutes there will come a low moan from the next bed. That is usually the groom, also in evening dress with the exception that he has tried to put on the trousers of your pajamas over his dress trousers. You then say, "What happened?" to which he replies, "Oh, Judas." You wait several minutes. In the next room you hear the sound of a shower bath and some one whistling. The bath stops; the whistling continues. The door then opens and there enters one of the ushers. He is the usher who always "feels great" the next day after the bachelor dinner. He says to you, "Well, boys, you look all in." You do not reply. He continues, "Gosh, I feel fine." You make no response. He then begins to chuckle. "I don't suppose you remember," he says, "what you said to the bride's mother when I brought you home last night." You sit quickly up in bed. "What did I say?" you ask. "Was I tight?" "Were you tight?" he replies, still chuckling. "Don't you remember what you said? And don't you remember trying to get the bride's father to slide down the banisters with you? Were you tight—Oh, my gosh!" He then exits, chuckling. Statistics of several important life insurance companies show that that type of man generally dies a violent death before the age of thirty.

THE REHEARSAL

THE rehearsal for the wedding is usually held in the church on the afternoon preceding the day of the nuptials. The ushers, of course, are an hour late, which gives the bridegroom (Bap.) an opportunity to meet the minister (Epis.) and have a nice, long chat about religion, while the best man (Atheist) talks to the eighty-three-year-old sexton who buried the bride's grandpa and grandma and has known little Miss Dorothy come twenty years next Michaelmas. The best man's offer of twenty-five dollars, if the sexton will at once bury the maid of honor, is generally refused as a matter of courtesy.

THE BRIDAL DINNER

IN the evening, the parents of the bride give the bridal dinner, to which all the relatives and close friends of the family are invited. Toasts are drunk in orange juice and rare old Virginia Dare wine, and much good-natured fun is indulged in by all. Speeches are usually made by the bride and groom, their parents, the best man, the maid of honor, the minister and Aunt Harriet.

Just a word about the speeches at a bridal dinner. Terrible!

A CHURCH WEDDING

ON the day of the wedding the ushers should arrange to be at the church an hour or so in advance of the time set for the ceremony. They should be dressed in cutaways, with ties, gloves and gardenias provided by the groom.

It is the duty of the best man to dress the bridegroom for the wedding. As you enter his room you see, lying half-dressed on the bed, a pale, wan, emaciated creature, who is staring fixedly at the ceiling. It is the happy bridegroom. His lips open. He speaks feebly. "What time is it?" he says. You reply, "Two-thirty, old man. Time to start getting dressed." "Oh, my God!" says the groom. Ten minutes pass. "What time is it?" says the groom. "Twenty of three," you reply. "Here's your shirt." "Oh, my God!" says the groom.

He takes the shirt and tries to put it on. You help him. "Better have a little Scotch, old man," you say. "What time is it?" he replies. "Five of three," you say. "Oh, my God!" says the groom.

At three-thirty you and he are dressed in cutaways and promptly at three-forty-two you arrive at the church. You are

ushered into a little side room where it is your duty to sit with
the corpse for the few brief hours which elapse between three-
forty-five and four o'clock. Occasionally he stirs and a faint
spark of life seems to struggle in his sunken eyes. His lips move
feebly. You bend over to catch his dying words. "Have—you—
got—the ring?" he whispers. "Yes," you reply. "Everything's
fine. You look great, too, old man." The sound of the organ
reaches your ears. The groom groans. "Have you got the ring?"
he says.

Meanwhile the ushers have been performing their duty of
showing the invited guests to the various pews. A correctly
trained usher will always have ready some cheery word or
sprightly bit of conversation to make the guests feel perfectly at
home as he conducts them to their seats. "It's a nice day, isn't
it?" is suggested as a perfectly safe and yet not too unusual topic
of conversation. This can be varied by remarking, "Isn't it a nice
day?" or in some cases, where you do not wish to appear too forward, "Is it a nice day, or isn't it?" An usher should also remember that although he has on a cutaway, he is neither a floor-
walker nor a bond salesman, and remarks such as "Something in
a dotted Swiss?" or "Third aisle over—second pew—next the
ribbon goods," are decidedly *non au fait*.

The first two pews on each side of the center aisle are always
reserved for members of the immediate family, but it is a firmly
established custom that the ushers shall seat in these "family
pews" at least three people with whom the family are barely on
speaking terms. This slight error always causes Aunt Nellie and
Uncle Fred to sit up in the gallery with the family cook.

With the arrival of the bride, the signal is given to the organist to start the wedding march, usually either Mendelssohn's
or Wagner's. About this time the mother of the bride generally
discovers that the third candle from the left on the rear altar has
not been lighted, which causes a delay of some fifteen minutes
during which time the organist improvises one hundred and
seventy-three variations on the opening strains of the march.

Finally all is adjusted and the procession starts down the aisle
led by the ushers swaying slowly side by side. It is always customary for three or four of the eight ushers to have absolutely no

conception of time or rhythm, which adds a quaint touch of uncertainty and often a little humor to the performance.

After the Scotch mist left by the passing ushers has cleared, there come the bridesmaids, the maid of honor, and then, leaning on her father's arm (unless, of course, her father is dead), the bride.

In the meantime, the bridegroom has been carried in by the best man and awaits the procession at the foot of the aisle, which is usually four hundred and forty yards long. The ushers and bridesmaids step awkwardly to one side; the groom advances and a hush falls over the congregation which is the signal for the bride's little niece to ask loudly, "What's that funny looking man going to do, Aunt Dotty?"

Then follows the religious ceremony.

Immediately after the church service, a reception is held at the bride's home, where refreshments are served and two hundred and forty-two invited guests make the same joke about kissing the bride. At the reception it is customary for the ushers and the best man to crawl off in separate corners and die.

The wedding "festivities" are generally concluded with the disappearance of the bride, the bridegroom, one of the uninvited guests and four of the most valuable presents.

H. L. Mencken

THE WEDDING: A STAGE DIRECTION

*T*he scene is a church in an American city of about half a million population, and the time is about eleven o'clock of a fine morning in early spring. The neighborhood is well-to-do, but not quite fashionable. That is to say, most of the families of the vicinage keep two servants (alas, more or less intermittently!), and eat dinner at half-past six, and about one in every four boasts a colored butler (who attends to the fires, washes windows and helps with the sweeping), and a last year's automobile. *The heads of these families are merchandise brokers; jobbers in notions, hardware and drugs; manufacturers of candy, hats, badges, office furniture, blank books, picture frames, wire goods and patent medicines; managers of steamboat lines; district agents of insurance companies; owners of commercial printing offices, and other such business men of substance—and the prosperous lawyers and popular family doctors who keep them out of trouble. In one block live a Congressman and two college professors, one of whom has written an unimportant textbook and got himself into "Who's Who in America." In the block above lives a man who once ran for Mayor of the city, and came near being elected.*

The wives of these householders wear good clothes and have a liking for a reasonable gayety, but very few of them can pretend to what is vaguely called social standing, and, to do them justice, not many of them waste any time lamenting it. They have, taking one with another, about three children apiece, and are good mothers. A few of them belong to women's clubs or flirt with the suffragettes, but the majority can get all of the intellectual stimulation they crave in the Ladies' Home Journal and the Saturday Evening Post, with Vogue added for its fashions. Most of them, deep down in their hearts, suspect their husbands of secret frivolity, and about ten per cent have the proofs, but it is rare for them to make rows about it, and the divorce rate among them is thus very low. Themselves indifferent cooks, they are unable to teach their servants the art, and so the food they set before their husbands and children is often such as would make a Frenchman cut his throat. But they are diligent housewives otherwise; they see to it that the windows are washed, that no one tracks mud into the hall, that the servants do not waste coal, sugar, soap and gas, and that the family buttons are always sewed on. In religion these estimable wives are pious in habit but somewhat nebulous in faith. That is to say, they regard any person who specifically refuses to go to church as a heathen, but they themselves are by no means regular in attendance, and not one in ten of them could tell you whether transubstantiation is a Roman Catholic or a Dunkard doctrine. About two per cent have dallied more or less gingerly with

Christian Science, their average period of belief being one year.

The church we are in is like the neighborhood and its people: well-to-do but not fashionable. It is Protestant in faith and probably Episcopalian. The pews are of thick, yellow-brown oak, severe in pattern and hideous in color. In each there is a long, removable cushion of a dark, purplish, dirty hue, with here and there some of its hair stuffing showing. The stained-glass windows, which were all bought ready-made and depict scenes from the New Testament, commemorate the virtues of departed worthies of the neighborhood, whose names appear, in illegible black letters, in the lower panels. The floor is covered with a carpet of some tough, fibrous material, apparently a sort of grass, and along the center aisle it is much worn. The normal smell of the place is rather less unpleasant than that of most other halls, for on the one day when it is regularly crowded practically all of the persons gathered together have been very recently bathed.

On this fine morning, however, it is full of heavy, mortuary perfumes, for a couple of florist's men have just finished decorating the chancel with flowers and potted palms. Just behind the chancel rail, facing the center aisle, there is a prie-dieu, and to either side of it are great banks of lilies, carnations, gardenias and roses. Three or four feet behind the prie-dieu and completely concealing the high altar, there is a dense jungle of palms. Those in the front rank are authentically growing in pots, but behind them the florist's men have artfully placed some more durable, and hence more profitable, sophistications. Anon the rev. clergyman, emerging from the vestry-room to the right, will pass along the front of this jungle to the prie-dieu, and so, framed in flowers, face the congregation with his saponaceous smile.

The florist's men, having completed their labors, are preparing to depart. The older of the two, a man in the fifties, shows the ease of an experienced hand by taking out a large plug of tobacco and gnawing off a substantial chew. The desire to spit seizing him shortly, he proceeds to gratify it by a trick long practised by gasfitters, musicians, caterer's helpers, piano movers and other such alien invaders of the domestic hearth.

That is to say, he hunts for a place where the carpet is loose along the chancel rail, finds it where two lengths join, deftly turns up a flap, spits upon the bare floor, and then lets the flap fall back, finally giving it a pat with the sole of his foot. This done, he and his assistant leave the church to the sexton, who has been sweeping the vestibule, and, after passing the time of day with the two men who are putting up a striped awning from the door to the curb, disappear into a nearby saloon, there to wait and refresh themselves until the wedding is over, and it is time to take away their lilies, their carnations and their synthetic palms.

It is now a quarter past eleven, and two flappers of the neighborhood, giggling and arm-in-arm, approach the sexton and inquire of him if they may enter. He asks them if they have tickets and when they say they haven't, he tells them that he ain't got no right to let them in, and don't know nothing about what the rule is going to be. At some weddings, he goes on, hardly nobody ain't allowed in, but then again, sometimes they don't scarcely look at the tickets at all. The two flappers retire abashed, and as the sexton finishes his sweeping, there enters the organist.

The organist is a tall, thin man of melancholy, uræmic aspect, wearing a black slouch hat with a wide brim and a yellow overcoat that barely reaches to his knees. A pupil, in his youth, of a man who had once studied (irregularly and briefly) with Charles-Marie Widor, he acquired thereby the artistic temperament, and with it a vast fondness for malt liquor. His mood this morning is acidulous and depressed, for he spent yesterday evening in a Pilsner ausschank with two former members of the Boston Symphony Orchestra, and it was 3 A.M. before they finally agreed that Johann Sebastian Bach, all things considered, was a greater man than Beethoven, and so parted amicably. Sourness is the precise sensation that wells within him. He feels vinegary; his blood runs cold; he wishes he could immerse himself in bicarbonate of soda. But the call of his art is more potent than the protest of his poisoned and quaking liver, and so he manfully climbs the spiral stairway to his organ-loft.

Once there, he takes off his hat and overcoat, stoops down to

*blow the dust off the organ keys, throws the electrical switch
which sets the bellows going, and then proceeds to take off his
shoes. This done, he takes his seat, reaches for the pedals
with his stockinged feet, tries an experimental 32-foot CCC, and
then wanders gently into a Bach toccata. It is his limbering-up
piece: he always plays it as a prelude to a wedding job. It thus
goes very smoothly and even brilliantly, but when he comes to
the end of it and tackles the ensuing fugue he is quickly in
difficulties, and after four or five stumbling repetitions of the
subject he hurriedly improvises a crude coda and has done.
Peering down into the church to see if his flounderings have
had an audience, he sees two old maids enter, the one very tall
and thin and the other somewhat brisk and bunchy.*

*They constitute the vanguard of the nuptial throng, and as
they proceed hesitatingly up the center aisle, eager for good
seats but afraid to go too far, the organist wipes his palms upon
his trousers legs, squares his shoulders, and plunges into the
program that he has played at all weddings for fifteen years past.
It begins with Mendelssohn's Spring Song, pianissimo. Then
comes Rubinstein's Melody in F, with a touch of forte toward
the close, and then Nevin's "Oh, That We Two Were Maying,"
and then the Chopin waltz in A flat, Opus 69, No. 1, and then
the Spring Song again, and then a free fantasia upon "The
Rosary" and then a Moszkowski mazurka, and then the Dvorák
Humoresque (with its heart-rending cry in the middle), and
then some vague and turbulent thing (apparently the disjecta
membra of another fugue), and then Tschaikowsky's "Autumn,"
and then Elgar's "Salut d'Amour," and then the Spring Song a
third time, and then something or other from one of the Peer
Gynt suites, and then an hurrah or two from the Hallelujah
chorus, and then Chopin again, and Nevin, and Elgar, and—*

*But meanwhile, there is a growing activity below. First
comes a closed automobile bearing the six ushers and soon after
it another automobile bearing the bridegroom and his best man.
The bridegroom and the best man disembark before the side entrance of the church and make their way into the vestryroom,
where they remove their hats and coats, and proceed to struggle
with their cravats and collars before a mirror which hangs on*

*the wall. The room is very dingy. A baize-covered table is in
the center of it, and around the table stand six or eight chairs of
assorted designs. One wall is completely covered by a bookcase,
through the glass doors of which one may discern piles of cheap
Bibles, hymn-books and back numbers of the parish magazine.
In one corner is a small washstand. The best man takes a flat
flask of whiskey from his pocket, looks about him for a glass,
finds it on the washstand, rinses it at the tap, fills it with a
policeman's drink, and hands it to the bridegroom. The latter
downs it at a gulp. Then the best man pours out one for himself.*

The ushers, reaching the vestibule of the church, have
handed their silk hats to the sexton, and entered the sacred
edifice. There was a rehearsal of the wedding last night, but
after it was over the bride ordered certain incomprehensible
changes in the plan, and the ushers are now completely at sea.
All they know clearly is that the relatives of the bride are to
be seated on one side and the relatives of the bridegroom on the
other. But which side for one and which for the other? They discuss it heatedly for three minutes and then find that they stand
three for putting the bride's relatives on the left side and three
for putting them on the right side. The debate, though instructive, is interrupted by the sudden entrance of seven women
in a group. They are headed by a truculent old battleship, possibly an aunt or something of the sort, who fixes the nearest
usher with a knowing, suspicious glance, and motions to him to
show her the way.

He offers her his right arm and they start up the center aisle,
with the six other women following in irregular order, and the
five other ushers scattered among the women. The leading
usher is tortured damnably by doubts as to where the party
should go. If they are aunts, to which house do they belong,
and on which side are the members of that house to be seated?
What if they are not aunts, but merely neighbors? Or perhaps
an association of former cooks, parlor maids, nurse girls? Or
strangers? The sufferings of the usher are relieved by the battleship, who halts majestically about twenty feet from the altar,
and motions her followers into a pew to the left. They file in

*silently and she seats herself next the aisle. All seven settle back
and wriggle for room. It is a tight fit.*

(*Who, in point of fact, are these ladies? Don't ask the question! The ushers never find out. No one ever finds out. They
remain a joint mystery for all time. In the end they become a
sort of tradition, and years hence, when two of the ushers meet,
they will cackle over old dreadnaught and her six cruisers.
The bride, grown old and fat, will tell the tale to her daughter,
and then to her granddaughter. It will grow more and more
strange, marvelous, incredible. Variorum versions will spring
up. It will be adapted to other weddings. The dreadnaught will
become an apparition, a witch, the Devil in skirts. And as the
years pass, the date of the episode will be pushed back. By
2017 it will be dated 1150. By 2475 it will take on a sort of
sacred character, and there will be a footnote referring to it in
the latest Revised Version of the New Testament.*)

*It is now a quarter to twelve, and of a sudden the vestibule
fills with wedding guests. Nine-tenths of them, perhaps even
nineteen-twentieths, are women, and most of them are beyond
thirty-five. Scattered among them, hanging on to their skirts,
are about a dozen little girls—one of them a youngster of eight
or thereabout, with spindle shanks and shining morning face,
entranced by her first wedding. Here and there lurks a man.
Usually he wears a hurried, unwilling, protesting look. He has
been dragged from his office on a busy morning, forced to rush
home and get into his cutaway coat, and then marched to the
church by his wife. One of these men, much hustled, has forgotten to have his shoes shined. He is intensely conscious of them,
and tries to hide them behind his wife's skirt as they walk up the
aisle. Accidentally he steps upon it, and gets a look over the
shoulder which lifts his diaphragm an inch and turns his liver
to water. This man will be court-martialed when he reaches
home, and he knows it. He wishes that some foreign power
would invade the United States and burn down all the churches
in the country, and that the bride, the bridegroom and all the
other persons interested in the present wedding were dead and
in hell.*

The ushers do their best to seat these wedding guests in some

*sort of order, but after a few minutes the crowd at the doors
becomes so large that they have to give it up, and thereafter all
they can do is to hold out their right arms ingratiatingly and
trust to luck. One of them steps on a fat woman's skirt, tearing
it very badly, and she has to be helped back to the vestibule.
There she seeks refuge in a corner, under a stairway leading up
to the steeple, and essays to repair the damage with pins produced from various nooks and crevices of her person. Meanwhile the guilty usher stands in front of her, mumbling apologies
and trying to look helpful. When she finishes her work and
emerges from her improvised drydock, he again offers her his
arm, but she sweeps past him without noticing him, and proceeds grandly to a seat far forward. She is a cousin to the
bride's mother, and will make a report to every branch of the
family that all six ushers disgraced the ceremony by appearing
at it far gone in liquor.*

*Fifteen minutes are consumed by such episodes and divertise-
ments. By the time the clock in the steeple strikes twelve the
church is well filled. The music of the organist, who has now
reached Mendelssohn's Spring Song for the third and last time,
is accompanied by a huge buzz of whispers, and there is much
craning of necks and long-distance nodding and smiling. Here
and there an unusually gorgeous hat is the target of many
converging glances, and of as many more or less satirical criticisms. To the damp funeral smell of the flowers at the altar,
there has been added the cacodorous scents of forty or fifty
different brands of talcum and rice powder. It begins to grow
warm in the church, and a number of women open their vanity
bags and duck down for stealthy dabs at their noses. Others,
more reverent, suffer the agony of augmenting shines. One, a
trickster, has concealed powder in her pocket handkerchief, and
applies it dexterously while pretending to blow her nose.*

*The bridegroom in the vestryroom, entering upon the sec-
ond year (or is it the third?) of his long and ghastly wait, grows
increasingly nervous, and when he hears the organist pass from
the Spring Song into some more sonorous and stately thing he
mistakes it for the wedding march from "Lohengrin," and is
hot for marching upon the altar at once. The best man, an*

old hand, restrains him gently, and administers another sedative from the bottle. The bridegroom's thoughts turn to gloomy things. He remembers sadly that he will never be able to laugh at benedicts again; that his days of low, rabelaisian wit and carefree scoffing are over; that he is now the very thing he mocked so gaily but yesteryear. Like a drowning man, he passes his whole life in review—not, however, that part which is past, but that part which is to come. Odd fancies throng upon him. He wonders what his honeymoon will cost him, what there will be to drink at the wedding breakfast, what a certain girl in Chicago will say when she hears of his marriage. Will there be any children? He rather hopes not, for all those he knows appear so greasy and noisy, but he decides that he might conceivably compromise on a boy. But how is he going to make sure that it will not be a girl? The thing, as yet, is a medical impossibility—but medicine is making rapid strides. Why not wait until the secret is discovered? This sapient compromise pleases the bridegroom, and he proceeds to a consideration of various problems of finance. And then, of a sudden, the organist swings unmistakably into "Lohengrin" and the best man grabs him by the arm.

There is now great excitement in the church. The bride's mother, two sisters, three brothers and three sisters-in-law have just marched up the center aisle and taken seats in the front pew, and all the women in the place are craning their necks toward the door. The usual electrical delay ensues. There is something the matter with the bride's train, and the two bridesmaids have a deuce of a time fixing it. Meanwhile the bride's father, in tight pantaloons and tighter gloves, fidgets and fumes in the vestibule, the six ushers crowd about him inanely, and the sexton rushes to and fro like a rat in a trap. Finally, all being ready, with the ushers formed two abreast, the sexton pushes a button, a small buzzer sounds in the organ loft, and the organist, as has been said, plunges magnificently into the fanfare of the "Lohengrin" march. Simultaneously the sexton opens the door at the bottom of the main aisle, and the wedding procession gets under weigh.

The bride and her father march first. Their step is so slow

(*about one beat to two measures*) *that the father has some difficulty in maintaining his equilibrium, but the bride herself
moves steadily and erectly, almost seeming to float. Her face is
thickly encrusted with talcum in its various forms, so that she
is almost a dead white. She keeps her eyelids lowered modestly,
but is still acutely aware of every glance fastened upon her—
not in the mass, but every glance individually. For example,
she sees clearly, even through her eyelids, the still, cold smile of
a girl in Pew 8 R—a girl who once made an unwomanly attempt upon the bridegroom's affections, and was routed and
put to flight by superior strategy. And her ears are open, too:
she hears every "How sweet!" and "Oh, lovely!" and "Ain't she
pale!" from the latitude of the last pew to the very glacis of the
altar of God.*

*While she has thus made her progress up the hymeneal
chute, the bridegroom and his best man have emerged from the
vestryroom and begun the short march to the prie-dieu. They
walk haltingly, clumsily, uncertainly, stealing occasional
glances at the advancing bridal party. The bridegroom feels of
his lower right-hand waistcoat pocket; the ring is still there.
The best man wriggles his cuffs. No one, however, pays any
heed to them. They are not even seen, indeed, until the bride
and her father reach the open space in front of the altar. There
the bride and the bridegroom find themselves standing side by
side, but not a word is exchanged between them, nor even a
look of recognition. They stand motionless, contemplating the
ornate cushion at their feet, until the bride's father and the
bridesmaids file to the left of the bride and the ushers, now
wholly disorganized and imbecile, drape themselves in an irregular file along the altar rail. Then, the music having died
down to a faint murmur and a hush having fallen upon the assemblage, they look up.*

*Before them, framed by foliage, stands the reverend gentle-
man of God who will presently link them in indissoluble chains
—the estimable rector of the parish. He has got there just in
time; it was, indeed, a close shave. But no trace of haste or of
anything else of a disturbing character is now visible upon his
smooth, glistening, somewhat feverish face. That face is wholly*

occupied by his official smile, a thing of oil and honey all compact, a balmy, unctuous illumination—the secret of his success in life. Slowly his cheeks puff out, gleaming like soap-bubbles. Slowly he lifts his prayer-book from the prie-dieu and holds it droopingly. Slowly his soft caressing eyes engage it. There is an almost imperceptible stiffening of his frame. His mouth opens with a faint click. He begins to read.

The Ceremony of Marriage has begun.

AMERICANS
ABROAD

" 'How much?' said our friend in English."

HENRY JAMES, *The Americans*

Americans Abroad

*F*rom this side of the Atlantic, Europe has variously appeared as a sink of iniquity, a museum of fine arts, a battle-
ground, a playground, a good-will project, and a sanctuary of
Western civilization. From the memorable entrance of Benjamin
Franklin at Versailles in a coon-skin hat to Mrs. Kennedy's
triumphal appearance in Paris in 1961 in a pill-box model,
Americans of all sorts have visited, resided in, fought in, and
worked in the place called "abroad." They have come on Grand
Tours, Wanderjahre, "Pleasure Excursions," cruise plans,
package tours, business missions, and State visits, invasions and
occupations. In all this variety of experience, only one thing is
common to all: the spectacle of one American abroad is up-
setting to another American abroad.

Mark Twain

GULLIBLE GUIDES
(from *The Innocents Abroad*, 1869)

I used to worship the mighty genius of Michael Angelo—
that man who was great in poetry, painting, sculpture, ar-
chitecture—great in everything he undertook. But I do not
want Michael Angelo for breakfast—for luncheon—for dinner
—for tea—for supper—for between meals. I like a change, occasionally. In Genoa, he designed everything; in Milan he or his
pupils designed everything; he designed the Lake of Como; in
Padua, Verona, Venice, Bologna, who did we ever hear of, from
guides, but Michael Angelo? In Florence, he painted everything,
designed everything, nearly, and what he did not design he
used to sit on a favorite stone and look at, and they showed us
the stone. In Pisa he designed everything but the old shot-tower,
and they would have attributed that to him if it had not been so
awfully out of the perpendicular. He designed the piers of
Leghorn and the custom-house regulations of Civita Vecchia.
But, here—here it is frightful. He designed St. Peter's; he designed the Pope; he designed the Pantheon, the uniform of the
Pope's soldiers, the Tiber, the Vatican, the Coliseum, the Capitol, the Tarpeian Rock, the Barberini Palace, St. John Lateran,
the Campagna, the Appian Way, the Seven Hills, the Baths of
Caracalla, the Claudian Aqueduct, the Cloaca Maxima—the
eternal bore designed the Eternal City, and unless all men and
books do lie, he painted everything in it! Dan said the other
day to the guide, "Enough, enough, enough! Say no more!
Lump the whole thing! say that the Creator made Italy from designs by Michael Angelo!"

I never felt so fervently thankful, so soothed, so tranquil, so
filled with a blessed peace, as I did yesterday when I learned
that Michael Angelo was dead.

But we have taken it out of this guide. He has marched us through miles of pictures and sculpture in the vast corridors of the Vatican; and through miles of pictures and sculpture in twenty other palaces; he has shown us the great picture in the Sistine Chapel, and frescoes enough to fresco the heavens—pretty much all done by Michael Angelo. So with him we have played that game which has vanquished so many guides for us —imbecility and idiotic questions. These creatures never suspect—they have no idea of a sarcasm.

He shows us a figure and says: "Statoo brunzo." (Bronze statue.)

We look at it indifferently and the doctor asks: "By Michael Angelo?"

"No—not know who."

Then he shows us the ancient Roman Forum. The doctor asks: "Michael Angelo?"

A stare from the guide. "No—a thousan' year before he is born."

Then an Egyptian obelisk. Again: "Michael Angelo?"

"Oh, *mon dieu*, genteelmen! Zis is *two* thousan' year before he is born!"

He grows so tired of that unceasing question sometimes, that he dreads to show us anything at all. The wretch has tried all the ways he can think of to make us comprehend that Michael Angelo is only responsible for the creation of a *part* of the world, but somehow he has not succeeded yet. Relief for overtasked eyes and brain from study and sight-seeing is necessary, or we shall become idiotic sure enough. Therefore this guide must continue to suffer. If he does not enjoy it, so much the worse for him. We do.

In this place I may as well jot down a chapter concerning those necessary nuisances, European guides. Many a man has wished in his heart he could do without his guide; but knowing he could not, has wished he could get some amusement out of him as a remuneration for the affliction of his society. We accomplished this latter matter, and if our experience can be made useful to others they are welcome to it.

Guides know about enough English to tangle everything up

so that a man can make neither head nor tail of it. They know their story by heart—the history of every statue, painting, cathedral, or other wonder they show you. They know it and tell is as a parrot would—and if you interrupt, and throw them off the track, they have to go back and begin over again. All their lives long, they are employed in showing strange things to foreigners and listening to their bursts of admiration. It is human nature to take delight in exciting admiration. It is what prompts children to say "smart" things, and do absurd ones, and in other ways "show off" when company is present. It is what makes gossips turn out in rain and storm to go and be the first to tell a startling bit of news. Think, then, what a passion it becomes with a guide, whose privilege it is, every day, to show to strangers wonders that throw them into perfect ecstasies of admiration! He gets so that he could not by any possibility live in a soberer atmosphere. After we discovered this, we *never* went into ecstasies any more—we never admired anything—we never showed any but impassible faces and stupid indifference in the presence of the sublimest wonders a guide had to display. We had found their weak point. We have made good use of it ever since. We have made some of those people savage, at times, but we have never lost our own serenity.

The doctor asks the questions, generally, because he can keep his countenance, and look more like an inspired idiot, and throw more imbecility into the tone of his voice than any man that lives. It comes natural to him.

The guides in Genoa are delighted to secure an American party, because Americans so much wonder, and deal so much in sentiment and emotion before any relic of Columbus. Our guide there fidgeted about as if he had swallowed a spring mattress. He was full of animation—full of impatience. He said:

"Come wis me, genteelmen!—come! I show you ze letter-writing by Christopher Colombo!—write it himself!—write it wis his own hand!—come!"

He took us to the municipal palace. After much impressive fumbling of keys and opening of locks, the stained and aged document was spread before us. The guide's eyes sparkled. He danced about us and tapped the parchment with his finger:

"What I tell you, genteelmen! Is it not so? See! handwriting Christopher Colombo!—write it himself!"

We looked indifferent—unconcerned. The doctor examined the document very deliberately, during a painful pause. Then he said, without any show of interest:

"Ah—Ferguson*—what—what did you say was the name of the party who wrote this?"

"Christopher Colombo! ze great Christopher Colombo!"

Another deliberate examination.

"Ah—did he write it himself, or—or how?"

"He write it himself!—Christopher Colombo! he's own hand-writing, write by himself!"

Then the doctor laid the document down and said:

"Why, I have seen boys in America only fourteen years old that could write better than that."

"But zis is ze great Christo—"

"I don't care who it is! It's the worst writing I ever saw. Now you mustn't think you can impose on us because we are strangers. We are not fools, by a good deal. If you have got any specimens of penmanship of real merit, trot them out!—and if you haven't, drive on!"

We drove on. The guide was considerably shaken up, but he made one more venture. He had something which he thought would overcome us. He said:

"Ah, genteelmen, you come wis me! I show you beautiful, oh, magnificent bust Christopher Colombo!—splendid, grand, magnificent!"

He brought us before the beautiful bust—for it *was* beautiful—and sprang back and struck an attitude:

"Ah, look, genteelmen!—beautiful, grand,—bust Christopher Colombo!—beautiful bust, beautiful pedestal!"

The doctor put up his eyeglass—procured for such occasions:

"Ah—what did you say this gentleman's name was?"

"Christopher Colombo!—ze great Christopher Colombo!"

* Ferguson is the sobriquet the travelers have chosen for their hired guide, whose real Italian name they find unpronounceable. —Editor's note.

"Christopher Colombo—the great Christopher Colombo. Well, what did *he* do?"

"Discover America!—discover America, oh, ze devil!"

"Discover America. No—that statement will hardly wash. We are just from America ourselves. We heard nothing about it. Christopher Colombo—pleasant name—is—is he dead?"

"Oh, *corpo di Baccho!*—three hundred year!"

"What did he die of?"

"I do not know!—I cannot tell."

"Smallpox, think?"

"I do not know, genteelmen!—I do not know *what* he die of!"

"Measles, likely?"

"Maybe—maybe—I do *not* know—I think he die of some-things."

"Parents living?"

"Im-posseeble!"

"Ah—which is the bust and which is the pedestal?"

"Santa Maria!—*zis* ze bust!—*zis* ze pedestal!"

"Ah, I see, I see—happy combination—very happy combina-tion, indeed. Is—is this the first time this gentleman was ever on a bust?"

That joke was lost on the foreigner—guides cannot master the subtleties of the American joke.

We have made it interesting for this Roman guide. Yester-day we spent three or four hours in the Vatican again, that won-derful world of curiosities. We came very near expressing in-terest, sometimes—even admiration—it was very hard to keep from it. We succeeded though. Nobody else ever did, in the Vatican museums. The guide was bewildered—nonplussed. He walked his legs off, nearly, hunting up extraordinary things, and exhausted all his ingenuity on us, but it was a failure; we never showed any interest in anything. He had reserved what he considered to be his greatest wonder till the last—a royal Egyptian mummy, the best-preserved in the world, perhaps. He took us there. He felt so sure, this time, that some of his old enthusiasm came back to him:

"See, genteelmen!—Mummy! Mummy!"

The eyeglass came up as calmly, as deliberately as ever.

"Ah,—Ferguson—what did I understand you to say the gentleman's name was?"

"Name?—he got no name!—Mummy!—'Gyptian mummy!"

"Yes, yes. Born here?"

"No! *'Gyptian* mummy!"

"Ah, just so. Frenchman, I presume?"

"No!—*not* Frenchman, not Roman!—born in Egypta!"

"Born in Egypta. Never heard of Egypta before. Foreign locality, likely. Mummy—mummy. How calm he is—how self-possessed. Is, ah—is he dead?"

"Oh, *sacré bleu*, been dead three thousan' year!"

The doctor turned on him savagely:

"Here, now, what do you mean by such conduct as this! Playing us for Chinamen because we are strangers and trying to learn! Trying to impose your vile second-hand carcasses on *us!*—thunder and lightning, I've a notion to—to—if you've got a nice *fresh* corpse, fetch him out!—or, by George, we'll brain you!"

We make it exceedingly interesting for this Frenchman. However, he has paid us back, partly, without knowing it. He came to the hotel this morning to ask if we were up, and he endeavored as well as he could to describe us, so that the landlord would know which persons he meant. He finished with the casual remark that we were lunatics. The observation was so innocent and so honest that it amounted to a very good thing for a guide to say.

There is one remark (already mentioned) which never yet has failed to disgust these guides. We use it always, when we can think of nothing else to say. After they have exhausted their enthusiasm pointing out to us and praising the beauties of some ancient bronze image or broken-legged statue, we look at it stupidly and in silence for five, ten, fifteen minutes—as long as we can hold out, in fact—and then ask:

"Is—is he dead?"

That conquers the serenest of them. It is not what they are looking for—especially a new guide. Our Roman Ferguson is the most patient, unsuspecting, long-suffering subject we have

had yet. We shall be sorry to part with him. We have enjoyed
his society very much. We trust he has enjoyed ours, but we
are harassed with doubts.

Don Marquis

mehitabel sees paris

(from *archy and mehitabel*)

Paris france
       i have not been
to geneva but i have been
talking to a french cockroach
who has just returned
from there traveling all the
way in a third class
compartment he says there is no
hope for insect or man in
the league of nations
what prestige it ever had is gone
and it never had any
the idea of one great brotherhood
of men and insects on earth
is very attractive to me
but mehitabel the cat
says i am a communist an
anarchist and a socialist
she has been shocked to the soul
she says by what the
revolutionists did here during
the revolution
i am always the aristocrat archy
she said i may go and play
around montmartre and that sort

of thing and in fact i was
playing up there with francy last
night but i am always the lady
in spite of my little larks
toujours gai archy and toujours
the lady that is my motto in
spite of
ups and downs
what they did to us aristocrats
at the time of the revolution
was a plenty archy
it makes my heart bleed
to see signs of it all
over town those poor
dear duchesses that got it
in the neck i can sympathize
with them archy i may not
look it now but i come of a
royal race myself
i have come down in the world
but wotthehell archy wotthehell
jamais triste archy jamais triste
that is my motto
always the lady and always
out for a good time
francy and i lapped up
a demi of beer in a joint
up on the butte last night
that an american tourist
poured out for us
and everybody laughed and it
got to be the fashion up there
to feed beer to us cats
i did not get a vulgar souse
archy no lady gets a vulgar
souse wotthehell i hope i am above
all vulgarity but i did get a
little bit lit up

and francy did too we came
down and got on top of the
new morgue and sang and did
dances there
francy seems to see
something attractive about
morgues when he gets lit up
the old morgue he says was
a more romantic morgue but
vandal hands have torn it down
but wotthehell archy this one
will do to dance on
francy is showing me a side of
paris he says tourists don t often
get a look at he has a little
love nest down in the
catacombs where
he and i are living now
he and i go down there
and do the tango amongst the
bones he is really a most
entertaining and agreeable
companion archy and he has some
very quaint ideas he is busy now
writing a poem about
us two cats filled with beer
dancing among the bones
sometimes i think francy
is a little morbid
when i see these lovely old places
that us aristocrats built archy
in the hands of the bourgeois it
makes me almost wild
but i try to bear up i try
to bear up i find agreeable
companions and put a good face
on it toujours gai that is my

motto toujours gai
francy is a little bit done up
today he tried to steal a
partridge out of a frying
pan in a joint up on the butte
we went back there for more beer
after our party
at the morgue
and the cook beaned him with
a bottle poor francy i
should hate to lose him
but something tells me i should
not stay a widow long
there is something in the air
of paris archy
that makes one young again
there s more than one
dance in the old dame yet
and with these words she
put her tail in the air and
capered off down the alley
i am afraid we shall never
get mehitabel back to america

                                        archy

Robert Frost

AN IMPORTER

Mrs. Someone's been to Asia.
  What she brought back would amaze ye.
Bamboos, ivories, jades, and lacquers,
Devil-scaring firecrackers,
Recipes for tea with butter,

Sacred rigmaroles to mutter,
Subterfuge for saving faces,
A developed taste in vases,
Arguments too stale to mention
'Gainst American invention;
Most of all the mass production
Destined to prove our destruction.
What are telephones, skyscrapers,
Safety razors, Sunday papers,
But the silliest evasion
Of the truths we owe an Asian?
But the best of her exhibit
Was a prayer machine from Tibet
That by brook power in the garden
Kept repeating Pardon, pardon;
And as picturesque machinery
Beat a sundial in the scenery—
The most primitive of engines
Mass producing with a vengeance.
Teach those Asians mass production?
Teach your grandmother egg suction.

Robert Benchley

FRENCH FOR AMERICANS

A HANDY COMPENDIUM FOR VISITORS TO PARIS

The following lessons and exercises are designed for the exclusive use of Americans traveling in France. They are based on the needs and behavior of Americans, as figured from the needs and behavior of 14,000 Americans last summer. We wish to acknowledge our indebtedness to American Express Co., 11 Rue Scribe, for some of our material.

THE FRENCH LANGUAGE

1. *Pronunciation*

Vowels	*Pronounced*
a	ong
e	ong
i	ong
o	ong
u	ong

2. *Accents*

The French language has three accents, the acute *e*, the grave *e*, and the circumflex *e*, all of which are omitted.

3. *Phrases most in demand by Americans*

English	*French*
Haven't you got any griddle-cakes?	*N'avez-vous pas des griddle-cakes?*
What kind of a dump is this, anyhow?	*Quelle espèce de dump is this, anyhow?*
Do you call that coffee?	*Appelez-vous cela coffee?*
Where can I get a copy of the N. Y. Times?	*Où est le N. Y. Times?*
What's the matter? Don't you understand English?	*What's the matter? Don't you understand English?*
Of all the godam countries I ever saw.	*De tous les pays godams que j'ai vu.*
Hey there, driver, go slow!	*Hey there, chauffeur, allez lentement!*
Where's Sister?	*Où est Sister?*
How do I get to the Louvre from here?	*Où est le Louvre?*
Two hundred francs? In your hat.	*Deux cents francs? Dans votre chapeau.*
Where's Brother?	*Où est Brother?*
I haven't seen a good-looking woman yet.	*Je n'ai pas vu une belle femme jusqu'à présent.*

3. *Phrases most in demand by Americans* (*Continued*)

English	French
Where can I get laundry done by six tonight?	*Où est le laundry?*
Here is where we used to come when I was here during the War.	*Ici est où nous used to come quand j'étais ici pendant la guerre.*
Say, this is real beer all right!	*Say, ceci est de la bière vrai!*
Oh boy!	*O boy!*
Two weeks from tomorrow we sail for home.	*Deux semaines from tomorrow nous sail for home.*
Then when we land I'll go straight to Childs and get a cup of coffee and a glass of ice-water.	*Sogleich wir zu hause sind, geh ich zum Childs und eine tasse kaffee und ein glass eiswasser kaufen.*
Very well.	*Très bien.*
Leave it in my room.	*Très bien.*
Good night!	*Très bien.*
Where did Father go to?	*Où est Papa?*

PLACES IN PARIS FOR AMERICANS TO VISIT

The Lobby of the Ritz

This is one of the most interesting places in Paris for the American tourist, for it is there that he meets a great many people from America. If he will stand by the potted palms in the corner he will surely find someone whom he knows before long and can enter into a conversation on how things are going at home.

The American Express Co., 11 Rue Scribe

Here again the American traveler will find surcease from the irritating French quality of most of the rest of Paris. If he comes here for his mail, he will hear the latest news of the baseball leagues, how the bathing is on the Maine coast, what the chances are for the Big Fight in September at the Polo Grounds, and whom Nora Bayes has married in August. There will be none

of this unintelligible *French* jabber with which Paris has become so infested of late years. He will hear language spoken as
it should be spoken, whether he come from Massachusetts or
Iowa.

WHERE TO EAT IN PARIS

Hartford Lunch

There has been a Hartford Lunch opened at 115 Rue Lord
Byron where the American epicure can get fried-egg sandwiches, Boston baked beans, coffee rings, and crullers almost
as good as those he can get at home. The place is run by Martin
Keefe, formerly of the Hartford Lunch in Fall River, Massachusetts, and is a mecca for those tourists who want good food
well cooked.

United States Drug Store

At the corner of Rue Bonsard and the Boulevard de Parteuille
there is an excellent American drug store where are served
frosted chocolates, ice-cream sodas, Coca-Cola, and pimento
cheese sandwiches. A special feature which will recall the beloved homeland to Americans is the buying of soda checks *before* ordering.

FRENCH CURRENCY

Here is something which is likely to give the American
traveler no little trouble. In view of the fluctuating value of
the franc, the following table should be memorized in order to
insure against mistakes:

Day of Week	*American value of Franc*
Monday	5 cents
Tuesday	5.1 cents
Wednesday	4.9 cents
Thursday	1 lb. chestnuts
Friday	2½ yds. linoleum
Saturday	What-have-you

The proper procedure for Americans in making purchases is as follows:

1. Ascertain the value of the franc.
2. Make the purchase of whatever it is you want.
3. Ask *"Combien?"* (How much?)
4. Say *"Trop cher."* (What the hell!)
5. Try to understand the answer.
6. Pay the asking price and leave the shop swearing in English, American or other mother tongue.

SIDE TRIPS FROM PARIS

There are many fascinating trips which may be made by the American sojourning in Paris which will relieve him of the tedium of his stay.

TRIP A.—Take the train at Paris for Havre and from there go by steamer to New York. The State of Maine Express leaves New York (Grand Central Station) at 7:30 P.M. and in the morning the traveler finds himself in Portland, Maine, from which many delightful excursions may be made up and down the rock-ribbed Atlantic coast.

TRIP B.—Entrain at Paris for Cherbourg, where there are frequent sailings westward. By the payment of a slight *pourboire* the ship's captain will put her in at the island of Nantucket, a quaint whaling center of olden times. Here you may roam among the moors and swim to your heart's content, unconscious of the fact that you are within a six-day run of the great city of Paris.

Ordinal Numbers and their Pronunciation

Numbers	*Pronounced*
1st. *le premier*	leh premyai
2nd. *le second*	leh zeggong
3rd. *le troisième*	leh trouazzeame
4th. *le quatrième*	leh kattreame
8th. *le huitième*	leh wheeteeame

Oh, well, you won't have occasion to use these much, anyway. Never mind them.

Other Words You Will Have Little Use For

Vernisser—to varnish, glaze.
Nuque—nape (of the neck).
Egriser—to grind diamonds.
Dromer—to make one's neck stiff from working at a sewing machine.
Rossignol—nightingale, picklock.
Ganache—lower jaw of a horse.
Serin—canary bird.
Pardon—I beg your pardon.

Ernest Hemingway

While not characteristically a satirical writer, Hemingway on occasion could produce superb caricatures. "Mr. and Mrs. Elliot" is one of his best abusive sketches; behind it one detects the smile of the Old European Hand.

MR. AND MRS. ELLIOT

Mr. and Mrs. Elliot tried very hard to have a baby. They tried as often as Mrs. Elliot could stand it. They tried in Boston after they were married and they tried coming over on the boat. They did not try very often on the boat because Mrs. Elliot was quite sick. She was sick and when she was sick she was sick as Southern women are sick. That is women from the Southern part of the United States. Like all Southern women Mrs. Elliot disintegrated very quickly under sea sickness, travelling at night, and getting up too early in the morning. Many of the people on the boat took her for Elliot's mother. Other people who knew they were married believed she was going to have a baby. In reality she was forty years old. Her years had been precipitated suddenly when she started travelling.

She had seemed much younger, in fact she had seemed not to have any age at all, when Elliot had married her after several weeks of making love to her after knowing her for a long time in her tea shop before he had kissed her one evening.

Hubert Elliot was taking postgraduate work in law at Harvard when he was married. He was a poet with an income of nearly ten thousand dollars a year. He wrote very long poems very rapidly. He was twenty-five years old and had never gone to bed with a woman until he married Mrs. Elliot. He wanted to keep himself pure so that he could bring to his wife the same purity of mind and body that he expected of her. He called it to himself living straight. He had been in love with various girls before he kissed Mrs. Elliot and always told them sooner or later that he had led a clean life. Nearly all the girls lost interest in him. He was shocked and really horrified at the way girls would become engaged to and marry men whom they must know had dragged themselves through the gutter. He once tried to warn a girl he knew against a man of whom he had almost proof that he had been a rotter at college and a very unpleasant incident had resulted.

Mrs. Elliot's name was Cornelia. She had taught him to call her Calutina, which was her family nickname in the South. His mother cried when he brought Cornelia home after their marriage but brightened very much when she learned they were going to live abroad.

Cornelia had said, "You dear sweet boy," and held him closer than ever when he had told her how he had kept himself clean for her. Cornelia was pure too. "Kiss me again like that," she said.

Hubert explained to her that he had learned that way of kissing from hearing a fellow tell a story once. He was delighted with his experiment and they developed it as far as possible. Sometimes when they had been kissing together a long time, Cornelia would ask him to tell her again that he had kept himself really straight for her. The declaration always set her off again.

At first Hubert had no idea of marrying Cornelia. He had never thought of her that way. She had been such a good friend of his, and then one day in the little back room of the shop they had been dancing to the gramophone while her girl friend was in the front of the shop and she had looked up into his eyes and he had kissed her. He could never remember just when it was decided that they were to be married. But they were married.

They spent the night of the day they were married in a Boston hotel. They were both disappointed but finally Cornelia went to sleep. Hubert could not sleep and several times went out and walked up and down the corridor of the hotel in his new Jaeger bathrobe that he had bought for his wedding trip. As he walked he saw all the pairs of shoes, small shoes and big shoes, outside the doors of the hotel rooms. This set his heart to pounding and he hurried back to his own room but Cornelia was asleep. He did not like to waken her and soon everything was quite all right and he slept peacefully.

The next day they called on his mother and the next day they sailed for Europe. It was possible to try to have a baby but Cornelia could not attempt it very often although they wanted a baby more than anything else in the world. They landed at Cherbourg and came to Paris. They tried to have a baby in Paris. Then they decided to go to Dijon where there was summer school and where a number of people who crossed on the boat with them had gone. They found there was nothing to do in Dijon. Hubert, however, was writing a great number of poems and Cornelia typed them for him. They were all very long poems. He was very severe about mistakes and would make her re-do an entire page if there was one mistake. She cried a good deal and they tried several times to have a baby before they left Dijon.

They came to Paris and most of their friends from the boat came back too. They were tired of Dijon and anyway would now be able to say that after leaving Harvard or Columbia or Wabash they had studied at the University of Dijon down in the Côte d'Or. Many of them would have preferred to go to Languedoc, Montpellier or Perpignan if there are universities there. But all those places are too far away. Dijon is only four and a half hours from Paris and there is a diner on the train.

So they all sat around the Café du Dôme, avoiding the

Rotonde across the street because it is always so full of foreigners, for a few days and then the Elliots rented a château in
Touraine through an advertisement in the New York *Herald.*
Elliot had a number of friends by now all of whom admired his
poetry and Mrs. Elliot had prevailed upon him to send over to
Boston for her girl friend who had been in the tea shop. Mrs.
Elliot became much brighter after her girl friend came and
they had many good cries together. The girl friend was several
years older than Cornelia and called her Honey. She too came
from a very old Southern family.

The three of them, with several of Elliot's friends who
called him Hubie, went down to the château in Touraine. They
found Touraine to be a very flat hot country very much like
Kansas. Elliot had nearly enough poems for a book now. He
was going to bring it out in Boston and had already sent his
check to, and made a contract with, a publisher.

In a short time the friends began to drift back to Paris.
Touraine had not turned out the way it looked when it started.
Soon all the friends had gone off with a rich young and un-
married poet to a seaside resort near Trouville. There they
were all very happy.

Elliot kept on at the château in Touraine because he had
taken it for all summer. He and Mrs. Elliot tried very hard to
have a baby in the big hot bedroom on the big, hard bed. Mrs.
Elliot was learning the touch system on the typewriter, but she
found that while it increased the speed it made more mistakes.
The girl friend was now typing practically all of the manu-
scripts. She was very neat and efficient and seemed to enjoy it.

Elliot had taken to drinking white wine and lived apart in his
own room. He wrote a great deal of poetry during the night and
in the morning looked very exhausted. Mrs. Elliot and the girl
friend now slept together in the big mediaeval bed. They had
many a good cry together. In the evening they all sat at dinner
together in the garden under a plane tree and the hot evening
wind blew and Elliot drank white wine and Mrs. Elliot and the
girl friend made conversation and they were all quite happy.

PROGRESS AND CIVILIZATION

On the U. S. A. in 1828: "In short, it is not possible to conceive a state of society in which more of the attributes of plain good sense, or fewer of the artificial absurdities of life, are to be found, than here."

JAMES FENIMORE COOPER, *Notions of the Americans*

Progress and Civilization

*T his wilderness of Sin . . . called Progress of Civiliza-
tion," fumed James Russell Lowell in* The Biglow Papers,
*thus foreshadowing in the 1850s a major theme of modern
American satire: the dogging question of whether material
progress in the U. S. has not somehow taken a wrong turn—
whether we may not be designing, pre-testing, fluoridizing,
brainstorming, consumer-researching, and color-scheming ourselves out of the human race. Of all the challenges to the critical
imagination, America's "chromo civilization" now stands at the
head of the list, and politics, religion and fashion all take secondary places as the twentieth-century satirist declares his mis-
trust of "civilization as we know it." Characteristically, our
satire persists in the belief that the individual counts for something and that all the armies of pigeonholers, group fetishists,
censors and dieticians have not quite turned him into a "mass
man." At bottom, American satire is engaged in a pitched battle
in defense of the vanishing individual.*

Finley Peter Dunne

MR. DOOLEY
ON THE VICTORIAN ERA
(1898)

A r-re ye goin' to cillybrate th' queen's jubilee?" asked Mr.
Dooley.

"What's that?" demanded Mr. Hennessy, with a violent
start.

"To-day," said Mr. Dooley, "her gracious Majesty Victorya,

Queen iv Great Britain an' that part iv Ireland north iv Sligo, has reigned f'r sixty long and tiresome years."

"I don't care if she has snowed f'r sixty years," said Mr. Hennessy. "I'll not cillybrate it. She may be a good woman f'r all I know, but dam her pollytics."

"Ye needn't be pro-fane about it," said Mr. Dooley. "I on'y ast ye a civil question. F'r mesilf, I have no feelin' on th' subject. I am not with th' queen an' I'm not again her. At th' same time I corjally agree with me frind Captain Finerty, who's put his newspaper in mournin' f'r th' ivint. I won't march in th' parade, an' I won't put anny dinnymite undher thim that does. I don't say th' marchers an' dinnymiters ar-re not both r-right. 'Tis purely a question iv taste, an', as the ixicutive says whin both candydates are mimbers iv th' camp, 'Pathrites will use their own discreetion.'

"Th' good woman niver done me no har-rm; an', beyond throwin' a rock or two into an orangey's procission an' sub-scribin' to tin dollars' worth iv Fenian bonds, I've threated her like a lady. Anny gredge I iver had again her I burrid long ago. We're both well on in years, an' 'tis no use carrying har-rd feelin's to th' grave. About th' time th' lord chamberlain wint over to tell her she was queen, an' she came out in her nitey to hear th' good news, I was announced into this wurruld iv sin an' sorrow. So ye see we've reigned about th' same lenth iv time, an' I ought to be cillybratin' me di'mon' jubilee. I wud, too, if I had anny di'mon's. Do ye r-run down to Aldherman O'Brien's an' borrow twinty or thirty f'r me.

"Great happenin's have me an' Queen Victorya seen in these sixty years. Durin' our binificent prisince on earth th' nations have grown r-rich an' prosperous. Great Britain has ixtinded her domain until th' sun niver sets on it. No more do th' original owners iv th' sile, they bein' kept movin' be th' polis. While she was lookin' on in England, I was lookin' on in this counthry. I have seen America spread out fr'm th' Atlantic to th' Pacific, with a branch office iv the Standard Ile Comp'ny in ivry hamlet. I've seen th' shackles dropped fr'm th' slave, so's he cud be lynched in Ohio. I've seen this gr-reat city desthroyed be fire fr'm De Koven Sthreet to th' Lake View pumpin' station, and thin rise felix-like fr'm its ashes, all but th' West Side, which was not burned. I've seen Jim Mace beat Mike McCool, an' Tom Allen beat Jim Mace, an' somebody beat Tom Allen, an' Jawn Sullivan beat him, an' Corbett beat Sullivan, an' Fitz beat Corbett; an', if I live to cillybrate me goold-watch-an'-chain jubilee, I may see some wan put it all over Fitz.

"Oh, what things I've seen in me day an' Victorya's! Think iv that gran' procission iv lithry men,—Tinnyson an' Long-fellow an' Bill Nye an' Ella Wheeler Wilcox an' Tim Scanlan an'—an' I can't name thim all: they're too manny. An' th' brave gin'rals,—Von Molkey an' Bismarck an' U. S. Grant an' gallant Phil Shurdan an' Coxey. Think iv thim durin' me reign. An' th' invintions,—th' steam-injine an' th' printin'-press an' th' cotton-gin an' th' gin sour an' th' bicycle an' th' flyin'-machine an' th' nickel-in-th'-slot machine an' th' Croker machine an' th' sody fountain an'—crownin' wur-ruk iv our civilization—th' cash raygisther. What gr-reat advances has science made in my time an' Victorya's! fr, whin we entered public life, it took three men to watch th' bar-keep, while to-day ye can tell within $8 an hour what he's took in.

"Glory be, whin I look back fr'm this day iv gin'ral rejoicin' in me rhinestone jubilee, an' see what changes has taken place an' how many people have died an' how much bether off th' wurruld is, I'm proud iv mesilf. War an' pest'lence an' famine have occurred in me time, but I count thim light compared with th' binifits that have fallen to th' race since I come on th' earth."

"What ar-re ye talkin' about?" cried Mr. Hennessy, in deep disgust. "All this time ye've been standin' behind this bar ladlin' out disturbance to th' Sixth Wa-ard, an' ye haven't been as far east as Mitchigan Avnoo in twenty years. What have ye had to do with all these things?"

"Well," said Mr. Dooley, "I had as much to do with thim as th' queen."

Ambrose Bierce

THE FLYING-MACHINE
(from *Fantastic Fables*, 1899)

An Ingenious Man who had built a flying-machine invited a great concourse of people to see it go up. At the appointed moment, everything being ready, he boarded the car and turned on the power. The machine immediately broke through the massive substructure upon which it was builded, and sank out of sight into the earth, the aeronaut springing out barely in time to save himself.

"Well," said he, "I have done enough to demonstrate the correctness of my details. The defects," he added, with a look at the ruined brickwork, "are merely basic and fundamental."

On this assurance the people came forward with subscriptions to build a second machine.

George Ade

THE *FABLE* OF THE *CADDY* WHO *HURT* HIS *HEAD* WHILE *THINKING*
(1899)

One Day a Caddy sat in the Long Grass near the Ninth Hole and wondered if he had a Soul. His Number was 27, and he almost had forgotten his Real Name.

As he sat and Meditated, two Players passed him. They were going the Long Round, and the Frenzy was upon them.

They followed the Gutta Percha Balls with the intent swiftness of trained Bird Dogs, and each talked feverishly of Brassy Lies, and getting past the Bunker, and Lofting to the

Green, and Slicing into the Bramble—each telling his own Game to the Ambient Air, and ignoring what the other Fellow had to say.

As they did the St. Andrews Full Swing for eighty Yards apiece and then Followed Through with the usual Explanations of how it Happened, the Caddy looked at them and Reflected that they were much inferior to his Father.

His Father was too Serious a Man to get out in Mardi Gras Clothes and hammer a Ball from one Red Flag to another.

His Father worked in a Lumber Yard.

He was an Earnest Citizen, who seldom Smiled, and he knew all about the Silver Question and how J. Pierpont Morgan done up a Free People on the Bond Issue.

The Caddy wondered why it was that his Father, a really Great Man, had to shove Lumber all day and could seldom get one Dollar to rub against another, while these superficial Johnnies who played Golf all the Time had Money to Throw at the Birds. The more he Thought the more his Head ached.

MORAL: *Don't try to Account for Anything.*

F.P.A.
(Franklin Pierce Adams)

OPTIMISTIC THOUGHTS ON THE COSMOS

I agree with the man whose molecular brain
    Is less than a goose's or gannet's
That this is a beautiful place, in the main,
    And the sweetest of possible planets.

No quarrel have I with the sillies and saps
    Who have intellectual traces
And say that the human, all over the maps,
    Is the finest of possible races.

And I am as certain as ever are they
Who used to be Russians or Thracians
That this, better known as the old U. S. A.,
Is the best of all possible nations.

O best of all planets and races and lands
If ye be the ultimate best of them,
The dullest among you, I hope, understands
How sad are the terrible rest of them.

Sinclair Lewis

"We cannot produce a national satire or character," declared James Russell Lowell, "because there is no butt visible to all parts of the country at once."

While accurate for the more provincial America of the mid-nineteenth century, Lowell's statement was contradicted in 1922 when Sinclair Lewis introduced George F. Babbitt, Esq., to American readers. Babbitt was as unmistakably Middle Western as Hosea Biglow was Down East; he was also an archetype of the American businessman. With his philistinism, his hustle, his "business ethics," his boosterism, his success-oriented social values, Babbitt is a devastating reflection of one segment of American civilization of the twenties.

THE REGULAR GUY
(from *Babbitt*)

In rising to address you, with my impromptu speech carefully tucked into my vest pocket, I am reminded of the story of the two Irishmen, Mike and Pat, who were riding on the Pullman. Both of them, I forgot to say, were sailors in the Navy. It seems Mike had the lower berth and by and by he heard a terrible racket from the upper, and when he yelled up to find out what the trouble was, Pat answered, "Shure an' bedad an' how can I ever get a night's sleep at all, at all? I been trying to get into this darned little hammock ever since eight bells!"

" 'Now, gentlemen, standing up here before you, I feel a good deal like Pat, and maybe after I've spieled along for a while, I may feel so darn small that I'll be able to crawl into a Pullman hammock with no trouble at all, at all!

" 'Gentlemen, it strikes me that each year at this annual occasion when friend and foe get together and lay down the battle-ax and let the waves of good-fellowship waft them up the flowery slopes of amity, it behooves us, standing together eye to eye and shoulder to shoulder as fellow-citizens of the best city in the world, to consider where we are both as regards ourselves and the common weal.

" 'It is true that even with our 361,000, or practically 362,-000, population, there are, by the last census, almost a score of larger cities in the United States. But, gentlemen, if by the next census we do not stand at least tenth, then I'll be the first to request any knocker to remove my shirt and to eat the same, with the compliments of G. F. Babbitt, Esquire! It may be true that New York, Chicago, and Philadelphia will continue to keep ahead of us in size. But aside from these three cities, which are notoriously so overgrown that no decent white man, nobody who loves his wife and kiddies and God's good out-o'-doors and likes to shake the hand of his neighbor in greeting, would want to live in them—and let me tell you right here and now, I wouldn't trade a high-class Zenith acreage development for the whole length and breadth of Broadway or State Street!—aside from these three, it's evident to any one with a head for facts that Zenith is the finest example of American life and prosperity to be found anywhere.

" 'I don't mean to say we're perfect. We've got a lot to do in the way of extending the paving of motor boulevards, for, believe me, it's the fellow with four to ten thousand a year, say, and an automobile and a nice little family in a bungalow on the edge of town, that makes the wheels of progress go round!

" 'That's the type of fellow that's ruling America to-day; in fact, it's the ideal type to which the entire world must tend, if there's to be a decent, well-balanced, Christian, go-ahead future for this little old planet! Once in a while I just naturally sit back and size up this Solid American Citizen, with a whale of a lot of satisfaction.

" 'Our Ideal Citizen—I picture him first and foremost as being busier than a bird-dog, not wasting a lot of good time in daydreaming or going to sassiety teas or kicking about things that are none of his business, but putting the zip into some store or profession or art. At night he lights up a good cigar, and climbs into the little old 'bus, and maybe cusses the carburetor, and shoots out home. He mows the lawn, or sneaks in some practice putting, and then he's ready for dinner. After dinner he tells the kiddies a story, or takes the family to the movies, or plays a few fists of bridge, or reads the evening paper, and a chapter or two of some good lively Western novel if he has a taste for literature, and maybe the folks next-door drop in and they sit and visit about their friends and the topics of the day. Then he goes happily to bed, his conscience clear, having contributed his mite to the prosperity of the city and to his own bank-account.

" 'In politics and religion this Sane Citizen is the canniest man on earth; and in the arts he invariably has a natural taste which makes him pick out the best, every time. In no country in the world will you find so many reproductions of the Old Masters and of well-known paintings on parlor walls as in these United States. No country has anything like our number of phonographs, with not only dance records and comic but also the best operas, such as Verdi, rendered by the world's highest-paid singers.

" 'In other countries, art and literature are left to a lot of shabby bums living in attics and feeding on booze and spaghetti, but in America the successful writer or picture-painter is indistinguishable from any other decent business man; and I, for one, am only too glad that the man who has the rare skill to season his message with interesting reading matter and who shows both purpose and pep in handling his literary wares has a chance to drag down his fifty thousand bucks a year, to mingle with the biggest executives on terms of perfect equality, and to show as big a house and as swell a car as any Captain of Industry! But, mind you, it's the appreciation of the Regular Guy who I have been depicting which has made this possible, and you got to hand as much credit to him as to the authors themselves.

" 'Finally, but most important, our Standardized Citizen, even if he is a bachelor, is a lover of the Little Ones, a supporter of the hearthstone which is the basic foundation of our civilization, first, last, and all the time, and the thing that most distinguishes us from the decayed nations of Europe.

" 'I have never yet toured Europe—and as a matter of fact, I don't know that I care to such an awful lot, as long as there's our own mighty cities and mountains to be seen—but, the way I figure it out, there must be a good many of our own sort of folks abroad. Indeed, one of the most enthusiastic Rotarians I ever met boosted the tenets of one-hundred-per-cent pep in a burr that smacked o' bonny Scutlond and all ye bonny braes o' Bobby Burns. But same time, one thing that distinguishes us from our good brothers, the hustlers over there, is that they're willing to take a lot off the snobs and journalists and politicians, while the modern American business man knows how to talk right up for himself, knows how to make it good and plenty clear that he intends to run the works. He doesn't have to call in some highbrow hired-man when it's necessary for him to answer the crooked critics of the sane and efficient life. He's not dumb, like the old-fashioned merchant. He's got a vocabulary and a punch.

" 'With all modesty, I want to stand up here as a representative business man and gently whisper, "Here's our kind of folks! Here's the specifications of the Standardized American Citizen! Here's the new generation of Americans: fellows with hair on their chests and smiles in their eyes and adding-machines in their offices. We're not doing any boasting, but we like ourselves first-rate, and if you don't like us, look out—better get under cover before the cyclone hits town!"

" 'So! In my clumsy way I have tried to sketch the Real He-man, the fellow with Zip and Bang. And it's because Zenith has so large a proportion of such men that it's the most stable, the greatest of our cities. New York also has its thousands of Real Folks, but New York is cursed with unnumbered foreigners. So are Chicago and San Francisco. Oh, we have a golden roster of cities—Detroit and Cleveland with their renowned factories, Cincinnati with its great machine-tool and soap products, Pittsburgh and Birmingham with their steel, Kansas City and Minneapolis and Omaha that open their bountiful gates on the bosom of the ocean-like wheatlands, and countless other magnificent sister-cities, for, by the last census, there were no less than sixty-eight glorious American burgs with a population of over one hundred thousand! And all these cities stand together for power and purity, and against foreign ideas and communism —Atlanta with Hartford, Rochester with Denver, Milwaukee with Indianapolis, Los Angeles with Scranton, Portland, Maine, with Portland, Oregon. A good live wire from Baltimore or Seattle or Duluth is the twin-brother of every like fellow booster from Buffalo or Akron, Fort Worth or Oskaloosa!

" 'But it's here in Zenith, the home for manly men and womanly women and bright kids, that you find the largest proportion of these Regular Guys, and that's what sets it in a class by itself; that's why Zenith will be remembered in history as having set the pace for a civilization that shall endure when the old time-killing ways are gone forever and the day of earnest efficient endeavor shall have dawned all round the world!

" 'Some time I hope folks will quit handing all the credit to a lot of moth-eaten, mildewed, out-of-date, old, European dumps, and give proper credit to the famous Zenith spirit, that clean fighting determination to win Success that has made the little old Zip City celebrated in every land and clime, wherever condensed milk and pasteboard cartons are known! Believe me, the world has fallen too long for these worn-out countries that aren't producing anything but boot-blacks and scenery and booze, that haven't got one bathroom per hundred people, and that don't know a loose-leaf ledger from a slip-cover; and it's just about time for some Zenithite to get his back up and holler for a showdown!

" 'I tell you, Zenith and her sister-cities are producing a new type of civilization. There are many resemblances between Zenith and these other burgs, and I'm darn glad of it! The extraordinary, growing, and sane standardization of stores, offices, streets, hotels, clothes, and newspapers throughout the United States shows how strong and enduring a type is ours.

" 'I always like to remember a piece that Chum Frink wrote for the newspapers about his lecture-tours. It is doubtless familiar to many of you, but if you will permit me, I'll take a chance and read it. It's one of the classic poems, like "If" by Kipling, or Ella Wheeler Wilcox's "The Man Worth While"; and I always carry this clipping of it in my note-book:

When I am out upon the road, a poet with a pedler's load, I mostly sing a hearty song, and take a chew and hike along, a-handing out my samples fine of Cheero Brand of sweet sunshine, and peddling optimistic pokes and stable lines of japes and jokes to Lyceums and other folks, to Rotarys, Kiwanis' Clubs, and feel I ain't like other dubs. And then old Major Silas Satan, a brainy cuss who's always waitin', he gives his tail a lively quirk, and gets in quick his dirty work. He fills me up with mullygrubs; my hair the backward way he rubs; he makes me lonelier than a hound, on Sunday when the folks ain't round. And then b' gosh, I would prefer to never be a lecturer, a-ridin' round in classy cars and smoking fifty-cent cigars, and never more I want to roam; I simply want to be back home, a-eatin' flap-jacks, hash, and ham, with folks who savvy whom I am!

But when I get that lonely spell, I simply seek the best hotel, no matter in what town I be—St. Paul, Toledo, or K. C., in Washington, Schenectady, in Louisville or Albany. And at that inn it hits my dome that I again am right at home. If I should stand a lengthy spell in front of that first-class hotel, that to the drummers loves to cater, across from some big film theayter; if I should look around and buzz, and wonder in what town I was, I swear that I could never tell! For all the crowd would be so swell, in just the same fine sort of jeans they wear at home, and all the queens with spiffy bonnets on their beans, and all the fellows standing round a-talkin' always, I'll be bound, the same good jolly kind of guff, 'bout autos, politics and stuff and baseball players of renown that Nice Guys talk in my home town!

Then when I entered that hotel, I'd look around and say, "Well, well!" For there would be the same news-stand, same magazines and candies grand, same smokes of famous standard brand, I'd find at home, I'll tell! And when I saw the jolly bunch

come waltzing in for eats at lunch, and squaring up in natty
duds to platters large of French Fried spuds, why then I'd stand
right up and bawl, "I've never left my home at all!" And all re-
plete I'd sit me down beside some guy in derby brown upon a
lobby chair of plush, and murmur to him in a rush, "Hello, Bill,
tell me, good old scout, how is your stock a-holdin' out?" Then
we'd be off, two solid pals, a-chatterin' like giddy gals of fliv-
vers, weather, home, and wives, lodge-brothers then for all our
lives! So when Sam Satan makes you blue, good friend, that's
what I'd up and do, for in these States where'er you roam, you
never leave your home sweet home.

" 'Yes, sir, these other burgs are our true partners in the great
game of vital living. But let's not have any mistake about this. I
claim that Zenith is the best partner and the fastest-growing
partner of the whole caboodle. I trust I may be pardoned if I
give a few statistics to back up my claims. If they are old stuff
to any of you, yet the tidings of prosperity, like the good news of
the Bible, never become tedious to the ears of a real hustler, no
matter how oft the sweet story is told! Every intelligent person
knows that Zenith manufactures more condensed milk and
evaporated cream, more paper boxes, and more lighting-fixtures,
than any other city in the United States, if not in the world. But
it is not so universally known that we also stand second in the
manufacture of package-butter, sixth in the giant realm of mo-
tors and automobiles, and somewhere about third in cheese,
leather findings, tar roofing, breakfast food, and overalls!

" 'Our greatness, however, lies not alone in punchful prosperity but equally in that public spirit, that forward-looking
idealism and brotherhood, which has marked Zenith ever since
its foundation by the Fathers. We have a right, indeed we have
a duty toward our fair city, to announce broadcast the facts
about our high schools, characterized by their complete plants
and the finest school-ventilating systems in the country, bar
none; our magnificent new hotels and banks and the paintings
and carved marble in their lobbies; and the Second National
Tower, the second highest business building in any inland city
in the entire country. When I add that we have an unparalleled

number of miles of paved streets, bathrooms, vacuum cleaners, and all the other signs of civilization; that our library and art museum are well supported and housed in convenient and roomy buildings; that our park-system is more than up to par, with its handsome driveways adorned with grass, shrubs, and statuary, then I give but a hint of the all-round unlimited greatness of Zenith!

" 'I believe, however, in keeping the best to the last. When I remind you that we have one motor car for every five and seven-eighths persons in the city, then I give a rock-ribbed practical indication of the kind of progress and braininess which is synonymous with the name Zenith!

" 'But the way of the righteous is not all roses. Before I close I must call your attention to a problem we have to face, this coming year. The worst menace to sound government is not the avowed socialists but a lot of cowards who work under cover—the long-haired gentry who call themselves "liberals" and "radicals" and "non-partisan" and "intelligentsia" and God only knows how many other trick names! Irresponsible teachers and professors constitute the worst of this whole gang, and I am ashamed to say that several of them are on the faculty of our great State University! The U. is my own Alma Mater, and I am proud to be known as an alumni, but there are certain instructors there who seem to think we ought to turn the conduct of the nation over to hoboes and roustabouts.

" 'Those profs are the snakes to be scotched—they and all their milk-and-water ilk! The American business man is generous to a fault, but one thing he does demand of all teachers and lecturers and journalists: if we're going to pay them our good money, they've got to help us by selling efficiency and whooping it up for rational prosperity! And when it comes to these blab-mouth, fault-finding, pessimistic, cynical University teachers, let me tell you that during this golden coming year it's just as much our duty to bring influence to have those cusses fired as it is to sell all the real estate and gather in all the good shekels we can.

" 'Not till that is done will our sons and daughters see that the ideal of American manhood and culture isn't a lot of cranks sitting around chewing the rag about their Rights and their Wrongs, but a God-fearing, hustling, successful, two-fisted Regular Guy, who belongs to some church with pep and piety to it, who belongs to the Boosters or the Rotarians or the Kiwanis, to the Elks or Moose or Red Men or Knights of Columbus or any one of a score of organizations of good, jolly, kidding, laughing, sweating, upstanding, lend-a-handing Royal Good Fellows, who plays hard and works hard, and whose answer to his critics is a square-toed boot that'll teach the grouches and smart alecks to respect the He-man and get out and root for Uncle Samuel, U. S. A.!' "

George Jean Nathan

and

H. L. Mencken

Here is a sampling of Nathan's and Mencken's satirical catalogue of basic American credences—the truths which we allegedly hold to be self-evident.

CREDOS

(selections from *The New American Credo*)

That tight corsets used to be the cause of many female ailments and that since women abandoned the wearing of them their general well-being has increased 100 per cent.

That a great many fires are caused annually by mice playing with matches.

That all the difficult feats ascribed to movie stars in the films are really done by doubles.

That the Irish are enormous consumers of whiskey, and that the average Irishman can singlehanded drink five Frenchmen, seven Englishmen and ten Jews under the table and then polish off the evening with another quart.

That too many soft foods are ruining the teeth of the race.

That when a society woman has a baby she is a complete wreck for months afterward, but that a washerwoman can have one at eleven o'clock in the morning and with perfect comfort go to a movie the same afternoon.

That General Robert E. Lee was exceptionally meticulous in the matter of dress and never went into battle without putting a clean collar on.

That every man should, if possible, read a little law, as it will safeguard him against swindlers.

That mathematics, while of no great practical value, are excellent discipline for the mind and will make one a deeper thinker.

That if you hurt your finger and promptly hold it under the hot water faucet, the pain will immediately vanish.

That a child who is brought up in filth is always more robust and lives to a greater age than one who is hygienically cared for.

That there are hundreds of letters in the Dead Letter Office whose failure to arrive at their intended destinations was instrumental in separating as many lovers.

That a man's stability in the community and reliability in business may be measured by the number of children he has.

That a doctor knows so much about women that he can no longer fall in love with one of them.

That when a comedian, just before the rise of the curtain, is handed a telegram announcing the death of his mother or only child, he goes on the stage and gives a more comic performance than ever.

That the old ladies on summer hotel verandahs devote themselves entirely to the discussion of scandals.

That all one has to do to gather a large crowd in New York is to stand on the curb a few moments and gaze intently at the sky.

That if a man takes a cold bath regularly every morning of his life he will never be ill.

That every circus clown's heart is breaking for one reason or other.

That when cousins marry, their children are born blind, deformed, or imbecile.

That the accumulation of great wealth always brings with it great unhappiness.

That a cat falling from the twentieth story of the Singer Building will land upon the pavement below on its feet, uninjured and as frisky as ever.

That a very small proportion of beggars posing as blind are actually blind.

That women with red hair or wide nostrils are possessed of especially passionate natures.

That when one twin dies, the other twin becomes exceedingly melancholy and soon also dies.

That French women use great quantities of perfume in lieu of taking a bath.

That whiskey is good for snake-bite.

That swearing is forbidden by the Bible.

That German peasants are possessed of a profound knowledge of music.

That a man married to a woman larger than himself is always henpecked.

That a Sunday school superintendent is always carrying on an intrigue with one of the girls in the choir.

That a policeman can eat *gratis* as much fruit and as many peanuts off the street-corner stands as he wants.

That onion breath may be promptly removed by eating a little parsley.

That whenever a woman receives a gift, she immediately goes downtown and prices it.

That if one drops a crust of bread into one's glass of champagne, one can drink indefinitely without getting drunk.

That if a dog is fond of a man it is an infallible sign that the man is a good sort, and one to be trusted.

That the average New Yorker, under his sophisticated and sinful exterior, is really an innocent, sentimental sucker.

That the more modest a young girl is, the more innocent she is.

That what a woman admires above everything else in a man is an upright character.

That the wife of a rich man always wistfully looks back into the past and wishes she had married a poor man.

That all criminals get caught sooner or later.

That crossword puzzles measurably increase one's store of knowledge, in addition to improving the mental faculties.

That the mistresses of monarchs in the old days always dictated the policies of the country.

That children were much better behaved twenty years ago than they are today.

That each year a man volunteers to take his children to the circus merely as a subterfuge to go himself.

That one feels very humble and insignificant when looking at the Grand Canyon.

That the chicken salad served in restaurants is always made of veal.

That chorus girls spend the time during the entr'actes sitting around naked in their dressing-rooms telling naughty stories.

That many soldiers' lives have been saved in battle by bullets lodging in Bibles which they have carried in their breast pockets.

That Jules Verne anticipated all the great modern inventions.

That a man of fifty-five is always more experienced than a man of thirty-five.

That all French women are very passionate, and will sacrifice everything to love.

Robert Benchley

WHOA!

Paul Revere leaped into his saddle.

"Through every Middlesex village and farm, Bess, old girl!" he whispered in his mare's ear, and they were off.

And, as he rode, the dauntless patriot saw as in a vision (in fact, it *was* a vision) the future of the land to which he was bringing freedom.

He saw a hundred and ten million people, the men in derbies, the women in felt hats with little bows on the top. He saw them pushing one another in and out of trolley-cars on their way to and from work, adding up figures incorrectly all morning and subtracting them incorrectly all afternoon, with time out at 12:30 for frosted chocolates and pimento cheese sandwiches. He saw fifty million of them trying to prevent the other sixty million from doing what they wanted to do, and the sixty million trying to prevent the fifty million from doing what *they* wanted to do. He saw them all paying taxes to a few hundred of their number for running the government very badly. He saw ten million thin children working and ten thousand fat children playing in the warm sands. And now and again he saw five million youths, cheered on by a hundred million elders with fallen arches, marching out to give their arms and legs and lives for Something to Be Determined Later. And over all he saw the Stars and Stripes fluttering in the artificial breeze of an electric fan operated behind the scenes.

So tugging at the reins he yelled, "Whoa, Bess! We're going back to the stable."

ISN'T IT REMARKABLE?

O n a recent page of colored reproductions of tomb-paintings and assorted excavations from holes in ancient Egypt there appears a picture of a goose with the following rather condescending caption:

Remarkably Accurate and Artistic Painting of a Goose from Pharaoh Akhenaten's Palace, Drawn 3300 Years Ago.

What I want to know is—why the "remarkable"? Why is it any more remarkable that someone drew a goose accurately 3300 years ago than that someone should do it today? Why should we be surprised that the people who built the Pyramids could also draw a goose so that it looked like a goose?

As a matter of fact, the goose in this particular picture looks more like a goose than that of many a modern master. Just what we think we are, in this age of bad drawing, to call an Egyptian painting "remarkably accurate and artistic" I don't know, but we have got to get over this feeling that anything that was done correctly in 1000 B.C. was a phenomenon. I say that we have got to get over it, but I don't know how.

People managed to drag along in ancient Egypt, from all that we can gather. They may not have known about chocolate malted milk and opera hats, but, what with one thing and another, they got by. And, presumably, every once in a while somebody felt like drawing a goose. And why not? Is there something exclusively twentieth-century about the art of goose-drawing?

We are constantly being surprised that people did things well before we were born. We are constantly remarking on the fact that things are done well by people other than ourselves. "The Japanese are a remarkable little people," we say, as if we were doing them a favor. "He is an Arab, but you ought to hear him play the zither." Why "but"?

Another thing, possibly not exactly in this connection, but in line with our amazement at obvious things. People are always saying, "My grandfather is eighty-two and interested in everything. Reads the paper every day and follows everything."

Why shouldn't he be interested in everything at eighty-two? Why shouldn't he be *especially* interested in everything at eighty-two? What is there so remarkable about his reading the paper every day and being conversant on all topics? If he isn't interested in everything at eighty-two when is he going to be? (I seem to be asking an awful lot of questions. Don't bother answering them, please.)

It is probably this naïve surprise at things that keeps us going. If we took it for granted that the ancient Egyptians could draw a goose accurately, or that Eskimos could sing bass, or that Grandpa should be interested in everything at eighty-two, there wouldn't be anything for us to hang our own superiority on.

And if we couldn't find something to hang our own superiority on we should be sunk. We should be just like the ancient Egyptians, or the Eskimos, or Grandpa.

S. J. Perelman

TO SLEEP, PERCHANCE TO STEAM

To anybody around here who is suffering from a touch of insomnia these days (surely no more than a hundred-to-one-shot), the sequence of events in my bedroom last night may have a certain clinical interest. About nine o'clock, after a brisk session with the newscasters, I shuddered for approximately half an hour to relax my nerves, plugged a pair of Flents into my ears, and tied on a sleep mask. I probably should have waited until I got into bed before doing so, as I took a rather nasty fall over a waste-basket, but in a few moments I was stretched out, busily reviewing the war news and adding up the family bank account, with my pulse furnishing a rich musical background.

When this palled, I read several chapters of Durfee's "Monasteries of the Rhône" with no success whatever until I discovered I had forgotten to remove my mask. As soon as I did, I was amply rewarded, for I found that with a little practice I was able to handle the strategy of the war and add up my bank account while vagabonding down the Rhône.

At this point, I regret to say, I tarnished an otherwise perfect record by falling into a slight doze. I must have been asleep almost fifteen minutes when I awoke suddenly and realized I had neglected to take a sedative before retiring. I promptly went out into the kitchen for a cup of hot milk with which to dissolve the nepenthe tablet and found Delia, our buxom cook, seated on the knee of her policeman friend. Actually, we have no cook called Delia, but we do have an impassive Englishman named Crichton and he was seated on the knee of a policewoman. The general effect was the same: a scene of coarse, steamy intimacy rivalling Hogarth's "Gin Lane." Muttering "This rivals Hogarth's 'Gin Lane,' " I stalked back to bed just in time to discover that the annual outing of the Clan-na-Gael was beginning directly beneath my window. Egged on by shrill cries of approval from the ladies' auxiliary, strapping bosthoons executed nimble jigs and reels, sang come-all-ye's, and vied with each other in hurling refuse cans the length of the street. The gaiety was so spontaneous and impulsive that I could not refrain from distributing several bags of water as favors. The gesture moved the crowd deeply, a few of its members even offering to come up and include me in their horseplay. Unfortunately, my good-natured refusal caused considerable pique and the revellers disbanded shortly. The sky and I were turning gray when, without any preamble, a woman in the apartment directly overhead began beating her husband mercilessly. Unable to withstand his screams, I finally gathered up all the available bedding, wrapped my head in it, and lay in a cedar chest in the foyer until routed out by the odor of coffee.

It is the notion of the General Electric Company, as set forth in a booklet I picked up at Lewis & Congers's Sleep Shop later in the morning, that this sordid series of events need never have occurred had I only been equipped with a recent discovery of theirs. Some anonymous genius in Schenectady (who will yet turn out to be Paul Muni, mark my words) has conjured up from his alembics and retorts an electrical comforter known as "The Blanket with a Brain." Just how General Electric came to be mixed up in blanket research is not too clear; perhaps it was one of those accidents we know take place daily in laboratories. I can readily imagine some brilliant young chemist bursting into the office of the head of the division, exultantly waving an Erlenmeyer flask. "What's cooking, Shaftoe —I mean Muni?" inquires his chief irritably. "Another one of those impractical daydreams of yours?" "N-n-no, sir," stammers Shaftoe in his excitement. "Do you recall that precipitate of blanketane, comfortate cellulose, and old voltage I left on my bench last night?" "Yes, it was the seven-hundred-and-forty-fifth combination you and Bazurdjian had tried, and although all the others failed, you doggedly persisted, scorning the mockery of older and wiser heads," replies the chief. "Look here, sir!" cries Shaftoe, holding the flask up to the light. "My God!" exclaims his usually imperturbable senior. "A little electrical quilt! Imperfect, incomplete, picayune, but still a quilt! What formula did you use, my boy?" "A very old one, sir," says Shaftoe quietly. "One part inspiration and ten of perspiration." "Success hasn't changed you, Shaftoe," observes the chief. "You're still a drip." And, pocketing the discovery, he kicks Shaftoe out into the corridor.

Outwardly, the G. E. Electric Comforter is a simple wool-and-taffeta affair which runs on the house current and automatically adjusts itself to the changing temperatures of the night. What emerges from a study of the booklet, however, is a weird complex of thermostats, transformers, and control boxes likely to frighten the putative customer out of his pants. "The heart of the Comforter," states the booklet, "is a web of 370 feet of fine flexible copper wire of low resistance arranged in a zigzag pattern." Set me down as a dusty old eccentric, but frankly, there would seem to be some more ideal haven nowadays than a skein of copper wire, no matter how fine or flexible. Nor is it any more reassuring to learn that "six rubber molded safety thermostats are placed at intervals in this web of insulated wire (you can feel these thermostats with your fingers beneath the cover of the Comforter)." It needs no vivid imagination to imagine oneself lying in the dark with eyes protruding, endlessly tallying the thermostats and expecting at any moment to be converted into roast Long Island duckling. The possibility is evidently far from academic, to judge from the question a little later on: "Can the Comforter overheat or give an electric shock?" The manufacturers shrug aside the contingency in a breezy 450-word essay, easily comprehensible to wizards like Steinmetz but unhappily just out of my reach. One passage, nevertheless, is all too succinct:

> Even if the full 115 volts went through the Comforter, the body would have to be moist . . . a worn spot on the web wire inside the Comforter would have to touch the body . . . and another part of the body, as a hand or leg, would have to come in contact with a piece of metal, in order to get the sensation of an electric shock.

Given half a chance, I know I could fulfill these conditions, difficult though they seem. As one who puts on a pair of rubbers when he changes a fuse, only to find himself recumbent on the floor with his eyelashes singed, I'll go further. I bet I could pass through a room containing an Electric Comforter in the original gift box and emerge with a third-degree burn.

The balance of the booklet, to tell the truth, held for me a purely formal interest, as I had already reached a decision regarding the Comforter. Such questions as "What causes the slight clicking noise in the control box?" are obviously intended to relieve the fears of neurotics, and, thank God, I'm no neurotic. All I know is, when I got that far I heard a slight clicking noise and experienced a distinct tingling sensation which could only have emanated from the booklet itself. Luckily, I had the presence of mind to plunge it into a pail of water and yell for help. Right now it's over at some expert's office, about to be analyzed. And so am I, honey, if I can lay my hands on a good five-cent psychiatrist.

E. B. White

THE PARABLE OF THE FAMILY WHICH DWELT APART

On a small, remote island in the lower reaches of Barnetuck Bay there lived a family of fisherfolk by the name of Pruitt. There were seven of them, and they were the sole inhabitants of the place. They subsisted on canned corn, canned tomatoes, pressed duck, whole-wheat bread, terrapin, Rice Krispies, crabs, cheese, queen olives, and homemade wild-grape preserve. Once in a while Pa Pruitt made some whiskey and they all had a drink.

They liked the island and lived there from choice. In winter, when there wasn't much doing, they slept the clock around, like so many bears. In summer they dug clams and set off a few pinwheels and salutes on July 4th. No case of acute appendicitis had ever been known in the Pruitt household, and when a Pruitt had a pain in his side he never even noticed whether it was the right side or the left side, but just hoped it would go away, and it did.

One very severe winter Barnetuck Bay froze over and the Pruitt family was marooned. They couldn't get to the mainland by boat because the ice was too thick, and they couldn't walk ashore because the ice was too treacherous. But inasmuch as no Pruitt had anything to go ashore for, except mail (which was entirely second class), the freeze-up didn't make any difference. They stayed indoors, kept warm, and ate well, and when there was nothing better to do, they played crokinole. The winter would have passed quietly enough had not someone on the mainland remembered that the Pruitts were out there in the frozen bay. The word got passed around the county and finally reached the Superintendent of State Police, who immediately notified Pathé News and the United States Army. The Army got there

first, with three bombing planes from Langley Field, which
flew low over the island and dropped packages of dried apricots
and bouillon cubes, which the Pruitts didn't like much. The
newsreel plane, smaller than the bombers and equipped with
skis, arrived next and landed on a snow-covered field on the
north end of the island. Meanwhile, Major Bulk, head of the
state troopers, acting on a tip that one of the Pruitt children had
appendicitis, arranged for a dog team to be sent by plane from
Laconia, New Hampshire, and also dispatched a squad of troopers to attempt a crossing of the bay. Snow began falling at sun-
down, and during the night three of the rescuers lost their lives
about half a mile from shore, trying to jump from one ice cake
to another.

The plane carrying the sled dogs was over southern New
England when ice began forming on its wings. As the pilot
circled for a forced landing, a large meat bone which one of the
dogs had brought along got wedged in the socket of the main
control stick, and the plane went into a steep dive and crashed
against the side of a powerhouse, instantly killing the pilot and
all the dogs, and fatally injuring Walter Ringstead, 7, of
3452 Garden View Avenue, Stamford, Conn.

Shortly before midnight, the news of the appendicitis reached
the Pruitt house itself, when a chartered autogiro from Hearst's
International News Service made a landing in the storm and
reporters informed Mr. Pruitt that his oldest boy, Charles, was
ill and would have to be taken to Baltimore for an emergency
operation. Mrs. Pruitt remonstrated, but Charles said his side
did hurt a little, and it ended by his leaving in the giro. Twenty
minutes later another plane came in, bearing a surgeon, two
trained nurses, and a man from the National Broadcasting
Company, and the second Pruitt boy, Chester, underwent an
exclusive appendectomy in the kitchen of the Pruitt home, over
the Blue Network. This lad died, later, from eating dried apricots too soon after his illness, but Charles, the other boy, recovered after a long convalescence and returned to the island in
the first warm days of spring.

He found things much changed. The house was gone, having
caught fire on the third and last night of the rescue when a flare

dropped by one of the departing planes lodged in a bucket of trash on the piazza. After the fire, Mr. Pruitt had apparently moved his family into the emergency shed which the radio announcers had thrown up, and there they had dwelt under rather difficult conditions until the night the entire family was wiped out by drinking a ten-per-cent solution of carbolic acid which the surgeon had left behind and which Pa Pruitt had mistaken for grain alcohol.

Barnetuck Bay seemed a different place to Charles. After giving his kin decent burial, he left the island of his nativity and went to dwell on the mainland.

THE WINGS OF ORVILLE

All through the courtship, the building of the nest, and even the incubation of the eggs, Orville had acted in what to the hen sparrow seemed a normal manner. He had been fairly attentive, too, as cock birds go. The first indication Orville's wife had of any quirk in his nature came one morning when he turned up before breakfast carrying a ginger-ale bottle-cap in his beak.

"I won't be home for lunch," he said. His mate looked at the bottle-cap.

"What's that for?"

Orville tried to act preoccupied, but it wasn't a success. He knew he'd better make a direct answer. "Well," he said, "I'm going to fly to Hastings-upon-Hudson and back, carrying this bottle-cap."

The hen looked at him. "What's the idea of carrying a bottle-cap up the river and back?"

"It's a flight," replied Orville, importantly.

"What do you mean, it's a *flight?* How else would you get there if you didn't fly?"

"Well, this is different," said Orville. "I want to prove the practicability of a round-trip flight between Madison Square and Hastings-upon-Hudson carrying a bottle-cap."

There wasn't anything she could say to that. Orville stayed around for a few minutes, then, after what seemed to his wife a great deal of unnecessary fluttering on the edge of the nest, he gripped the bottle-cap firmly in his bill and departed. She noticed that he was flying faster than his usual gait, and was keeping an unusually straight course. Dutifully she watched him out of sight. "He'll be all tuckered out when he gets back," she thought to herself.

Orville, as the hen sparrow had expected, was tired that evening; but he seemed pleased with the results of the day.

"How did it go?" asked his wife, after he had deposited the bottle-cap on the base of the statue of Admiral Farragut.

"Fine," said Orville. "I ran into a little rain the other side of Yonkers, but kept right on into fair weather again. It was only bad once, when ice began to form on my wings."

His wife looked at him intently. "I don't believe for a minute," she said, "that any ice started to form on your wings."

"Yes, it did," replied Orville.

He mooched about the nest for a while, and went into a few details for the benefit of his three children.

The nest occupied by Orville's family was in a tree in Madison Square near the Farragut statue. It was no neater than most sparrows' nests, and had been constructed eagerly of a wide variety of materials, including a kite-string that hung down. One morning, a few days after the Hastings affair, Orville came to his wife with a question. "Are you through with that string?" he asked, nodding toward the trailing strand.

"Are you crazy?" she replied, sadly.

"I need it for something."

His wife gazed at him. "You're going to wreck the nest if you go pulling important strings out."

"I can get it out without hurting anything," said Orville. "I want it for a towline."

"A what?"

"Listen," said Orville, "I'm going to fly to 110th Street tomorrow, towing a wren."

The hen sparrow looked at him in disgust. "Where are you going to get a wren?"

"I can get a wren," he said, wisely. "It's all arranged. I'm going to tow it till we get up about three thousand feet and then I'm going to cut the wren loose and it will glide down to a landing. I think I can prove the feasibility of towing a wren behind a sparrow."

Orville's wife did not say anything more. Grudgingly she helped him pull the kite-string from the nest. Pretty strange doings, it seemed to her.

That evening Orville experimented alone with his string, tying it first to one foot and then the other. Next morning he was up at the crack of dawn and had the string all lashed to his right leg before breakfast. Putting in the half hitches had occasioned an immense lot of kicking around and had been fairly uncomfortable for the youngsters.

"For goodness' sake, Orville," said the hen sparrow, "can't you take it down to the ground and tie it on there?"

"Do me a favor," said Orville. "Put your finger on this knot while I draw it tight."

When the towline was arranged to his complete satisfaction, he flew down to the Square. There he immediately became the centre of attention. His wife, noticing how other birds gathered around, was a bit piqued to see all this fuss made over Orville. Sparrows, she told herself, will gape at anything queer. She didn't believe that Orville had actually located a wren, and was genuinely surprised when one showed up—a tiny brown bird, with sharp eyes and a long, excitable tail. Orville greeted the wren cordially, hopping briskly round and round dragging the line. When about fifty sparrows and pigeons had congregated, he took the wren to one side. "I don't want to take off," he said, "till we get a weather report."

The news that the flight was to be delayed pending a report on weather conditions increased the interest of the other birds, and one of them volunteered to fly up to Central Park and back to find out how things were. He was back in ten minutes, and said the weather was clear. Orville, without any hesitation, motioned to the wren, who seized the towline in its beak, spread its wings rigidly, and waited. Then, at a signal from Orville, they both ran as fast as they could along the grass and jumped wildly into the air, Orville beating his wings hard. One foot, two feet, three feet off the ground they soared. Orville was working like a horse. He put everything he had into it, but soon it became clear that they hadn't enough altitude to clear a park bench that loomed up directly ahead—and the crash came. Orville landed with the string tangled in one wing, and the wren fell to the ground, stunned.

No further attempt to tow a wren was made that day. Orville felt sick, and so did the wren. The incident, however, was the talk of the Square, and the other birds were still discussing it when night fell. When Orville's wife settled herself on the roosting branch beside her mate for the twittering vespers, she turned to him and said: "I believe you could have made it, Orville, if that darn bench hadn't been there."

"Sure we could have."

"Are you going to try again tomorrow?" There was a note of expectation in her voice.

"Yes."

The hen sparrow settled herself comfortably beside him. He, if any sparrow could, would prove the feasibility of towing a wren. For a minute she roosted there, happily. Then, when Orville had dropped off to sleep, she stole quietly down to the kitchen and busied herself making two tiny sandwiches, which she tied up in wax paper.

"I'll give him these tomorrow," she murmured, "just before he takes off."

Ogden Nash

I WILL ARISE AND GO NOW

In far Tibet
There live a lama
He got no poppa,
Got no momma,

He got no wife,
He got no chillun,
Got no use
For penicillun,

He got no soap,
He got no opera,
He don't know Irium
From copra,

He got no songs,
He got no banter,
He don't know Hope,
He don't know Cantor,

He got no teeth,
He got no gums,
Don't eat no Spam,
Don't need no Tums.

He love to nick him
When he shave;
He also got
No hair to save.

Got no distinction,
No clear head,
Don't call for Calvert;
Drink milk instead.

He use no lotions
For allurance,
He got no car
And no insurance,

No Alsop warnings,
No Pearson rumor

For this self-centered
Nonconsumer.

Indeed, the
Ignorant Have-Not
Don't even know
What he don't got.

If you will mind
The box-tops, comma,
I think I'll go
And join that lama.

James Thurber

THE PREOCCUPATION OF MR. PEFFIFOSS

In a time when everything should be made as simple and un-
complicated as possible, the Connecticut Telephone Company
has taken to changing a lot of peaceful old rural phone numbers
which had been doing all right the way they were. For several
years I have known by heart the number of some friends of mine
who live in a quiet little house out in the country, eight miles
from town—New Milford 905 Ring 4, a pleasant number,
easily remembered and easily spoken. When I called it the other
day, I was told the number had been changed to New Milford
1006 W-1. New Milford One Oh Oh Six Double-U One.

Lots worse things have happened to me, but not many that
I keep thinking about more often. I have slowly built up in my
mind a picture of the official in Hartford who thought up that
change. His name, as it comes to me in dreams, is Rudwooll Y.
Peffifoss. Peffifoss, who has had to go through a lot of hell, not
only on account of the name Peffifoss, but also on account of
Rudwooll (the Y is for Yurmurm), has had to compensate for
what has happened to him in this life. Working up relentlessly
and maliciously to an important post in the Number Changing
Department of the Connecticut Telephone Company, he has decided to get back at the world for what he conceives it has

done to him. He spends the day going through phone books looking for simple, easily remembered numbers, like 905 Ring 4, and when he finds one, he claps his hands and calls in his secretary, a Miss Rettig.

"Take a number change, Miss Rettig," he says with an evil smile. "New Milford 905 Ring 4 to be changed to Pussymeister W-7 Oh 8 Oh 9 6 J-4."

Miss Rettig, who has gone through this every day for months, sits patiently and waits for his fiendish glee to subside, and then reminds him, as she has to do a dozen times a day, that such a number is not yet possible under the company's regulations. She hastily adds that of course it will be possible when Mr. Peffifoss finally gets complete charge of the company.

Somewhat mollified, Peffifoss snarls for a while, but in the end agrees to stay within bounds. He writes down all the tough arrangements of authorized numbers he can think of and tries them out on Miss Rettig. When she stumbles several times trying to say New Milford One Oh Oh Six Double-U One, he claps his hands and okays the change. It hasn't been such a bad day after all, and Rudwooll Yurmurm Peffifoss goes home in what for him are high spirits, to kick his children's rabbits around a while before sitting down to dinner.

Marya Mannes

MODERN CHANTY
OR
THE SOFT BERTH

"Rise in Neurotic Seamen Called
Challenge to Merchant Marine."
—New York *Times*

Two years before the mast
And one on the couch, my lad;
It's the bounding main and the whistle's blast
That drives a seaman mad.

Heave ho and away we go,
    Ready to blow the stack;
Up in the fo'c'sle folks'll know
    One of 'em's going to crack.

One of 'em's going to crack, poor soul!
    For lonely is the sea,
With the wrong kind of rock and roll
    And fathoms without TV.

Two years before the mast,
    And one on the couch, my boy;
You'll never last on the briny vast
    So nuts to the ship ahoy!

John Cheever

THE PSYCHIATRIC TEST
(from *The Wapshot Chronicle*)

Early the next morning Coverly reported to Grafley and Harmer, where he was given a common intelligence-quotient test. There were simple arithmetical problems, blocks to count and vocabulary tests, and he completed this without any difficulty although it took him the better part of the morning. He was told to come back at two. He ate a sandwich and wandered around the streets. The window of a shoe-repair place on the East Side was filled with plants and reminded him of Mrs. Pluzinski's kitchen window. When he returned to Grafley and Harmer he was shown a dozen or so cards with drawings or blots on them—a few of them colored—and asked by a stranger what the pictures reminded him of. This seemed easy, for since he had lived all his life between the river and the sea the drawings reminded him of fish bones, kelp, conch shells and other simples of the flood. The doctor's face was inexpressive and he couldn't tell if he had been successful. The doctor's reserve seemed so impenetrable that it irritated Coverly that two strangers should be closeted in an office to cultivate such an atmosphere of inhumanity. When he left he was told to report in the morning for two more examinations and an interview.

In the morning he found himself in stranger waters. Another gentleman—Coverly guessed they were all doctors—showed him a series of pictures or drawings. If they were like anything they were like the illustrations in a magazine although they were drawn crudely and with no verve or imagination. They presented a problem to Coverly, for when he glanced at the first few they seemed to remind him only of very morbid and unsavory things. He wondered at first if this was a furtive strain of morbidity in himself and if he would damage his chances at a job in the carpet works by speaking frankly. He wondered for only a second. Honesty was the best policy. All the pictures dealt with noisome frustrations and when he was finished he felt irritable and unhappy. In the afternoon he was asked to complete a series of sentences. They all presented a problem or sought an attitude and since Coverly was worried about money—he had nearly run through his twenty-five dollars —he completed most of the sentences with references to money. He would be interviewed by a psychologist on the next afternoon.

The thought of this interview made him a little nervous. A psychologist seemed as strange and formidable to him as a witch doctor. He felt that some baneful secret in his life might be exposed, but the worst he had ever done was masturbate and looking back over his life and knowing no one of his age who had not joined in on the sport he decided that this did not have the status of a secret. He decided to be as honest with the psychologist as possible. This decision comforted him a little and seemed to abate his nervousness. His appointment was for three o'clock and he was kept waiting in an outer room where many orchids bloomed in pots. He wondered if he was being observed through a peephole. Then the doctor opened a double or soundproof door and invited Coverly in. The doctor was a young man with nothing like the inexpressive manners of the others. He meant to be friendly, although this was a difficult feeling to achieve since Coverly had never seen him before and would never see him again and was only closeted with him because he wanted to work in the carpet factory. It was no climate for friendship. Coverly was given a very comfortable chair to sit in, but he cracked his knuckles nervously. "Now, suppose you tell me a little about yourself," the doctor said. He was very gentle and had a pad and a pencil for taking notes.

"Well, my name is Coverly Wapshot," Coverly said, "and I come from St. Botolphs. I guess you must know where that is. All the Wapshots live there. My great-grandfather was Benjamin Wapshot. My grandfather was Aaron. My mother's family are Coverlys and . . ."

"Well I'm not as interested in your genealogy," the doctor said, "as I am in your emotional make-up." It was an interruption, but it was a very courteous and friendly one. "Do you know what is meant by anxiety? Do you have any feelings of anxiety? Is there anything in your family, in your background that would incline you to anxiety?"

"Yes sir," Coverly said. "My father's very anxious about fire. He's awfully afraid of burning to death."

"How do you know this?"

"Well, he's got this rig up in his room," Coverly said. "He's got this suit of clothes—underwear and everything—hanging up beside his bed so in case of fire he can get dressed and out of the house in a minute. And he's got buckets full of sand and water in all the hallways and the number of the fire department is painted on the wall by the telephone and on rainy days when he isn't working—sometimes he doesn't work on rainy days— he spends most of the day going around the house sniffing. He thinks he smells smoke and sometimes it seems to me that he spends nearly a whole day going from room to room sniffing."

"Does your mother share this anxiety?" the doctor asked.

"No sir," Coverly said. "My mother loves fires. But she's anxious about something else. She's afraid of crowds. I mean she's afraid of being trapped. Sometimes on the Christmas holidays I'd go into the city with her and when she got into a crowd in one of those big stores she'd nearly have a fit. She'd get pale and gasp for breath. She'd pant. It was terrible. Well then she'd grab hold of my hand and drag me out of there and go up some side street where there wasn't anybody and sometimes it would be five or ten minutes before she got her breath back. In any place where my mother felt she was confined she'd get very uneasy. In the movies, for instance—if anybody in the movies was sent to jail or locked up in some small place why my mother would grab her hat and her purse and run out of that theater before you could say Jack Robinson. I used to have to sprint to keep up with her."

"Would you say that your parents were happy together?"

"Well, I really never thought of it that way," Coverly said. "They're married and they're my parents and I guess they take the lean with the fat like everybody else but there's one thing she used to tell me that left an impression on me."

"What was that?"

"Well, whenever I had a good time with Father—whenever he took me out on the boat or something—she always seemed to be waiting for me when we got home with this story. Well, it was about, it was about how I came to be, I suppose you'd say. My father was working for the table-silver company at the time and they went into the city for some kind of banquet. Well, my mother had some cocktails and it was snowing and they had to spend the night in a hotel and one thing led to another but it seems that after this my father didn't want me to be born."

"Did your mother tell you this?"

"Oh, yes. She told me lots of times. She told me I shouldn't trust him because he wanted to kill me. She said he had this abortionist come out to the house and that if it hadn't been for her courage I'd be dead. She told me that story lots of times."

"Do you think this had any effect on your fundamental attitude toward your father?"

"Well, sir, I never thought about it but I guess maybe it did. I sometimes had a feeling that he might hurt me. I never used to like to wake up and hear him walking around the house late at night. But this was foolish because I knew he wouldn't hurt me. He never punished me."

"Did she punish you?"

"Well, not very often, but once she just laid my back open. I guess perhaps it was my fault. We went down to Travertine swimming—I was with Pete Meacham—and I decided to climb up on the roof of the bathhouse where we could see the women getting undressed. It was a dirty thing to do but we hadn't even hardly got started when the caretaker caught us. Well my mother took me home and she told me to get undressed and she took my great-grandfather's buggy whip—that was Benjamin—and she just laid my back open. There was blood all over the wall. My back was such a mess she got scared, but of course she didn't dare call a doctor because it would be embarrassing, but the worst thing was I couldn't go swimming for the rest of that summer. If I went swimming people would see these big sores on my back. I wasn't able to go swimming all that summer."

"Do you think this had any effect on your fundamental attitude toward women?"

"Well, sir, where I come from, I think it's hard to take much pride in being a man. I mean the women are very powerful. They are kind and they mean very well, but sometimes they get very oppressive. Sometimes you feel as if it wasn't right to be a man. Now there's this story they tell about Howie Pritchard. On his wedding night he's supposed to have put his foot into the chamber pot and pissed down his leg so his wife wouldn't hear the noise. I don't think he should have done that. If you're a man I think you ought to be proud and happy about it."

"Have you ever had any sexual experiences?"

"Twice," Coverly said. "The first time was with Mrs. Maddern. I don't suppose I should name her but everybody in the village knew about her and she was a widow."

"Your other experience?"

"That was with Mrs. Maddern too."

"Have you ever had any homosexual experiences?"

"Well, I guess I know what you mean," Coverly said. "I did plenty of that when I was young but I swore off it a long time ago. But it seems to me that there's an awful lot of it around. There's more around anyhow than I expected. There's one in this place where I'm living now. He's always asking me to come in and look at his pictures. I wish he'd leave me alone. You see, sir, if there's one thing in the world that I wouldn't want to be it's a fruit."

"Now would you like to tell me about your dreams?"

"I dream about all kinds of things," Coverly said. "I dream about sailing and traveling and fishing but I guess mostly what you're interested in is bad dreams, isn't it?"

"What do you mean by bad dreams?"

"Well, I dream I do it with this woman," Coverly said. "I never saw this woman in real life. She's one of those beautiful women you see on calendars in barbershops. And sometimes," Coverly said, blushing and hanging his head, "I dream that I do it with men. Once I dreamed I did it with a horse."

"Do you dream in color?" the doctor asked.

"I've never noticed," Coverly said.

"Well, I think our time is about up," the doctor said.

"Well, you see, sir," Coverly said, "I don't want you to think that I've had an unhappy childhood. I guess what I've told you doesn't give you a true picture but I've heard a little about psychology and I guessed what you wanted to know about were things like that. I've really had an awfully good time. We live on a farm and have a boat and plenty of hunting and fishing and just about the best food in the world. I've had a happy time."

"Well, thank you, Mr. Wapshot," the doctor said, "and good-by."

On Monday morning Coverly got up early and had his pants pressed as soon as the tailor shop opened. Then he walked to his cousin's office in midtown. A receptionist asked if he had an appointment and when he said that he hadn't she said that she couldn't arrange one until Thursday. "But I'm Mr. Brewer's cousin," Coverly said. "I'm Coverly Wapshot." The secretary only smiled and told him to come back on Thursday morning. Coverly was not worried. He knew that his cousin was occupied with many details and surrounded by executives and secretaries and that the problems of this distant Wapshot might have slipped his mind. His only problem was one of money. He didn't have much left. He had a hamburger and a glass of milk for supper and gave the landlady the rent that night when he came in. On Tuesday he ate a box of raisins for breakfast, having heard somewhere that raisins were healthful and filling. For supper he had a bun and a glass of milk. On Wednesday morning he bought a paper, which left him with sixty cents. In the help-wanted advertisements there were some openings for stock clerks and he went to an employment agency and then crossed town to a department store and was told to return at the end of the week. He bought a quart of milk and marking the container off in three sections drank one section for breakfast, one for lunch and one for dinner.

The hunger pains of a young man are excruciating and when Coverly went to bed on Wednesday night he was doubled up with pain. On Thursday morning he had nothing to eat at all and spent the last of his money having his pants pressed. He walked to his cousin's office and told the girl he had an appointment. She was cheerful and polite and asked him to sit down and wait. He waited for an hour. He was so hungry by this time that it was nearly impossible for him to sit up straight. Then the receptionist told him that no one in Mr. Brewer's office knew about his appointment but that if he would return late in the afternoon she might be able to help him. He dozed on a park bench until four and returned to the office and while the receptionist's manner remained cheerful her refusal this time was final. Mr. Brewer was out of town. From there Coverly went to Cousin Mildred's apartment house but the doorman stopped him and telephoned upstairs and was told that Mrs. Brewer couldn't see anyone; she was just leaving to keep an engagement. Coverly went outside the building and waited and in a few minutes Cousin Mildred came out and Coverly went up to her. "Oh yes, yes," she said, when he told her what had happened. "Yes, of course. I thought Harry's office must have told you. It's something about your emotional picture. They think you're unemployable. I'm so sorry but there's nothing I can do about it, is there? Of course your grandfather was second crop." She unfastened her purse and took out a bill and handed it to Coverly and got into a taxi and drove away. Coverly wandered over to the park.

It was dark then and he was tired, lost and despairing—no one in the city knew his name—and where was his home—the shawls from India and the crows winging their way up the river valley like businessmen with brief cases, off to catch a bus? This was on the Mall, the lights of the city burning through the trees and dimly lighting the air with the colors of reflected fire, and he saw the statues ranged along the broad walk like the tombs of kings—Columbus, Sir Walter Scott, Burns, Halleck and Morse—and he took from these dark shapes a faint comfort and hope. It was not their minds or their works he adored but the kindliness and warmth they must have possessed when they lived and so lonely and so bitter was he then that he would take those brasses and stones for company. Sir Walter Scott would be his friend, his Moses and Leander.

Then he got some supper—this friend of Sir Walter Scott—and in the morning went to work as a stock clerk for Warburton's Department Store.

Frank Sullivan

THE CLICHÉ EXPERT TESTIFIES ON THE ATOM

Q—Mr. Arbuthnot, you're the very man I want to see. I've been longing to examine you on atomic energy.

A—Well, my boy, you've come to the right party. I believe I can say that I know all the clichés on the subject.

Q—How can you say that?

A—Without fear of successful contradiction.

Q—I'm glad to hear it. I suspected you would be making a study of the atomic cliché.

A—A study! Why I've been doing nothing since V–J Day

but listen to the experts explain atomic energy and the bomb on the air, or editorialize about them in the newspapers. Indeed I *am* the cliché expert of the atom. You realize of course what the dropping of that test bomb in the stillness of the New Mexico night did.

Q—What did it do?

A—It ushered in the atomic age, that's what it did. You know what kind of discovery this is?

Q—What kind?

A—A tremendous scientific discovery.

Q—Could the atomic age have arrived by means of any other verb than "usher"?

A—No. "Usher" has the priority.

Q—Mr. Arbuthnot, what will never be the same?

A—The world.

Q—Are you pleased?

A—I don't know. The splitting of the atom could prove a boon to mankind. It could pave the way for a bright new world. On the other hand it may spell the doom of civilization as we know it.

Q—You mean that it has—

A—Vast possibilities for good or evil.

Q—At any rate, Mr. Arbuthnot, as long as the bomb had to be discovered, I'm glad we got it first.

A—If you don't mind, I will be the one to recite the clichés here. You asked me to, you know.

Q—I'm sorry.

A—Quite all right. I shudder to think.

Q—What?

A—Of what might have happened if Germany or Japan had got the bomb first.

Q—What kind of race was it between the Allied and German scientists?

A—A close race.

Q—What pressed?

A—Time pressed.

Q—With what kind of energy did the scientists work in their race to get the bomb?

A—Feverish energy. Had the war lasted another six months the Germans might have had the bomb. It boggles.

Q—What boggles?

A—This tremendous scientific discovery boggles the imagination. Also stirs same.

Q—Where do we stand, Mr. Arbuthnot?

A—At the threshold of a new era.

Q—And humanity is where?

A—At the crossroads. Will civilization survive? Harness.

Q—Harness, Mr. Arbuthnot? What about it?

A—Harness and unleash. You had better learn to use those two words, my boy, if you expect to talk about the atom, or write about it, either. They are two words very frequently used. With pea, of course.

Q—Why pea?

A—Oh, everything is in terms of the pea. You know how much U-235 it would take to drive a car to the moon and back?

Q—No, sir. How much?

A—A lump the size of a pea. Know how much U-235 it would take to ring your electric doorbell for twenty million years?

Q—How much, God forbid?

A—A lump the size of a pea. Know how much it would take to lift the Empire State Building twelve miles into the air?

Q—I wish you would let the Empire State Building alone, Mr. Arbuthnot. It is all right where it is.

A—Sorry. It must be lifted twelve miles into the air. Otherwise, do you know who would not be able to understand the practical application, or meaning, of atomic energy?

Q—No. Who?

A—The average layman.

Q—I see. Well, in that case, up she goes. I gather that a lump the size of a pea would do it.

A—Exactly.

Q—You wouldn't settle for a lump the size of a radish, or a bean?

A—Sorry. The pea is the accepted vegetable in these explanations. Do you know what the atomic energy in the lobe of your left ear could do?

Q—What?

A—If harnessed, it could propel a B-29 from Tokyo to San Francisco.

Q—It *could!*

A—Do you know that the energy in every breath you take could send the Twentieth Century Limited from New York to Chicago?

Q—Mercy on us, Mr. Arbuthnot!

A—And the atomic energy in your thumbnail could, if unleashed, destroy a city twice the size of three Seattles. Likewise, the energy in your . . .

Q—For God's sake, stop, Mr. Arbuthnot! You make me feel like a menace to world security in dire need of control by international authority in the interests of world peace. Kindly leave off explaining atomic energy to me in terms so simple a layman can understand. Explain it to me in scientific terms, and the more abstruse the better.

A—Well, listen carefully and I'll give you a highly technical explanation. In the first place the existence of the atom was only suspected. Then Einstein . . . equation . . . nucleus . . . electron . . . bombard . . . proton . . . deuteron . . . radioactive . . . neutron . . . atomic weight . . . beta rays . . . matter . . . split . . . chain reaction . . . gamma rays . . . alpha particles . . . Mme. Curie . . . break down . . . energy . . . end products . . . control . . . impact . . . uranium . . . Dr. Niels Bohr . . . barium . . . orbit . . . Dr. Lise Meitner . . . knowledge pooled . . . Dr. Enrico Fermi . . . military possibilities . . . Dr. Vannevar Bush . . . U-235 . . . isotopes . . . U-238 . . . autocatalytic . . . heavy water . . . New Mexico . . . mushroom-shaped cloud . . . awesome sight . . . fission . . . William L. Laurence . . . and there you had a weapon potentially destructive beyond the wildest nightmares of science. Do I make myself clear?

Q—Perfectly. Now, Mr. Arbuthnot, what is nuclear energy the greatest discovery since?

A—It is the greatest discovery since the discovery of fire. You will find that "Promethean" is the correct adjective to use here.

Q—What does this tremendous scientific discovery do to large armies?

A—It spells the doom of large armies. It also spells the doom of large navies. Likewise, it spells the doom of large air forces. Similarly, as I mentioned earlier, it may spell the doom of civilization. I doubt if so many dooms have been spelled by anything since the phrase was first coined.

Q—When was that, sir?

A—I should imagine at the time gunpowder spelled the doom of the bow and arrow.

Q—What is the atomic bomb a menace to?

A—World order, world peace, and world security.

Q—What must be done to it?

A—It must be controlled by an international authority. The San Francisco Charter must be revised to fit the Atomic Age.

Q—What does the bomb make essential?

A—It makes world unity essential. It makes an international league for peace essential if the world is not to be plunged into a third war which will destroy civilization.

Q—In short, its use must be—

A—Banned.

Q—What kind of plaything is the bomb?

A—A dangerous plaything. A dangerous toy.

Q—What kind of boomerang is it?

A—A potential boomerang.

Q—What else is it?

A—It is the greatest challenge mankind has yet faced. It is also the greatest destructive force in history. It has revolutionary possibilities and enormous significance and its discovery caused international repercussions.

Q—What does the splitting of the atom unleash?

A—The hidden forces of the universe. Vast.

Q—Vast?

A—That's another word you'd better keep at hand if you expect to talk or write about this tremendous scientific discovery.

Vast energy, you know. Vast possibilities. Vast implications.
Vast prospects; it opens them.

Q—I see. What cannot grasp the full significance of the
tremendous scientific discovery?

A—The human mind.

Q—Whose stone is it?

A—The philosopher's stone.

Q—Whose dream?

A—The alchemist's dream.

Q—And whose monster?

A—Frankenstein's monster.

Q—What does it transcend?

A—It transcends the wildest imaginings of Jules Verne.

Q—And of whom else?

A—H. G. Wells.

Q—The fantastic prophecies of these gentlemen have become
what?

A—Stern reality.

Q—What does it make seem tame?

A—The adventures of Superman and Flash Gordon.

Q—Very good, Mr. Arbuthnot. Now, then, in addition to
ushering in the Atomic Age, what else does this T.S.D. do?

A—It brightens the prospect for the abolition of war but in-
creases the possibility of another war. It adds to the store of
human knowledge. It unlocks the door to the mysteries of the
universe. It makes flights into interstellar space a possibility. It
endangers our security and makes future aggression a tempta-
tion.

Q—What has it done to warfare?

A—It has revolutionized warfare, and outmoded it, and may
outlaw it. It has changed all existing concepts of military power.
It has made current weapons of war obsolete.

Q—And what may it do to cities?

A—It may drive cities underground.

Q—Mr. Arbuthnot, in the happy event that atomic energy
is not used destructively, what kind of role will it play?

A—A peacetime role.

Q—Meaning?

A—Meaning cheap power, cheap fuel. A lump of U-235—

Q—The size of a pea?

A—No, not this time—the size of forty pounds of coal would run the entire nation's heating plants all winter.

Q—What would that result in?

A—Sweeping changes in our daily life and unemployment on a hitherto unheard-of scale.

Q—Bringing about what kind of revolution?

A—An industrial revolution.

Q—Mr. Arbuthnot, should we share the secret with other nations?

A—Yes and no.

Q—If the latter, why?

A—Because we can be trusted with it.

Q—Why can we be trusted with it?

A—Because we would use it only in self-defense and as a last resort.

Q—Who could not be trusted with it?

A—Some future Hitler. Some gangster nation. Some future aggressor.

Q—If we should share it, why that?

A—As a gesture of confidence in other nations.

Q—And anyhow—

A—Anyhow, every nation will possess the secret within five years.

Q—Now, Mr. Arbuthnot, can you tell us what is ironic?

A—It is ironic that several of the major contributions to the bomb were made by scientists whom Hitler and Mussolini had exiled.

Q—In other words, Hitler cooked—

A—His own goose.

Q—What else is ironic?

A—The spending of two billions on the bomb, in contrast to the amounts spent on education, public health, slum clearance, and research on cancer and other diseases.

Q—What kind of commentary is that?

A—A sad commentary on our so-called, or vaunted, civilization.

Q—Mr. Arbuthnot, how ready is man for the Atomic Age?

A—As ready as a child is to handle dynamite.

Q—What kind of little boys do the atomic scientists remind you of?

A—Of little boys playing with matches.

Q—What is a possibility of the future?

A—Atomic bombs a hundred times more destructive than the one dropped on Nagasaki.

Q—What is such a discovery known as?

A—It is known as man's conquest of natural forces.

Q—What does such a discovery advance?

A—It advances the frontiers of science.

Q—And what does the invention of this key to world suicide constitute?

A—It constitutes scientific progress.

Index

ABOUT THE EDITOR

HENRY C. CARLISLE, JR., was born in San Francisco in 1926 and was educated at the Sorbonne and at Stanford University, from which he received his M.A. in 1954. Subsequently he became an editor for a New York book publisher and began his researches on American satire. He says wryly, "Once, the incomparable Mencken, solicitously prescribing artistic hobbies in place of golf or Kiwanis for bored and dissatisfied businessmen, suggested among other therapies that Babbitt '. . . take a stiff drink and try *vers libre*. Or, if his tastes run to more sober things, let him collect early American humor . . .' "

Mr. Carlisle is married to the former Olga Andreyev and has one son, Michael.